'With our politicians refusing to confront the climate cris▓
the increasingly influential role being played by military pla▓▓▓▓▓ a▓▓ ▓▓▓▓▓▓▓ ▓▓▓▓. ▓ ▓▓▓
want to understand why we can't leave it to the Pentagon to shape our response to climate
change, then you need to read this book.'

Naomi Klein, author of *This Changes Everything* and *The Shock Doctrine*

'Will climate change prove the downfall of capitalism? Or can the corporate world harness
even the threat of ecological meltdown to its advantage? Do the security risks it will unleash
undermine conventional geopolitics, or enhance their hold on us all? As this riveting analysis
makes clear, climate change will have winners as well as losers. This is far too important to be
left to the scientists.'

Fred Pearce, environment consultant, *New Scientist*

'The compelling arguments in this volume show very clearly that linking climate change to
security is not the simple matter political elites now so frequently assume. As these chapters
show in detail it may perpetuate precisely the dangers that we need to confront. Unless, that
is, much more attention is paid to who precisely is deciding what kind of future we need to
secure for which parts of humanity in a very unequal world. This book is a "must read" for
anyone concerned to secure ecological futures for more than just the rich and powerful few
in the global system.'

Simon Dalby, CIGI Chair in the Political Economy of Climate Change,
Balsillie School of International Affairs

'We're at a crucial moment. We can deal with the climate crisis either as a moment to build
new global unity, or to further divide the planet between wealthy profiteering elites and
everyone else. This book will help you understand the possibilities, and hopefully move you
to join the fight for justice.'

Bill McKibben, Environmental journalist and co-founder of 350.org

'A tremendous book that shows how the few intend to profit from climate change and how the
many can stop it happening.'

John Vidal, *Guardian*

'Responding to climate change is increasingly seen as a security issue not a matter of human
rights and justice. As long as elite communities are protected – the proper job of the military -
then security professionals are doing what they should, with the control paradigm the only way
forward. *The Secure and the Dispossessed* challenges that head-on, bringing together a series of
excellent contributions to take apart the dangers and short-sightedness of securitising climate
change. This is a badly needed book and a hugely important contribution to one of the most
significant issues of our age.'

Paul Rogers, Professor of Peace Studies at University of Bradford

'Among the books that attempt to model the coming century, this one stands out for its sense of plausibility and danger. It examines several current trends in our responses to climate change, which if combined would result in a kind of oligarchic police state dedicated to extending capitalist hegemony. This will not work, and yet powerful forces are advocating for it rather than imagining and working for a more just, resilient, and democratic way forward. All the processes analysed here are already happening now, making this book a crucial contribution to our cognitive mapping and our ability to form a better plan.'

Kim Stanley Robinson, Award-winning science fiction writer

'Buxton and Hayes make clear that climate justice activists must be careful about making alliances with strange bedfellows such as the military in the fight for climate justice. While the military does recognise climate change as a threat, their solutions often create new dangers for the most vulnerable, by curtailing civil liberties and democratic space. It is the task of climate justice activists to seize the crisis as an opportunity for building a more just world – a job that is made more difficult by partnerships with repressive institutions.'

Payal Parekh, Global Campaigns Director, 350.org

'A brilliantly conceived and edited volume that warns us of the dire political and ecological consequences of accepting a security rationale for the control of climate change policy that entrusts the human future to the main culprits of our era: corporate neoliberalism and geopolitical militarism.'

Richard Falk, American Professor Emeritus of
International Law at Princeton University

'This book provides a deep and wide-ranging analysis of the securitization of climate change and its military and corporate sponsors and beneficiaries. It is must reading for activists, scholars, researchers and policymakers working to build a different kind of present and future, where peace, equality and justice are at the center of responses to climate change – not men with guns or corporate balance sheets. The authors mount an important challenge to environmentalists willing to play the national security card in order to get more attention to climate change at the highest levels of government. The risks of such framings far outweigh the benefits.'

Betsy Hartmann, Professor Emerita of Development Studies and
Senior Policy Analyst of the Population and Development Program,
Hampshire College, Amherst, MA

'We already see the climate crisis unfolding worldwide. How we react will be the challenge of our age. Will we respond with the politics of fear and business as usual – and in so doing condemn millions? Or will we wrest power from the corporations and the military in order to develop the radical just solutions we need? This book is an indispensable guide to the dystopian forces we must confront and the alternative just solutions we will need to advance.'

Pablo Solón, Former Ambassador to the Plurinational Government
of Bolivia and lead climate negotiator to the UN

'This book shows that preventing worsening climate change in the face of business-as-usual is more urgent than ever. More importantly, it shows that the struggles for environmental justice and civil liberties, for refugee rights and #blacklivesmatter, will only be won if we unite together against a system that preserves the privileges of the few against the rights of the many.'

Asad Rehman, Head of International Climate, Friends of the Earth

'While millions of people, in Transition groups, community energy groups, and many others, are looking at the climate crisis and seeing opportunity amidst the crisis, so, sadly, are other less altruistic forces. Familiarising ourselves with the madness that sees retreating ice as potential oil fields, and a warming world as a business opportunity, is vital. *The Secure and the Dispossessed* shines a bright light into corners we'd rather avoid, and in doing so, does us a huge service.'

Rob Hopkins, Transition Network and author of *The Power of Just Doing Stuff*

'The war business is constantly on the hunt for new opportunities to profit from death. This illuminating book unveils how military and corporate planners are capitalising on the climate crisis to introduce new deadly technologies to police our borders, repress peaceful protestors and undermine human rights. But it also shows how – just as in the movement to ban landmines – ordinary people everywhere are standing up to reject violence and to propose real lasting peaceful and just solutions to the climate crisis.'

Jody Williams, Nobel Peace Prize winner, awarded for her work to ban landmines

"This is a great contribution to the much-needed connection between war and climate chaos."

Medea Benjamin, award winning peace activist, founder of Code Pink and author of *Drone Warfare: Killing by Remote Control*

'The link between security and climate change has long been regarded by the global security status quo as a pretext for hardening security measures on local, national and international scales. Buxton and Hayes have crafted an important book that both acknowledges the climate crisis and takes a critical approach toward managing its human consequences. Climate change – like many of the new insecurities in the news today – first and foremost reveals the social and political inequalities of our time. *The Secure and the Dispossessed* documents and analyses the multiple facets of the new – but perhaps actually very old – configuration of power, economic resources, social standing and political access that have shaped the most recent climate-change events. It is the first work of its kind that undertakes such a critical mapping, culminating in a set of recommendations, both wise and sharp, for addressing climate-based crises in the age of the security-industrial-media-entertainment complex.'

J. Peter Burgess, Professor of Philosophy, Vrije Universiteit Brussel

'*The Secure and the Dispossessed* warns of the looming "perfect storm" of climate chaos, global inequality, and mass dispossession of vulnerable people – but above all exposes a growing corporate military and security complex determined to protect the worst of the status quo. Thankfully the authors also offer us a very different future rooted in justice, community rights to land, water and energy, and a sustainable peace. A powerful collection.'

Maude Barlow, National Chair of the Council of Canadians and author of *Blue Future*

'At a time when too many in the climate movement are quick to celebrate military and corporate forces acknowledging the reality of climate change, *The Secure and the Dispossessed* asks the critical questions about the fundamental difference between climate security and climate justice. This is an important reminder that we need to change not just our energy system, but our power structures as well.'

Tim DeChristopher, Fossil fuel abolition activist,
founder of the Climate Disobedience Center

'This excellent and powerful book explores the rise of "climate security" – a state and corporate-led reframing of climate change from a predominantly environmental and social justice paradigm into one defined primarily by military security. We should all be deeply concerned by the rise of "climate security" and this important collection of essays from scholars and activists explains in graphic detail why. Buxton and Hayes have curated a deeply disturbing and compelling analysis in which environmental crisis, unbridled neoliberalism and militarism are converging to ignite global conflicts and normalise exceptional security regimes.'

Penny Green, Professor of Law and Globalisation at Queen Mary
University of London and Director of the International State Crime Initiative

'In responding to climate change, not all actors are equal: while most of us (and especially the poor) will suffer egregiously, many corporations and military organizations will seek to benefit from the devastation. There's no better guide to these differentiated responses than *The Secure and the Dispossessed*. Each chapter provides valuable insights into the social and economic dimensions of the unfolding climate catastrophe.'

Michael Klare, author of *The Race for What's Left*

'This is the missing link the climate justice movement has needed, mainly without knowing it: the corporatisation and militarisation of our changing weather. Given how much the Pentagon and firms like Shell are investing in their own secretive research, and given the free-to-pollute pass that the world's militaries get during UN climate summits, it is vital for us all to learn what Buxton and Hayes eloquently explain in this excellent book.'

Patrick Bond, Professor of Political Economy, University of the Witwatersrand,
Johannesburg and author of *Politics of Climate Justice*

THE SECURE AND THE DISPOSSESSED

Ideas into movement

The Transnational Institute (TNI) is an international research and advocacy institute committed to building a just, democratic and sustainable world. For more than 40 years, TNI has served as a unique nexus between social movements, engaged scholars and policy makers.

www.tni.org

Also available:

The New Latin American Left: Utopia Reborn
Edited by Patrick Barrett, Daniel Chavez and César Rodríguez-Garavito

Agrofuels: Big Profits, Ruined Lives and Ecological Destruction
François Houtart

The Bases of Empire: The Global Struggle against U.S. Military Posts
Edited by Catherine Lutz

THE SECURE AND THE DISPOSSESSED

How the Military and Corporations are
Shaping a Climate-Changed World

Edited by Nick Buxton and Ben Hayes

Foreword by Susan George

PlutoPress
www.plutobooks.com

First published 2016 by Pluto Press
345 Archway Road, London N6 5AA

www.plutobooks.com

British Library Cataloguing in Publication Data
A catalogue record for this book is available from the British Library

ISBN   978 0 7453 3691 6   Hardback
ISBN   978 0 7453 3696 1   Paperback
ISBN   978 1 7837 1720 0   PDF eBook
ISBN   978 1 7837 1722 4   Kindle eBook
ISBN   978 1 7837 1721 7   EPUB eBook

This book was generously supported by Occupy.com which contributed to its production and is promoting its analysis. Occupy.com is a multi-media channel providing independent, international news for the global 99%: www.occupy.com.

Typeset by Stanford DTP Services, Northampton, England
Text design by Melanie Patrick

Simultaneously printed in the European Union and United States of America

CONTENTS

PART I: THE SECURITY AGENDA

PART II: SECURITY FOR WHOM?

PART III: ACQUISITION THROUGH DISPOSSESSION

Online chapters
We had so much good analysis for this book, we were unable to fit it all into the final version. However we are glad to say that additional material, not included in the book, is available free of charge on the accompanying website: www.climatesecurityagenda.org.

Two minutes to midnight: Why the intergovernmental process has failed
Nick Buxton

'We thought it was oil, but it was blood': Resistance to the military-corporate wedlock in Nigeria and beyond
Nnimmo Bassey

Seeing red: state responses to environmental protests
Chris Jones

Conversion to a low-carbon economy from 'below' and 'inside': New alliances and transformative trade unionism
Hilary Wainwright and Jacklyn Cock

Climate, commons and hope: The Transition Movement in global perspective
Justin Kenrick and Tom Henfrey

LIST OF FIGURES AND BOXES

ACKNOWLEDGEMENTS

We'd like first to thank the Transnational Institute (TNI) – a fabulous research institute with four decades of history embedded in social movement struggles – for its support in helping us put this book together. In particular, we are deeply appreciative of TNI's Fellows and staff that have inspired our thinking and its director Fiona Dove who has given us both tremendous support.

We are deeply indebted to the hundreds of individuals who showed their confidence in our book by crowdfunding its production and promotion. Their willingness to believe in the importance of the project was even more valuable than the critical resources it raised. The full list of contributors is below. We want to give a special thanks to Lawrence Taubman and Occupy.com for their particularly generous support.

A very kind group of academics, scholars and activists generously gave their time to peer review chapters. These are in alphabetical order: Fidelis Allen, Juliette Beck, Steffen Boehm, Saturnino 'Jun' Borras, Ben Brangwyn, Elizabeth Bravo, Rose Cairns, Katy Fox, Jennifer Franco, Harriet Friedmann, Emily Gilbert, Patrick Kane, Satoko Kishimoto, Edgardo Lander, Daniel Moss, Daanish Mustafa, Alex Randall, Janet Redman, Rachel Smolker, Pascoe Sabido, Vish Satgar, Sara Sexton, Dimitris Stevis, Larry Swatuck, Kathleen Tierney and Tim Wise.

We would particularly like to thank Simon Dalby, a wonderful long-term scholar on environmental security issues who has given us invaluable advice from start to finish of this project.

We are also grateful to David Castle at Pluto Books for taking on and publishing this book at very short notice, for all the work done by Melanie Patrick and Emily Orford to produce and market it, Jeanne Brady for her copyedit and Dave and Sue Stanford for the typesetting and proofreading.

Nick would like to give a special thanks to two key activists that started him on the journey of exploration that led to this book. The first is Pablo Solon, a friend and former Bolivian climate negotiator, whose courage in standing up for a truly just solution to the climate crisis at UN climate conferences and convening of the historic World Peoples' Summit on Climate Change and the Rights of Mother Earth in Cochabamba, Bolivia in 2010 showed that nothing less than a different politics and economics can help us address the climate crisis.

The second is Tim DeChristopher, an inspiring American activist whose amazing disruption of an oil auction in 2008 inspired thousands of activists to take direct action. An interview with Tim also prompted Nick to look beyond the issue of stopping climate change to who is shaping its impacts. As he said: 'We need to start working now on putting in place power structures that share our values as we enter difficult times.'

Nick also thanks Sara Rogers, Matt Fluty and Eric Doud for providing beautiful hideaways to write and edit, Roberta McNair for her editing and moral support and Sally Hensel for helping with the nightmare endnotes.

Ben would like to thank the very many people who have inspired and encouraged him to think critically about civil liberties and state power over the years. In particular his mum, Judy, and the many people involved in Statewatch, especially Tony Bunyan, Trevor Hemmings, Ann Singleton, Paddy Hillyard, Steve Peak, Heiner Busch and Nadine Finch. He also wishes to express a huge thanks to Nick, for without his patience, commitment and encouragement of all involved, this project would never have been completed

While it's traditional to acknowledge long suffering partners in a book, it's not until you take on a challenge like this that you realise how much of a nightmare it is for those who manage alone when you're working instead of doing other things. So we are more than eternally grateful for their support, and hugely appreciative of the years of conversations with Juliette and Gina that have helped shape our thinking. We hope that the future of our four young children will reflect the dreams and actions of the movements now fighting for a better future, and not the dystopian visions of the 'securocrats' who inspired this book.

Finally, we would like to dedicate the book to the memory of Praful Bidwai, who died suddenly in Amsterdam in June 2015, a wonderful TNI Fellow whose work on climate change and security issues was an inspiration to everyone who knew him.

Full list of crowdfunders

Caroline Clark, Maxim Narbrough, Travis Driessen, Julian Jacobs, Anuradha Vittachi, Dan Boorman, Helen Wolfson, Dan Montuschi, Sara Rogers, Beatriz Martinez, Greg Wright, Dixon Caspar, N. Capellini, Julian Filochowski, Payal Parekh, Mauricio Vargas, Dave Patterson, Kathryn Johnson, John Adams, Kara Moore O'Leary, Theresa Wolfwood, Matthew Hodson, Ralph Suikat, William Carroll, Fred Faust, Dan Caines, Tom and Katy Buxton, Chris Venables, Nicola Rogers, David Heath, Katharine Collenette, Adam Boulter, Jason Gehrig, Tom Kruse, Maximilian Leroux, Julia Ruxton, Joanna Bernie, Maia Baconguis, Nina Iszatt, Larry Lohmann, Ben Lowe, Lia van Wijk, Martin Roberts, Rita Huybens, Gonzalo Berron, Michael Klare, Sally Hill, John Farrar, Mike Gould, Monisha Bhaumik, Alan Dube, Sabrina Aguiari, Brid Brennan, Sarah Garden, Aaron Nitzkin, Peter Wright, Nuria Del Viso, Ben Dangl, Esther Lexchin, Yonit Percival, Jolyon White, Kris Abrams, David Alexander, Kristian Smith, Amira Armenta, Nicolien Scholtens, Kevin Odell, Bernard Meijfroidt, Michel Fleur, Nele Marien, Barbara Crowther, Mary Light, James and Kari Stewart, Angela Burton, Peter Carter, Catherine Dilley, Fergus McInnes, András Novoszáth, Ignace van der Meijden, Sarah Barfoot, James Smith, Ulrich Karthaus, Steve McGiffen, Louis Reynolds, Lindsay Simmonds, Steffen Boehm, Daniel Chavez, Bill Powers and Melissa Draper, Peter Stone, Donna McGuire, Franz Bonsema, Rafael Alejandro Salvador, Aaron Nitzkin, Barry Gills, Marlene Barrett, Jonathan Brough,

Martina Weitsch, Kirsten Moller, Deb Mason, Joachim Rollhaeuser, Cindy Blaney, Aidan Patrick White, Liz Scurfield, Grietje Baars, Saleh Mamon, Linda McPhee, Jean Jackman, Kathrin Barta, Claire Black Slotton, Luis Sierra, Susan Bizeau, Elisabeth Robbins, Julian Eaton, Nina Iszatt, Corinne Voilquin, Francis Buxton, Linda Farthing, David Hallowes, Jeff Rudin, Alexander Leipold, Rejo Zenger and the many anonymous donors or those who didn't leave a full name.

All URLs cited in this volume were accessed in August 2015.

Nick Buxton and Ben Hayes
August 2015

FOREWORD

Susan George

As I read the chapters of this book commissioned by editors Nick Buxton and Ben Hayes, I had a nagging feeling of *déjà vu*, even *déjà su* [known]. Not because the contributions were unoriginal – to the contrary, they were full of new, often scary information and written by people I seldom encounter in the vicinity of 'my' subjects. But they were all, each in its own way, facing the reader with a sort of existential contradiction and hard, borderline impossible, choices that go to the roots of who we are, individually and collectively; who we want to remain or to become as – if the term is still valid – the human family.

We know that no single factor is ever the single cause of a complex phenomenon, but as the military say, climate change is, at the very least, a 'threat multiplier' and seems now also to be a human disaster multiplier in both frequency and intensity. The tension that lies between the threats and the human disasters is at the nexus of the hard choices and the contradictions.

An example: How can one possibly condone what is happening to migrants, to poor people, to unnumbered innocents as their livelihoods are destroyed by flood or erosion augmented by war and their place in the world becomes unliveable? But how can one not simultaneously agree with the famous remark by former French Prime Minister Michel Rocard, justifying the reinforcement of his immigration policy in 1989: 'France cannot welcome the whole world's misery.'

Twenty-five years later, Kos, Kalymnos, Samos, Chios and Lesbos – the Greek islands closest to the Turkish border – in June 2015 were trying to cope with about 3,500 new arrivals landing their sputtering Zodiacs on the Greek beaches every 48 hours. The European Union with its rule of first European touchdown point apparently considers that austerity-stricken Greece by itself should manage to care for these people who have lost everything. Climate change and failed crops are recognised as one of the causes of the huge inflows of desperate Syrians, Eritreans and Somalis who are also fleeing war and inter-religious and ethnic strife. The populations of these Greek islands range from 10,000-33,000 people, except for Lesbos (86,000). But as first stop in the EU, it falls to them to manage sharing resources with an extra 10,000 destitute people each week. Is it just? Could I? Could you? It's out of sight and of mind for most Europeans.[1]

How can one not feel pity for the people in some neighbouring European country whose houses have been flooded and their automobiles washed away? They generally emerge alive; help arrives more quickly. Seeing their plight on television, doesn't one also feel a sort of guilty relief? 'It's awful, but this time it wasn't for me or my children and grandchildren. Maybe our turn won't come after all.' I cannot say I've never had that reflex. Can you? It's human to want to be protected from the elements and, if need be, from other people. And it works both ways. A young Syrian refugee on Kos told a reporter, 'My parents brought me up to be a good man. I had everything to be a good person but this war makes us do things you can't even imagine.' And who can protect you from yourself and from others and from the elements if not the government? The government hasn't saved us from increasing inequality, financial crisis and joblessness, but they seem to know what they're doing in protecting us from nature's backlash. And if for that they're making full use of the military, then we assume the military must be necessary.

The ravages and unexpected perils of climate change provide a dress rehearsal for acting out the Hobbesian scenario and we know how that play ends. In the state of Nature to which climate change threatens to reduce us – first locally, then perhaps universally – and the war of all against all, the Leviathan demands a sovereign who may be despotic but shields us from the war in which, otherwise, everyone is a loser.

So whence came the sense of *déjà vu, déjà su* I referred to at the beginning? It took me a while to realise it came from a well-documented but fake narrative I had written in 1999 as my contribution to the Millennium. I ask the reader to forgive me this brief foray into my own work. The title of this book was *The Lugano Report*, which I called a 'factual fiction', because all the facts were seriously sourced but the context, the scenario was my own. Ten experts in as many disciplines are recruited by a factotum and commissioned by mysterious but clearly extremely powerful decision makers to provide a report on a matter of paramount importance to the Commissioners: 'Preserving capitalism in the 21st century'. In their comfortable villa in Lugano, the experts first establish the baseline of potential factors that will threaten capitalism in the twenty-first century: these naturally include climate change. They establish the basic equation $I = C \times T \times P$, which stands for Impact (on the earth) equals Consumption x Technology x Population. Since capitalism is a subsystem operating within, and not outside of or beyond a finite biosphere whose capacity cannot be increased; protection of this total natural system – and thus of its economic capitalist subsystem – depends upon 1) the number of people in the world, 2) the quantity, quality and nature of their consumption, and 3) the technology employed to produce and distribute what they consume and to dispose of the waste they engender.

These experts have been selected because they are trustworthy neoliberals and can be counted on to be sympathetic to the Commissioners' aims. In solving their equation, they quickly eliminate the notion that consumption can somehow be made fairer, transferred from North to South, or from Haves to Have-nots to any significant degree. They note that choices dictated by morality and more generally ethical behaviour in all circumstances have never, and will never become mass phenomena. Meanwhile, numbers of new, more affluent consumers are rising (for example, China) and under such circumstances, the two products for which demand immediately increases are energy and meat. This has proven true regardless of culture: richer people invariably place more demands on their – and the world's – environment.

As for technology, although it may be constantly improved, this will not guarantee a smaller impact on the planet since increased efficiency is continually cancelled out by the sheer numbers of, say, automobiles or airplanes. With these and other arguments, the experts establish that the solution to the equation depends crucially on the 'P' factor, or Population, which is overwhelmingly located in the poorer countries where people's consumption may be less high-tech but where anything seemingly 'free', such as trees or soil will fall victim to deforestation or erosion. Furthermore, these people usually have several children for reasons which may be perfectly valid in their individual circumstances but are not collectively justifiable.

I'm drastically summarising here much longer and entirely logical arguments. The upshot is that Malthus is not dead, population will outrun resource capacity, a smoothly functioning capitalist system cannot coexist with 8 billion people in the world and since these experts explicitly decline to belong to the caste of 'coopted thinkers … whose livelihoods chiefly depend on maintaining the illusions that the (ruling) class holds about itself', they go straight to the solutions.[2] Whatever you may have guessed, these solutions do not include Hitlerian methods, which the experts gathered in Lugano deem primitive and unsophisticated but none the less costly and resource-intensive. Drastic population reduction can, however, be achieved, mostly by allowing, or encouraging, nature to take its course, in the personae of the Four Horsemen of the Apocalypse: Conquest (or War), Pestilence, Famine and Death.

And this is why, patient reader, I had the eerie feeling that today's neoliberal politicians, corporate brass and military strategists had literally taken a leaf from my book, as recounted in this one. I meant my book as a biting, dystopian satire and had to recognise that something much more sinister, such as a serious, realistic scenario is under construction and is literally documented here in *The Secure and the Dispossessed*. And as Marx observed, today's co-opted thinkers, both military and civilian, are still telling the ruling class exactly what it wants to hear. It wants to hear that the planet can no longer tolerate hundreds of millions – perhaps billions – of unnecessary, superfluous, useless, unwelcome and disposable people who cannot be permitted to burden the earth. Therefore it is morally permissible to maintain order, discipline and manageable human societies by whatever means reveal themselves as necessary.

Climate change is the backdrop and the proximate cause of this offensive, as well as its justification. It will require rationalisation with new rhetoric and soothing language, but the neoliberals have been nurturing experts in such matters in innumerable think tanks.

Fortunately, the on-the-ground reality of climate change's impact can be counted upon to produce, spontaneously or with a little help from its friends, any number of mostly internecine conflicts, many of which will produce significant fatalities. The producers of higher-tech walls, barriers, fences and related impediments to free movement will flourish as will other branches of capitalist endeavour such as communications equipment, surveillance gear, or crowd-control equipment. Capitalism will continue to prosper – at least until New York is submerged – and by then, the present politicians will be out of office. With many foreign destinations newly off-limits, internal tourism will grow. The Fortress State will have its charms for many. People will, for a time, feel safe.

Naturally, citizens of Northern countries will have to suffer part of the impact, but only in rare cases will it be fatal and even then, unattributable to forces other than natural ones. And lest we forget, the rich countries, too, have their share of the useless and disposable. The military will find a new lease on life after myriad failures in its more classic conflicts of the Middle East.

Where the Southern, poorer countries are concerned, studies also show that in many cases, no outside agency will be necessary for assisting millions of the unnecessary and unwelcome to annihilate each other. After severe droughts, for example, new conflicts emerge, or old ones rise from their ashes and once more claim many lives.

What I am trying to say is that the ice-cold logic of the ruling class isn't going to change course. The world-as-we-know-it will henceforth be plunged into a situation in which climate change is at the centre but engulfs us also in the certainty that capitalism will not give up, and not just the fossil-fuel corporations. Contrary to ordinary people, the masters of the universe will not be ordered to 'adapt' or to become more 'resilient'. We, not they, are the adjustable variable. It may not be exactly *après nous le déluge,* but neither the US nor China nor any other rich, greenhouse gas-emitting country is going to cancel their subsidies to the major polluters or stop making policy in their favour, at least not spontaneously or voluntarily.

I won't go so far as to say that unless we can get rid of capitalism we can't win on keeping global warming under 2°C. I will say that we must recognise that relocalisation and local action, however essential, cannot replace the state. Only the state can force capitalism to comply with the laws of survival and only the people can force the state to force the companies to obey.

This means that the people must bond and consciously, purposefully merge their individual struggles under the banner of compassion. The hopeful pages in this book show us people reacting with spontaneous altruism to relieve distress and intervening with ordinary kindness, where the authorities can think only of sending in the troops.

Climate change has got to be on the hymn sheet or manifesto or charter of every citizen effort from now on and it doesn't matter if it's the local football club or the movement to separate banks and close down tax havens or promote human (gay, women's, minority) rights or save the whales or anything else you care to name. Find the angle and include it in your struggle. Ignore the constant diet of fear which Power feeds us to make us quiescent and frozen. Tell the shameful little voice within to shut up when it murmurs in the face of tragedy, 'Thank God it wasn't me this time', or 'We can't afford to share with these outsiders'. Join with others, place the accent on what unites you, not what separates you. Time is short.

Auden said it best: 'We must love one another or die.'[3]

Notes

1. Kourounis, A. and Jacobi, T. (11 June 2015). 'Kos, l'autre porte de l'Europe', *Politis*. *Politis* is a smallish left French weekly.
2. Marx, K. and Engels, F. (1970). *The German Ideology*, Vol. 1, *Materialist Theory, Dominant Classes and Ideas*. New York: International Publishers Co.
3. From 'September 1, 1939' (the day Germany invaded Poland and started the Second World War). Later, Auden disavowed the line, said the poem was 'trash' and everyone was going to die anyway. Yet somehow I feel he would not object to its use here in the radically new context this book reveals. Retrieved from http://www.poets.org/poetsorg/poem/september-1-1939.

INTRODUCTION: SECURITY FOR WHOM IN A TIME OF CLIMATE CRISIS?

Nick Buxton and Ben Hayes

> Our challenge has changed. It is no longer about just reducing emissions. We have to work out how to hold on to our humanity as we head to increasingly difficult times.
>
> *Tim DeChristopher, environmental activist arrested and imprisoned*
> *for disrupting an auction of oil and gas leases in Utah in 2008*

The year 2008 will go down in history as the year that the Lehman Brothers filed for bankruptcy, bringing the world within a breath of a global banking meltdown and prompting the world's most serious economic crisis since the 1930s. It was also the year in which two of the world's most powerful forces started planning for a dystopian future in a time of climate crisis. On one side of the Atlantic, in The Hague and London, the oil giant Shell's internal 'scenarios team' were asked to look into their crystal ball to see how their business model would fare in a climate-changed world. On the other side of the Atlantic, in Washington, DC, a powerful group of political elites including former US assistant defence secretaries, the ex-chief of the CIA and a leading Democrat policy advisor gathered to assess the likely impacts of climate change for US national security interests.

Neither group would be considered prime candidates for environmental leadership. The positions adopted by the oil industry and the US military have hitherto been associated with the diversionary tactics of the deniers and gas-guzzling warmongers. Yet here they were taking climate change very seriously and in Shell's case tacitly acknowledging the cost of the world's fossil-fuel addiction.

Shell's team, led by Jeremy Bentham, forecast two scenarios: 'Scramble' and 'Blueprint'.[1] Scramble envisages a future where the growing demand for energy, fuelled by India and China's rapid growth, leads to increasing competition, rivalry and tensions between states, and ensuing conflicts and social and environmental crises. Blueprint imagines that public concern about the environment and the rise of renewable energy leads to significant reduction of carbon emissions, leading by 2050 to a 'world of electrons rather than molecules'. In other words, a world fuelled largely by renewable sources, rather than fossil fuels.

Unusually, Shell, which has published global forecasts for more than forty years without ever publicly stating its energy policy preferences, declared this time that it was in favour of Blueprint. This was heralded at the time as a sign that oil companies could be part of the solution to climate change rather than the principal cause.

However, a closer look at the Blueprint's small print showed that Shell did not envisage that this scenario would involve curtailing their own fossil fuel production. Instead, their scenario relies heavily on two policy sleights-of-hand: first a cap-and-trade scheme that in 2013 had all but collapsed in ignominy, having both failed to reduce emissions and rewarded the world's worst polluters. Second, it depends on a huge increase in Carbon Capture and Storage technologies that have yet to be proven to work and are unlikely to do so anytime soon. In other words, Shell believed that a renewable world would come into being without requiring any fundamental change in Shell's operations; instead, the problem of carbon dioxide would be magically resolved with the help of a few technofixes and the use of carbon credits to get others to reduce their emissions. Given that the International Energy Agency states that two-thirds of existing fossil fuel reserves will need to stay in the ground to have a chance to keep global temperature rises below the internationally agreed goal of 2°C, Shell's so-called Blueprint was in fact a plan for continuing business-as-usual – even if it leads to a world considered dangerous by many climate scientists.

As if to prove Shell's underlying cynicism, within two years – and in the wake of the collapsed UN climate talks in Copenhagen – Shell admitted that it had effectively joined the 'Scramble' for the resources that could be accessed thanks to the melting ice in the Arctic. Any pretence that the company cared about anything other than profit was laid bare for all to see.[2]

The military strategists, meanwhile, published their scenarios for the future in a book, *Climate Cataclysm: The Foreign Policy and National Security Implications of Climate Change*. The research built on a study released a year before that warned that humankind had now entered the 'Age of Consequences' that would 'increasingly be defined by the intersection of climate change and the security of nations.'[3] In that report (see further Chapter 2), the researchers sketched out three scenarios of possible climate impacts: an 'expected' one based on temperature rise of 1.3°C (2.3°F) by 2040, a 'severe' one (2.6°C/4.7°F) and a 'catastrophic' one' (5.6°C/10.1°F) by 2100.

The authors issued stark warnings about entire populations fleeing or perishing, particularly across Africa, South and Central Asia, Central America, the Caribbean, South America and South East Asia. The report forecast civil unrest, conflicts, millions of migrants on the move, and the growing use of martial law to control unrest. 'As first thousands and then millions and then hundreds of millions of starving people begin flooding toward Europe,' warns the book, 'the EU will try to retreat behind high walls and naval blockades, a containment strategy that will be seen as morally indefensible and will provoke tremendous internal unrest and impoverishment, but also will be seen as a matter of survival.' It concluded laconically, 'Altruism and generosity would likely be blunted.' (Disturbingly the path we are currently on in terms of emissions growth lies closer to the 'severe' than 'expected' scenarios.)

Their report does not provide *concrete* recommendations for US military responses, but the authors were clear that this posed an unprecedented security threat, in their words, to 'our society, our way of life, and our liberty'. They explained that 'In national security planning, it generally can take about 30 years to design a weapons system and bring it to the battlefield, so it is important to anticipate future threat environments. It is no less important to anticipate and prepare for the challenges we may face in the future as a result of climate change.'

This report is now but one of many we could have chosen to introduce this book. And the messages in each of them are being repeated ever more widely in the media and in the corridors of power: that climate change is a 'threat multiplier' that will make current global conflicts and social tensions far worse, leading to a far more insecure world. The immediate call is for more urgent action to tackle climate change, but the obvious subtext is that the military better get ready and be given the resources to deal with a messier and more conflict-ridden world. In the words of a US Department of Defense report, 'We have entered an era of persistent conflict ... a security environment much more ambiguous and unpredictable than that faced during the Cold War.'[4]

We believe that when the world's foremost military power and one of the world's most powerful corporations start predicting the future in ways that dovetail, it is worthwhile listening to what they say. For the way they forecast the future also influences how these powerful institutions are now shaping policies to deal with climate impacts, which has huge and still largely undiscussed consequences for the rest of us.

The genesis of this book emerged from our own experiences, working in social movements fighting for justice on issues related to climate change and civil liberties respectively. We are linked to the Transnational Institute (TNI), a progressive international institute based in Amsterdam that has, for four decades, provided research and logistical support for struggles for social and environmental justice. For the past decade, TNI has worked to confront the corporate interests that have sought to stall effective action on climate change by blocking progress or diverting energies into false, ineffective and unjust solutions such as carbon trading.

After the collapse of the Copenhagen talks in 2009, when it became obvious that there was little political will to take the bold steps needed to tackle climate change, we were struck by the potential implications of parallel attempts to recast climate change as a security issue. Clearly this new 'security' agenda will have a growing impact – not just for people involved in environmental or peace and civil liberty movements – but also for everyone concerned with maintaining or creating a livable future. In December 2011, coinciding with the UN climate talks in Durban, South Africa, we convened a workshop bringing together climate scientists, security scholars, social and political scientists and activists. Out of that seminar, a series of working papers were developed and the proposal for a book emerged. In autumn 2013, we organised a crowdfunding campaign[5] that successfully raised €10,000 to fund the production of this book. We have also produced online chapters and a living website to accompany this book (www.climatesecuritya-genda.org).

This book poses the same fundamental question that we asked at the seminar in Durban: What are the implications of institutions such as the Pentagon or corporations such as Shell re-framing climate change from an environmental and social justice issue to a security one?

This begs several related questions of a 'what if' nature. First, what does a climate-changed world look like, and what are the social, political and economic implications of 'business as usual'? Second, who are the winners and losers of the new 'climate security' strategies – or, put another way, what is being secured, for whom, from whom, and at what cost?

A small collection like this cannot, of course, hope to provide comprehensive answers to questions that many scholars and researchers have long been asking. What we hope it can do is provide food for thought about how these new security strategies relate to existing concerns about the environment, social justice, adaptation and resilience, and the implications of failing to prevent runaway climate change. We also hope the accompanying website can be a place where this discussion can continue and be enriched.

It is important to stress that this is not a book about how to stop climate change. Climate change is already happening, having an impact particularly on the vulnerable, and it is going to worsen. This does not mean we have given up hope that concerted action can still avert a worsening catastrophe; in fact we believe the opposite. We are actively engaged and fully in support of all movements and communities taking direct action against fossil fuel interests and working to create alternative low-carbon futures. Our actions can still affect how bad climate change will be. However, we think it is crucial to cast a critical eye on the climate change and international security discourse, because we believe that progressives need to engage in these debates and articulate the necessary alternatives. Leaving the planning of a climate-changed future in the hands of corporate and military elites has far too dangerous implications for all of us, as subsequent chapters will testify.

In turning the spotlight on climate-change impacts, the book exposes more clearly the agents that are both causing the climate crisis and seeking to benefit from its consequences – be they states, corporations, or private security companies. It is no coincidence that many of these same entities are engaged in the subversion or repression of precisely the kinds of activism and ideas that are necessary to avert any future climate chaos. Exposing the veil of legitimacy that 'security' can give these efforts is one of the key motivations for our work.

One issue we have constantly had to grapple with, as editors, is that the subject matter in this book can at times be dispiriting. At a time when concerted action to combat climate change is needed more than ever, it may appear counter-intuitive to produce a book that could compound the sense of relative powerlessness that many believe underpins contemporary apathy.

We certainly do not wish to add to the sense of doom, nor give dystopian and catastrophic narratives a legitimacy or sense of inevitability they do not deserve. But we do not wish to self-censor the dangers, either. For if we don't engage critically with these state-corporate narratives in order to understand how this fear is being exploited to perpetuate injustice, we are not going to be in a position to challenge, confront, or reshape the future as we want it to be.

We therefore asked two things of the contributors to this collection. First, to make these trends and power-plays visible by carefully analysing the political and economic forces that make a militarised and corporatised future possible. Second, to inspire resistance by exposing the cracks in the system, giving voice to progressive alternatives and experiences and recounting the stories of hope and self-determination that are so often overlooked by media commentators. Interestingly, many of the alternatives to a security narrative, outlined in each chapter, provide not only a more just response to climate change impacts but are also solutions that can help to prevent further climate change.

Heating up and no end in sight

If we are to look at how we respond to climate impacts, we need first to look at what the best consensus of science says are the likely consequences of our current trajectory of carbon emissions. We also need to understand why the international community has so far failed to act to curtail emissions and the way this has bolstered a security-led response.

The evidence of rising emissions shows that we are currently on a treacherous one-way slope. Moreover, there is little sign that we are even heading in the right direction. Greenhouse gas emissions grew nearly twice as fast from 2000 to 2010 as in the previous thirty years, and in 2013, they grew at their fastest rate since 1984.[6] As carbon dioxide stays in the atmosphere for hundreds of years, every increase locks in an increase in global warming, which means that even if we stopped carbon emissions tomorrow, we would still continue to see increases in global warming for decades to come. UK climate scientists Kevin Anderson and Alice Bows say that the only way to keep temperatures within the globally agreed target of 2°C of warming will be for industrialised countries to peak their emissions soon after 2015 and then enforce a 10 per cent cut in emissions year after year, starting in 2020.[7] They admit this kind of cut is unprecedented in human history; it is a target that even the most praised 'green' economies such as Germany have failed to achieve.

This means that whatever we do – and must do – to end the fossil-fuel economy, we are still going to be living in a climate-changed world, so we must simultaneously prepare for its consequences.

The rapid degradation of our planetary home is not just an issue of carbon emissions. A team of 28 scientists in 2009 identified nine separate biophysical systems crucial to humanity's flourishing, and marked out boundaries within which we must remain in order to prevent 'irreversible and in some cases abrupt environmental change'.[8] We have already crossed the boundaries for climate change, biodiversity loss, and interference with the nitrogen cycle; we are fast approaching the boundaries for freshwater use, land-use changes, ocean acidification, and interference with the global phosphorus cycle. In fact, humans are having such a significant impact on the planet that some geologists are now saying we have moved into a new epoch – the 'Anthropocene' – marked by the fact that humans are now shaping the entire planet's ecosystem, oceans and atmosphere, leaving nothing untouched. We agree that it would be better called the 'Capitalocene', given that the responsibility for continued destruction lies with contemporary alignments of power and capital, rather than humanity as a whole.[9]

The Intergovernmental Panel on Climate Change (IPCC) report is the most widely acknowledged reflection of consensus among scientists, even though its statements and predictions are frequently on the conservative side, given the difficulty in reaching consensus among 195 countries. Nevertheless, their report released in March 2014 starkly chronicled some of the changes scientists across the world are reporting – and the likely impacts as these trends continue. These include extreme weather, rising sea levels that will flood many coastal cities, food insecurity and 'the breakdown of food systems', declining water supplies, increases in 'ill-health in many regions,' and ongoing collapse of biodiversity.[10]

The report notes that climate impacts will be not be evenly spread, hitting those in the Global South and vulnerable populations the hardest. This points to the profound injustice at the heart of the climate crisis: that those who played the least role in causing the crisis will feel its impact hardest. People living at the edge of subsistence have few resources to deal with additional stresses caused by climate change. Frank Rijsberman, head of the international Consultative Group for International Agricultural Research (CGIAR) 15 crop-research centres, explains how it will impact food production:

> The annual production gains we have come to expect ... will be taken away by climate change. We are not so worried about the total amount of food produced so much as the vulnerability of the one billion people who are without food already and who will be hit hardest by climate change. They have no capacity to adapt.[11]

The financial capacity to respond to climate change impacts is also starkly different between North and South. The US government spent $68 billion on the aftermath of Hurricane Sandy, but all the richest countries together have barely raised $30 billion a year to help the poorest countries cope with climate change impacts, despite a pledge to raise $100 billion in 2009.[12] Former Filipino climate negotiator Yeb Sano despairs when he thinks of how much money and resources it will take to prepare his country for climate impacts:

> The fact is we are not ready. We have a coastline of 37,000 miles. How can we possibly defend that from sea level rise? Sixty per cent of our people live in low-lying areas which may flood. It will be probably be 4C warmer – that will seriously impact on our fisheries, our cities, our coral reefs, our food supplies, our economy. Everything we know will be compromised.[13]

Planning for the future is not made any easier by the fact that understanding our climate is still, in the words of environmental policy professor Joseph DiMento, 'a film with many blurry images and empty frames'.[14] We know it will lead to increased extreme weather, heatwaves, flooding and rising seas, but predicting where and when is an elusive science. The most disturbing scientific predictions now suggest that as climate change accelerates, it could prompt self-reinforcing feedback loops that would create a tipping point and lead to a sudden surge in emissions. There is particular concern at the speed of melting permafrost in the Arctic and Northern Siberia, which could cause a major and sudden release of methane, one of the most powerful greenhouse gases.

In spite of impressive innovation and take-up of renewable energy production, our current trajectory, if not altered, could see temperature increases of up to 4 degrees Celsius, which, according to the World Bank, would mean that by 2080, the coolest months of the year would be substantially warmer than the warmest months now, and we would experience 'a completely new class of heat waves, with magnitudes never experienced before in the 20th century'.[15] As Australian scholar Clive Hamilton argues, these kind of scenarios force us to consider the ability of humanity to adapt, even with all the financial resources in the world.[16]

Hot air and no action

The big question is why – given the alarm bells sounded by the world's science community and the acceptance of the facts by most politicians – there has been so little action commensurate with the threat. In an online chapter that accompanies this book, Nick Buxton and Pablo Solon explore the reasons in more depth.[17] To summarise their arguments, rising corporate power, the constant drive for capital expansion, and a mistaken focus on emissions rather than extraction and production of fossil fuels have blocked an effective dismantling of a deeply embedded fossil fuel economy. International governance, weakened by years of US unilateralism, has spectacularly failed to rise to the challenge. Annual UN climate conferences have become an abysmal charade. Behind the grand speeches and posturing, it is clear that the whole point of the annual spectacle is cosmetic; the decision to avoid any commitment that could possibly put a country and its national and corporate interest at an economic disadvantage has already been taken.

The result of these systemic failures has been a catastrophic political stasis, that allows the current fossil fuel complex to run amok. The dangerous impacts of inaction play out in the context of growing corporate power and diminishing popular accountability while the same forces that caused the crisis are also looking to shape its impact, increasingly behind the barrel of a gun. It means for concerned citizens that the struggles to combat climate change and to address its impacts are no longer separate issues but need to be addressed together.

The new security agenda

The first part of this book examines the way in which states and corporations are seeking to leverage climate change to their own ends. Chapter 1 is abridged from Christian Parenti's book, *The Tropic of Chaos*,[18] and explores these 'new geographies of violence' and the links between climate, conflict and insecurity. A US journalist and scholar, Parenti argues that climate change has been an overlooked factor in a whole range of conflicts, particularly in the world's central latitudes, which are affected most by changes in weather patterns.

To his evidence gathered in Afghanistan, Kenya and India, one can also add recent research that suggests that the civil war in Syria was also fuelled, at least in part, by an extreme drought that affected the country from 2006 to 2009, most likely due to climate change. Rising food prices linked to climate change are also seen as a significant source of the mass frustrations that boiled over into the so-called 'Arab Spring'.

Parenti's chapter demonstrates how the environmental crisis is colliding with the twin legacies of Cold War militarism and unbridled free market economics to inflame existing conflicts and create new patterns of violence – and how countries of the Global North and others in the South are responding with greater repression, surveillance and a program of permanent counter-insurgency.

Much of the violence that Parenti describes also has roots in the conflicts embedded within the global fossil fuel economy: violence has consistently followed extraction of oil, ranging from repression of residents in extraction zones to the giant geopolitical conflicts that have devastated and distorted politics in the Middle East.

In a powerful online chapter that accompanies this book,[19] Nigerian environmental campaigner Nnimmo Bassey explores how militarisation has accompanied oil extraction in Nigeria, causing devastation to the environment and local communities. The chapter provides an insight into the dynamics of resource wars in the twenty-first century and shows how militarisation in distressed regions is becoming the given geopolitical backdrop for our times.[20] At the same time, Bassey also draws attention to the creative and powerful resistance that has emerged and against the odds has won significant victories.

In Chapter 2, security researcher Ben Hayes examines the security strategies seeking to address the impacts of climate change. He unpicks the 'threat multiplier' doctrine adopted by NATO, the Pentagon, the EU and the UN and others that frame climate change as a security issue in order to cement their role in managing its impacts. Long-term threat assessment is something that military and security agencies claim they are mandated to do in the public interest, however, there is an inherent danger to liberty and democracy in letting these agencies play a leading role in this area, because they are structurally and ideologically predisposed to a limited set of hard security responses. These are based on a 'paradigm that seeks to maintain control rather than address the underlying problems'.[21]

This ideology and practice also serves the interests of those who have power and resources; by its very nature, it militates against actions that would seek to redistribute power and wealth and thereby address the inequities that are at the heart of the climate crisis. This can be seen most obviously in the detail of military security strategies that focus on how to protect assets, resources and supply chains against the social instability caused by climate change. What unites all these strategies is their externalisation of threat. As scholar Robyn Eckersley notes, 'environmental threats are something that foreigners do to Americans or to American territory', and they are never something caused by US or Western domestic policies.[22] By its very nature, then, the military/security approach disregards the systemic causes of climate change and therefore the changes that need to be made in US and Western institutions, structures and policies. As usual, the enemy is elsewhere.

The chapter also explores the relationship between the politics of security and the politics of scarcity, which have together spawned a whole set of sub-narratives – food security, water security, energy security, and so on. These narratives largely persist with the military 'control' paradigm, ignoring issues of justice and equity, and seeking to ensure that those with resources, no matter how, why, and at what cost, continue to keep them.

While many people still view 'security' in benign terms – being able to walk safely at night or having the security of a job or income – the term has been co-opted radically since 9/11 and is increasingly deployed to justify coercive measures *against* people. As later chapters explore, we are starting to see, for example, the notion of 'food security' being used to justify land grabbing, or 'energy security' used as a reason to take pre-emptive action against environmental campaigners. Cornerhouse research group suggest a useful distinction between 'Upper-Case' Security which secures property and privilege, and 'lower-case' security, which is the right to have the means to survive and to defend territory and livelihoods. Not only has Upper-Case Security been used to 'subdue recalcitrant or colonised peoples, to provide physical and political infrastructure, to assure the flow of raw materials, [and] to break apart old social relationships in order to lubricate increasingly global channels of commerce,' it has also become a 'scarce, global commodity ... of which there can never be enough.'[23] Given the application of 'security' measures usually ends up creating further insecurity, security rapidly becomes a panoptic vision covering everything and everywhere. This much is now patently clear thanks to Edward Snowden.

Chapter 3 by climate scholar and activist Oscar Reyes takes up the corporate side of the new security agenda through the lens of managing 'risk' and promoting corporate 'resilience', in other words, continued profit making. Reyes explains how the narrative of security has been usurped by corporate elites to defend the status quo and consolidate their power. Climate change brings both risks to corporations such as flooding of warehouses or disruption of trade routes – to be addressed through corporate resilience – and opportunities – expressed in terms of new markets, new supply routes and changes in patterns of consumption. Resilience accepts worsening climate change as fact and, rather than seeking to take the radical actions to prevent it, seeks to adapt to it. Used with equal vigour in the military-industrial complex, it embraces 'disequilibrium as a point of organisation', in which populations are helped to 'survive' while corporations and capitalism are supported to 'thrive.'[24]

Corporations are also hedging their bets on climate change, promoting a number of 'sustainable' activities to attempt to appease consumer concerns and protecting themselves from specific threats such as rising sea levels. Yet in financial terms, these same corporations continue to invest in deeply unsustainable activities and in political terms exercise their influence to prevent radical *dirigiste* climate interventions, promoting their technocratic expertise as the solution to any problem that emerges.

Walmart is a typical example of this corporate greenwashing. The retail giant received plaudits for setting a goal of being 'supplied by 100 percent renewable energy', before an investigation by *Grist* magazine found that at its current pace of converting to renewables the company would take about 300 years to achieve this.[25] Similarly, divestment campaigners forced Exxon Mobil to analyse its climate-change risk exposure, given that burning all of its reserves would undermine internationally agreed climate goals and therefore risked their becoming 'stranded assets'. Exxon Mobil's report concluded that government action forcing Exxon to keep any of its oil reserves in the ground was 'highly unlikely', and argued that it could therefore continue to search for more oil and gas without restraint. Reyes concludes:

> That type of response represents a complacent – indeed, arrogant – disregard for the planet. But it is based on a confident bet that transnational corporations will continue to have significant influence on public policy-making, both through their lobbying, and as a result of the anti-regulatory neoliberalism shared by politicians of both the centre-left and centre-right in most industrialised countries.

Meanwhile, other companies are lining up to profit from the impacts of climate change. One such company is Arcadis, a Dutch engineering firm that offers flood-protection services. The company has embarked on a buying spree, snapping up ETEP, a Brazilian water-engineering and consulting firm, winning contracts in New York to bring water-treatment facilities online after Hurricane Sandy, and working with New Orleans and San Francisco to raise levees and plan for rising sea levels. Arcadis's revenue rose 26 per cent in 2012 to €2.5 billion ($3.25 billion). Services such as flood protection will be critical, but the rise of these new climate-change profiteers does reflect an economic model in which corporations and elites are best placed to prosper from climate change while the vast majority of the planet will have no such protection. As explored later in the book, some of the solutions that corporations provide to address climate change end up intensifying the dispossession of peasants and marginalized communities. When Michael Richardson, head of business development at Land Commodities, who advises rich investors and sovereign wealth funds, says that 'there is an overemphasis of its [global warming's] negative impacts' and celebrates its potential to increase the value of land and create new markets, you can be sure that he is not thinking about the impacts of climate change on peasant farmers.

The corporate capacity to shape our climate-changed world reflects the growing power that corporate elites have accumulated in the past two decades. A report by TNI in 2014 showed that the world's wealth is concentrated to an even greater extent than is popularly understood: not in the hands of the 1 per cent but the 0.001 per cent, that is, the 111,000 people who control $16.3 trillion. This is equivalent to a fifth of the world's GDP. Moreover, 37 of the world's largest economies are corporations, not nations. But the concentration of power goes deeper still: in a study of 43,000 corporations, mathematicians at the Zurich Polytechnic Institute found just 147 companies control 40 per cent of the economic value of the entire sample. Most of these are banks, hedge funds, or other financial services corporations. Even an advisor to Deutsche Bank, George Sugihara, admitted that 'It's disconcerting to see how connected things really are.'[26]

The unprecedented concentration of economic and military power is not only an indication of the forces that will seek to dominate a climate-changed world, it is also an indication of systemic vulnerabilities in our globalised world. Geographer Mazen Labban explains: 'The vulnerability of the network derives not only from its vastness ... of the (physical) concentration of the infrastructure, but also from its connectivity: disruption of supply in one place might create shocks at the regional, or even global scale.'[27] On the flip side, though, these vulnerabilities are also opening new spaces for social innovation and challenges to corporate power.

Adaptation and security for whom?

The second part of this book examines four specific features of the state-corporate climate-change agenda as they relate to adaptation to climate change. Climate adaptation is understood as efforts made to reduce the vulnerability of human, natural and social systems to the impacts of climate change. Cities, institutions, governments clearly need to invest in adaptation efforts to protect people from negative climate impacts. However, as environment and security scholar Geoff Dabelko and others have argued, both mitigation and adaptation efforts handled badly are likely to aggravate social unrest and conflict.[28] While climatic events may be the catalyst for future conflicts, ham-fisted elite adaptations are likely to make them even worse. An EU-funded study of conflicts in the Mediterranean, Sahel and Middle East showed, for example, that the principal causes of conflict in these countries was not hydro-climatic conditions, but rather democratic deficits, distorted and unjust economic development and poor adaptation efforts to climate change that end up worsening the situation.[29] A militarised response is – as we have already seen all too clearly – only likely to make this situation worse.

Many people watched in horror as 58,000 troops were deployed to New Orleans in the wake of Hurricane Katrina, together with privatised security forces such as the notorious Blackwater commandos. While many civilians were rescued, others found themselves shot at and arrested. Seven police were eventually indicted for killing two African Americans and wounding four others. Many more killings by the military, security guards and vigilantes still await justice. Rebecca Solnit, who has analysed many disasters, including New Orleans, notes that militarisation normally occurs because of what she calls 'elite panic' – the fear of social disorder and fear of the poor, minorities and immigrants. This fear prompts police and military to prioritise protecting property over human lives. The US military continues to see potential disorder where others see injustice, suggesting New Orleans is not an unusual one-off case: a US Army Strategic Studies Institute report in 2008 said that in the wake of civil unrest caused by climate change, the 'DoD would be, by necessity, an essential enabling hub for the continuity of political authority in a multi-state or nationwide civil conflict or disturbance.'[30]

In Chapter 4, writer and journalist Nafeez Ahmed (writing with Nick Buxton and Ben Hayes) looks at how governments are preparing for 'natural' disasters with 'civil contingencies' and 'disaster preparedness'. Across the world, states have added new statutes to their books that provide for the suspension of democratic institutions and the restriction of civil liberties in times of crisis. In many cases, this legislation builds upon and even extends powers previously adopted in wartime. At the same time, the standard for invoking those powers has slipped from state of emergency to any time of 'crisis'. While it is both legitimate and desirable for governments to plan for the worst, it is clear that a significant part of this planning is concerned with the 'threat' that citizens are seen to pose to governments. Ahmed shows how these 'emergency' powers build upon the exceptional and now permanent measures introduced under the 'war on terror'. In a post-Occupy, post-Arab Spring world, security agencies have become increasingly preoccupied with managing and anticipating social unrest, which inevitably rests on targeting 'radical' social activism. One example is the Pentagon Minerva initiative, which is funding researchers to develop advanced data-mining tools that can automatically categorise activist groups and rank them on a threat-scale and determine their alleged propensity for violence or terrorism by automatically tracking and analysing their social media posts. Within these models, the threat comes not from climate change or the iniquities of the neoliberal system, but now from those who oppose it. There is of course nothing new in states casting 'radicals' as a threat, but the threat is now green as well as red.[31]

These tendencies have put environmental activists in particular on the front line of state repression, as one of the online chapters that accompany this book explores.[32] Global Witness reports in 2014 and 2015 indicated that there has been a dramatic rise in killings of people protecting the environment and defending land rights, as competition for natural resources intensifies.[33] Around three-quarters of these deaths took place in Central and South America, often during the repression of resistance to hydropower projects, mining, agribusiness and logging. Meanwhile in the US and UK, climate-change activists have been defined along with terrorist suspects and armed militias as 'domestic extremists', or 'eco-terrorists', with enormous resources now devoted to identifying, tracking and spying on them.

Meanwhile, those who flee their countries due to climate disruption confront even bigger military obstacles and dangers, as many nations follow the lead of Europe and the US in building ever-stronger fences to keep refugees at bay. Journalist Todd Miller calls the borderlands of the US 'constitution-free zones' and says the borderlands are providing a useful 'on-the-ground laboratory for the development of a surveillance state ... one of the police and the policed'.[34] The disturbing militarisation of borders, using ever more dangerous technologies to ward off those forced to migrate from climate instability, is explored by security scholar Steve Wright, border security expert April Humble and co-editor Ben Hayes in Chapter 5. They argue that what is needed is less a new legal category of 'environmental refugee' than sustained resistance to the 'border industrial complex'.

In Chapter 6, Kathy Jo Wetter and Sylvia Ribeiro of ETC group examine the corporate and military interests that promote geo-engineering of the climate to reduce temperatures and prevent their damaging impacts. The fact that these proposals are gathering momentum is a reflection of both the support of Big Oil and the influence of those in power who believe that bizarre experiments with sunshades in space is a more sensible course of action than confrontation of the fossil-fuel industry.

Wetter and Ribeiro explain how geo-engineering advocates – or, as they prefer to call them, 'geopirates' – are backed in the US and Europe by some of the same conservative institutes and politicians that are sceptical about climate change. Perhaps that explains why geo-engineering's impact is perversely the same or worse than climate change, legitimising further human meddling with the climate, creating profits for a small few and leaving those most affected out of the discussions. Despite its dangers, geo-engineering is gaining ever more traction and government support. The Central Intelligence Agency funded a 21-month $630,000 scientific study in 2013 to analyse the prospects for and potential impacts of geo-engineering.[35]

The final chapter in this part of the book, by Dutch peace activist Mark Akkerman, looks at some of the broader responses of the global military-industrial complex to climate change. In the wake of 9/11, what is more accurately described as the military-*security* industrial complex has become extraordinarily powerful. In 2013, global military spending reached about $1.7 trillion dollars, 130 times that of planned humanitarian spending and dwarfing any investment in climate change. US military spending is roughly equal to the next nine top global spenders combined, with ever more corporations seeking to grab a slice of the pie.[36] A *Washington Post* investigation in 2010 revealed the existence of 1,931 private companies benefiting from a $75 million government intelligence budget that had more than doubled since 9/11.[37] Corporations reaping handsome rewards from this burgeoning fear-based industry clearly have a vested interest in fuelling a media and political debate that forecast an insecure dangerous future in order to promote their 'security' solutions.

Europe is involved in a similar security-industrial arms race. TNI's report *Neoconopticon* revealed, for example, that arms manufacturers are benefiting from €1.4 billion of EU largesse to develop research into how to integrate land, air, maritime, space and cyber-surveillance systems. As the report noted, we are not just 'sleepwalking into ... a surveillance society', but also 'turning a blind eye to the start of a new kind of arms race, one in which all the weapons are pointing inwards'.[38]

Despite the interests at stake, the military embrace of climate change as a new *raison d'être* has been warmly welcomed by some in the environmentalist community. Climate scientist John Schellnhuber,[39] for example, expresses his relief that 'the military do not deal with ideology. They cannot afford to: They are responsible for the lives of people and billions of pounds of investment in equipment.' Certainly in the US, the military is seen as one of the few possible voices that could get a hearing by Republican climate sceptics. Nick Mabey, formerly of World Wildlife Fund, has urged military officials to become louder 'communicating the security implications and costs of uncontrolled and extreme climate change to political leaders and the public', saying it would protect their interests, open up new markets, and drive technological innovation.[40] Others point to the potential role for the military in dealing with climate disasters, with the US Operation Damayan in the aftermath of the Typhoon Haiyan in the Philippines in 2012, as one recent example.

We see the unfolding love affair between some environmentalists and the military as deeply problematic. Akkerman's closer look at the military's 'green pivot' shows that it is mainly driven by energy, not environmental concerns – and the need to identify a new 'threat' that will fill army coffers in case the threat of terrorism no longer suffices. The military have also welcomed new allies from the environmental movement and efforts to paint themselves 'green', as it helps detract attention from the deeply unpopular wars in Afghanistan and Iraq and the much less publicised, but constant, public opposition to their vast global infrastructure of military bases.

Acquisition through dispossession

The third part of the book casts a critical eye on the new state-corporate discourses on food, water and energy security. The common theme is a Malthusian vision of scarcity that predicts shortages in the future due to population growth combined with climate constraints. The dominant proposed solution to these 'InSecurities' is always the same: expand production, encourage more private investment and participation and use new technologies to overcome obstacles. Issues of distribution, injustice and environmental exploitation or the values of self-reliance or local control, where considered at all, are dismissed as unfeasible or irrelevant.

Yet the scarcity most describe is not an absolute scarcity – there continues to be enough food and water for everyone – but is mainly created by how these resources are shared. In our global food system, 30–50 per cent of food produced globally is wasted; moreover while an estimated 1 billion people today suffer from hunger, 500 million people in both the Global North and South are obese. Despite this chronic mal-distribution of resources, the bulk of research and investment continues to go into production and technological development. The result is that real-life experiences of present injustices in our energy, food and water systems are ignored, not learnt from. As research group Cornerhouse point out, this also means we are doomed to repeat and deepen the problems with our current systems of food, water and energy:

> As the future will grow out of the present, a better way of dealing with 'future [resource] crisis' is not imagining a future Malthusian world that bears no relationship to what exists now or ever has existed, and then imagining how to stave off that hypothetical Malthusian destiny, but rather dealing with current scarcities now on the realistic assumption that what causes scarcity today is going to go on causing scarcity in the future.[41]

The advocacy and implementation of plans for food security, water security and energy security in the name of climate change has also in many cases perversely accelerated climate change. In Chapter 8, Zoe Brent and Annie Shattuck of the think tank Food First, together with co-editor Nick Buxton, note that the World Bank's and others' calls for 'sustainable intensification' of agriculture in future decades will consolidate an industrial agricultural model that is decidedly unsustainable in its dependence on cheap fossil fuels and global transportation. Moreover, peasants are having their land grabbed in the name of 'food security' at an unprecedented rate.

In Chapter 9, researcher and activist Mary Ann Manahan of Focus on the Global South reveals how water scarcity has become a major driver in corporations and banks securing water rights in order to lock-in guaranteed profits as the precious resource becomes scarce. This leads to situations where companies like Pepsi have glossy brochures about reducing their water footprint, yet have quietly secured rights to water in water-stressed regions of India. 'Water security' is also invoked in California to back 'climate-friendly' water infrastructure that will mainly benefit agribusiness and fracking firms.

Meanwhile in the world of energy, dwindling resources have fuelled a calamitous 'race for what's left',[42] as companies enter regions like the Arctic, Amazonian rainforests, protected national parks and often indigenous territories to extract the very last drop of oil and gas. In Chapter 10, UK oil campaigner Emma Hughes and the Platform research collective show how, despite the obvious role our energy system has played in causing climate change, most government and corporate energy planners have used energy security to justify ongoing fossil-fuel exploitation, to legitimise military intervention in defence of supply, to repress environmental activists and to prioritise energy for corporations rather than people.

From security to justice

The final chapter in the book asks what our response to climate-change impacts should be once we reject the notion of security. After critically examining two popular concepts of 'adaptation' and 'resilience', the last chapter outlines some of the driving principles and practices that could embody a people's just response to climate change. Many of the alternatives are described in each of the preceding chapters and have arisen out of resistance to corporate and security-led strategies as well as through attempts by communities to take back control of key resources in a way that embodies principles of justice, democracy and sustainability. Two accompanying online chapters explore these themes further – one by labour scholars Hilary Wainwright and Jacklyn Cock points to the importance and potential of trade unions to address climate change and its impacts, the other by Justin Kenrick and Tom Henfrey who have been deeply involved in the Transition Town movement draws out the lessons for commons-based movements worldwide.[43] The book ends on a note of hope, drawing on the inspiration from the way people throughout history in times of disaster have more often responded with creativity and in defence of justice than with repression and violence.

For a long time, environmental advocates have ducked the issue of how we should respond to the impact of climate change because it was seen as a tacit admission of defeat, an admission that we had failed. But as climate impacts become increasingly obvious, that is ever more a self-defeating strategy. When it becomes clear that this void has been filled mainly by the military and corporations seeking to cash in on catastrophe, it is even more short-sighted.

We hope this book, which analyses those forces, and points to the dangers of viewing all our basic necessities such as food and water through the lens of 'security' will build support for alternative approaches. These alternatives already exist as many of this book's authors makes clear. Indeed, climate disruption may well provide the opportunities to put them on the table as never before. The key will be to connect them from the bottom up and build the inclusive local, regional and global movements that can tackle systemic injustice. We need to ensure that as difficult times emerge, our societies respond with justice and compassion, rather than fear and repression.

Notes

1. *Shell Energy Scenarios to 2050.* (2008). The Hague, Netherlands: Shell International BV.
2. In 2013, Shell provided two more scenarios, this time divided into 'Mountains' and 'Oceans'. While Scramble and Blueprint had focused on inter-state rivalries and energy sources, Mountains and Oceans honed in on power dynamics and class tensions within states and the interconnection of water with energy and food. Like its predecessor, the scenario assumes an ongoing 'race for what's left', but interestingly perceives the main fault-lines to be along 'class' or social-strata lines. Mountains imagines a world where 'status quo power is locked in and held tightly by the currently influential', leading to more stability but also inequality and social unrest. Oceans, on the other hand, is where 'power is devolved, competing interests are accommodated and compromise is king'; it paints a more messy world with a strange mix of rampant market forces, revitalised civil society and inaction on climate change. Again, neither scenario can imagine a world where corporate power is constrained and fossil-fuel use radically reduced.

3. Campbell, K.M., ed. (2009). *Climate Cataclysm: The foreign policy and national security implications of climate change.* Washington, DC: Brooking Institute Press; Campbell, K.M., Gulledge, J., McNeil, J., Podesta, J., Ogden, P., Fuerth, L., Mix, D. (n.d.). *The Age of Consequences: The foreign policy and national security implications of global climate change,* pp. 1–124. Retrieved from http://csis.org/files/media/csis/pubs/071105_ageofconsequences.pdf.

4. Department of Defense. (2008). *2008 Army Modernization Strategy.* Retrieved from http://downloads.army.mil/docs/08modplan/Army_Mod_Strat_2008.pdf.

5. The crowdfunding appeal can be seen here: https://www.indiegogo.com/projects/cashing-in-on-catastrophe.

6. IPCC. (2014). Climate change 2014: Mitigation of climate change. *Summary for Policymakers,* p. 6. Retrieved from http://ipcc.ch/pdf/assessment-report/ar5/wg3/ipcc_wg3_ar5_summary-for-policymakers.pdf ; World Meteorological Organization. (9 September 2014). Record Greenhouse Gas Levels Impact Atmosphere and Oceans. Retrieved from https://www.wmo.int/pages/mediacentre/press_releases/pr_1002_en.html.

7. Anderson, K. (2012). *Real Clothes for the Emperor: Facing the challenges of climate change,* pp. 1–86. Retrieved from http://kevinanderson.info/blog/wp-content/uploads/2012/11/Cabot-Seminar-anderson-ppt.pdf.

8. For descriptions of the Planetary Boundaries Project, including their latest report released in 2015, visit http://www.stockholmresilience.org/21/research/research-programmes/planetary-boundaries.html.

9. Moore, J.W. (2010). Ecology, capital, and the nature of our times: Accumulation and crisis in the capitalist world-ecology. *Umeå University,* 108–47. Retrieved from http://www.jasonwmoore.com/uploads/Moore__Ecology_Capital_and_the_Origins_of_Our_Times__JWSR__2011_.pdf.

10. IPCC. (2014). Summary for policymakers. *Climate Change 2014: Impacts, Adaptation, and Vulnerability,* 9(1), 1–34. Retrieved from http://ipcc-wg2.gov/AR5/images/uploads/WG2AR5_SPM_FINAL.pdf.

11. Vidal, J. (13 April 2013). Millions face starvation as world warms, say scientists. *The Guardian.* Retrieved from http://www.theguardian.com/global-development/2013/apr/13/climate-change-millions-starvation-scientists.

12. US Department of Commerce. (2013). Service assessment: Hurricane/post-tropical cyclone Sandy, October 22–29, 2012, pp. 1–66. Retrieved from http://www.nws.noaa.gov/os/assessments/pdfs/Sandy13.pdf; World Resources Institute. (December 2013). Adaptation finance tracking. Retrieved from http://www.wri.org/resources/presentations/adaptation-finance-tracking.

13. Vidal, J. (1 April 2014). Yeb Sano: Unlikely climate justice star. *The Guardian.* Retrieved from http://www.theguardian.com/environment/2014/apr/01/yeb-sano-typhoon-haiyan-un-climate-talks.

14. DiMento, J.F. (2014). *Climate Change: What it means for us, our children, and our grandchildren.* Cambridge, MA: MIT Press.

15. World Bank. (2014). *Turn Down the Heat: Confronting the new climate normal,* pp. 1–320. Retrieved from http://www-wds.worldbank.org/external/default/WDSContentServer/WDSP/IB/2014/11/20/000406484_20141120090713/Rendered/PDF/927040v20WP0OOOull0Report000English.pdf.

16. Hamilton, C. (2010). *Requiem for a Species: Why we resist the truth about climate change.* London: Earthscan.

17. See www.climatesecurityagenda.com.

18. Parenti, C. (2012). *Tropic of Chaos: Climate change and the new geography of violence.* New York: Nation Books.

19. See www.climatesecurityagenda.org.

20. Welzer, H., and Camiller, P. (2012). *Climate Wars: Why people will be killed in the twenty-first century.* Cambridge: Polity Press.

21. Rogers, P. (2009). *Climate Change and Security.* The Hague: Advisory Council on International Affair. Retrieved from http://rcpjournal.org/content/9/2/108.full.pdf.

22. Eckersley, R. (2009) Environmental security, climate change, and globalizing terrorism, in D. Greenfel and P. James, eds. *Rethinking Insecurity, War and Violence: Beyond savage globalization?* London: Routledge, p. 87.

23. Hildyard, N., Lohmann, L., Sexton, S., and The Corner House. (2012). Energy security for what? For whom? Retrieved from doi:10.1080/19934270.2012.675191.

24. The term 'resilience' has been uncritically embraced by many civil-society organisations, but as Jeremy Walker and Melissa Cooper warn, it has strong neoliberal and Darwinian roots and 'risks becoming the measure of one's fitness to survive in the turbulent order of things'. It certainly tells us nothing about the exercise of power and the need for transformation. See Walker, J. and Cooper, M. (2011). Genealogies of resilience from systems ecology to the political economy of crisis adaptation. *Security Dialogue*, 42(2), 143–60.

25. Mitchell, S. (18 November 2011). Think Walmart uses 100% clean energy? Try 2%. Retrieved from http://grist.org/business-technology/2011-11-17-walmarts-progress-on-renewables-has-been-very-slow/.

26. Coghlan, A. and MacKenzie, D. (24 October 2011). Revealed – the capitalist network that runs the world. Retrieved from http://www.newscientist.com/article/mg21228354.500-revealed--the-capitalist-network-that-runs-the-world.html#.VUNCf_DE-Dk.

27. Labban, M. (2009). The struggle for the heartland: Hybrid geopolitics in the Transcaspian. *Geopolitics*, 14(1), 1–25. doi:10.1080/14650040802578641.

28. Dabelko, G.D., Herzer, L., Null, S. and Sticklor, R., eds. (2013). *Backdraft: Conflict potential of climate change adaptation and mitigation* (2nd edn, Vol. 14). Washington, DC: Woodrow Wilson International Center for Scholars.

29. Zographos, C., Goulden, M.C. and Kallis, G. (November 2014). Sources of human insecurity in the face of hydro-climatic change. Retrieved from http://www.sciencedirect.com/science/article/pii/S0959378013001933.

30. Freier, N. (2008). Known unknowns: Unconventional 'strategic shocks' in defense strategy development [Abstract]. *Strategic Studies Institute*, pp. 1–52. Retrieved from http://www.strategicstudiesinstitute.army.mil/pdffiles/PUB890.pdf.

31. Potter, W. (2011). *Green is the New Red: An insider's account of a social movement under siege.* San Francisco, CA: City Lights Books.

32. See www.climatesecurityagenda.org.

33. Global Witness. (2015). How many more? 2014's deadly environment: The killing and intimidation of environmental and land activists, with a spotlight on Honduras. *Global Witness Limited*. Retrieved from https://www.globalwitness.org/documents/17882/how_many_more_pages.pdf.

34. Miller, T. (17 August 2013). War on the border. *New York Times*. Retrieved from http://www.nytimes.com/2013/08/18/opinion/sunday/war-on-the-border.html?pagewanted=all&_r=1.

35. Dunlea, E. (n.d.). Geoengineering climate: Technical evaluation and discussion of impacts. Retrieved from http://www8.nationalacademies.org/cp/projectview.aspx?key=49540.

36. Kutsch, T. (13 April 2014). Global military spending falls overall, but rises outside the West. Retrieved from http://america.aljazeera.com/articles/2014/4/13/global-military-spending.html.

37. Priest, D. and Arkin, W.M. (19 July 2012). A hidden world, growing beyond control. Retrieved from http://projects.washingtonpost.com/top-secret-america/articles/a-hidden-world-growing-beyond-control/.

38. Hayes, B. (2009). *NeoConOpticon: The EU security-industrial complex*, p. 5. Retrieved from http://www.tni.org/sites/www.tni.org/files/download/neoconopticon_0.pdf.

39. Carrington, D. (30 June 2013). Climate change poses grave threat to security, says US envoy. *The Guardian*. Retrieved from http://www.theguardian.com/environment/2013/jun/30/climate-change-security-threat-envoy.

40. Mabey also suggested that military action on climate change could help thwart more radical groups and their potential growing 'resentment against the current international order'. Mabey, N. (23 April 2008). Delivering climate security: International security responses to a climate changed world. Retrieved from https://www.rusi.org/publications/whitehall/ref:I480E2C638B3BC/#.VUPDRfDE-Dk.

41. The Corner House. (2006). Colonizing the future: 'Scarcity' as political strategy. *Different Takes*, 43, 1–4. Retrieved from http://popdev.hampshire.edu/sites/default/files/uploads/u4763/DT%2043%20-%20Corner%20House.pdf.

42. Klare, M.T. (2012). *The Race for What's Left: The global scramble for the world's last resources*. New York: Metropolitan Books.

43. See www.climatesecurityagenda.org.

PART I

THE SECURITY AGENDA

I

THE CATASTROPHIC CONVERGENCE: MILITARISM, NEOLIBERALISM AND CLIMATE CHANGE

Christian Parenti

Water flows or blood.
Slogan of the banned Pakistani political party Jamaat-u-Dawa

Introduction

Climate change arrives in a world primed for crisis.[1] And the political responses to climate change increasingly take the form of ethnic, religious, or class violence in the form of banditry, rebellion, warfare, state repression and general militarisation. This is because the current and impending dislocations of climate change intersect with the already existing crises of poverty and inequality left by thirty years of neoliberalism, and the violence and tattered social fabric left by Cold War-era military conflicts. I call this collision of political, economic and environmental disasters the 'catastrophic convergence'. By catastrophic convergence, I do not merely mean that several disasters happen simultaneously, one problem atop another. Rather, I am arguing that problems compound and amplify each other, one expressing itself through another.

Societies, like people, deal with new challenges in ways that are conditioned by the traumas of their past. Thus damaged societies, like damaged people, often respond to new crises in ways that are irrational, short-sighted and self-destructive. In the case of climate change, the past traumas that set the stage for bad adaptation – a destructive social response – are Cold War-era militarism and the economic pathologies of neoliberal capitalism. Over the last forty years, both these forces have distorted the state's relationship to society – removing and undermining the state's collectivist, regulatory and redistributive functions – while overdeveloping its repressive and military capacities. And this, I contend, seriously challenges society's ability to avoid violent dislocations as climate change kicks in.

Climate crisis

The scientific consensus about climate takes institutional form in the Intergovernmental Panel on Climate Change (IPCC). The IPCC does not conduct independent research but is instead a government- and UN-supported international clearinghouse. It collects and summarises all published scientific literature on climatology and related issues in biology, hydrology and glaciology to facilitate governments' response to climate issues based on fully vetted research.

The IPCC has been attacked by climate denialists as alarmist and wrong, due to several minor errors in its 2007 Fourth Assessment Report. But correcting these minor errors did not change the report's overall conclusions. In fact, because the IPCC operates on the basis of consensus, its conclusions are quite conservative and its reports lag years behind the latest scientific developments. The IPCC represents the lowest-common-denominator, fully accepted conclusions of the scientific mainstream.

The IPCC has concluded that our civilisation's dependence on burning fossil fuels has boosted atmospheric concentrations of carbon dioxide from around 280 parts per million (ppm) before the Industrial Revolution to 400 ppm today. Analyses of ancient ice cores show 400 ppm to be the highest that atmospheric CO_2 has been for 10,000 years.

Atmospheric CO_2 functions like the glass in a greenhouse, allowing the sun's heat in but preventing much of it from radiating back out to space. We need atmospheric CO_2 – without it, the earth would be an ice-cold lifeless rock. However, over the last 150 years, we have been loading the sky with far too much CO_2, and the planet is heating up.

As the Center for Climate and Energy Solutions explains, 'The Earth's average surface temperature has increased by 1.4°F (0.8°C) since the early years of the 20th century. The 10 warmest years on record (since 1850) have all occurred since 1998, and all but one have happened since 2000.'[2]

Less than 1 degree Celsius warmer over a hundred years? That may not sound like much, but scientists believe it is enough to begin disrupting the climate system's equilibrium. The negative feedback loops that keep the earth's climate stable are increasingly giving way to destabilising positive feedback loops, in which departures from the norm build on themselves instead of diminishing over time. As a result, climate change is happening faster than initially predicted and its impacts are already upon us in the form of more extreme weather events, desertification, ocean acidification, melting glaciers and incrementally rising sea levels. The scientists who construct the computer models that analyse climate data agree that even if we stop dumping greenhouse gases into the atmosphere, CO_2 levels are already so high that we are locked into a significant increase in global temperatures. Disruptive climate change is a certainty even if we make the economic shift away from fossil fuels.

Incipient climate change is already starting to express itself in the realm of politics. Extreme weather events and off-kilter weather patterns are causing more humanitarian crises. The UN estimates that 70 per cent of humanitarian disasters are climate related, up from 50 per cent two decades ago. Already climate change adversely affects 300 million people a year, killing 300,000 of them. By 2030 – as floods, drought, forest fires and new diseases grow worse – as many as 500,000 people a year could be killed by climate change, and the economic cost of these disruptions could reach $600 billion annually.[3]

This dangerous mix of extreme weather and water scarcity could inflame and escalate already existing social conflicts. Columbia University Earth Institute's Center for International Earth Science Information Network (CIESIN) and the International Crisis Group combined databases on civil wars and water availability, and found that 'When rainfall is significantly below normal, the risk of a low-level conflict escalating to a full-scale civil war approximately doubles the following year.'[4] The project cites the example of Nepal, where the Maoist insurgency was most severe after droughts and almost nonexistent in areas that had normal rainfall. In some cases, when the rains were late or light, or came all at once, or at the wrong time, 'semi-retired' armed groups often re-emerged to start fighting again.

Between the Tropic of Capricorn and the Tropic of Cancer lies what I have called the 'Tropic of Chaos', a belt of economically and politically battered post-colonial states girding the planet's equatorial latitudes. In this band around the tropics, climate change is beginning to hit hardest. The societies in this belt are heavily dependent on agriculture and fishing, thus very vulnerable to shifts in weather patterns. According to a Swedish government study, 'There are 46 countries – home to 2.7 billion people – in which the effects of climate change interacting with economic, social and political problems will create a high risk of violent conflict.'[5] Their list covers that same terrain. These latitudes are now being most affected by the onset of anthropocentric climate change.

In my book, *Tropic of Chaos*, I described numerous conflicts that are being exacerbated by climate change, beginning with the escalation of violence among East African pastoralists, most specifically the Turkana. Moving farther eastward, Afghanistan is facing the worst drought conditions in a hundred years. On to India, where a map of Naxalite guerrilla activity correlates almost perfectly with the most drought-affected districts. More recently, other climate conflicts have become well known: Syria's civil war in 2011, for example, was precipitated in part by a horrific drought from 2006 to 2009.

Rising sea levels provide another major challenge for our capacity to adapt. In 2007, the IPCC projected sea levels could rise by an average of 7–23 inches this century. These numbers were soon amended and scientists now believe that sea levels could rise by an average of five feet over the next ninety years. Such sea-level rises will lead to massive dislocations. One 2014 study from Columbia's CIESIN projects that 700 million 'climate refugees' will be on the move by 2050, although most of these will not cross borders and will move within their country of birth (see Chapter 5).[6]

Perhaps the modern era's first 'climate refugees' were the 500,000 Bangladeshis left homeless when half of Bhola Island flooded in 2005. In Bangladesh, 22 million people could be forced from their homes by 2050 because of climate change. India is already building a militarised border fence along its 2,500-mile frontier with Bangladesh.[7]

And the student activists of India's Hindu Right are pushing vigorously for the mass deportation of (Muslim) Bangladeshi immigrants.

Meanwhile, 22 Pacific island nations, home to 7 million people, are planning for relocation as rising seas threaten them with national annihilation. What will happen when China's cities begin to flood? When the eastern seaboard of the US starts to flood, how will people and institutions respond?

Military legacy of the Cold War

The vulnerability of the Global South to climate change cannot be fully understood without noting that this region was also the frontline of the Cold War's hot proxy battles and the laboratory for neoliberal, violent economic restructuring. The main pre-existing crisis of the catastrophic convergence is the legacy of Cold War militarism. In the Global South, the Cold War was hot. Revolution and counter-insurgency were its methods. Conventional warfare in which the military and infrastructures are targeted is, despite all its horrors, often associated with increased social solidarity, as witnessed in Britain during the Second World War, where Nazi bombardment was met with evacuation, rationing, conscription and an unprecedented levelling of class differences. Asymmetrical socio-military conflicts, such as those waged across the Global South at the height of the Cold War were quite different, eroding and destroying the social fabric.

For the most part, the rebellion in the Global South was a home-grown affair, and the reaction from the US was – in the eyes of US planners – defensive. As a doctrine, counter-insurgency is the theory of internal warfare; it is the strategy of suppressing rebellions and revolution. Counter-insurgency mimics revolution: Its object is *civilian society* as a whole, and the social fabric of everyday life. Whereas traditional aerial bombing (which is notoriously ineffective) targets bridges, factories and command centres, counter-insurgency targets – *pace* Foucault – the 'capillary' level of social relations. It ruptures and tears (but rarely re-makes) the intimate social relations among people, the ability to cooperate, the lived texture of solidarity – in other words, the bonds that are society's sinews.

Conventional warfare seeks to control territory and destroy the opposing military, but counter-insurgency seeks to control society. In an insurgency, the military force – the state or the occupying power – already has (at least nominal) control of the battle space, but it lacks control of the population. Guerrillas, irregular forces, even small unpopular terrorist groups all rely on the populace, or parts of it, for recruits, food, shelter, medical care, intelligence and, if nothing else, simple cover. Mao Zedong summed it up: 'The guerrilla must move amongst the people as a fish swims in the sea.' Thus, the counter-insurgent's task is to isolate and destroy the guerrillas by gaining control of the population through violence as well as psychological and ideological control. Society is the target, and as such, society is damaged.

Irregular, proxy conflicts – insurgency and counter-insurgency in the Third World – defined the American and Soviet methods during the Cold War. Those methods primed many areas of the world for serious instability. The UN documented around 150 armed conflicts in the Third World between 1945 and 1990. In these 'small wars', 20 million people died, 60 million were injured, and 15 million were deracinated as refugees by 1991. Derek Summerfield, a psychiatrist and academic who specialises in the mental-health effects of modern war, described the situation as follows:

> Five percent of all casualties in the First World War were civilians; the figure for the Second World War was 50 percent, and that for the Vietnam War was over 80 percent. In current armed conflicts over 90 percent of all casualties are civilians, usually from poor rural families. This is the result of deliberate and systematic violence deployed to terrorize whole populations … Population, not territory, is the target, and through terror the aim is to penetrate into homes, families, and the entire fabric of grassroots social relations, producing demoralization and paralysis. To this end terror is sown not just randomly, but also through targeted assaults on health workers, teachers and co-operative leaders, those whose work symbolizes shared values and aspirations. Torture, mutilation, and summary execution in front of family members have become routine.[8]

Nowhere saw a more devastating counter insurgency than Guatemala. Beginning in 1981, the military government of General Rios Mont combined a genocidal scorched-earth campaign against civilians with a classic 'secure and hold' development strategy. The strategy was called '*frijoles y fusiles*' (kidney beans and guns). After destroying Indian villages and massacring many of their inhabitants, the military would gather the surviving civilians and concentrate them in 'model villages'. Male survivors were forced to participate in civil patrols, lightly armed vigilante forces that were the eyes and ears of the military – and often their human shield. An estimated 100,000 civilians were murdered during the Guatemalan civil war, the vast majority of them by government forces.

I had an opportunity to see this war first-hand, in 1988, when I hiked across the Ixill Triangle in the highlands war zone. The trails were littered with government and guerrilla propaganda – small handbills exhorting the people to join one side or the other. The area was still at war but the guerrillas were in retreat. Everywhere we saw the methods of counter-insurgency: trails cleared of trees on all sides, air patrols, civilian militia checkpoints, burnt villages, and newly constructed ones under strict government control. Later, in 1991, I travelled with and reported on the *Resistencia Nacional*, part of the FMLN, in the hills of Cabañas, El Salvador; similar physical and social scars were evident.

Today, the Guatemalan highlands and the small towns of El Salvador are still violent, but instead of guerrilla operations and counter-insurgency, crime is the plague. The global average homicide rate is less than eight per 100,000. But the 2012 UN Office on Drugs and Crime report on Central America cites the rates that murder increased between 2000 and 2011: from 51 to 92 per 100,000 in Honduras; from 60 to 69 per 100,000 in El Salvador; and from 26 to 39 per 100,000 in Guatemala, with a spike to 46 per 100,000 in 2008 and 2009.[9]

All three of those countries were sites of intense counter-insurgency from the late 1970s to early 1990s, and the legacy of that is a society weakened, social fabric frayed: gun culture; large populations of unemployed men trained and habituated to violence, discipline, secrecy, pack loyalty, brutality, and the arts of smuggling, extortion, robbery and assassination. The political class is also steeped in violence, and much of it sees society as warfare: enemies must be destroyed, social problems eliminated by force. Walls and armed guards define the landscape. The police are steeped in traditions of torture, disappearance and drug running.[10]

Relative deprivation defines the psychological terrain: these societies are more unequal than ever, but the revolutionaries and progressive social movements, in raising class-consciousness, have made the masses aware of the inherent unfairness of the situation.[11] The spectacle of modern media, in advertising riches and fame, make them aware of what they lack – all of which now feed criminogenic relative depravation.

Post-Cold War

Famously, the US defeat in Vietnam turned the US military away from the study of counter-insurgency, though the methods of irregular warfare were still part of the instruction for US proxy forces in El Salvador, the Philippines, Colombia and elsewhere. Counter-insurgency doctrine began to make a return after US Army Rangers got into trouble in Mogadishu, Somalia, in 1993, during a botched raid on the compound of Somali warlord Mohamed Farrah Aidid. A Black Hawk helicopter was shot down in the city and a seat-of-the pants rescue mission eventually shot its way in and then back out of the city, but not without considerable loss of life – particularly for the Somali militiamen, 800–1,300 of whom were killed – and a spectacular humiliation for the US Army.[12]

After that, the Pentagon began to think more seriously about how to fight irregulars in cities and failed states. Soon the RAND corporation put out a study called *The Urbanization of Insurgency*, and a December 1997, National Defense Panel review

> … castigated the Army as unprepared for protracted combat in the near impassable, maze-like streets of the poverty-stricken cities of the Third World. As a result, the four armed services, coordinated by the Joint Staff Urban Working Group, launched crash programs to master street-fighting under realistic third-world conditions.[13]

Greg Grandin's *Empire's Workshop: Latin America, the United States, and the rise of the new imperialism* made clear the links between counter-insurgency in Iraq and its antecedents in Central America. Grandin quotes an American counter-insurgency expert, who described the ferocity of US-funded and trained forces in Central America as 'going primitive'.

As Grandin explains:

> With the United States failing to defeat the rebels [in Iraq] on its own, the Pentagon came to debate the 'Salvadorian option', that is the use of local paramilitary forces otherwise known as death squads, to do the kind of dirty work that it was either unwilling or unable to do. It turned to men like James Steele, who in the 1980s led the Special Forces mission in El Salvador and worked with Oliver North to run weapons and supplies to the Nicaraguan Contras … .[14]

The Shiite death squads of Iraq's Maliki government were the result. They were also a disturbing harbinger of a world wracked by climate insecurity, as we will explore later.

In the meantime, let us now turn to the other great crisis: the rise of neoliberalism.

The political economy of neoliberalism

From the 1930s until the 1980s, many developing economies in the Global South followed a model of state-directed import-substitution industrialisation, or ISI. This form of capitalist development involved an uneasy compact between business and labour, brokered by an interventionist state. The rise of Communism in the USSR, the spread of radical left movements, and the collapse of markets for traditional exports during the Great Depression, all encouraged an embrace of the model. In exchange for discipline on the shop floor, the state created social security programmes and allowed rising wages for the aristocracy of labour. Investment and finance were regulated, and banks were often state owned. Examples of this mix are found from Brazil to Mexico to Morocco to South Africa to India. Overall – and contrary to the assertions of today's economic orthodoxy – labour productivity, living standards and the economy as a whole increased under ISI.[15]

By the mid-1960s, however, signs of trouble emerged. There started to be too much stuff and not enough demand.[16] By 1970, 99 per cent of American homes had refrigerators, electric irons and radios. More than 90 per cent had washing machines, vacuum cleaners and toasters. As one economist put it:

> Saturation in one market led to saturation in others as producers looked abroad when the possibilities for domestic expansion were exhausted. The results were simultaneous export drives by companies in all advanced countries, with similar, technologically sophisticated products going into one another's markets … Increasing exports … from developing countries such as Taiwan, Korea, Mexico and Brazil further increased the congestion of mass markets in the advanced economies.[17]

By the early 1970s, capitalism was suffocating from industrial success.[18] In 1973, the other shoe dropped: Arab defeat in the Yom Kippur War led to an oil boycott by many key exporters. The price of oil quadrupled in less than a year. That hit countries like Brazil hard. Though it is now a major oil producer, it was then importing 80 per cent of its petroleum. Before prices could subside, the Shah of Iran fell to a revolution and there was a second oil shock in 1979. Prices nearly doubled again.

These petrodollars flooded the world financial markets and were lent out to anyone who would borrow at very low, but variable interest rates. In Latin America, this translated into mounting debt. Overcapacity and a collapse in the rate of return on investment prompted Paul Volker, the chairman of the US Federal Reserve, to begin a dramatic rise in interest rates from 7.9 per cent in 1979, to 16.4 per cent in 1981. This had the effect of cutting borrowing throughout the economy; with that, investment and consumer spending also ratcheted down abruptly. Unemployment in the US reached 10.8 per cent by December 1982.[19] At the same time, both Reagan and Thatcher launched offensives against the power of organised labour, cut social spending and slashed taxes on the wealthy.

In Latin America, the new monetary policy also meant that interest payments on existing debt soared. Thus began the Latin American debt crisis. From 1978 to the end of 1982, total Latin American debt more than doubled, from $159 billion to $327 billion. Debt servicing – that is, paying the interest – grew even faster: The average Latin American country was using more than 30 per cent of its export earnings just to service its debts – Brazil paid nearly 60 per cent.[20]

... Austerity

The solution to the debt crisis came in the form of IMF- and World Bank-enforced austerity. Though the pattern played out differently in each affected country, I will focus on the paradigmatic examples of Brazil and Mexico.

In 1983, Brazil had the largest foreign debt of the developing world – $83.8 billion. Just to service its debts, it had to borrow more and more in a downward spiral. In early 1983, Brazil went to the IMF for $6 billion, which was then the single largest loan in the Fund's history. But in return, Brazil agreed to a brutal austerity program: To cut inflation, growth was strangled, public spending was cut, the currency devalued, imports restricted, public assets privatised, exports boosted.[21] In Sao Paulo, workers were soon rioting.[22]

Unfortunately, Brazil's export drive took place amidst falling commodity prices. Two factors contributed to this. The Bretton Woods institutions were simultaneously pressuring other Third World debtors to export more; meanwhile, deep recessions and high interest rates in the richer countries held down consumption. Increased supply plus reduced demand meant plummeting prices. Sugar, copper, aluminium and other raw materials all hit deep lows.

The IMF's structural adjustment programme resulted in higher unemployment, rising poverty and growing urbanisation – as the rural poor went to cities in search of work. From 1980 to 1990, Rio's overall population growth rate was 8 per cent, but the *favela* (slum) population surged by 41 per cent. As economist and Latin America expert Mark Weisbrot explained, 'From 1960 to 1980, income per person – the most basic measure that economists have of economic progress – in Brazil grew by about 123 per cent. From 1980 to 2000, it grew by less than 4 per cent.' Weisbrot estimates that had Brazil not embraced neoliberalism, 'the country would have European living standards today. Instead of about 50 million poor people as there are today, there would be very few. And almost everyone would today enjoy vastly higher living standards, educational levels, and better health care.'[23]

In Mexico, the debt crisis played a similar role, but was exacerbated by trade policies. Mexico's crisis broke on 12 August 1982, when Mexico announced that it could not pay its bills and took the first steps towards default, declaring a 90-day moratorium on repayment. The peso was devalued 30 per cent and before the year's end would drop another 53 per cent.[24] The crisis was prompted a year earlier though, when the effect of Volker's monetarist squeeze went international: oil prices began to slide and Mexico faced badly diminished revenues and the world's largest foreign debt: $70 billion. Mexican economists had projected the country would have oil revenues of $20 billion in 1981 and $27 billion in 1982, but in 1981 oil brought in a mere $14 billion and the next year was also below target.[25] The cost of debt servicing now consumed most of Mexico's projected petroleum sales, and thus most of its foreign earnings. By the summer of 1982, Mexico owed almost $81 billion to foreign banks, and that sum was rising. To avoid default, the peso was devalued and the government imposed limited capital controls. It was the second devaluation of the year. Rich individuals and private firms began to panic and shift their wealth out of the country, prompting a default and the fear that it would clearly spread to the US banking system and worldwide.

Bailout '82

A deal between the US Federal Reserve, the IMF and most of the eight hundred banks to which Mexico owed money led that country to be granted $12 billion in credit, in exchange for a programme of economic liberalisation and imposed austerity. Out went Keynes; in came Hayek. The government sold 106 state-owned companies and agencies. These included sugar mills, shipyards, textile plants and power plants, as well as the parastatal processing plants and the export-marketing firms.[26]

Privatisation brought new owners, who broke unions, fired workers and drove down wages. By decade's end, Mexico's 1,155 state businesses had shrunk to only 400. The government earned less than $2 billion from these privatisations, which went to service debts.[27] At the same time, food subsidies were slashed; those for eggs, milk, cooking oil, sugar, beans and rice were eliminated completely. The retail price of gasoline and natural gas doubled.[28] By 1986, the purchasing power of the average Mexican was about half of what it had been in 1982.[29]

Mexico's trial by debt began the long march to the North American Free Trade Agreement (NAFTA) that came into effect on 1 January 1994. At the same time, in the southern Mexican state of Chiapas, the Zapatista National Liberation Army – a group of mostly indigenous peasants – rose up against the government, calling NAFTA a death sentence for Indians.[30]

What did 'free trade' really do for Mexico? An almost quizzical article published in the *New York Times* in 2009 answered this as follows:

> In some cases, NAFTA produced results that were exactly the opposite of what was promised. For instance, domestic industries were dismantled as multinationals imported parts from their own suppliers. Local farmers were priced out of the market by food imported tariff-free. Many Mexican farmers simply abandoned their land and headed north.[31]

The piece went on to note that although the value of Mexico's exports had quintupled in 15 years, almost half a million people each year were migrating in search of work, a disproportionate number of them from the countryside. With only one-quarter of Mexico's total population, the countryside accounts for 44 per cent of all Mexican immigrants moving to the United States.[32]

Under NAFTA, the government dismantled most of the agencies that offered assistance and administered subsidies to small farmers: 'Lending by both government and private-sector rural credit programs declined 75 per cent after 1994, when NAFTA took effect, while rural bankruptcies increased six-fold.'[33] The reformed Article 27 now allows the sale of *ejido* (common) lands, which has increased landlessness.[34] According to a 2010 report by Oxfam, Mexico has spent $80 billion on food imports and now has a deficit in food trade of $435 million.[35] Mexican agricultural production has turned away from food for people and internal markets toward animal feed for export.[36] Markets for corn, the staple food, protected by government policy until NAFTA, have been completely opened.[37] Peasant organisations have demanded a renegotiation of the treaty.[38]

Since 1994, Mexico's economic growth has slowed. It now averages only about 3 per cent. From 1921 to 1967, annual growth averaged 5.2 per cent, and for much of that period it was over 6 per cent.[39] According to World Bank figures, 'in 2004, 28 per cent of rural dwellers were extremely poor and 57 per cent moderately poor.'[40]

By the late 1980s and early 1990s, the neoliberal model imposed on Brazil and Mexico was enforced all over the planet. Sometimes it was associated with a high rate of growth, as in India, sometimes with stagnation, as in Latin America, but it always created increased inequality.

The suffering and social polarisation produced by neoliberalism has fostered corruption and exacerbated relative deprivation. This is the stage, pre-set, onto which now enters the issue of climate change to converge with the economic crises and the legacy of political repression. In combination, all of these factors help drive migration to the United States and to northern Mexico, where the chaotic drug war now eats away at society.

Militarised adaptation

The anticipation of increased conflict in a world remade by climate change has led the militaries of the Global North toward an embrace of militarised adaptation.

Military planning is conceived of as a response to events, but it also shapes events. Planning too diligently for war can preclude peace. The US's overdeveloped military capacity – its military-industrial complex – has created powerful interests that are dependent on war and therefore promote it. Today, the old military-industrial complex – companies such as General Electric, Lockheed and Raytheon, with their fabulously expensive weapons systems – are joined by a swarm of smaller security firms offering hybrid services. Blackwater, DynCorp and Global come to mind, but private prison companies such as Corrections Corporation of America, Management and Training Corporation and the Geo Group are also involved. This new security-industrial complex offers an array of services for home and abroad: surveillance, intelligence, border security, detention, facility and base construction, anti-terrorism consulting, military and police logistics, analysis, planning, training and, of course, personal security.

Their operations are found wherever the US projects power: in Afghanistan, running supply convoys, serving food and providing translators; in Colombia, spraying coca fields and training the military; in the Philippines, training the police; in Mexico, guarding businesspeople; and all along the US-Mexico border, processing immigrant detainees. This new economy of repression helps promulgate a xenophobic and bellicose ideology. For example, private prison companies lobbied hard for passage of SB1070, Arizona's tough anti-immigration law, in 2010.[41]

As a politics of climate change begins to develop, this matrix of parasitic interests has begun to shape adaptation to the militarised management of civilization's violent disintegration. Returning to the brutal legacy of the Cold War, they also have revived US commitment to strategies of counterinsurgency.

The apocalypse on paper

One of the first government investigations on the security impacts of climate change to make news was a 2004 Pentagon-commissioned study titled *An abrupt climate change scenario and its implications for United States national security*.[42] It was authored by Peter Schwartz, a CIA consultant and former head of planning at Royal Dutch Shell, and Doug Randall of the California-based Global Business Network. Schwartz and Randall forecast a new Dark Ages:

> Nations with the resources to do so may build virtual fortresses around their countries, preserving resources for themselves ... As famine, disease, and weather-related disasters strike due to the abrupt climate change, many countries' needs will exceed their carrying capacity. This will create a sense of desperation, which is likely to lead to offensive aggression in order to reclaim balance ... Europe will be struggling

internally, large numbers of refugees washing up on its shores and Asia in serious crisis over food and water. Disruption and conflict will be endemic features of life. Once again, warfare would define human life.[43]

A 2007 report by the Pentagon-connected think tank CNA Corporation envisioned permanent counter-insurgency on a global scale. Here is a salient excerpt:

> Climate change acts as a threat multiplier for instability in some of the most volatile regions of the world. Many governments in Asia, Africa and the Middle East are already on edge in terms of their ability to provide basic needs: food, water, shelter and stability. Projected climate change will exacerbate the problems in these regions and add to the problems of effective governance. Unlike most conventional security threats that involve a single entity acting in specific ways at different points in time, climate change has the potential to result in multiple chronic conditions, occurring globally within the same time frame. Economic and environmental conditions in these already fragile areas will further erode as food production declines, diseases increase, clean water becomes increasingly scarce and populations migrate in search of resources. Weakened and failing governments, with an already thin margin for survival, foster the conditions for internal conflict, extremism and movement toward increased authoritarianism and radical ideologies. The US may be drawn more frequently into these situations to help to provide relief, rescue and logistics, or to stabilize conditions before conflicts arise.[44]

Other developed states have conducted similar studies, most of them classified. The European Council's report in 2008 noted, in familiar language, that 'climate change threatens to overburden states and regions which are already fragile and conflict prone.' And this leads to 'political and security risks that directly affect European interests'.[45] It also noted the likelihood of conflict over resources due to reduction of arable land and water shortages; economic damage to coastal cities and critical infrastructure, particularly Third World megacities; environmentally induced migration; religious and political radicalisation, and tension over energy supply.[46]

Western military planners, and growing numbers of political leaders, are speaking out about the dangers in the convergence of political disorder and climate change. Instead of worrying about conventional wars over food and water, they see an emerging geography of climatologically driven civil war, migration, pogroms and social breakdown. In response, they envision a project of open-ended counter-insurgency on a global scale.[47]

Mitigation and adaptation

The watchwords of the climate discussion are *mitigation* and *adaptation*. We must mitigate the causes of climate change, while adapting to its effects. *Mitigation* means drastically cutting our production of carbon dioxide and other greenhouse gases – such as methane and chlorofluorocarbons – that prevent the sun's heat from radiating back out to space. Mitigation means moving towards clean energy sources such as wind, solar power, geothermal and tidal kinetics. It means closing coal-fired power plants, weaning our economy off oil and building a smart electrical grid.

Adaptation, on the other hand, means preparing to live with the *effects* of climatological changes, some of which are already underway, and some of which are inevitable, that is, 'in the pipeline'. Adaptation is both a technical and a political challenge.

Technical adaptation means transforming our relationship to nature as nature transforms: learning to live with the damage we have wrought by building seawalls around vulnerable coastal cities, giving land back to mangroves and everglades so they may act to break tidal surges during giant storms, opening wildlife migration corridors so species can move north as the climate warms and developing sustainable forms of agriculture that can function on an industrial scale, even as weather patterns gyrate wildly.

Political adaptation, on the other hand, means transforming humanity's relationship to itself, transforming social relations among people. Successful political adaptation to climate change will mean developing new ways of containing, avoiding and de-escalating the violence that climate change fuels. That will require economic redistribution and development. It will also require a new diplomacy of peace building.

But the military-led strategy for dealing with climate change suggests another type of political adaptation is already under way, which might be called the 'politics of the armed lifeboat': responding to climate change by arming, excluding, forgetting, repressing, policing and killing. One can imagine a green authoritarianism emerging in rich countries, while the climate crisis pushes the Third World into chaos. Already, as climate change fuels violence in the form of crime, repression, civil unrest, war and even state collapse in the Global South, the North is responding with a new authoritarianism. The Pentagon and its European allies are actively planning a militarised adaptation, which emphasises the long-term, open-ended containment of failed or failing states – counter-insurgency forever.

This sort of 'climate fascism' – a politics based on exclusion, segregation and repression – is horrific and bound to fail. The struggling states of the Global South cannot collapse without eventually taking down wealthy economies with them. If climate change is allowed to destroy whole economies and nations, no amount of walls, guns, barbed wire, armed aerial drones and permanently deployed mercenaries can save elites from a planet in collapse.

Conclusion

The catastrophic convergence offers a way to think about climate change that can help reveal its more obscured political impacts. The catastrophic convergence also has implications for how we should adapt and mitigate. If climate change acts through and by exacerbating pre-existing crises, then it is imperative that climate adaptation and mitigation act upon those same crises. Proper adaptation requires addressing the pre-existing crises – militarism and neoliberalism – through planning and socially necessary investment.

Societies suffering from continued neoliberal austerity measures, and a new round of counter-insurgency now delivered under the framework of the war on terror, cannot be expected to address the implications of climate change. Real mitigation likewise requires moving away from an unbridled free market economic orthodoxy that is only hindering our attempts to cope with climate change.

Notes

1. From *Tropic of Chaos: Climate change and the new geography of violence* by Christian Parenti, copyright © 2011. Reprinted by permission of Nation Books, a member of The Perseus Books Group.
2. Science and impacts. (n.d.). Retrieved from http://www.c2es.org/science-impacts.
3. Vidal, J. (29 May 2009). Global warming causes 300,000 deaths a year, says Kofi Annan thinktank. *The Guardian*. Retrieved from http://www.theguardian.com/environment/2009/may/29/1.
4. Quoted in Susan George, Globalisation and war. *International Congress of IPPNW*, New Delhi, 10 March 2008. Retrieved from https://www.tni.org/en/archives/act/18042.
5. Smith, D. and Vivekananda, J. (2007). A climate of conflict. *International Alert*. Retrieved from http://www.international-alert.org/sites/default/files/publications/A_climate_of_conflict.pdf.
6. Warner, K., De Sherbinin, A., Adamo, S. and Chai-Onn, T. (May 2009). *In Search of Shelter: Mapping the effects of climate change on human migration and displacement* (report). Center for International Earth Science Information Network. Retrieved http://ciesin.columbia.edu/documents/clim-migr-report-june09_media.pdf.
7. Stefanova, K. (19 April 2009). Rising sea levels in Pacific create wave of migrants. *Washington Times*. Retrieved from http://www.washingtontimes.com/news/2009/apr/19/rising-sea-levels-in-pacific-create-wave-of-migran/.
8. Summerfield, D. (1991). The psychosocial effects of conflict in the Third World. *Development in Practice*, 3, 159–73.
9. *Transnational Organized Crime in Central America and the Caribbean* (report). United Nations Office on Drugs and Crime (September 2012). Retrieved http://www.unodc.org/documents/data-and-analysis/Studies/TOC_Central_America_and_the_Caribbean_english.pdf.
10. Here is a random sampling of news stories on the post-war violence: Gunmen slaughter 14 football players, *Independent* (UK), 1 November 2010, retrieved from http://www.independent.co.uk/news/world/americas/gunmen-slaughter-14-football-players-in-honduras-2121861.html; Danilo Valladares, Central America: Youth gangs – Reserve army for organized crime, *Inter Press Service* (English), 21 September 2010; Miroff, N., and Booth, W. (27 July 2010). See also Wolf, S. (2009). Subverting democracy: Elite rule and the limits to political participation in post-war El Salvador. *Journal of Latin American Studies*, 41(3), 429, doi:10.1017/S0022216X09990149.

11. Rogers, T. (September 2000). The spiral of violence in Central America. *Z Magazine*. Retrieved from http://www.thirdworldtraveler.com/Central_America/Spiral_Violence_CA.html.

12. Bowden, M. (1999). *Black Hawk down: A story of modern war*. Berkeley, CA: Atlantic Monthly Press.

13. Davis, M. (19 April 2004). The Pentagon as global slumlord. *TomGram*. Retrieved from http://www.tomdispatch.com/blog/1386/tomgram%3A_mike_davis_on_the_pentagon%27s_urban_war_planning.

14. Grandin, G. (2006). *Empire's Workshop: Latin America, the United States, and the rise of the new imperialism*. New York: Metropolitan Books.

15. Colistete, R.P. (2010), Revisiting Import-Substituting Industrialisation in Post-War Brazil, MPRA Paper 24665, University Library of Munich, Germany.

16. Schor, J. (1992). *The Overworked America: The unexpected decline of leisure*. New York: Basic Books, p. 111.

17. Charles Sable, quoted in Harrison, B. and Bluestone, B. (1990). *The Great UTurn: Corporate restructuring and the polarizing of America*. Boulder, CO: Basic Books, p. 10.

18. On excess capacity or over-accumulation see Armstrong, P., Glyn A., and Harrison J., (1991) *Capitalism Since 1945*. Oxford: Basil Blackwell, esp. Chapter 11.

19. Morris, J. (6 December 1982). Markets recover from losses, but outlook is grim. *American Banker*.

20. Federal Deposit Insurance Corporation. (5 June 2000). History of the eighties: An examination of the banking crises of the 1980s and early 1990s. Retrieved from https://www.fdic.gov/bank/historical/history/vol1.html.

21. Brooke, J. (18 April 1983). Growth of southern giants stifled by austerity plans. *Miami Herald*.

22. Oppenheimer, A. (18 April 1984). Recession, debt batter Americas. *Miami Herald*.

23. Weisbrot, M. (27 August 2010). Who will allow Brazil to reach its economic potential? *Folha de Sao Paulo*. Retrieved from http://www.cepr.net/index.php/op-eds-&-columns/op-eds-&-columns/who-will-allow-brazil-to-reach-econ-potential.

24. Riding, A. (19 February 1982). Mexico devalues peso 30%. *New York Times*; Riding, A. (14 August 1982). Worry spreads after peso curbs. *New York Times*.

25. Ross, O. (6 August 1982). Dropping oil prices leave Mexico in economic limbo. *Toronto Globe and Mail*.

26. Mexico plans 106 closings. *New York Times*. (17 November 1982); on Ocean Garden Products, see Young, E. (2001). State intervention and abuse of the commons: Fisheries development in Baja California Sur, Mexico. *Annals of the Association of American Geographers*, 91(2), 283–306. doi:10.1111/0004-5608.00244.

27. Ellison, K. (22 October 1989). Mexico sheds its assets. *San Jose Mercury News*.

28. Riding, A. (3 December 1982). Bankers cheer Mexico's austerity plan. *New York Times*.

29. Crewdson, J., and Schodolski, V.J. (23 November 1986). Price of reform cripples Mexico. *Chicago Tribune*.

30. Chomsky, N. (1999). *Profit Over People*. New York: Seven Stories Press.

31. Malkin, E. (23 March 2009). Nafta's promise, unfulfilled. *New York Times*.

32. Ibid.

33. Wise, T. (December 2003) Fields of Free Trade: Mexico's Small Farmers in a Global Economy. *Dollars & Sense*.

34. Dyer-Leal, G. and Yúnez-Naude, A. (2003). *NAFTA and conservation of maize diversity in Mexico* (report). Commission for Environmental Cooperation of North America, 2003. Retrieved from http://www.cec.org/Storage/49/4150_Dyer-Yunez-ExSum_en.pdf.

35. Perez U. M. (2 January 2010). En materia alimentaria para México, el TLCAN está reprobado: Oxfam. *La Jornada*. Retrieved from http://www.jornada.unam.mx/2010/01/02/index.php?section=politica&article=008n2pol.

36. Chomsky, N. (1999).

37. Dyer-Leal, G. and Yúnez-Naude, A. (2003).

38. Pavón, O. (20 December 2007). Afrontar con mucho corazón apertura total del TLC, aconseja Alberto Cárdenas. *La Crónica de Hoy*. Retrieved from http://www.cronica.com.mx/nota.php?id_nota=338675.

39. Gilly, A. (2005) *The Mexican Revolution*. New York: New Press, p. 337.

40. *Mexico – Income generation and social protection for the poor. Volume 4. A study of rural poverty in Mexico* (p. 170, Rep. No. 32867MX) (2005–08). Retrieved https://openknowledge.worldbank.org/handle/10986/8286; The CIA World Fact Book (2012) lists poverty rates as 52.3 per cent using food-based definition of poverty. Asset-based poverty amounted to more than 47 per cent. Retrieved from https://www.cia.gov/library/publications/download/download-2012/.

41. Sullivan, L. (28 October 2010). Prison economics help drive Arizona immigration law (Radio series episode). In *All Things Considered*. NPR. Retrieved from http://www.npr.org/2010/10/28/130833741/prison-economics-help-drive-ariz-immigration-law.

42. This report was prepared for Pentagon Office of Net Assessment. It is widely available on the web, for example: Schwartz, P. and Randall, D. (October 2003). *An abrupt climate change scenario and its implications for United States national security* (Report No. ADA469325). Retrieved from http://www.dtic.mil/cgi-bin/GetTRDoc?Location=U2&doc=GetTRDoc.pdf&AD=ADA469325.

43. Schwartz, P. and Randall, D. (October 2003), p. 2.

44. *National security and the threat of climate change*. (April 2007), p. 44, report. Retrieved from http://www.cna.org/sites/default/files/National%20Security%20and%20the%20Threat%20of%20Climate%20Change%20-%20Print.pdf.

45. *Climate Change and International Security: Paper from the High Representative and the European Commission to the European Council*. (2008), pp. 1–2, report. Retrieved from http://www.consilium.europa.eu/ueDocs/cms_Data/docs/pressData/en/reports/99387.pdf.

46. Ibid., pp. 3–4.

47. Statistically, battle-related deaths worldwide have declined since the Second World War and especially since the end of the Cold War – which in the frontline states of the Global South was often quite hot. But other amorphous types of violence linked to social breakdown are spreading. Take the case of El Salvador: twelve years of civil war ended in 1993, but deaths by homicide in the post-war era at one point surpassed the death rate during the war. And they remain almost as high today. Or consider Caracas: in the 1970s, Venezuela suffered a series of small guerrilla insurgencies; in fact, the young paratrooper Hugo Chavez fought Maoist guerillas around Lake Maricaibo. Today, Venezuela is at peace, but the hillside barrios of Caracas are hyper-violent with crime; Caracas is far more violent than during the era of civil war. The Caracas murder rate is about 130 per 100,000.

2

COLONISING THE FUTURE: CLIMATE CHANGE AND INTERNATIONAL SECURITY STRATEGIES

Ben Hayes

Imagining the unthinkable

The two most likely reactions to a sudden drop in carrying capacity due to climate change are defensive and offensive.

The United States and Australia are likely to build defensive fortresses around their countries because they have the resources and reserves to achieve self-sufficiency. With diverse growing climates, wealth, technology, and abundant resources, the United States could likely survive shortened growing cycles and harsh weather conditions without catastrophic losses. Borders will be strengthened around the country to hold back unwanted starving immigrants from the Caribbean islands (an especially severe problem), Mexico, and South America. Energy supply will be shored up through expensive (economically, politically, and morally) alternatives such as nuclear, renewables, hydrogen, and Middle Eastern contracts. Pesky skirmishes over fishing rights, agricultural support, and disaster relief will be commonplace. Tension between the U.S. and Mexico will rise as the U.S. reneges on the 1944 treaty that guarantees water flow from the Colorado River. Relief workers will be commissioned to respond to flooding along the southern part of the east coast and much drier conditions inland. Yet, even in this continuous state of emergency the U.S. will be positioned well compared to others. The intractable problem facing the nation will be calming the mounting military tension around the world.

As famine, disease, and weather-related disasters strike due to the abrupt climate change, many countries' needs will exceed their carrying capacity. This will create a sense of desperation, which is likely to lead to offensive aggression in order to reclaim balance...

In that event the United States will need to take urgent action to prevent and mitigate some of the most significant impacts. Diplomatic action will be needed to minimize the likelihood of conflict in the most impacted areas, especially in the Caribbean and Asia. However, large population movements in this scenario are inevitable. Learning how to manage those populations, border tensions that arise and the resulting refugees will be critical. New forms of security agreements dealing specifically with energy, food and water will also be needed. In short, while the U.S. itself will be relatively better off and with more adaptive capacity, it will find itself in a world where Europe will be struggling internally, large numbers of refugees washing up on its shores and Asia in serious crisis over food and water. Disruption and conflict will be endemic features of life.

P. Schwartz, and D. Randall (2003). An Abrupt Climate Change Scenario and Its Implications for United States National Security[1]

From environmental security to secure environments

The idea of 'environmental security' emerged in the 1980s. It was consolidated in the 1990s as the United Nations (UN) and others incorporated the adverse impacts of environmental degradation into its 'human security' agenda.[2] More recently, over the past decade or so, climate change has been cast as an international and national security issue in its own right. While this discourse shares some basic theoretical assumptions with the concepts of environmental and human security, it differs markedly in its prognosis and remedy.

From the crude projections in the early Pentagon climate-security scenarios (above) – in which some rich countries can adapt while those on the periphery of the global economy buckle under the weight of climate change, resource wars and failed states, imperilling the Western way of life with their uncivilised and refugee-producing ways – a new political discourse that takes conflict for granted and places self-preservation and risk management ahead of measures to address the root causes of environmental insecurity has emerged.

Because aspects of the climate-security agenda appear to dovetail with the environmental justice movement's demands for mitigation, adaptation and transition, many social justice activists have welcomed the military and security establishment's new-found concern for the environment – either as a victory for common sense, a fillip for campaigns to limit emissions (including by the military, famously the 'world's biggest polluter'), and/or as necessary planning for a climate-changed world. This is particularly the case in the US, where progressives have tried (and largely failed) to use the re-framing of climate change as a security issue to by-pass the deniers in the Republican Party and gain traction on other climate-change issues.

Climate considerations are now firmly embedded in a much wider set of security imperatives that have taken hold of public policy in the Global North. As noted in the introduction to this book, some of the security threats now typically associated with climate change have spawned their own sub-narratives – including those explored in chapters 8–10 on 'energy security', 'food security', 'water security' – while the language of *rights* (the right to food, to water, etc.) and *sovereignty* (for example, food sovereignty, energy sovereignty and other struggles for democratic control over critical resources) is being usurped by the logic of 'security', and more recently, 'resilience'.

This language brings its own seductive logic: who doesn't want to be more secure or resilient in the face of heightened insecurity or devastating climate change, which, left unchecked, is by any measure indeed the biggest security threat our species faces? But this logic also comprises a particular way of mitigating threats and managing risk that inevitably prioritises the resilience of the system – that is, business as usual; the market supported by the state – ahead of other human and environmental security concerns. In this model, poverty, injustice and the protests and resistance this causes are seen not as fundamental social-policy failures, but as a source of potential social unrest to be predicted, managed and countered.

While there are perfectly sound and welcome reasons for states to think critically about how to ensure the continued supply of public goods and the protection of critical infrastructure from a security perspective, there are good reasons to be wary of national security establishments appearing to bear gifts for climate-change campaigners.

This chapter attempts to unpick the climate-security agenda. First, by exploring the framing of climate change as a security issue: who is doing it and why? What do climate change and inter/national security strategies say? Second, by looking critically at the kind of security that is envisaged through the transformation of security apparatuses since 9/11. Third, by looking at the ways in which the new climate-security narratives are related to wider processes of securitisation under neoliberalism; this is really a question of how the new security-scarcity nexus benefits elites. The issue of what kind of strategy is needed to challenge securitisation and militarisation in the name of climate change is deferred to the conclusion to this collection.

The 'Age of Consequences'

The discourse on climate change as a security threat has emerged from various quarters: social, political and environmental scientists looking at the implications of climate change; national and international security agencies tasked with identifying and mitigating future threats; a growing interest in issues related to climate change on the part of the military; journalists reporting (and sensationalising) these issues, and a growing number of think tanks and NGOs.

The idea of climate change as a 'threat multiplier' appeared briefly in a 2004 report by a UN High-level Panel on Threats, Challenges and Change,[3] but it wasn't until 2007 – just as emphasis on the 'war on terror' was receding – that influential security actors in Europe and the US began to outline foreign policy options for addressing climate change as a security threat. From here, the idea was steadily written into the national and international security strategies of nation states and intergovernmental organisations.

Age of Consequences: The Foreign Policy and National Security Implications of Global Climate Change, produced by two influential US think tanks in 2007, is typical of these climate-security briefings.[4] The report begins by citing potential conflict over newly accessible resources in the Arctic, floods in Bangladesh, and the genocide in Darfur as examples of climate change-fuelled conflict. An expert panel is then asked to consider the national security implications for the US of three climate-change scenarios.

The first scenario, entitled 'expected climate change' envisages an average global temperature increase of 1.3°C by 2040 and is described as 'the least we ought to prepare for'. It brings the prospect of

> ... heightened internal and cross-border tensions caused by large-scale migrations; conflict sparked by resource scarcity, particularly in the weak and failing states of Africa; increased disease proliferation, which will have economic consequences; and some geopolitical reordering as nations adjust to shifts in resources and prevalence of disease.

The second scenario, 'severe climate change', brings a 2.6°C temperature rise by 2040, which sees

> ... nations around the world ... overwhelmed by the scale of change and pernicious challenges, such as pandemic disease ... Armed conflict between nations over resources, such as the Nile and its tributaries, is likely and nuclear war is possible. The social consequences range from increased religious fervor to outright chaos.

The third, 'catastrophic scenario' is a 5.6°C temperature rise by 2100. Unsurprising as it may be to seasoned observers of US foreign policy, the world is now characterised by 'strong and surprising intersections between the two great security threats of the day – global climate change and international terrorism waged by Islamist extremists'. This scenario 'would pose almost inconceivable challenges as human society struggled to adapt'.

For what it's worth, the last report of the Intergovernmental Panel on Climate Change (IPCC) suggests that in terms of expected temperature rises, we are still closer to the first scenario (a 1.3°C rise,[5] although less conservative and more recent assessments, particularly those concerned with the potential effect of feedback loops, suggest that we are more likely to be on track for the second 'severe' scenario. But in climate-security thinking, the scientific prognosis is far less important than the geopolitical one, and the defining feature of the 'Age of Consequences' and its ilk is that the world's underdeveloped areas are most vulnerable – and hence most threatening – because climate change can be expected to exacerbate existing international crises and problems.

All of this is couched in neo-Malthusian scares – too many people, not enough to go around – about disaster-induced migration: 'the most worrisome problems associated with rising temperatures and sea levels are from large-scale migrations of people.' The report finishes with the stark warning that '"national security" may be woefully inadequate to convey the ways in which state authorities might break down in a worst-case climate change scenario.' For all intents and purposes, this is the 'failed state' narrative, which serves primarily to legitimise Western and now other military interventions in sovereign states, transplanted onto the entire Global South.

The threat multiplies

It was summer 2007 when the Council of the European Union (EU) invited the High Representative for EU Common Foreign and Security Policy and the European Commissioner for External Relations to jointly assess the potential security implications of climate change from an EU perspective. Their joint paper, *Climate Change and International Security*, published in March 2008, picks up the themes of *Age of Consequences*: conflict over resources, economic damage and risk to coastal cities and critical infrastructure, loss of territory and border disputes, environmentally induced migration, situations of fragility and radicalisation, tension over energy supply, and pressure on international governance.[6] Although the paper stops well short of *Age of Consequences'* hyperbolic predictions about nuclear war and civilisational collapse, it confirms the view that climate change is 'best viewed as a threat multiplier', which carries 'political and security risks that directly affect European interests'. The paper was thin on detail in terms of how best to protect 'European interests' beyond the strengthening of existing EU development, security and climate-change policies. It has since been integrated into the wider 'European Security Strategy.'[7]

While the Pentagon took an early interest in climate change, it wasn't until Barack Obama's administration took office that the national security establishment could attach significant importance to climate-related issues. In his December 2009 Nobel Prize acceptance speech, Obama called on the world to 'come together' to confront climate change. 'There is little scientific dispute that if we do nothing, we will face more drought, more famine, more mass displacement – all of which will fuel more conflict for decades', he said. 'For this reason, it is not merely scientists and environmental activists who call for swift and forceful action – it's military leaders in my own country and others who understand our common security hangs in the balance.'[8] Two months earlier, Obama had issued Executive Order 13514, mandating all federal agencies to establish greenhouse gas emission reduction plans and meet energy, water and waste targets.

The Department of Defense's 2010 Quadrennial Defense Review (QDR) then identified 'energy security and climate change' as one of four issues requiring imperative reform.[9] On the one hand, US energy security would serve as a 'force multiplier', increasing 'the range and endurance of forces in the field' and reducing 'the number of combat forces diverted to protect energy supply lines';[10] on the other hand, climate change would act as 'an accelerant of instability or conflict', placing a burden to respond on civilian institutions and militaries around the world'.[11] Four years later, the QDR states that climate change 'will aggravate stressors abroad such as poverty, environmental degradation, political instability, and social tensions – conditions that can enable terrorist activity and other forms of violence'.[12] Later in 2014, a Department of Defense 'Report on Climate Change Readiness' categorised climate conflict as a *near-term* strategic challenge for the first time.[13]

The US Navy's Military Advisory Board also concluded that climate change was a 'threat multiplier' in 2007.[14] By 2013, Admiral Samuel J. Locklear III, head of US Pacific Command (PACOM), had identified climate change as the biggest security threat facing the Asia-Pacific region. 'We have interjected into our multilateral dialogue – even with China and India – the imperative to kind of get military capabilities aligned [for] when the effects of climate change start to impact these massive populations,' he explained.[15] Other senior PACOM officials have been more candid about their motivations: 'climate change is a great soft power engagement tool – just like medical is, just like logistics is. That's why we are embracing this so wholeheartedly right now.'[16] In its latest report, the Navy's Advisory Board has upgraded climate change from a 'threat multiplier' to a 'catalyst for conflict',[17] to reflect a slightly more nuanced approach to climate security.

The US intelligence community has also embraced climate change. *Global Trends 2025: A Transformed World*, published by the Director of National Intelligence (DNI) and National Intelligence Council (NIC) in 2008, included a chapter entitled 'Scarcity in the Midst of Plenty', which predicted that 'global inattention to climate change leads to major unexpected impacts, thrusting the world into a new level of vulnerability.'[18] Of course it would be the banking crisis and not climate change that would reveal the fragility of this 'world of plenty' a few months later.

Subsequent DNI and NIC reports have included *The Impact of Climate Change to 2030* (2009),[19] *Global Water Security* (2012),[20] and *Natural Resources in 2020, 2030, and 2040: Implications for the United States* (2013).[21] The CIA has also commissioned several reports into the security implications of climate change,[22] and in 2014, the US National Intelligence Strategy addressed the issue for the first time.[23] 'Many countries important to the United States are vulnerable to natural resource shocks that degrade economic development, frustrate attempts to democratize, raise the risk of regime-threatening instability, and aggravate regional tensions', said former Director of National Intelligence, James Clapper, in subsequent testimony to a Senate Committee on Intelligence.[24]

The US's allies have adopted their national security strategies along similar lines. In the UK, the 2006 review of the 'Economics of Climate Change', led by Lord Stern, famously put the cost of adaptation to climate change at 1 per cent of GDP (as compared to potential losses of 5 and even 20 per cent for failing to adapt).[25] The 'Stern Review' also raised the spectre of 200 million climate refugees for the UK to help deal with. In 2008, the UK's first ever National Security Strategy described climate change as 'potentially the greatest challenge to global stability and security, and therefore to national security'. The premise that climate change is a threat multiplier that will exacerbate all major existing insecurities has also been incorporated into the national security strategies of France, Germany, Denmark, Sweden, and other EU member states as well as Australia. The

German Advisory Council on Global Change's 2007 report was noteworthy for stressing that while climate change carried the threat of destabilisation and violence, it 'could also unite the international community, provided that it recognizes climate change as a threat to humankind and soon sets the course for the avoidance of dangerous anthropogenic climate change by adopting a dynamic and globally coordinated climate policy'.[26]

Most of the major Western foreign-policy think tanks, with the exception of the climate sceptical organisations in the US, have embraced this agenda as well, spawning dedicated climate-security programmes and organisations.[27] In 2009, for example, the Institute for Environmental Security established the Global Military Advisory Council on Climate Change (GMACCC) in order to engage international policy makers, environmental decision makers and military strategists globally on climate change and security, and to foster increased interest in the role the military can play in humanity's effort to surmount abrupt climate change.

'When I meet with my colleagues at the GMACC – generals and admirals from around the world, all with career-long experience in military planning and operations – I am struck by the similarity of our concerns', said A.N.M. Muniruzzaman, the Council's chairman.[28] 'All countries of the world are experiencing changes that are destabilizing communities and increasing security concerns. Diseases are spreading, wells are drying up, storms are smashing cities and destroying crops, and rain is either a distant memory or an acute danger.' The first GMACCC public statement called on all governments to ensure that security implications of climate change are integrated into their respective military strategies, and on the military to reduce its own carbon 'bootprint'.

Despite the hype, the climate-security discourse has been less well received at the United Nations Security Council (UNSC), though not for the want of trying on the part of its advocates. In 2007, at the request of the UK, a discussion on 'Climate, energy and security' took place in the Security Council. In 2009, the Brookings Institution, Chatham House and the Institute for Environmental Security organised a special session on 'Climate change and the military' at the COP15 proceedings of the UN Framework Convention on Climate Change in Copenhagen (UNFCCC). In 2011, the UN Security Council (UNSC) recorded its concern that 'possible adverse effects of climate change *may*, in the long run, aggravate certain existing threats to international peace and security'.[29] But in 2013, China and Russia rejected a concerted attempt to have climate change recognised as an international security threat by the UNSC. Together with India and many other developing countries, they fundamentally object to climate change becoming a UNSC issue because the Council does not operate under the principle of Common But Differentiated Responsibility which underpins the UNFCCC (this is the principle that recognises that those who have contributed more to greenhouse gas emissions (that is, developed and industrialised states) have a greater role to play in terms of mitigation efforts). While acknowledging that 'climate change is one of the greatest challenges facing humankind', the BRICS dialogue has spurned the climate-security agenda for the same reasons.[30]

Moreover, when the Intergovernmental Panel on Climate Change last reported, the 2014 reports of Working Group II on 'Impacts, adaptation, and vulnerability' (AR5) focused not on national security or defence concerns about international conflict, but local and regional threats to food production, human security, health and livelihoods.[31] The GMACC put its own spin of the report, however, 'translating' the IPCC's 'key findings' as recognising that climate change:

i)   'poses an increasing threat to peace and security in the world',
ii) 'acts as a "threat multiplier"',
iii) threatens to overwhelm the 'global or regional capacity to manage [the] responses peacefully',
iv) challenges states' ability to share resources and provide human security, and
v)   'directly affects ... military forces'.[32]

However, although the IPCC did acknowledge a threat to peace and security, the military was not even mentioned in the AR5 reports.

A threat to whom?

With varying emphasis on the national, military, or human security implications of climate change, the G7/G8, G20, OECD, OSCE, NATO, the World Bank and the Davos Forum have also embraced key elements of the climate-security agenda. But why does all of this matter? Before attempting to answer that question, it is important to point out that the arguments put forward by the security and military strategists are neither homogeneous nor universally accepted. As noted earlier, there are various perspectives on environmental security and the potential for climate change to fuel violent conflict and instability. What they share is a belief that climate change will have – or is already having – an impact on peace and security, and that these issues must be addressed by policy makers. And it is not just the 'securocrats' who are making these arguments: critical security scholars such as Michael Klare, Christian Parenti (see Chapter 1) and Nafeez Ahmed (see Chapter 4) strongly endorse a realist interpretation of 'threat multiplier' theory. Where their analyses strongly diverge from those of the 'securocrats', however, is on the fundamental causes of contemporary insecurity and what should be done in terms of adaptation and mitigation.

That rising temperatures, sea levels, food prices and all the rest pose a genuine *threat* to basic human security (as defined by the UN as 'freedom from fear, freedom from want') may not be in dispute, but the core belief that climate change will lead inevitably to chaos and conflict is contested. Leading environmental security scholar Simon Dalby has consistently pointed out that many of the security forecasts, that posit scarcity as a cause of conflict, are not supported by social-scientific evidence. Similarly, the fact that environmental change may lead to forms of conflict does not necessarily imply they are threats to national or global security.[33] While some evidence of a correlation between temperature variation and civil conflict in specific regions has been produced, the issue remains hotly disputed.[34] But there is certainly no evidence base to support the Malthusian hypotheses in the likes of *Age of Consequences* which sees climate change leading to mass international migration and war in the next couple of decades.

On the contrary, a majority of scholars argue that governance and policy failure are, and will remain, far more important drivers of conflict than climate change. Similarly, in respect to international migration, which is the focus of Chapter 5, it is suggested that not only have fears about environmental migration been massively overblown and sensationalised, it is in practice very difficult to discern a 'climate refugee' or 'climate-induced migrant' from any other kind, because the reasons people move around are much more complex and based on multiple factors. And what research has been produced to date suggests that most migration that can be plausibly related to climate change occurs, at least so far, mostly within states.[35]

Critics of climate-security narratives have also pointed out that the discourse is in hock with a range of questionable military, authoritarian and developmental agendas, and consistently misrepresents the causes of contemporary violence.[36] Others have linked it to a more 'radical interventionist agenda – first and foremost carried out by the West in the Global South'.[37] But whereas critical scholars and activists have sown the seeds of resistance to the framing of climate change as a national security and defence issue, 'most Northern governments, militaries, think tanks and NGOs continue to believe that climate change will worsen existing social stresses and either directly or indirectly advocate for appropriate security-centred responses to those problems'.[38]

These perspectives are inexorably related to the failure of the international community to agree upon a significant curbing of CO_2 emissions. As long as this hiatus continues, it must be assumed that in these paranoid times, the very insecurity created by the failure to tackle climate change will continue to drive the institutional framing of climate change as a security issue. Put another way: absent radical action to combat climate change, the realist take on climate insecurity could become something of a self-fulfilling prophecy.

What kind of security?

In addressing these insecurities, what kind of 'security' should we expect? The concepts and practices associated with inter/national security have changed markedly since the end of the Cold War and especially since the terrorist attacks in the United States on 9/11, so it is in this context that new climate-security strategies should be critically appraised. This period has been characterised by the growing reach of internal and external security mandates, the blurring of the traditional boundaries between security and defence, and an obsession with new security technologies.

In terms of external security, policy makers in the Global North have come to believe that they are embroiled in some kind of 'long war' to contain the threat of terrorism, failing states and now climate change. This kind of thinking grew out of NATO's intervention in the Balkans and the neo-conservative Project for a New American Century; it took hold as the neo-cons then kicked off the very wars they had dreamed of, dragging their NATO allies and client states with them. Most now share the conviction that the US-led alliance has a mandate to intervene, militarily if necessary, anywhere on the globe, in the name of combating those threats to 'international security'.

In terms of internal security, it is the twin development of frameworks for mass surveillance – revealed so strikingly by Edward Snowden in 2013 – and an ever greater emphasis on public order and civil unrest that have characterised the post-9/11 period. In terms of information technology, security agencies, empowered by battlefield developments, ubiquitous surveillance and 'big data' analytics, are now firmly in the business of trying to predict and act against threats before they materialise, be they terrorist attacks, food price riots or popular uprisings.

These features are by no means limited to their spiritual homeland in the US; the constant refining of internal and external security to encompass more and more 'threats' have gripped democratic and authoritarian regimes alike. A new mantra of 'crisis management' and 'inter-operability' throughout the 'crisis cycle' is integrating previously disparate state functions such as public order and 'social unrest' (the police), 'situational awareness' (intelligence gathering), resilience/preparedness (civil planning) and emergency response (including first responders, counter-terrorism; chemical, biological, radiological and nuclear defence; critical infrastructure protection, military planning, and so on) under new 'command-and-control' structures (see further Chapter 4).

The emergence of Islamic State out of the ruins of the disastrous invasion of Iraq and the flawed intervention in the Syria crisis has discredited both 'neo-con' foreign policy and 'liberal interventionalism' – while severely undermining the UN's 'Responsibility to Protect' doctrine.[39] But this has not reduced the appetite for intervention per se. Bush and Blair's promises of spreading democracy and human rights have simply been replaced by a narrative of containment and risk management. The goal has essentially been reduced to what security scholar Paul Rogers has long called 'liddism' (that is, keeping the lid on things), a strategy that is 'both pervasive and accumulative, involving an intense effort to develop new tactics and technologies that can avert problems and suppress them should they arise'.[40] In practice, this has included, inter alia, the violent repression of political Islam, support for dictators, fuelling civil wars, engaging in covert operations and conducting the kinds of 'Dirty Wars' exposed by journalist Jeremy Scahill.[41]

In terms of keeping the lid on the fallout from climate change, as one military man put it, 'it's like getting embroiled in a war that lasts 100 years. That's the scariest thing for us. There is no exit strategy that is available for many of the problems.'[42] It's also a scary thing for the rest of us. As *Rolling Stone* was moved to ponder:

> ... the U.S. military is the only force on Earth with the ability to police, process, house, feed and move refugees on a mass scale. But you can see how this picture could turn dark fast – one of the biggest long-term threats climate change poses could be to

civil liberties and freedom. 'It's not a question of what the military can do for climate change,' says one former Pentagon official. 'It's what climate change will do to the military and its mission.' It's a scary notion, but that's where we are headed.[43]

There are good reasons to fear the growing involvement of the military in disaster relief. After Hurricane Katrina overwhelmed New Orleans in 2005, the world witnessed how quickly a democratic superpower could to turn to military force in the face of domestic disaster, as impoverished black communities were treated like aggressors by their own government.[44] Following the earthquake in Haiti in 2010 – which the UN described as the worst it had ever faced – police opened fire on people taking provisions from supermarkets and other stocks of food and water. In the Philippines in 2013, after the devastation of Typhoon Haiyan (aka Yolanda), one of the strongest tropical cyclones ever recorded, the authorities imposed de facto martial law.

One must be careful to stress that state responses to disaster do not always bring out the worst in the authorities and emergency services. On the contrary, much disaster response clearly brings out the best in humanity. As writers like Rebecca Solnit have explained, while government responses may at times be characterised by 'elite panic',

[m]ost people behave beautifully in disasters … The majority in Katrina took care of each other, went to great lengths to rescue each other – including the 'cajun navy' of white guys with boats who entered the flooded city the day after the levees broke – and were generally humane and resourceful. A minority that included the most powerful believed they were preventing barbarism while they embodied it.[45]

Nevertheless, for journalist Richard Seymour, the tale of disaster response has become

… depressingly familiar. The agonisingly slow delivery of aid. Desperate survivors scratching out messages pleading for help, seemingly getting none. Soon, the panic about social breakdown provides a justification for militarising the disaster zones. And at the centre of it all, a morally loaded narrative about 'looters'.[46]

These narratives, he argues, 'tap into animating myths about human civilisation being only a few hot meals away from total breakdown. By mobilising that common sense, often in a racialised way, they exert real effects in organising violent interventions into disaster zones.'

As Simon Dalby has explained, 'consideration of ways of adapting without inducing conflict is now part of the environmental-security agenda.'[47] But disaster response is only half the story of a growing 'ensemble of techniques for taking control of crisis situations', which serves primarily to maintain 'existing authority structures and property arrangements' and render people 'passive, dependent and thus governable'.[48] The global mania for all things 'Homeland Security' that has gripped the world since 9/11 corresponds with increasingly frequent and repressive clampdowns on freedom of expression and association across the world. While ostensibly democratic governments in the West now publicly lament the 'closing of political space' for civil society, and wonder how to create an 'enabling environment' in the rest of the world,[49] many are as embroiled in the systematic undermining of activism and repression of political protest as the authoritarian regimes they bemoan.

Public order

In *Take Back the Streets*, the International Network of Civil Liberties Organisations concludes that 'Governments all around the world too often treat protest as at best an inconvenience to be controlled or discouraged, and at worst a threat to be extinguished.'[50] The policing in Ferguson, Missouri and Baltimore, Maryland, which exposed the high levels of deaths of black men at the hands of the police and led to widespread 'Black Lives Matter' protests throughout 2015, is rightly seen as a fundamental issue of racial injustice, but it is also intimately connected to the 'militarization of America's police forces' and 'the blurring distinctions between the police and military institutions and between war and law enforcement'.[51] This is blamed in no small part on the obsession with security and 'federal programs that create incentives for state and local police to use unnecessarily aggressive weapons and tactics designed for the battlefield'.[52] Although research is sorely lacking, the same process can be observed in security-obsessed states the world over.[53]

The policy and practice of militarisation has profound implications for 'crisis management', particularly the development of so-called 'less lethal weapons'. Justified on the grounds that these devices provide the police with an 'alternative' to lethal force, they have merely added new tools of political and social control to the state's still-lethal armoury. Crowd-control technologies and directed/acoustic energy weapons may provide the authorities with a less lethal way of 'taking back the streets' than the slaughter witnessed in the squares of Tiananmen, Andijan and Rabaa, but the goal is every bit the same. US police forces have thus been using military-grade 'sonic weapons' (long-range acoustic devices) to disperse crowds since the protests in Ferguson against police violence in 2014–15.[54] These technologies are already touted by the companies that developed them for everything from crisis management to border control.

Two years after US intelligence operative Edward Snowden laid bare the mass surveillance capabilities of the US and its closest allies in mid-2013, there has been no significant intelligence or surveillance reform anywhere outside of the US itself (which has only moved to limit spying on US citizens by US agencies – the rest of the world remains fair game).[55] Snowden unveiled how intelligence agencies now operate on the principles of collecting 'all of the signals, all of the time', 'by any means necessary' – or what former National Security Agency (NSA) Director James Clapper acknowledged as the capacity to search the 'haystack of global telecommunications', including retro-spectively. Yet across the world, an entire political generation, with a few honourable exceptions, has effectively acquiesced to everything Snowden revealed, as national security trumped human rights concerns for the umpteenth time since 9/11. That includes the surveillance of NGOs and activists – including people campaigning for action to prevent climate change – who, according to the Snowden documents, were routinely targeted.

Paralleling developments in government, corporate security is now characterised by corporate espionage, thanks to a revolving door between state-security agencies and the private sector. In *Secret Manoeuvres in the Dark*, Eveline Lubbers has begun to document the way in which corporations are undermining legitimate actions and investigations by activists using tactics such as spying and infiltration, pursuing injunctions, damages claims and manifestly unfounded court cases, disinformation, 'stakeholder dialogue' and bogus 'corporate social responsibility'.[56] She argues that corporate intelligence gathering – like that done by the state – has shifted from being reactive to pro-active, and shows how companies like Nestlé, Shell and McDonald's use covert methods to evade scrutiny and accountability.

Terrorism laws have also been used against environmental change activists, and 'eco-terrorism' has entered the threat lexicon (to describe activists, not environmental destruction). In 'Seeing red: state responses to environmental protests', published online to accompany this book,[57] Chris Jones shows how internal security structures developed in the name of counter-terrorism have increasingly been deployed against those opposed to destructive attempts to extract new and more traditional fossil fuels. Indeed, the two things most likely to get you an intelligence record in democratic countries is being deemed an 'Islamist' or participating in environmental direct action.

These are worldwide trends. According to Global Witness, 116 environmental activists were murdered in 2014 – almost double the number of journalists reported killed in the same period.[58] Forty per cent of these victims were indigenous peoples, 'with most people dying amid disputes over hydropower, mining and agri-business', and nearly three-quarters of the deaths were in Central and South America. In India, often lauded as the biggest democracy on earth, Prime Minister Modi froze Greenpeace's bank accounts in 2015 on the grounds that their 'anti-development' agenda is contrary to the public good, and the organisation has threatened to quit the country. Add to this repressive picture the gusto with which the Occupy movement was removed from streets and squares across the world and what emerges since 9/11 is an increasingly fine-tuned system of repression and control that views all citizens as suspects to be monitored, and all activists as threats to be countered. As Heidi Boghosian has explained, it is inevitable that such systems come to be used 'to suppress the most essential tools of democracy: the press, political activists, civil rights advocates and conscientious insiders who blow the whistle on corporate malfeasance and government abuse'.[59]

It is this backdrop to preparations for more frequent disasters that should concern us. But in climate change and national security strategies, the widespread restriction of civil rights is something that happens in the future, when climate change gets out of hand and civilisation starts to crumble. Of course, they are very much part of the status quo; the very same organisations warning about the security implications of climate change are also spying on perfectly legitimate and democratic activity to make sure that it doesn't get in the way of business as usual. Philosophers have long identified this as a fundamental problem with 'security': at its core is the essentially repressive goal of *making things stay the same* – no matter how unjust they may be.

Security through 'resilience'

Discussions about preparations for a climate-changed world seldom pass without demands for society to become more 'resilient' – particularly in national security contexts. The concept of 'resilience' was marshalled in the wake of terrorist attacks in the US, and subsequent attacks in Europe, but since climate change appeared on the threat horizon, it has taken on epic proportions. Now the concept of 'resilience' is everywhere: President Obama's newly inaugurated Council on Climate Preparedness and Resilience (co-chaired by the Assistant to the President for Homeland Security and Counterterrorism); the UK's National Resilience Capabilities Programme (a sub-project of the National Security Council); the UN Plan of action on disaster risk reduction for resilience; and the EU Secure societies programme, which is 'protecting freedom and security of Europe and its citizens' by 'enhancing the resilience of our society against natural and man-made disasters'.[60]

The basic premise of resilience is to better prepare for, respond to, and recover from disasters, which in the context of climate change sounds like a very sensible idea. But like being 'more secure', the new resilience does not occur in a vacuum. Rather, it is as if 'the demand of security and for security is somehow no longer enough … It is as though the state is fast becoming exhausted by its own logic of security and wants a newer concept, something better and bolder', writes Mark Neocleous in the *Journal of Radical Philosophy*.

Neocleous explains that:

> The state now assumes that one of its key tasks is to imagine the worst-case scenario, the coming catastrophe, the crisis-to-come, the looming attack, the emergency that could happen, might happen and probably will happen, all in order to be better prepared … In this task resilience plays heavily on its origins in systems thinking, explicitly linking security with urban planning, civil contingency measures, public health, financial institutions, corporate risk and the environment in a way that had previously been incredibly hard for the state to do.[61]

This obsession with imagining everything that could go wrong has also come to permeate state planning at every level: April 2015 was Critical Infrastructure Security and Resilience Month at the Department of Homeland Security; it is part of the policing of so-called 'megavents' such as the Olympics (the London 2012 Organizing Committee had a 'Security and Resilience' section); the term is even applied to state-building itself (which the OECD has styled as 'from fragility to resilience'). At every turn, of course, the securitisation of infrastructure or public policy provides a boon for the security and resilience specialists, consultants and systems developers.

More profoundly, writes Neocleous, the concept of resilience now stretches from the security state through business and the financial system to the management of personal problems. Consultants PricewaterhouseCoopers publish a *Resilience Journal* to help 'reliance builders' stay 'attuned to both opportunities and threats' and prepare their 'enterprises to be more resilient to change'. Since the 2008 financial crisis, the overwhelming emphasis in the banking fraternity has been to resist significant policy reform in favour of 'Building a more Resilient Financial System', so that the financial system is 'capable of absorbing shocks from the economy'.[62] And this is the nub of resilience: the focus is stealthily transferred from the *production* of crises by capital toward the *management* of crises by capitalism – from sustainable development to sustainable capitalism, as it were.

Paralleling developments in the wider political economy of 'business as usual' is personal resilience. With its origins in the endless supply of 'self-help' books, resilience promises to help you overcome emotional or physical trauma, or just to be a better, stronger, more resilient person. As Neocleous explains, resilience thus 'connects the emotional management of personal problems with the wider security agenda'. This is embodied, for example, in the UK government's decision to send ex-service personnel into schools to teach kids 'grit and resilience',[63] and the RAND Corporation selling services for 'individuals and community organizations wishing to learn more about resilience and to implement strategies to help communities prepare, withstand, and recover from disasters'.[64]

RAND has identified no less than eight 'levers of community resilience': 'wellness' (pre- and post-incident population health), 'access' (to health and social services), 'education' (about preparedness and risk), 'engagement' (participatory decision making), 'self-sufficiency' (responsibility for preparedness), 'partnership' (between government and NGOs), 'quality' (improve community resilience through constant evaluation), and 'efficiency' (leveraging resources). What is striking is not just how the 'soldiers of reason' now proffer an off-the-shelf solution for vulnerable communities to mitigate the threat posed by climate change,[65] but how conceptually similar it is to the Transition Town movement's definition, which views 'resilience' as a desired state centred upon 'strengthen[ing] our communities from within in order to reduce our vulnerability and increase our ability to respond, survive and prosper'.[66]

To be clear, there is nothing intrinsically wrong with the premise of being more resilient: of course, we should wish that in the face of legitimate fears about the potentially devastating impacts of climate change. There is equally nothing new about the appropriation of alternative/autonomous cultural and political action for corporate gain. The question that we must keep asking, however, is who or what gets to be resilient, and who or what gets left behind? Is the goal to keep the lights on or to keep the profits flowing?

The concept of 'adaptation' can be no less problematic, with the onus for change placed on vulnerable communities instead of powerful interests who might instead be asked to adapt their practices so they no longer harm people. The dangers are self-evident: those who lack the resources to adapt and become more resilient are forgotten, while calls for more radical social and political change are marginalised. As Neocleous explains, 'Resilience wants acquiescence, not resistance. Not a passive acquiescence, for sure, in fact quite the opposite. But it does demand that we use our actions to accommodate ourselves to capital and the state, and the secure future of both, rather than to resist them.'[67]

Policing the imagination: Dystopia and scarcity

If 'security' boils down to making things stay (largely) the same, and 'resilience' is about marshalling activism (or at least volunteerism) in the service of this endeavour, the dystopian narratives about climate change and insecurity that underpin them take on an added significance by feeding into a wider culture of political apathy.

Reflecting on the capacity of well-educated individuals to simultaneously grasp the threat and impact of climate change while doing nothing whatsoever about it, British novelist Zadie Smith jokes that 'It's hard to keep apocalypse consistently in mind, especially if you want to get out of bed in the morning.'[68] The quip belies a more profound observation; it is as if our current spirit of resilience is encapsulated in the supremely irritating 'Keep calm and carry on' meme. Or perhaps it is that the world is already suffering 'catastrophe fatigue'?

Regardless, dystopia is now an important cultural and political phenomenon in its own right. The 'hopeless' fight against greed, excess and corporate plunder has itself become a hackneyed backdrop to popular culture, spurred on by those branches of right- and left-wing thought that adopt essentially Malthusian approaches to the current crisis – approaches framed by some future day of reckoning, be it with God, Mother Earth, or some plucky Hollywood hero.

The 'doomers' have been widely criticised in recent times. The authors of *Catastrophism: The apocalyptic politics of collapse and rebirth* do not just critique the way in which these discourses are embroiled in the production of apathy, but how they dovetail with the agendas of the powerful, and the political choices their rhetoric promotes, from localism to green capitalism to gun-toting 'survivalism'.[69] 'Catastrophists', they argue, believe that 'an ever-intensified rhetoric of disaster will awaken the masses from their long slumber': the left hoping for the collapse of capitalism and a radical rebirth, the right looking for divine intervention and retribution – neither strategy having much to commend it. Leigh Phillips has taken this critique a step further by linking green-left dystopia to a retreat from Enlightenment values and calls for 'de-growth', which he suggests is paving the way for an era of permanent 'eco-austerity', sounding the death knell for socialists and progressives alike.[70]

But the climate-security discourse suggests that dystopia is also a top-down strategy related to the consolidation of power and the reproduction of inequality. Two things are particularly important here. First, by 'shifting the responsibility for the crisis to the masses of poor people in the world', 'Malthusian environmentalism' eases the pressure on those corporations, nation-states and militaries who bare significant responsibility for current insecurity.[71] Second, as Jackie Orr has intimated in 'making civilian soldiers', by suggesting conflict and catastrophe is predictable or even inevitable, 'civil society can be psychologically conditioned for the production of violence.'[72] In this context, preparing for violent confrontation and civilisational collapse appears the very worst of foundations for thinking about just and proportionate responses to current insecurities, let alone trying to organise radical politics. Rather, it offers an excellent platform for states to exploit authoritarian populism in the name of scarcity.

Here we can be confident that the appropriation and exploitation of land, water, mineral and hydrocarbon resources will lead to *local* conflict and social unrest because it already does so. This is not only a struggle that frequently pitches states and corporations *against* local communities, but one in which those states and corporations often triumph with support from security forces. As Nnimmo Bassey makes clear in an online essay prepared for this collection, the military and the fossil-fuel industry in Nigeria have worked in a symbiotic relationship for decades. The military has grown fat on the back of its promise to keep oil flowing, while the oil industry has happily turned to the military for action whenever supply was threatened. This is, of course, a microcosm of a much wider 'energy-security' policy that has blighted the Middle East and North Africa.

Rather than seek to avoid the 'race for what's left' of our natural resources, the security establishments of powerful countries and regional blocs continue to support the extraction and consumption patterns responsible for climate change and insecurity with as much zeal as ever. The melting ice-caps in the Arctic region – an almost ever-present topic in climate-security debates – are a case in point. 'As we consider how to make the most of the emerging economic opportunities in the region, we recognize that we must exercise responsible stewardship … promoting healthy, sustainable, and resilient ecosystems over the long term', wrote Barack Obama in 2013, before setting out a national 'Arctic strategy' predicated on the US's commercial, security and defence interests.[73] The following year this would become a fully-fledged Arctic military strategy.

And as the Middle East lurches from one crisis to the next, European and US inter/national security interests remain embroiled with those of Saudi Arabia and the Gulf states. Is this a credible way of mitigating the threats of climate change and resource wars (never mind dealing with right-wing Islamic fundamentalism)? Of course it isn't. As research collective Corner House explains:

> … future crises are likely to be rooted in the same dynamics in which they are rooted today: political conflict, exploitative distributive institutions, sexism, racism, human rights abuses and environmentally destructive practices. If society wants to prepare for future resource crises (and there surely will be future scarcity of one kind or another), it would be more prudent to look to the present rather than to some theoretical model of the future. As the future will grow out of the present, a better way of dealing with

'future crisis' is not imagining a future Malthusian world that bears no relationship to what exists now or ever has existed, and then imagining how to stave off that hypothetical Malthusian destiny, but rather dealing with current scarcities now on the realistic assumption that what causes scarcity today is going to go on causing scarcity in the future.[74]

In climate change and security strategies, although some of the structural problems underpinning current crises are acknowledged, the future is used to 'thrust them into the background, casting them as petty distractions of purely academic interest', in comparison to the coming shit storm. In this way, argues Corner House, threats to the environment and society are 'being used to colonize the future and thereby capture the present'. 'Resilience', the new handmaiden of security, can be seen as another fundamental mechanism for what they describe as 'policing the imagination', with the 'constant re-imagining of the myriad ways in which [threats] might be realized' amounting to 'nothing less than the attempted colonization of the political imagination by the state'.[75]

Insecurity as opportunity

To suggest that it is not all doom-and-gloom is to risk being written off as delusional, or a techno-utopian, but many climate-change campaigners do see transition as an opportunity to build a more equitable and socially just world (back to Zadie Smith's 'why else get out of bed' conundrum). As Simon Dalby has explained, recent research emphasises that 'environmental difficulties frequently facilitate co-operation rather than conflict, as dealing with stratospheric ozone depletion made especially clear.' He makes the point that 'collaboration has frequently proven much more effective than conflict in managing scarce resources', providing 'considerable cause for optimism in terms of security planning'.[76]

The climate crisis could also be a boon for advocates of Keynesian economic and social policy – or what their detractors call 'big government'. As Christian Parenti has explained:

> During natural disasters, society regularly turns to the state for help, which means such immediate crises are a much-needed reminder of just how important a functional big government turns out to be to our survival … After all, there is only one institution that actually has the capacity to deal with multibillion-dollar natural disasters on an increasingly routine basis. Private security firms won't help your flooded or tornado-struck town. Private insurance companies are systematically withdrawing coverage from vulnerable coastal areas. Voluntary community groups, churches, anarchist affinity groups – each may prove helpful in limited ways, but for better or worse, only government has the capital and capacity to deal with the catastrophic implications of climate change.[77]

'Catastrophism', however, sounds a warning of the more likely implications of an expansion of the state:

> The Keynesian stimulus hoped for by proponents of a Green New Deal is more likely to be a further expansion of border fences, naval patrols, military contractors, privatised security services, surveillance systems, and climate monitoring drones. Indeed, since 2008, the security industry has grown at 5% annually despite a worldwide recession and its projected global revenue was estimated to be somewhere in the region of $20 billion in 2013.[78]

Little more needs to be said about the predatory and pervasive logic of 'disaster capitalism' at this point, except perhaps to warn, as others have, that failure to prevent climate change could persuade the security establishment to support future geo-engineering projects.

That corporate profiteers and private individuals will continue to feather their own nests on the back of disaster is a given. What is perhaps more interesting in terms of climate change and inter/national security strategy is the way in which disaster capitalism brings with it a particular way of viewing the world. As Naomi Klein observed in her book *The Shock Doctrine*:

> At first I thought the Green Zone phenomenon was unique to the war in Iraq. Now, after years spent in other disaster zones, I realize that the Green Zone emerges everywhere that the disaster capitalism complex descends, with the same stark partitions between the included and the excluded, the protected and the damned.[79]

Dividing the world into red zones and green zones and the like is something elites have always done. But ubiquitous surveillance and risk management have taken this enterprise to new heights. Green technology and the military's new-found concern for climate change will take it further still. The US Department of Defense now boasts a programme that

> ... visualizes multiple dimensions of climate vulnerability and risks in a single map. Data about conflicts, aid, governance and climate are overlaid to give a dynamic view of the continent's risk factors, as well as development projects such as World Bank initiatives to buffer or adapt to climate change. Users can select and layer any combination of data to see how climate change intersects with risks over time. Local conflicts, for example, can be related to climate-induced food insecurity.[80]

Surely nothing encapsulates our current malaise better than the images depicted in the Department of Defense's screenshots (see http://tinyurl.com/securitymap). We have satellites and drones and algorithms to help us measure and connect each and every dimension of the disasters to come, but we can't muster the political will to try to prevent them. We are mapping vulnerability – not to help the vulnerable, but to seek out opportunity for the disaster-industrial complex. Meet the new dystopia, same as the old one, insulating the rich from the threat of the poor.

Notes

1. Schwartz, P. and Randall, D. (2003). *An Abrupt Climate Change Scenario and its Implications for United States National Security.* Washington, DC: US Department of Defense.
2. As stated in paragraph 143 of the 2005 World Summit Outcome (A/RES/60/1), entitled 'Human Security', the Heads of State and Government stressed 'the right of all people to live in freedom and dignity, free from poverty and despair', and recognised that 'all individuals, in particular vulnerable people, are entitled to freedom from fear and freedom from want, with an equal opportunity to enjoy all their rights and fully develop their human potential.'
3. High-level Panel on Threats, Challenges and Change. (2004). *A More Secure World: Our shared responsibility: Report,* p. 15.
4. Campbell, K.M. et al. (2007). *The Age of Consequences: The foreign policy and national security implications of global climate change.* Center for Strategic & International Studies.
5. Kirtman, B., Power, S. B., Adedoyin, A. J., Boer, G. J., Bojariu, R., Camilloni, I., and Wang, H. (2013). *Near-term climate change: Projections and predictability. Climate Change 2013: The Physical Science Basis.* doi:10.1017/cbo9781107415324.023
6. *Climate Change and International Security.* (2008). Retrieved from http://www.consilium.europa.eu/uedocs/cms_data/docs/pressdata/en/reports/99387.pdf.
7. 'A secure Europe in a better world – the European Security Strategy' was approved by the European Council held in Brussels on 12 December 2003. A *Report on the implementation of the European Security Strategy – providing security in a changing world,* incorporating the report on *Climate Change and International Security,* was approved by the European Council held in Brussels on 11 and 12 December 2008.
8. Remarks by President Obama at the acceptance of the Nobel Peace Prize. (10 December 2009). Retrieved from https://www.whitehouse.gov/the-press-office/remarks-president-acceptance-nobel-peace-prize.
9. US Department of Defense. (2010). *Quadrennial Defense Review Report.* p. 73. Retrieved from http://www.defense.gov/QDR/QDR%20as%20of%2029JAN10%201600.pdf.
10. Ibid., p. 87.
11. Ibid., p. 85.
12. Ibid., p. 8.
13. US Department of Defense. (2014). *2014 Climate Change: Adaptation roadmap.* Retrieved from http://s3.documentcloud.org/documents/1312288/dod-report-on-climate-change-readiness-october.pdf; McDonnell, T. (13 October 2014). Pentagon: We could soon be fighting climate wars. Retrieved from http://www.motherjones.com/blue-marble/2014/10/pentagon-climate-change-shift-wars.
14. Center for Naval Analyses. (2007). *National Security and the Threat of Climate Change,* report. Retrieved from http://www.cna.org/reports/climate.
15. Bender, B. (9 March 2013). Admiral Samuel Locklear, commander of Pacific forces, warns that climate change is top threat. Retrieved from http://www.bostonglobe.com/news/nation/2013/03/09/admiral-samuel-locklear-commander-pacific-forces-warns-that-climate-change-top-threat/BHdPVCLrWEMxRe9IXJZcHL/story.html.

16. Olson, W. (10 August 2014). PACOM not waiting on politics to plan for climate change challenges. Retrieved from http://www.stripes.com/news/pacom-not-waiting-on-politics-to-plan-for-climate-change-challenges-1.297433.

17. Center for Naval Analyses. (2007). *National Security and the Accelerating Risks of Climate Change*, report. Retrieved from https://www.cna.org/reports/accelerating-risks.

18. Office of the Director of National Intelligence. (2008). Global trends 2025: A transformed world. *National Intelligence Council*, 2008(3), 77. Retrieved from http://www.dni.gov/files/documents/Newsroom/Reports%20and%20Pubs/2025_Global_Trends_Final_Report.pdf.

19. National Intelligence Council. (n.d.). Commissioned research and conference reports. Retrieved from http://www.dni.gov/index.php/about/organization/national-intelligence-council-nic-publications/the-impact-of-climate-change-to-2030-commissioned-research-and-conference-reports.

20. Defense Intelligence Agency, National Geospatial-Intelligence Agency, Central Intelligence Agency, Bureau of Intelligence and Research of the US State Department, and United States Department of Energy. (2012). *Global Water Security*. Retrieved from http://www.dni.gov/files/documents/Newsroom/Press%20Releases/ICA_Global%20Water%20Security.pdf.

21. National Intelligence Council. (2013). Natural resources in 2020, 2030 and 2040: Implications for the United States. *National Intelligence Council Report*, 2013(5). Retrieved from http://www.dni.gov/files/documents/NICR%202013-05%20US%20Nat%20Resources%202020,%202030%202040.pdf.

22. US Government Intelligence. (n.d.). Climate and security resources: U.S. government, intelligence. Retrieved from http://climateandsecurity.org/resources/u-s-government/intelligence/.

23. Office of the Director of National Intelligence, and US Intelligence Community. (2014). *The National intelligence Strategy of the United States of America 2014*, p. 5.

24. Klare, M. (2013, 21 April). Tomgram: Michael Klare, the coming global explosion. Retrieved from http://www.tomdispatch.com/blog/175690/.

25. Stern Review: The economic effects of climate change [Abstract]. (2006). *Population & Development Review Population and Development Review*, p. vi. Retrieved from http://mudancasclimaticas.cptec.inpe.br/~rmclima/pdfs/destaques/sternreview_report_complete.pdf.

26. German Advisory Council on Global Change. (2007). World in transition: Climate change as a security risk. Retrieved from http://www.wbgu.de/en/flagship-reports/fr-2007-security/.

27. For example, in the US: Center for Climate and Security (http://climateandsecurity.org), Wilson Center 'New Security Beat' http://www.newsecuritybeat.org/.

28. Muniruzzaman, A. (17 October 2013). Global warming and global security. Retrieved from http://www.project-syndicate.org/commentary/muniruzzaman-khanon-climate-change-as-a-military-problem.

29. Security Council. (20 July 2011). Security council, in statement, says 'contextual information' on possible security implications of climate change important when climate impacts drive conflict. Retrieved from http://www.un.org/press/en/2011/sc10332.doc.htm.

30. BRICS Ministry of External Relations. (15 July 2014). Sixth BRICS summit: Fortaleza declaration. Retrieved from http://brics6.itamaraty.gov.br/media2/press-releases/214-sixth-brics-summit-fortaleza-declaration.

31. IPCC. (30 March 2014). Summary for policymakers (approved) and final draft (accepted). Retrieved from http://ipcc-wg2.gov/AR5/report/final-drafts/.

32. Global Military Advisory, Council on Climate Change, University of Cambridge's Institute for Sustainability Leadership and European Climate Foundation. (June 2014). *Climate change: Implications for defence.* Retrieved from http://www.academia.edu/7454647/Climate_Change_Implications_for_Defence_June_2014.

33. Dalby, S. (June 2013). Climate change: New dimensions of environmental security. Retrieved from https://www.rusi.org/publications/journal/ref:A51CC1B1090750/#.VXIdgFLE-Dm. See also Selby, J. and Hoffman, C. (30 October 2014). Rethinking climate change, conflict and security. Retrieved from http://www.tandfonline.com/toc/fgeo20/19/4.

34. Randall, A. (17 February 2014). There's little evidence that climate migration will lead to global conflict. Retrieved from http://www.carbonbrief.org/blog/2014/02/despite-the-guardians-front-page,-theres-little-evidence-climate-change-will-lead-to-global-conflict/.

35. Dalby, S. (June 2013). Climate change: New dimensions of environmental security, p. 36. Retrieved from https://www.rusi.org/publications/journal/ref:A51CC1B1090750/#.VXIdgFLE-Dm

36. Selby, J. and Hoffmann, C. (30 October 2014). Rethinking climate change, conflict and security. Retrieved from http://www.tandf.net/books/details/9781138915398/#description.

37. Söderbaum, F. and Sörensen, J. (2012). Introduction: The end of the development-security nexus? Retrieved from http://www.gu.se/english/research/publication?publicationId=170904.

38. Selby, J. and Hoffman, C. (30 October 2014).

39. Office of the Special Adviser on the Prevention of Genocide. (n.d.). The responsibility to protect. Retrieved from http://www.un.org/en/preventgenocide/adviser/responsibility.shtml.

40. Rogers, P. (1 April 2010). Beyond 'liddism': Towards real global security. Retrieved from https://www.opendemocracy.net/paul-rogers/beyond-%E2%80%9Cliddism%E2%80%9D-towards-real-global-security.

41. Scahill, J. (9 May 2013). Dirty Wars: The world is a battlefield (Wellcome). London: Serpent's Tail. Retrieved http://www.amazon.co.uk/Dirty-Wars-world-battlefield-Wellcome/dp/1846688507.

42. Holthaus, E. (n.d.). 'Climate change war' is not a metaphor. Retrieved from http://www.slate.com/articles/technology/future_tense/2014/04/david_titley_climate_change_war_an_interview_with_the_retired_rear_admiral.html.

43. Goodell, J. (12 February 2015). The Pentagon and climate change: How deniers put national security at risk. Retrieved from http://www.rollingstone.com/politics/news/the-pentagon-climate-change-how-climate-deniers-put-national-security-at-risk-20150212#ixzz3TMD1JwUS.

44. Riefer, T. (2007). Blown away: U.S. militarism and Hurricane Katrina, in H. Potter (ed.), *Racing the Storm: Racial implications and lessons learned from Hurricane Katrina.* Lanham, MD: Lexington Books.

45. Solnit, R. (25 August 2009). Four years on, Katrina remains cursed by rumour, cliche, lies and racism. Retrieved June 5, 2015, from http://www.theguardian.com/commentisfree/2009/aug/26/katrina-racism-us-media; Riefer, T. (2007).

46. Seymour, R. (15 November 2013). The real story of 'looting' after a disaster like typhoon Haiyan. Retrieved from http://www.theguardian.com/commentisfree/2013/nov/15/looting-typhoon-haiyan-philippines-new-orleans-haiti.

47. Dalby, S. (June 2013), p. 45.

48. Seymour, R. (15 November 2013).

49. Hayes, B. (25 April 2013). How international rules on countering the financing of terrorism impact civil society. Retrieved from http://socs.civicus.org/?p=3823.

50. International Network of Civil Liberties Organization (INCLO). (2013). *Take Back the Streets: Repression and criminalization of protest around the world*, p. 61. Retrieved from https://www. aclu.org/sites/default/files/field_document/global_protest_suppression_report_inclo.pdf.

51. Greenwald, G. (14 August 2014). The Militarization of U.S. police: Finally dragged into the light by the horrors of Ferguson. Retrieved from https://firstlook.org/theintercept/2014/08/14/ militarization-u-s-police-dragged-light-horrors-ferguson/.

52. American Civil Liberties Union. (2014). War comes home: The excessive militarization of American policing. Retrieved from https://www.aclu.org/sites/default/files/assets/jus14-warcomeshome-report-web-rel1.pdf.

53. Hörnqvist, M. (2004). The birth of public order policy. *Race & Class*, 46(1), 30–52. doi:10.1177/0306396804045513.

54. Cantú, A. (2014, 5 December). Video: NYPD uses military-grade sonic weapon on Eric Garner protesters. Retrieved from http://www.alternet.org/news-amp-politics/video-nypd-uses-military-grade-sonic-weapon-eric-garner-protesters.

55. Hayes, B. (2014). State of surveillance: The NSA files and the global fightback. Retrieved from http://www.tni.org/sites/www.tni.org/files/download/state_of_surveillance_chapter.pdf.

56. Lubbers, E. (2012). *Secret Manoeuvres in the Dark: Corporate and police spying on activists*. London: Pluto Press; Lilley, S., McNally, D., Yuen, E. and Davis, J. (2012). *Catastrophism: The apocalyptic politics of collapse and rebirth*. Oakland, CA: PM Press.

57. See www.climatesecurityagenda.com.

58. Global Witness. (20 April 2015). How many more? Retrieved from https://www.globalwitness. org/campaigns/environmental-activists/how-many-more/.

59. 'Not only is it easy for the U.S. and its contractors to focus on activists, it is imperative that they do so. They must target social advocates in order to justify maintaining their budgets and their livelihoods. There are simply not enough "terrorists" in existence for the government to warrant the current level of intelligence spending. As a result, enormous federal resources are devoted to identifying and tracking activists who are portrayed as "extremists." Individuals who have helped bring about changes in corporate policies, such as animal rights or environmental advocates, are labelled domestic terrorist threats by the FBI. The more individuals the security industry can identify as posing a national security threat – often based on tenuous, inaccurate or misleading information – the more it becomes possible to secure sizable government contracts' Karlin, M. (21 August 2013). From spying on 'terrorists abroad' to suppressing domestic dissent: When we become the hunted. Retrieved from http://truth-out.org/news/ item/18292-from-spying-on-terrorists-abroad-to-using-massive-surveillance-to-suppress-domestic-dissent-when-we-become-the-hunted.

60. European Commission. (n.d.). Secure societies – Protecting freedom and security of Europe and its citizens. Retrieved from http://ec.europa.eu/programmes/horizon2020/en/ h2020-section/secure-societies-%E2%80%93-protecting-freedom-and-security-europe-and-its-citizens.

61. Neocleous, M. (March 2013). Resisting resilience. Retrieved from http://www. radicalphilosophy.com/commentary/resisting-resilience.

62. Bank of England. (2009). Building a more resilient financial system. Retrieved from http:// www.bankofengland.co.uk/publications/Documents/fsr/2009/fsr25sec3.pdf.

63. Paton, G. (16 December 2014). Nicky Morgan: Lessons in character 'just as important' as academic grades. Retrieved from http://www.telegraph.co.uk/education/educationnews/11296280/Nicky-Morgan-lessons-in-character-just-as-important-as-academic-grades.html.

64. Rand Corporation. (n.d.). Resilience in action. Retrieved from http://www.rand.org/multi/resilience-in-action.html.

65. Abella, A. (2009, 4 May). *Soldiers of Reason: The Rand Corporation and the rise of the American empire*. Retrieved from http://www.amazon.co.uk/Soldiers-Reason-Corporation-American-Empire/dp/0156033445.

66. Transition Town Totnes. (n.d.). What is resilience? Retrieved from http://www.transitiontowntotnes.org/about/what-is-transition/what-is-resilience/.

67. Neocleous, M. (March 2013).

68. Smith, Z. (3 April 2014). Elegy for a country's seasons. Retrieved from http://www.nybooks.com/articles/archives/2014/apr/03/elegy-countrys-seasons/.

69. Lilley, S., McNally, D., Yuen, E. and Davis, J. (2012).

70. Phillips, L. (2015). *Austerity Ecology & the Collapse-porn Addicts: A Left defence of economic growth, progress and stuff*. Zero Books.

71. Lilley, S., McNally, D., Yuen, E. and Davis, J. (2012), p. 29.

72. Orr, J. (2005). Making civilian soldiers: The militarisation of inner space, in Hartmann, B., Subramaniam, B. and Zerner, C., eds, *Making Threats: Biofears and environmental anxieties*. Lanham, MD: Rowman & Littlefield, pp. 47–70.

73. White House. (2013). *National Strategy for the Arctic Region*. Retrieved from https://www.whitehouse.gov/sites/default/files/docs/nat_arctic_strategy.pdf.

74. The Corner House. (2006). Colonizing the future: 'Scarcity' as political strategy. *Different Takes*, 43. Retrieved from http://popdev.hampshire.edu/sites/default/files/uploads/u4763/DT%2043%20-%20Corner%20House.pdf.

75. Neocleous, M. (March 2013).

76. Dalby, S. (June 2013).

77. Parenti, C. (n.d.). Why climate change will make you love big government. Retrieved from http://www.thenation.com/article/165885/why-climate-change-will-make-you-love-big-government#.

78. I-Connect 007. (23 January 2013). High value in security drives global border security market growth. Retrieved from http://smt.iconnect007.media/index.php/article/71335/high-value-in-security-drives-global-border-security-market-growth/71338/?skin=smt.

79. Klein, N. (2008). The Shock Doctrine: The rise of disaster capitalism. London: Penguin, p. 414.

80. Coren, M. (18 April 2012). U.S. Defense Department maps future climate turmoil in Africa. Retrieved from http://www.fastcoexist.com/1679682/us-defense-department-maps-future-climate-turmoil-in-africa.

3

CLIMATE CHANGE INC.: HOW TNCs ARE MANAGING RISK AND PREPARING TO PROFIT IN A WORLD OF RUNAWAY CLIMATE CHANGE

Oscar Reyes[1]

I'm not disputing that increasing CO2 emissions in the atmosphere is going to have an impact ... [but] we believe those consequences are manageable ... Changes to weather patterns that move crop production areas around – we'll adapt to that. It's an engineering problem, and it has engineering solutions.

(Rex Tillerson, CEO of Exxon Mobil)[2]

Introduction

Transnational corporations (TNCs) account for the majority of global trade and investment in today's economy, which is often taken as a sign that we should look to them as leaders in addressing both the causes and impacts of climate change.

Large corporations themselves are generally fond of extolling their climate-change credentials. For example, Walmart, the world's largest retailer, and EDF, the world's largest electricity producer, both claim their climate policies make them a 'leader in sustainability'.[3] Meanwhile, some nongovernmental organizations like the Environmental Defense Fund, the World Wildlife Fund and The Nature Conservancy have long sought partnerships with (and funding from) some of the world's largest TNCs. 'We work closely with business leaders and hold them accountable to ambitious goals while also celebrating their environmental gains,' explains Tom Murray, vice president of the Environmental Defense Fund's Corporate Partnerships Program.[4]

This chapter offers a different view. It shows how TNCs' investment strategies seek to escape accountability for their role in causing the climate crisis, consistently fail to address the systemic risks that business-as-usual poses, and do very little to support a just transition to a low-carbon economy. Rather than embracing corporate leadership, the key to addressing climate change and its growing impacts on our lives and society will lie in diminishing the power of the transnationals.

A dirty business

Where TNCs stand on climate change largely depends on the investments they are sitting on. Oil and gas corporations have concluded that they would benefit far more from building up huge reserves – exploiting new sites and unconventional fuels – than they would from spearheading a renewable energy transition. As Naomi Klein puts it, 'Wrecking the planet is their business model.'[5] Similarly, the banking sector currently has too much invested in fossil-fuel stocks to pay much more than lip service to cleaner alternatives. Even the insurance sector, which often takes the lead in calling for action on climate change, is positioning itself to gain from inaction: extremes of weather can serve as a marketing opportunity to sell more products, the risks of which are outsourced to other companies or, ultimately, underwritten by states.

Transnational corporations are not just gearing up to profit from climate change, but they were disproportionately responsible for causing the problem in the first place. Just ninety corporations produced almost two-thirds of the CO_2 and methane emissions produced during the industrial era.[6]

Many of the same transnational corporations, and a small clutch of newer ones, maintain their leading role in causing climate change – as is well-documented by researchers at the Carbon Tracker Initiative (CTI). Their analysis shows that financial markets are carrying an enormous 'carbon bubble' with 'more fossil fuels listed on the world's capital markets than we can afford to burn if we are to prevent dangerous climate change.'[7] The 200 largest polluters listed on public stock markets in 2013 own 762 Gigatonnes of carbon dioxide $(GtCO_2)$ in untapped reserves of oil, gas and coal. By way of comparison, a global carbon budget for limiting climate change to 2°C (which may still lead to climate disaster) would be around 565–886 $GtCO_2$ to 2050.[8]

While these figures usefully shed light on the scale of the problem the world's largest fossil fuel companies pose, the CTI analysis of how to address this problem is more limited. Their aim is to persuade investors that the carbon content of investments should be counted and to highlight the risk of holding onto stranded assets if states put restrictions on extraction in line with their international commitments. Since most of the value on oil and gas companies' balance sheets relates to upstream investments that will pay off in over a decade's time, a consideration of the long-term risks could dent their share value and encourage a rethink on longer-term strategies. At the same time, the aim is to compel institutional investors to push for greater action, to encourage ratings agencies to factor in climate risk and to pressure regulators to demand mandatory carbon reporting.

This may provide a compelling argument for activists and concerned citizens, but it is unlikely to convince fossil-fuel companies and financial sector investors to change tack.

They are betting on (and often encouraging) states to take actions on climate change that are weak, at best, while projecting the lucrative possibilities from remaining invested in fossil fuels. To illustrate this point, let's look more closely at a few particular sectors: oil and gas, banking, and insurance.

A new oil age?

According to projections from the International Energy Agency, as well as those of the oil industry itself, energy demand could triple by 2050, with the greatest share of this increase coming from emerging economies.[9] With the significant risk that this demand could outstrip the available supply, particularly of liquid fuels, most future scenarios predict a world of higher energy prices – despite the significant oil price falls in 2015. Far from moving the world beyond fossil fuels, however, these increased prices could make extreme energy sources (notably deep-sea offshore installations, tar sands, oil shale and shale gas) ever more profitable, as well as increasing the profitability and extending the lifespan of existing fields. Oil, gas and coal companies are investing accordingly in new oil and gas exploration, production facilities and refineries.[10]

It is worth underscoring just how marginal climate change is as a factor in directing fossil-fuel investment decisions, which are based on a 'price deck', that is, a series of price projections centred on future oil prices and production cost estimates. Projected demand – as well as potential conflicts in producing regions – are the main factors affecting long-term oil prices. Those companies that project a high-demand, high-price future tend to see unconventional (and dirtier) production as more attractive. Although climate change is increasingly taken into account in the form of a potential carbon price, the ability to pass on this (relatively marginal) cost to consumers, alongside strong predicted growth, leaves most oil companies unworried.

Take the example of Royal Dutch Shell, the world's largest non-state oil company by revenue, which likes to portray itself as an industry leader on climate change. Looked at from an investment perspective, it is clear that Shell is both ramping up conventional oil and gas production (in Nigeria, Kazakhstan and Iraq, in particular), while simultaneously expanding oil-sands operations in Canada, gas-to-liquids (GTL) extraction in Qatar, liquid natural gas operations globally, offshore drilling in the Gulf of Mexico and Brazil, and offshore exploration in the Arctic. As the company itself acknowledges, this strategy will lead to 'more energy-intensive' production and an 'associated increase in direct CO_2 emissions' from the company's facilities.[11]

Even Shell's claims to manage the company's carbon footprint are built around fossil-fuel extraction, with an emphasis placed on its gas-sector investments and carbon capture and storage. This reflects a strategic choice made in 2009 to back away from solar and wind power, claiming that they were uneconomical.[12] The company has since increased its agrofuel operations instead, despite a large body of evidence that these put pressure on food crops whilst failing to contribute to climate mitigation.[13]

Shell treats the threat of climate change largely as a risk-management exercise, with the main components being reputational and regulatory risk. The latter includes taking into account the possible influence of CO_2 prices, although as 'a leading trader of carbon', the company can also profit from carbon markets.[14] The company has a small, 25-person team working on climate strategy, which is organisationally removed from the company's 'upstream' (exploration and production) activities.[15] In its Carbon Disclosure Project (CDP) report, Shell claims that the increased risk of storm surges as a result of climate change is a contributing factor in the refitting and operation of some offshore platforms.[16]

With less fanfare but greater consequence, however, Shell's CDP reporting also notes that climate modelling of 'future sea ice conditions' (for 2030–50) is a consideration in its Arctic oil explorations.[17] At a cost of well over $5 billion since 2005, Shell's Arctic explorations are most likely the largest single financial commitment it is making to adapt its operations in light of climate change, as it bets on rapid reductions in ice cover and sustained high oil prices, making offshore oil recovery from the region profitable – despite repeated failures and setbacks.[18] Elsewhere, Peter Slaiby, the vice-president of Shell Alaska, stated the company's view in less guarded terms: 'I will be one of those persons most cheering for an endless summer in Alaska,' he said, the day after climate scientists reported a record decline in Arctic sea ice.[19]

A major part of the company's climate-related work takes the form of modelling future energy scenarios. It has mapped out various scenarios in which either new international social 'blueprints' emerge for addressing climate change and energy security or, more likely, national governments 'scramble' to secure their own supplies (See Introduction).[20] Pursuing Arctic drilling conforms to this scenario, helping the company to hedge its supply bets in a context where national oil companies are generally taking greater control of their countries' natural resources.

While no two companies are the same, a similar pattern can be observed in the case of other oil majors, which have all concluded that it is worth pursuing further oil and gas reserves.

Saudi Aramco, the world's largest oil company in terms of both its 'proven reserves' and the daily rate of oil production, is committed to exploiting its reserves while developing offshore and unconventional gas and oil as fast as possible. At the same time it is seeking greater returns from refinery or (oil-based) chemical industries. It treats the potential impacts of climate change as a 'carbon management' issue, focusing its efforts on 'carbon capture and injection'.[21] This is not simply about reducing emissions: such technology is also anticipated to enhance the ability to recover more oil.

Banking on climate change

While the oil industry has a clear vested interest in continuing extraction for as long as possible, the same is not obviously true with the banking sector. If their own literature is to be believed, major banks are taking great strides towards addressing climate change. Citibank declares itself the 'most innovative investment bank for climate change and sustainability'. Morgan Stanley claims to support measures to tackle climate change, and sponsors its own Institute for Sustainable Investing, while Bank of America talks of 'financing a low-carbon economy'. Yet these same three banks are the world leaders in providing finance for coal mining.[22]

The details of the lending portfolios of major banks are shrouded in commercial secrecy. This allows them to put forward ambitious-sounding claims about their future climate lending. For example, Bank of America (BoA) claims to have in place a $70 billion commitment (over 16 years) to financing energy-efficiency projects, renewable energy and other 'low-carbon' initiatives.[23] But this (non-binding) target is so vague as to be almost meaningless. Climate-related investment is not defined, although we know from BoA's own presentations that it can include structured financial instruments (the kind of speculative products that were behind the 2008 financial crash) that have only tenuous relations to climate change. If publicly accounted climate finance is taken as a guide, it may also be used for anything from installing air conditioning to expanding oil refineries. Moreover, BoA is not suggesting that it will change its investment policies and track climate lending in its overall portfolio, leaving open the possibility that most of the figure it claims is simply a question of re-branding routine business.

A similar lack of transparency affects most banks' fossil-fuel lending, although researchers have reconstructed known details of their portfolio to shed some light on how this works. They found that banks play a key role in providing corporate loans, as well as underwriting bond and share issues that mobilise finance for fossil-fuel extraction and fossil-fuel-based electricity generation.[24] In a series of reports, Banktrack has looked at financial support provided to both coal mining and coal-fired power stations. It found that JPMorgan Chase, Citi, Bank of America, Morgan Stanley and Barclays had the worst record globally in lending in support of coal projects (including power plants).[25] Notably, all major banks continue to heavily fund both coal-fired power stations and coal mining – even against the advice of a minority of their own analysts. The same picture is broadly true in relation to oil and gas lending, with the proviso that those sectors tend to see a greater proportion of investment cross-financed by their own profits, rather than the financial sector.

In short, the banking sector remains heavily invested in fossil fuels and other infrastructure that accentuates climate change. Climate change remains largely an issue of reputation management, with vague and aspirational targets sometimes generated to face down criticisms of fossil-fuel lending, or used as 'greenwash' for the PR damage done by the financial crisis.[26] But banks are not required to report upon or make any strategic assessment of the climate-change risks that are posed by their overall investment portfolios, nor does there seem much realistic chance that this would happen without regulation.

Insurance: Passing the buck

Insurance is the one major business sector where the impacts of climate change on profit margins and investment decisions should be the most obvious, with the greater frequency of extreme weather already resulting in significant increases in pay-outs for related loss and property damage. For example, Allianz forecast US$80–120 billion of annual damage globally from weather-related disasters over the period 2010–19.[27]

Yet the structure of the world's largest insurances companies means that they do not always take a direct interest in steering investments away from climate-change risks. In some assessments, a steady stream of climate-related disasters may actually be good for business, as critical geographer Neil Smith points out, in so far as 'they recharge home-owner fear and insecurity concerning financial loss and trigger a surge of policies at inflated premiums.'[28] While this is not consistently the case, other factors also mitigate against more ambitious action across the whole sector.

Significant divergences of approach can be seen within the insurance industry. AIG, which once saw itself as a corporate leader on climate change, changed tack and closed its climate programme in 2009 – a case of boardroom dynamics reflecting broader denials of the impact of climate change on the right of the US political spectrum.[29] Others have followed a similar path, with Berkshire Hathaway CEO Warren Buffett even going so far as to claim that 'climate change is not a material risk' to the company.[30]

Amongst the other industry leading companies, AXA is seeking to quantify the 'emerging risks' from climate change (which it regards as 'proven beyond doubt').[31] Aside from the risks that more frequent extremes of weather pose to property insured by the company, it is working to identify its implications for insurance in agriculture, the transport sector, and private healthcare services.

Allianz goes further, offering investors the option of sustainability-focused financial products, whilst increasing its own holdings of renewable energy stocks.[32] It has started to experiment with catastrophe bonds – a means to alleviate risks for insurance companies in cases where major disasters occur – driven, in part, by climate-change concerns.[33] Its other climate-adaptation activities, according to a report Allianz made to the UNFCCC, include an expanding micro-insurance business in six developing countries, which have gained the company 100,000 new clients in India alone.[34] Yet these are all niche interests in an industry whose largest players still often pay little heed to climate change and whose overall business strategy continues to be business-as-usual.

In the case of climate disasters, the buck rarely stops with the frontline insurance companies. Most large corporates take out cover from reinsurance companies, specialising in selling insurance to insurers, in order to cover their risk. It is these re-insurers that have provided corporate leadership on adaptation to climate change. Munich Re, the world's largest re-insurance firm, set up the Munich Climate Insurance Initiative in 2005, which has concentrated on the inclusion of micro-insurance and other insurance-based approaches in international policy. It has also published numerous reports on the climate impacts on the insurance industry, showing that re-insurers pick up the largest share of a bill of around $200 billion per year, hitting their balance sheets in the short term, while stimulating some cost restructuring that ultimately passes through to increased costs to policy holders.

At the same time, re-insurance companies are expanding their offering of products that keep the wheels firmly on the fossil-fuels wagon. Alongside the World Bank Group's Multilateral Investment Guarantee Agency, re-insurers routinely now offer 'political risk' insurance products, which have extractive industries as their main clients. Their core business also includes underwriting loans, loan guarantees and other investments made in infrastructure projects, including offshore oil exploration and production, and other projects controversially (and misleadingly) labelled 'climate friendly'. For example, the Belo Monte dam in Brazil, which could decimate a large area of the Amazon and displace up to 40,000 people, is being underwritten by the Spanish insurance company MAPFRE, Brazil Re, Munich Re and a host of others.[35] Re-insurance firms have also begun to offer 'reputational risk' insurance, which would pay out to subsidise a PR campaign in response to damages sustained to brands by events such as the Deepwater Horizon oil spill.

More generally, insurance companies are becoming indistinguishable from asset managers, with insurance just one of several business lines that include managing stock holdings, trading futures, commodities and currency. The vast majority of the thousands of stock market funds created by these companies contain investments in fossil-fuel industries, while they are also increasingly involved in oil futures markets.[36] For example, AllianceBernstein (majority owned by AXA) holds oil, gas and mining stocks worth over US$13 billion.[37] As with the banks, there remains a stark disconnect between their pro-nouncements on climate change and their investment portfolio. And for as long as the value of these assets is centrally linked to projections on the value and accessibility of proven reserves, the insurance sector (like other businesses) is unlikely to be a reliable ally in controlling and adapting to climate change.

Reducing climate change to 'climate risk'

It is difficult to generalise about the investment motives of transnational corporations as a whole, a problem that would look still more acute if we were to cover a range of other business sectors, such as food and beverages, car manufacturing or information technology. But a common methodology can nevertheless be observed.

When climate change is factored into corporate investment strategies at all, it usually takes the form of a 'climate risk [that] must be understood and managed in the same way as any other corporate risk'.[38] The major elements of this include regulatory risk, referring to 'the impact on the company of current and anticipated laws and regulations relating to climate change', reputational risk, and a variety of physical risks, including the current or future impacts on supply chains of changing weather patterns, rising sea levels or diminishing water supplies, and indirect risks posed by technological developments. Companies running this analysis have noted potential impacts in terms of higher operating costs or reduced demand for certain products and services. Abercrombie & Fitch estimates, for example, that it lost out on $10.7 million in store and direct sales when Superstorm Sandy hit the US in 2012.[39] But the models for quantifying any individual risks abstract from the systemic impact that climate change as a whole will have.

A risk-management approach may have its uses in helping corporations think through the climate-change implications of specific investment choices, but it also has significant limitations. By reducing climate impacts to isolated categories of 'risk', corporate risk management offers a framework through which climate change can be normalised and then dealt with by means of everyday, technocratic fixes: a big-box store may be cited on marginally higher ground in a coastal city, a car plant may be moved inshore, an oil rig may have increased stress testing, and so on. Risk management parcels out the climate problem into isolated factors affecting particular assets and specific organisational processes, but in doing so, it can make it more difficult for firms to see the bigger-picture effects of their actions, both to their own longer-term viability in a climate-constrained world, and to society more generally.

Such measures spread the risks posed to an individual corporation, but also generate systemic risk in reducing the incentives faced by any one corporate actor to do any differently. Risk management can serve as a sort of safety valve that allows corporations to continue to spread the systemic damage that their fossil-fuel-related investments pose. It almost never cautions: should we invest or not? But simply: having decided to invest, how can we safeguard this investment?

A failure to address the bigger picture on climate change is compounded by the fact that most corporations don't consider that current or future climate-change regulations are likely to make a significant difference, either in terms of directly restricting certain polluting practices, or through energy taxation, subsidy shifts, or carbon pricing rendering certain practices uncompetitive.

The case of Exxon Mobil offers a clear example here. In April 2014, divestment campaigners forced the company to analyse its climate-change risk exposure. The resulting report noted the rigour with which the company considered 'the risk of climate change in our planning bases and investments', including stress testing against a conservative range of economic assumptions and factoring in a cost of carbon in investment evaluations.[40] It nevertheless concluded that government action forcing Exxon to keep any of its oil reserves in the ground was 'highly unlikely', and argued that it could therefore continue to search for more oil and gas without restraint. 'Based on this analysis, we are confident that none of our hydrocarbon reserves are now or will become "stranded"', the company proclaimed.

That type of response represents a complacent – indeed, arrogant – disregard for the planet. But it is based on a confident bet that TNCs will continue to have significant influence on public policy making, both through their lobbying, and as a result of the anti-regulatory neoliberalism shared by politicians of both the centre-left and centre-right in most industrialised countries.

A lack of regulatory constraint, or even fear of future regulations, is a significant problem because, left to their own devices, transnational corporations are profit-seeking machines that have little incentive to curb their contributions to climate change. That can mean not simply ignoring climate change, but also positioning themselves to profit from some of its worst effects.

Profiteering from climate change

The 'booming business of global warming' was recently exposed by journalist McKenzie Funk, whose book *Windfall* journeys around the world in search of the people and corporations looking to benefit from the impacts of climate change. In the Alps, he finds an Israeli company capitalising on the greater variability of snow conditions by producing snowmaking equipment, in what is now a billion dollar a year business.[41] Over in California, private firefighters are teaming up with insurance companies to capitalise on the growing risks that wildfires pose to private property.[42] Climate change has also proven to be good business for specialist consultants, such as catastrophe-modelling companies advising the insurance sector on where to raise premiums in response to climate risks.

The main opportunities to profit from climate change lie in relation to energy, food production and water distribution (explored in chapters 8, 9 and 10). As was recently documented by the Intergovernmental Panel on Climate Change, global warming could be devastating for food production, destroying crop yields and pushing up prices to the extent of driving millions of people into poverty.[43] But it is also a key factor driving farm land grabs in large parts of the world. From Canada to Romania, farm land is changing hands on the assumption that climate change will increase yields at higher latitudes.[44] In South Sudan, Funk meets an investment fund manager positioning himself to profit from climate-induced conflict, as well as rises in food prices.[45]

The threat of drought, meanwhile, is driving a 'climate-patent' race between many of the world's biggest biotech companies. Water scarcity is also high on the agenda for those investing on the assumption of worsening climate change, with analysts talking up the chances of water-management multinationals such as Suez and Veolia.[46]

In recent years, that investment has been formalised via a variety of climate-change and environmental investment funds, which advertise themselves as directing capital towards building a greener world through investments in wind and solar energy as well as, more controversially, biofuels. But these same funds tend to expend as much or more capital on bets on accelerating climate change: 'companies that fit the portfolio not because they could help fight climate change but because the warmer the world, the less habitable it became, the bigger the windfall.'[47] Funk tracks the case of the Deutsche Bank's $2.9 billion DWS Climate Change Fund, whose portfolio includes Monsanto and Syngenta, biotech giants hoping to expand a market in genetically modified 'drought-resistant crops', as well as water-treatment and fertilizer companies.

Elsewhere, Wall Street investors have interpreted the effects of climate change as a green light for investment in gas extraction. 'They're predicting more weather extremes,' noted gas index investor Skip Aylesworth, in response to the landmark 2014 US National Climate Assessment report: 'Weather extremes are good for the energy business. More energy use, better for the earnings.'[48]

Market structure

The structure of modern stock markets offers a further reason why investors continue myopically bankrolling climate change and avoiding more fundamental change. Transnational corporations are, for the most part, listed on public exchanges, where institutional investors (pension, savings and insurance funds) control most shares. The majority of these are held in funds that invest on the basis of short-term measures of economic performance. That translates into firms placing increasing pressure on senior executives to deliver on short-term financial performance. The pressure is reinforced by an incentives culture in which share options can represent the largest share of multi-million dollar pay settlements for senior executives.

Investments in oil and gas companies are a partial exception to this trend, in so far as their value is measured against reserves, which would only be exploited over the longer term. But this does not lessen the short-term imperative to maximise the expansion of such reserves, against which company value is created and bonuses are paid.

A further, structural issue relates to the interconnectedness of the major fossil-fuel companies and the financial sector. In 2011, a group of Swiss researchers conducted the largest-ever study of the architecture of international corporate ownership, and found that 'nearly 4/10 of the control over the economic value of TNCs in the world is held, via a complicated web of ownership relations, by a group of 147 TNCs in the core.'[49] Their conclusion was that 'transnational corporations form a giant bow-tie structure and that a large portion of control flows to a small tightly-knit core of financial institutions.' Those firms, in turn, have significant assets invested in both fossil-fuel companies and speculation on commodities (oil is the world's most heavily traded commodity). What that creates, on a global scale, is a significant vested interest in the continuation of the status quo: while big financial corporations could survive a transition to renewable energy, their powerful status within the economy affords them the ability to survive without having to learn or significantly adapt.

From climate denial to corporate myth making

When climate change came to be recognised as a global problem, many of the world's largest corporations sensed a fundamental threat to their economic interest. US-based corporations in the fossil-fuel, automobile, electricity-generation and chemical sectors led the way.[50] They funded extensive efforts to delegitimise climate science, using tried and tested tactics summarized by the Union of Concerned Scientists as

> ... exaggerating the uncertainty associated with climate change while ignoring what is known, funding contrarian scientists and think tanks engaged in spreading misinformation and blocking policy, and contributing to politicians who proclaim they do not believe in the science of global warming.[51]

At the same time, US politicians were subjected to fierce lobbying against climate legislation, or ratifying the 1997 Kyoto Protocol, on the basis of claims that the high costs of reducing emissions would destroy US competitiveness.

Most notably, the Global Climate Coalition (GCC) – a front group for about forty major oil, coal, auto and chemical corporations and trade associations – played a key role in delaying and weakening international climate agreements. The GCC successfully lobbied Washington to ensure that no binding targets were included in the UN Framework Convention on Climate Change, agreed to at the 1992 Rio Earth Summit. It also promoted a 1997 Senate resolution where US legislators expressed unanimous opposition to legally binding greenhouse-gas reductions unless developing countries (responsible for a fraction of the current and historical emissions) accepted similar limits.

The tactics identified with the GCC and its allies are still occasionally seen today. Most notably, the Koch brothers, whose Koch Industries group is the second-largest privately held company in the US, bankroll climate denial and provide millions of dollars annually to lobby Washington politicians against adopting climate legislation.

For the most part, though, corporate responses to climate change have shifted. Since the early 2000s, most large corporations have acknowledged that climate change is happening, although there remains considerable diversity in what policy responses, if any, they are willing to countenance. And there is still greater reluctance, as we have seen, to make significant changes to their own business practice.

Ecological modernisation

We have already seen how investment based on the continuation of fossil fuels tries to secure a path for business as usual to continue. But this is often accompanied by a 'win-win' discourse on ecological modernisation.[52]

From a marketing point of view, at least, it is now usually seen as good practice to acknowledge that climate change is a problem and to highlight how corporations are acting in response to it. In a recent study on 'corporate responses to climate change as political myths', business-school researchers Christopher Wright and Daniel Nyberg interviewed a number of senior corporate managers and summarized the new 'corporate environmentalism' thus: 'while most of the businesses we studied acknowledged the issue of climate change as a threat and challenge, they emphasised their central role in "solving" climate change through technological innovation and the development of "green" products and services.'[53]

This was clearly observable in our examples from both the oil and gas and financial sectors – and similar cases are easily found elsewhere, from airlines pioneering 'climate-friendly' agrofuels, to breweries developing 'carbon-neutral' beer. A survey of S&P 500 companies (the 500 largest companies listed on the New York Stock Exchange or NASDAQ), based on self-reporting, found that they had $50 billion invested in 'emissions-reduction' and 'energy-savings' activities, about 4 per cent of their total capital expenditure.[54]

For example, Walmart, the world's largest retailer, talks loudly about sustainability, slashing emissions in its supply chain, and switching to renewable energy. To this end, the company produces a 'global responsibility' report, documenting pockets of progress on reducing its CO_2 emissions intensity (for example, by reducing waste). Yet at the same time, its annual greenhouse-gas emissions continue to grow.[55]

A related aspect is that corporations tend to be flexible and nonspecific in defining the scale of their action – expressing aspirational emissions reductions, or announcing programmes running into billions of dollars that sound impressive in press releases but are dwarfed by the actual impact of the company's operations. The Bank of America example cited above gives one illustration, and Walmart provides yet another. Despite receiving media plaudits for setting a goal of being 'supplied by 100 per cent renewable energy', the company would actually take about 300 years to achieve this at its current pace of converting to renewables.[56] At present, Walmart derives just 4 per cent of the electricity for its US stores from wind and solar power.

More damningly, the unsustainable nature of these major corporations' business models remains unchallenged. In the case of Walmart, that is manifested most obviously in its contribution to a globalised, industrial food system that is reliant on long supply chains – the company does not count the impacts of international shipping in its emissions accounting – as well as in its contribution to urban sprawl and increased car travel.

It is easy to dismiss the efforts of Walmart and others as little more than publicity stunts designed to greenwash their corporate image. But a key part of their resonance relates to the way it has legitimised TNCs' attempts to be considered good corporate citizens, seen as acting not just in the narrow interests of their shareholders but a broader range of stakeholders such as employees, customers, suppliers, communities – indeed, global society as whole. Against a backdrop of neoliberal policy making, this positioning can serve as cover for corporate lobbying and increased corporate involvement in national and international governance.

Corporate lobbying

Although climate change is the ultimate global problem, and transnational corporations by definition operate across national boundaries, the core focus of climate lobbying remains domestic policy making, with the partial exception of the EU, where Brussels is a key focus.

Domestic lobbying happens both directly and indirectly. TNCs directly submit their own proposals to legislators, host public or closed-door meetings with senior civil servants and ministers, place staff on secondment to relevant government departments, and (where national rules allow) directly fund political parties to create leverage over decision makers. But they also work through industry associations covering individual sectors or (as in the case of groups like the Confederation of British Industry, BusinessEurope or the American Chamber of Commerce) lobby for the interests of 'business' as a whole.

These lobby activities have been extensively documented, but it is worth underscoring that the messaging of individual corporations and business associations has often diverged, and corporations often take positions that are contradictory. The most notable example in the US is the case of the proposed climate and energy bill in 2010, where 14 large corporations formed the US Climate Action Partnership in support of the bill, while the US Chamber of Commerce pitched its stall against the legislation. A number of corporations, including ConocoPhillips and the General Electric Company, were represented on both sides of this divide.[57]

The market-based framing of the US climate bill – which eventually fell victim to climate sceptics – and of other carbon market schemes before it is also, in part, a result of corporate agenda setting. Emissions trading schemes (ETS) are intended to give polluters flexibility: instead of simply putting a limit on greenhouse-gas emissions, companies are given permits to pollute that they can use, sell if they don't need them, or purchase so that they can pollute more. Corporations have played an important role in securing the adoption of this 'cap-and-trade' approach. For example, oil giant BP ran an internal carbon-trading scheme, which was intended to demonstrate its viability to European policy makers and so encourage them to create a carbon market rather than setting a carbon tax. Historians of the scheme have shown how employees of BP, Shell and a handful of other corporations formed part of an informal 'issue-specific policy network' with members of the European Commission's DG Environment that advocated for the scheme.[58]

Once the EU ETS was established, lobbying on the allocation of emissions permits quickly became a form of rent-seeking, with the power sector and heavy industries gaining generous allocations of permits to pollute. By a mix of selling these permits and hiking prices for consumers on the back of over-stated assumptions about what such permits would cost, the power sector and heavy industries have gained billions in unearned windfall profits from the ETS, while doing little to reduce emissions and nothing to restructure the economy away from a reliance on fossil fuels.[59] The scheme has also been invoked time and again to undermine or block the adoption of a wide range of other environmental policies.

Pushing at an open door: Transnational corporations and the state

This brings us, finally, to the role of the state in reinforcing the power of transnational corporations and their business practices that neglect or exacerbate climate change. National governments often take a lead in lobbying on behalf of industries they deem to be strategically important. For example, Germany routinely lobbies on behalf of its 'national' car industry (which produces vehicles across the globe) against regulations on vehicle emissions within the European Union.[60] Lobbying by nation states on behalf of transnational corporations is a common feature, too, of international climate negotiations. At the UN Climate Conference in Poland, the Polish Ministry of Economy even teamed up with the World Coal Association to stage an International Coal and Climate Summit, to promote the continued use of coal in power production.[61]

Foot-dragging on the international stage can also be a result of state ownership. More than 10 per cent of the world's 2,000 largest companies are majority state owned.[62] Public ownership is particularly prevalent in the case of fossil fuels, with state-owned corporations owning about 86 per cent of known global reserves and accounting for around 55 per cent of current production.[63] State-owned enterprises are also particularly prevalent in the mining sector, including mining for coal and lignite. Many of these state-owned companies are highly corporatised entities 'whose management has internalised the logic of the private sector, via the adoption of a market rationality primarily focused on financial gains, with the subsequent deterioration of the public ethos.'[64] In short, such companies see a profitable future in fossil fuels.

But the main contribution of the state to corporate inertia on climate change arguably has less to do with fossil fuels than it does with an ideological distaste for social and environmental regulation. Notably, this is not the same as distaste for regulation per se. While neoliberal theory suggests that markets should be self-regulating and freely functioning, the more common practice of neoliberal state interventions is to ensure a 'good business or investment climate'.[65] At a domestic level, for example, the UK government scrapped a code for sustainable homes that mandated energy as part of a drive to 'simplify' regulation to help stimulate private investment. The Spanish government cut renewables subsidies and placed a hefty tax on households and landowners who produce their own electricity from solar panels, as a result of lobbying from large utilities (under the guise of austerity).[66]

The real damage is done internationally, though, in the terrain of trade policy. The Trans-Pacific Partnership (TPP), under negotiation in 2015, could include rules that would 'harmonise' environmental regulations, levelling them down to a lowest common denominator.[67] Its proposed 'investment chapter' would grant transnational corporations impunity, allowing them to bypass local courts, opting for international tribunals stacked in their favour.[68]

The EU's existing and proposed free-trade agreements also serve to weaken the hand of legislators in adopting tougher regulations. For example, the 2015-proposed Transatlantic Trade and Investment Partnership (TTIP) would put pressure on the EU to reduce its energy efficiency standards to US levels.[69] It would also strengthen the hand of energy-intensive industries, which are arguing strongly against the EU increasing its greenhouse-gas targets without similar commitments from other industrialised countries.

More generally, the consequences of the EU's pursuit of market liberalisation can be seen in terms of its increasing 'emissions embodied in trade', a consumption-based measure of responsibility for greenhouse-gas emissions, which shows that the bloc's global share of responsibility for climate change has continued to rise. A plethora of free-trade agreements and bilateral investment treaties (BITs) that allow the EU to import goods from unsustainable energy sources and evade environmental regulations have encouraged this outsourcing of emissions.[70]

The state frequently acts as a backstop for corporate profit making, sometimes even opening up new business opportunities by force. This manifests itself most obviously in the willingness of states to engage in warfare to secure energy resources. The Iraq War of 2003 remains the most notable recent example, and whilst oil was not the sole motive for the US and its allies in forcing that conflict, bringing Iraq's reserves onto international markets in the hands of private corporations was a leading strategic interest.

The connection between military expansionism and securing oil reserves is even clearer in the case of state oil companies, with the China National Offshore Oil Corporation (CNOOC) laying claim to oil concessions in the South China Sea on territory claimed by the Philippines and Vietnam, which has led to military skirmishes.[71] The East China Sea has seen a similar stand-off involving China, Japan and Taiwan. And with military operations increasingly being supplemented by private security, corporations are also budgeting for increases in their security operations in a climate-constrained world. For example, Shell spent at least $1 billion on security between 2007 and 2009, according to internal documents leaked to the campaign group Platform.[72]

Conclusion: Beyond corporate control

We have seen in this chapter how deeply entrenched the corporate addiction to fossil fuels is, and how a series of factors serve to further embed corporations' choice to keep investing in runaway climate change and avoid any fundamental changes in business practice, putting economic growth above all other priorities. Risk-management techniques parcel up climate impacts into quantifiable chunks, which, once thrown into a cost-benefit mixer, rarely emerge as sufficiently indigestible to demand much action. Financial-sector connections with fossil-fuel firms, and investment norms that favour short-term financial performance irrespective of its environmental costs, create a powerful bloc with vested interests in continued greenhouse-gas pollution. At the same time, some companies are readying themselves to profit from crisis with new services and products to address climate-change impacts, as well as offering corporate solutions to any perceived insecurity that might result from climate change.

TNCs 'greenwash' their business practices with eye-catching initiatives that do little of substance, on closer inspection, to change their destructive business models. At the same time, corporations and industry associations lobby governments to water down environmental legislation, or avoid regulation in favour of market-based solutions that allow them to buy their way out of enacting environmental policies. Often, this lobbying is pushing at an open door, with politicians and civil servants acting to avoid strong climate commitments at an international level, while at the same time promoting free-trade agreements that undermine regulation and afford transnational corporations impunity from domestic legal regimes.

It should be clear from this mesh of factors reinforcing corporate inaction on climate change and the evasion of responsibility for its impacts that no simple, single remedy can be applied – but it is equally clear that efforts must be made to rein in corporate power, if climate change and its impacts are to be addressed effectively.

Nation states can play a key role here, legislating to phase out fossil-fuel subsidies (starting with producer subsidies in industrialised countries) and directly regulating greenhouse emissions from the power sector and industry.[73] They can also legislate to change the rules according to which the financial sector operates, such that central banks consider fossil-fuel investments as systemic risks and regulate accordingly, or even by applying capital and credit controls to investments that produce high levels of greenhouse-gas emissions. Chinese banking regulations already do this domestically, albeit with significant lapses in implementation. At the same time, states could use public procurement policies to invest massively in measures to reduce greenhouse-gas emissions and lessen the impacts of climate change. But to do so requires challenging the ideological dominance of austerity and 'balanced budgets', which encourage infrastructure investment to be pushed off the public books and long into the future by means of public-private partnerships. These schemes routinely deliver poor value for taxpayers while, over the long term, they compromise the ability of states to invest in projects that could help them adapt to the effects of climate change – be those flood defences, coastal protection, or improved health systems.

Reclaiming the public sphere is also vital in the case of the energy sector, and is already happening in the case of water services worldwide and, to a lesser extent, in the form of municipal energy grids (in Germany in particular). Increasing public ownership, in particular when that takes the form of re-municipalisation, can help to break the stranglehold of the large corporate utilities that are delaying the transformation of the energy system.[74] That points the way to a second area where the transformation of the state is closely linked to a more ambitious tackling of climate change and a more just adaptation agenda. As we have seen, corporate lobbyists can set agendas and influence rule making on the environment, trade and broader economic policy. Tackling that means democratising the state (and regional blocs, notably the EU), through new rules to enhance transparency and accountability, and to rein in trade and investment treaties that bias laws in favour of corporate polluters rather than citizens.[75] Various campaigns and proposals, including that promoted by the Global Campaign against Corporate

Impunity, also exist that are pushing for legal changes to hold transnational corporations and senior corporate leaders to account for environmental and human-rights abuses committed under their watch.[76]

A third dimension of 'reclaiming the state' is the de-corporatisation of state-owned enterprises: restructuring them so that they are no longer held as joint-stock, partially privatised companies on stock exchanges, and given instead a public-interest mandate that is reflected in their investment priorities. In the case of public-energy companies, that means retooling them away from extracting fossil fuels, or producing power from those fuels, and towards renewable energy infrastructure – in the process, breaking the increased interdependency between public and private firms in the extractives sector.[77]

In practice, it remains extremely unlikely that states that depend heavily upon fossil-fuel extraction would take such action on their own initiative. International pressure, in the form of a strong and legally binding international climate agreement, therefore remains a necessary step to changing state fossil-fuel enterprises – and the achievement of such an agreement, in turn, requires strong domestic pressure from social movements to shift the perspective of negotiators.

A fourth front in transforming the state rests on changing how public money is invested. Considerable revenues from fossil-fuel extraction (principally oil and gas) have been placed in Sovereign Wealth Funds (SWFs), which manage over $5 trillion in investments globally.[78] These are invested in a range of assets, from shares in transnational corporations to infrastructure and real estate. SWFs have the potential to invest long term and in climate-friendly just transition measures that their more commercial counterparts find unattractive. In 2013, for example, the Norwegian Government Pension Fund Global (the world's largest SWF) divested from 27 mining companies and 23 oil palm companies (which fuel deforestation).[79] This was followed with the declaration of a new 'renewable investment mandate', although a parallel effort to investigate whether to withdraw its billions from fossil-fuel stocks altogether recommended only a weak 'conduct-based exclusion' that falls a long way short of divestment.[80]

More directly, pension funds could also provide some of the billions needed to fund a just transition and address adaptation needs – although it's worth recalling that there are clear limits in the transformative potential of such funds, though, not least in their marked preference for market-based solutions.[81]

The transformation of the role of corporations in our society requires more than just state action, however. States do not act without pressure from their citizens, and while the solutions to reining in corporations and addressing climate change lie mainly at the level of changes in national and international laws and policies, it is social movements and citizens' organisations that drive such changes. To some extent, the emphasis should be on reasserting democratic control, which includes redefining legal definitions of what corporations are. Instead of corporations claiming 'corporate personhood', whilst acting as pathological profit-maximising machines, they could be legally mandated to seek benefits beyond profit – similar to the model of 'benefit corporations' that already exists in a handful of US states.[82] Alongside legal changes, corporate governance could also be shifted to enhance employee ownership (including along cooperative lines) or mandating that workers take at least half the seats in corporate boardrooms (following the German model).[83]

But reforming corporations is no substitute for diminishing their power altogether, which remains a key goal of many social movements and citizens' groups. The tactics are too numerous to mention, but in the case of climate-change activism alone, these have included referendums to retake control of energy systems, fossil-fuel divestment campaigns, protests and shareholder activism at corporate Annual General Meetings, legal cases against environmental and rights abuses, occupations of corporate offices or corporate-sponsored spaces, culture jamming, social-media campaigning, and direct action (including occupations) to stop land clearing, pipeline building, and mining and drilling operations. The creative space for intervention is fairly limitless, but there are some common threads to what works, starting with a refusal to countenance support from the corporate players that are the source of much of the problem, accompanied by a refusal to be constrained by what corporations and governments deem pragmatic at any given moment. Only by rejecting corporate control and dependence on fossil fuels can we create the space for a just response to the climate crisis.

Notes

1. Thanks to Steffen Boehm, Janet Redman and Pascoe Sabido for their comments on earlier versions of this chapter.
2. Tillerson, R. (2012). The new North American energy paradigm: Reshaping the future. Speech presented at Council on Foreign Relations. Retrieved from http://www.cfr.org/north-america/new-north-american-energy-paradigm-reshaping-future/p2863.
3. Walmart (22 April 2013). Walmart highlights sustainability progress in its 2013 Global Responsibility Report (press release). Retrieved from http://news.walmart.com/news-archive/2013/04/22/walmart-highlights-sustainability-progress-in-its-2013-global-responsibility-report; EDF Energy. (n.d.). *Our Sustainability Commitments* (report). Retrieved http://www.edfenergy.com/sustainability/our-sustainability-commitments/.
4. Upham, D. (2014). Trust us: Savvy businesses understand their role in fighting climate change. Retrieved from http://www.edf.org/blog/2014/02/20/trust-us-savvy-businesses-understand-their-role-fighting-climate-change/.
5. McKibben, B. (2012). Global warming's terrifying new math. *Rolling Stone*, p. 1162. Retrieved from http://www.rollingstone.com/politics/news/global-warmings-terrifying-new-math-20120719#ixzz2BAAEi09H.
6. Heede, R. (2014). Tracing anthropogenic carbon dioxide and methane emissions to fossil fuel and cement producers, 1854–2010. *Climatic Change*, 122(1–2), 229–41. Retrieved from doi:10.1007/s10584-013-0986-y.
7. Leaton, J. (2011). *Unburnable Carbon – Are the world's financial markets carrying a carbon bubble?* London: Carbon Tracker Initiative, p. 4.
8. Carbon Tracker also uses a figure of 900 Gt, but that figure assumes some proportion of carbon capture and storage by 2050, which is controversial. Leaton, J. et al. (2013). *Unburnable Carbon 2013: Wasted capital and stranded assets*. London: Carbon Tracker Initiative, p. 4.

9. *World Energy Outlook 2014*. Paris: International Energy Agency.

10. For example, Petrobras's current investment strategy anticipates a long-term price of $90 to $100 per barrel of Brent crude. See Petrobras (2012). *2012–2016 Business Plan*, pp. 1–8 (p. 6). Shell uses $80–100 as its medium-term price estimate (through to the end of 2015), see Royal Dutch Shell. (2012a). *Building an Energy Future: Annual Report 2011*. The Hague: Shell, 2012, p. 20; Royal Dutch Shell. (August 2010). *Evidence on the Supply and Demand for Oil*, p. 4. Retrieved from http://www.decc.gov.uk/assets/decc/what%20we%20do/global%20 climate%20change%20and%20energy/international%20energy/energy%20security/1789- shells-response-to-cfe-oil.pdf.

11. Royal Dutch Shell (2012a), p. 50.

12. Simms, A. (1 May 2012). Shell's stance on wind power reveals a profound truth of capitalism. The *Guardian*.

13. Friends of the Earth International. (2013). *Good Energy, Bad Energy: Transforming our energy system for people and the planet*. Amsterdam: Friends of the Earth International. Retrieved from http://www.foei.org/wp-content/uploads/2013/09/Good-energy-bad-energy.pdf.

14. Royal Dutch Shell. 2012b. *Carbon Disclosure Project 2012: Royal Dutch Shell*, p. 9. Retrieved from http://www-static.shell.com/static/environment_society/downloads/environment/ climate_change/cdp_response_050912.

15. Royal Dutch Shell. (2012a), p. 3; Royal Dutch Shell. (2012b), p. 49.

16. Royal Dutch Shell. (2012b), p. 18.

17. Ibid., p. 20.

18. Foster, J. (30 January 2014). Shell suspends 2014 offshore drilling plans in Arctic. *Climate Progress*. Retrieved from http://thinkprogress.org/climate/2014/01/30/3225831/shell- arctic-drilling-2014/. For a critical view of Shell's arctic explorations, see Platform et al. (2012) *Out in the Cold: Investor risk in Shell's Arctic exploration* London: Greenpeace.

19. Bourne, J. (10 September 2012). Ice-breaking: U.S. oil drilling starts as nations mull changed Arctic. *National Geographic*. Retrieved from http://news.nationalgeographic.com/news/ energy/2012/09/120910-shell-begins-arctic-drilling.

20. Royal Dutch Shell. (2011), p. 30.

21. Al-Anazi, D. (2009). Carbon management efforts in Saudi Aramco. *EnviroNews*, 18, 2–3. Retrieved from http://www.saudiaramco.com/content/dam/Publications/Environews/ Environews%20Summer%202009/EnviroNewsSummer2009.pdf.

22. Schücking, H. (2013). *Banking on Coal*. Urgewald, Sassenberg: BankTrack, CEE Bankwatch Network and Polska Zielona Sieć, p. 17.

23. Bank of America (2015). U.S. Environmental Protection Agency recognizes Bank of America for climate change leadership. Retrieved from http://about.bankofamerica.com/en-us/global- impact/environmental-sustainability.html#fbid=icpqTLb07Z6.

24. Schücking (2013), p. 10; see also Reyes, O. (2013). *Carbon Capital: How the City bankrolls climate change*. London: WDM.

25. Schücking, H., Kroll, L., Louvel, Y. and Richter, R. (2011). *Bankrolling Climate Change*. Urgewald, Sassenberg: groundWork, Earthlife Africa Johannesburg and BankTrack, p. 15.

26. Reuters (24 May 2012). Goldman Sachs outlines $40bn clean energy investment plan. *Climate Spectator*.

27. Allianz (n.d.). Insuring against climate impacts and rewarding sustainable business practices. Retrieved from http://unfccc.int/files/adaptation/nairobi_work_programme/private_ sector_initiative/application/pdf/allianz.pdf.

28. Smith, N. (2007). Disastrous accumulation. *South Atlantic Quarterly*, 106(4), 775.

29. Lehmann, E. (9 July 2009) The climate for climate-related insurance at AIG turns bleak. *ClimateWire*.

30. Buffett's statement is contradicted by other calculations, which show that $30.6 billion, or 29 per cent, of Berkshire Hathaway's revenue is heavily contingent on climate and energy issues. See Lichtenheld, M. (10 February 2012). Warren Buffett's billions at risk; Berkshire Hathaway is lowest-rated on sustainability. *HIP Investor*.

31. AXA (2012). *Annual Report 2011*. Paris: AXA, p. 222.

32. Sandhövel, A. (2012). *Low-carbon Investments: Perspective of an institutional investor*. Singapore: Allianz, p. 11.

33. Insurance companies issue 'catastrophe bonds' (underwritten by investment banks), which pay a coupon (a periodic payment) to investors if no catastrophe occurs. If a major disaster does occur during the period of the bond, the principal (the original amount of the bond) is returned to the insurance company, which then uses this money to pay claimants. For a critical take, see Phillips, L. (2014). *Cat Bonds: Cashing in on catastrophe*. Retrieved from: http://roadtoparis.info/2014/11/18/cat-bonds-cashing-catastrophe/.

34. Allianz (n.d). *Insuring Against Climate Impacts and Rewarding Sustainable Business Practices*. Retrieved from http://unfccc.int/files/adaptation/nairobi_work_programme/private_sector_initiative/application/pdf/allianz.pdf.

35. Banktrack (2014, April 20). Dodgy deals: Belo Monte Dam. Retrieved from http://www.banktrack.org/manage/ajax/ems_dodgydeals/createPDF/belo_monte_dam.

36. Fattouh, B. and Mahadeva, L. (2012). *Financialization in Oil Markets: Lessons for policy*. Oxford: Oxford Institute for Energy Studies.

37. Capel, A. (2011). AllianceBernstein likes these basic materials stocks the most in 13F filing. Retrieved from http://wallstcheatsheet.com/trading/alliancebernstein-likes-these-basic-materials-stocks-the-most-in-13f-filing.html/.

38. CBI (2009). *Future Proof: Preparing your business for a changing climate*. London: CBI, p. 1.

39. Bardeline, J. (23 September 2013). Number of 'climate leaders' doubles in new CDP report. *Green Biz*. More generally, see www.riskybusiness.org.

40. ExxonMobil (2014) *Energy and Carbon – Managing the risks*, p. 21. Retrieved from http://cdn.exxonmobil.com/~/media/Files/Other/2014/Report%20-%20Energy%20and%20Carbon%20-%20Managing%20the%20Risks.pdf.

41. Funk, M. (2014). *Windfall: The booming business of global warming*. New York: Penguin, pp. 80, 101.

42. Ibid., pp. 97–107.

43. Intergovernmental Panel on Climate Change (2014) *Climate Change 2014: Impacts, Adaptation, and Vulnerability. Summary for policymakers*. Geneva: IPCC.

44. Funk, M. (2014), p. 152.

45. Ibid., pp. 139–51.

46. Ibid., p. 21.

47. Ibid., p. 3.

48. Polson, J. (9 May 2014). Cleanest fossil fuel Is Wall Street's bet on climate change. *Bloomberg*.

49. Vitali, S., Glattfelder, J.B. and Battiston, S. (2011). The network of global corporate control. *PLoS ONE*, 6(10), 4. See also Draffan, G. (2013). *Dirty Money: The finance and fossil fuel web*. Amsterdam: Transnational Institute.

50. Newell, P. and Paterson, M. (1998). A climate for business: Global warming, the state and capital. *Review of International Political Economy*, 5, 682; Levy, D. and Egan, D. (2003). A neo-Gramscian approach to corporate political strategy: Conflict and accommodation in the climate change negotiations. *Journal of Management Studies*, 40, 804.

51. Union of Concerned Scientists. (2012). *A Climate of Corporate Control: How corporations have influenced the U.S. dialogue on climate science and policy* (report). Retrieved http://www. ucsusa.org/our-work/center-science-and-democracy/fighting-misinformation/a-climate-of-corporate-control.html#.VIGL01mIZco.

52. Hajer, M. (1995). *The Politics of Environmental Discourse: Ecological modernization and the policy process.* Oxford: Oxford University Press.

53. Wright, C. and Nyberg, D. (2014). Creative self-destruction: Corporate responses to climate change as political myths. *Environmental Politics*, 23, 210.

54. *Investment, transformation and leadership: CDP S&P 500 climate change report 2013* (report). (23 September 2013), p. 19. Retrieved from https://www.cdproject.net/CDPResults/CDP-SP500-climate-report-2013.pdf.

55. *2013 Walmart Global Responsibility Report* (report). (2013). Retrieved from http://corporate. walmart.com/microsites/global-responsibility-report-2013/; Sheppard, K. (13 November 2013). Walmart's sustainability results don't match promises, report finds. Retrieved from http://www.huffingtonpost.com/2013/11/13/walmart-sustainability_n_4263032.html.

56. Mitchell, S. (13 November 2013). *Walmart's Assault on the Climate: The truth behind one of the biggest climate polluters and slickest greenwashers in America* (report). Retrieved from http:// ilsr.org/downloads/Walmart%27s+Assault+on+the+Climate.

57. Union of Concerned Scientists. (2012), pp. 13–14.

58. Braun, M. (2009). The evolution of emissions trading in the European Union – The role of policy networks, knowledge and policy entrepreneurs. *Accounting, Organizations and Society*, 34(3–4), 469–87; Corporate Europe Observatory. (2009). *Putting the Fox in Charge of the Henhouse: How BP's emissions trading scheme was sold to the EU.* Brussels: Corporate Europe Observatory; Victor, D. and House, J. (2006). BP's emissions trading system. *Energy Policy*, 34.

59. Reyes, O. (2012). What goes up must come down – Carbon trading, industrial subsidies and capital market governance, in Hallström, N., ed. *What Next: Climate, development and equity.* Uppsala: Dag Hammarskjöld Foundation.

60. Hey, C. (2010). The German paradox: Climate leader and green car laggard, in S. Oberthür and M. Pallemaerts, eds. *The New Climate Policies of the European Union.* Brussels: VUB Press; Germany wins backing of EU ministers to block car emissions law. (15 October 2013). *Euractiv.* Retrieved from www.euractiv.com/ … /germany-wins-backing-eu-minister-news-531085.

61. *The COP19 guide to corporate lobbying: Climate crooks and the Polish government's partners in crime.* (2013). Amsterdam: Corporate Europe Observatory and Transnational Institute, p. 19.

62. Kowalski, P., et al. (2013). State-owned enterprises: Trade effects and policy implications. *OECD Trade Policy Papers*, 147, 9. OECD Publishing. doi:10.1787/5k4869ckqk7l-en.

63. Mitchell, J., Marcel, V. and Mitchell, B. (2012). *What next for the oil and gas industry?* London: Chatham House, p. 18.

64. Chavez, D. (2014). State of the state, in Buxton, N. (ed.). *State of Power 2014: Exposing the Davos class.* Amsterdam: TNI/Occupy, p. 51.

65. Harvey, D. (2007). *A Brief History of Neoliberalism.* Oxford: Oxford University Press, p. 70.

66. Galanova, M. (6 October 2013). Spain's sunshine toll: Row over proposed solar tax. *BBC*; Dunham, A. (21 March 2014). Energy giants out to kill off Spain's solar sector. *The Local.*

67. Solomon, I. (2012). *Raw Deal: How the Trans-Pacific Partnership could threaten our climate.* Washington, DC: Sierra Club; Wikileaks. (24 November 2013). *TPPA Environment Chapter and Chair's Commentary* (report). Retrieved from https://wikileaks.org/tppa-environment-chapter.html.

68. Wallach, L. and Tucker, T. (2012). Public interest analysis of leaked Trans-Pacific Partnership (TPP) investment text. *Public Citizen.* Retrieved from www.citizen.org/documents/Leaked-TPP-Investment-Analysis.pdf.

69. Riley, B. (6 June 2013). Personal interview.

70. Peters, G., Minx, J., Weber, C. and O. Edenhofer, O. (2011). Growth in emission transfers via international trade from 1990 to 2008. *PNAS,* 108(21), 5.

71. US Energy Information Administration. (7 February 2013). *South China Sea: EIA Analyst Briefs.* Retrieved from: http://www.eia.gov/countries/analysisbriefs/South_China_Sea/south_china_sea.pdf.

72. Amunwa, B. (2012). *Dirty Work: Shell's security spending in Nigeria and beyond.* London: Platform, p. 3.

73. Bast, E., Kretzmann, S., Krishnaswamy, S. and Romine, T. (2013). *Low-hanging Fruit: Fossil fuel subsidies, climate finance, and sustainable development* (report). Washington, DC: Oil Change International for the Heinrich Böll Stiftung North America.

74. Whitfield, D. (2010) *Global Auction of Public Assets: Public sector alternatives to the infrastructure market and public private partnerships.* Nottingham: Spokesman.

75. See, for example: Alter-EU Steering Committee. (2010). A way forward, in H. Burley, W. Dinan, K. Haar, O. Hoedeman and E. Wesselius, eds. *Bursting the Brussels Bubble.* Brussels: Alter-EU, pp. 197–9.

76. See the website: http://www.stopcorporateimpunity.org.

77. In fact, the emerging pattern in the oil and gas sectors is of private and public firms acting together at different points in the supply chain. Private companies control most of the world's refinery capacity and distribution infrastructure for oil and gas. The picture gets blurred even further by the increase in cooperation agreements between the major private and public companies. See Mitchell, J., Marcel, V. and Mitchell, B. (2012), pp. 19, 38.

78. Sovereign wealth fund assets surpass $5tn. (11 October 2013). *Emirates 24/7.* Retrieved from http://www.emirates247.com/business/economy-finance/sovereign-wealth-fund-assets-surpass-5tn-2013-10-11-1.524222.

79. Lang, C. (7 March 2014). It's certainly profitable. But how green is Norway's Government Pension Fund Global? *REDD Monitor.*

80. Holvand, K. (13 March 2014). Norway to raise oil fund's exposure to renewable energy. *Wall Street Journal;* Lokhandwala (10 April 2015). Norwegian oil fund adopts 'broad criteria' for climate change exclusion. *Investment & Pensions Europe.*

81. Lang, C. (7 March 2014).

82. Eberlein, S. and Baida, D. (9 February 2012). California's new triple bottom line. *Yes! Magazine.* Retrieved from http://www.yesmagazine.org/new-economy/californias-new-triple-bottom-line.

83. For a series of practical suggestions on how to reform and rein in corporations, see Marx, M., Margil, M., Cavanagh, J., Anderson, S., Collins, C., Cray, C. and Kelley, M. (2007). *Strategic Corporate Initiative: Toward a Global Citizens' Movement to Bring Corporations Back Under Control.* Washington, DC: Corporate Ethics International. See also www.neweconomyworkinggroup.org.

PART II

SECURITY FOR WHOM?

4

A PERMANENT STATE OF EMERGENCY: CIVIL CONTINGENCIES, RISK MANAGEMENT AND HUMAN RIGHTS

Nafeez Mosaddeq Ahmed, Ben Hayes and Nick Buxton

Let us look at the case of Nazi Germany. Just after Hitler came to power (or, to be more precise, just after he was offered power) he proclaimed, on February 28, 1933, the Decree for the Protection of the People and the State. This decree suspends all the articles in the Weimar Constitution maintaining individual liberties. Since this decree was never revoked, we can say that the entire Third Reich from a legal point of view was a twelve-year-long state of emergency. And in this sense we can define modern totalitarianism as the institution, by way of a state of emergency, of a legal civil war that permits the elimination not only of political adversaries, but whole categories of the population that resist being integrated into the political system. Thus the intentional creation of a permanent state of emergency has become one of the most important measures of contemporary States, democracies included. And furthermore, it is not necessary that a state of emergency be declared in the technical sense of the term.

(Giorgio Agamben, Italian philosopher and author of State of Exception*)*

Introduction

Over eight days in September 2000, a small band of lorry drivers protesting fuel prices shocked the government, the public and perhaps even themselves when they almost brought the United Kingdom to a halt. Their blockades of several oil terminals not only forced 90 per cent of petrol stations to close, but also led to rationing in supermarkets and cancellation of hospital surgeries. Above all, they demonstrated how dependent the UK's economy and society was on oil processed in a few refineries and how vulnerable the entire population was in its reliance on a highly centralised food system all set up to deliver goods 'just in time'. Lord Cameron of Dillington, head of the UK Countryside Agency, said the experience showed the UK was 'just 9 meals away from anarchy'.

In this case, it was a group of lorry drivers that exposed the thin veneer that holds modern civilisation together. More recently, climate change has been cited as one of the main drivers for potential societal disruption. A study by Anglia Ruskin University's Global Sustainability Institute (GSI) for Lloyds of London, released in June 2015, warned that a combination of just three catastrophic weather events could lead to shortfalls in the production of staple crops, prompt price spikes and unleash food riots and political instability worldwide. The global food system, the authors argue, is 'under chronic pressure to meet an ever-rising demand, and its vulnerability to acute disruptions is compounded by factors such as climate change, water stress, ongoing globalisation and heightening political instability.'[1]

As much of this book explores, the state's response to these threats can end up exacerbating them. The threats posed by disasters and emergencies – real or imagined – are no different. In fact, as this chapter exposes, states have started to see risks everywhere and are determined to prepare for the worst. Yet these preparations appear capable only of producing legislation and contingencies that override democratic processes and undermine civil liberties.

In the UK, the lorry protest, which was followed by severe flooding and the outbreak of foot-and-mouth disease, catalysed the UK government into upgrading its emergency response and powers. The events of 9/11 and the incorporation of climate change issues into the UK's first National Security Strategy (see Chapter 2) have circumscribed these emergency preparations. In a similar vein, states worldwide have similarly ramped up their 'states of emergency' preparations to address vulnerabilities exposed by globalisation and the threat of climate change and new 'complex emergencies'. The draconian contingencies envisaged have been another boon for an ever-expanding military-security-industrial complex, but are deeply concerning for anyone committed to a progressive just response to climate-change impacts.

As this chapter examines, these strategies are likely to fail as they do not appear to understand, let alone address, the causes of complex emergencies, nor identify who is made vulnerable in the process. The irony is that the vulnerability of contemporary capitalism has created vast new markets for crisis management that are predicated on increasing the resilience of the capitalist system as a whole, thus perpetuating the cycle of crisis. This self-defeating cycle has set the scene for a permanent state of emergency that must be resisted.

Extreme weather and climate change

Natural disasters appear ever more present. And it is not just down to perception or 24 hour rolling news. Total natural disasters reported each year have been steadily rising in recent decades, from 78 in 1970, to 348 in 2004. The average number of disasters throughout the 1980s was 400. It increased to 630 in the 1990s and to 730 in the past ten years. The highest recorded number of natural disasters, 960, occurred in 2007.[2]

Of course part of this increase is artificial – due to rapid advances in communications technologies providing better reporting of disasters – but about two-thirds of the increase is real and linked primarily to hydro-meteorological disasters, namely droughts, tsunamis, hurricanes, typhoons and floods. In contrast, natural geologic disasters, such as volcanic eruptions, earthquakes, landslides and avalanches have remained steady in recent decades.

Over the last three decades, reports of major floods have increased from an average of less than fifty to just below two hundred per year. Tropical storms have increased from around ten to roughly fifteen, and the annual total of US tornadoes and global tsunamis has also risen dramatically – and along with them, so have the financial costs. Gerhard Berz, former head of Geo Risks at the German reinsurance corporation Munich Re, reports that 'losses from natural disasters have increased eightfold in economic terms during the last four decades. The insured losses have even increased by a factor of fourteen.'[3]

Climate change is a critical factor in this rise of hydro-meteorological disasters – although it has always been difficult to quantify. In their review of the scientific literature, Anderson and Bausch noted cautiously that:

> ... in some cases, like heat waves and intense rainfall, the influence [of climate change] is already clear; in others, like hurricanes, the evidence is just emerging; in some other cases there are as yet no clear indications. However, in all cases the trend toward the future is worrying: modelling indicates that unless serious action is taken, global warming will reach levels at which several types of extreme events are much more likely.[4]

They also noted 'important impacts from 'secondary' effects of climatic events – for example, avalanches, rock falls, landslides due to flooding, and forest fires in areas of drought.[5]

For a long time, climate scientists refused to attribute specific disasters to climate change, however a study by renowned climate scientist James Hansen and others in 2012 showed that the frequency of extreme weather events (which has increased by a factor of 50 in the last decade compared to the decades prior to 1980) has made certain disasters unexplainable without the influence of climate change. They conclude:

> We can state, with a high degree of confidence, that extreme anomalies such as [the heatwaves] in Texas and Oklahoma in 2011 and Moscow in 2010 were a consequence of global warming because their likelihood in the absence of global warming was exceedingly small.[6]

Building vulnerability

Yet while the frequency of natural disasters is certainly fuelled by over-dependence on fossil fuels and corresponding global warming, it is also a reflection of other anthropogenic actions – in particular, population growth, urbanisation and the destruction of ecological and social resilience.

Half of the global population currently lives in cities. If current trends continue, this figure will reach 75 per cent by mid-century.[7] Many of these cities are on coasts, or near earthquake fault zones, or deltas prone to flooding. A 2007 OECD study predicts that by 2070, the impact of climate change and urbanisation could more than triple the number of people exposed to coastal flooding, to about 150 million. The most vulnerable cities include Miami, Guangzhou, New York, Calcutta, Shanghai, Mumbai, Tianjin, Tokyo, Hong Kong and Bangkok.[8] Moreover, many vulnerable cities are home to some of the world's 1 billion poorest people, who live in slums in 'barely imaginable' conditions of absolute poverty.[9]

The rise of the city has not only increased the vulnerability of certain populations, it has also increased the economic costs of those disasters. According to global risk analysis firm, Control Risks: 'The concentration of human, physical, and financial capital in cities renders them especially vulnerable to both immediate devastation and lingering disruption to transport, commerce, and communications in the aftermath of major disasters.'

Another cause of worsening disasters has been the destruction of ecological landscapes that traditionally protected populations. For example, in the constant search for economic growth, and under pressure to serve growing populations, developers, businesses and governments frequently eradicate the natural buffers, such as sand dunes, mangrove swamps and flood plains that traditionally protected populations. As even the libertarian *Economist* reported in 2012, private individuals and firms, 'left to pursue their own self-interest, put all of society at risk'.[10] The *Economist* went on to argue that 'growth is the best disaster-mitigation policy of all', as it would provide the 'human and physical infrastructure needed to protect against, and respond to, natural disaster'.[11]

This might make sense if the benefits of economic growth and the efforts that go in to mitigation and prevention were shared equally, or if growth did not come with its own costs, but this is patently not the case. The global inequalities embedded in contemporary capitalism mean that large swathes of the world's population have become more vulnerable as more prosperous areas grow. And even within the wealthiest societies, decisions about allocating the resources needed to reduce vulnerability are highly politicised, short-termist and often inadequate. It was, for example, never a question of *if* the levees in New Orleans would be breached, but *when*.

The threats that climate change, urbanisation and economic growth produce were famously described by British sociologist Anthony Giddens as 'manufactured risks', in which the threats facing modern societies are no longer external acts of 'God' or 'Nature', but manufactured by the modernisation process itself. Nuclear disaster, the emergence of vaccine-resistance diseases and the 'blowback' of contemporary 'Islamist' terrorism can all be seen as manufactured risks – unintended consequences of modern, industrial societies that we have little experience in confronting. As Giddens notes, 'At a certain point ... we started worrying less about what nature can do to us, and more about what we have done to nature. This marks the transition from the predominance of external risk to that of manufactured risk.'[12]

Ultimately, however, these impacts only become a disaster if people are unprepared and unable to deal with them. In and of itself, then, climate-change-induced extreme weather is not a disaster; it is a hazard – that is, an environmental condition whose harm will depend on where it happens and how prepared its population is to deal with those conditions. The varying impact of extreme weather on poor and rich can be seen in every disaster, from Hurricane Katrina in 2005 to the extreme drought in Brazil in 2015. In other words, it is not just risk that is manufactured, but vulnerability. It is the way in which societies try to address those risks – or lack the resources to do so, or in some cases chose simply to ignore them – that ultimately determines whether those harms and losses materialise, and if so, whom they will affect. As a Pakistani official observed in relation to the earthquake that devastated large areas of northern Pakistan in October 2005: 'It is not earthquakes that kill people but building regulations and the failures of aid and rescue.'[13]

Facing up to complex emergencies

Under globalisation, the reliance of modern societies on global supply lines, industrial food production, transnational infrastructure and high-tech communications have exacerbated vulnerability by ensuring that disaster or catastrophe in one place now reverberates far beyond the initial point of contact, producing what are known as 'complex emergencies'.[14] Put another way: as climate change, urbanisation, and man-made vulnerability interact with other elements of the global system – such as energy and food production – there is an increased risk of knock-on effects that could ultimately challenge the capacity of states to maintain social stability.

The provision of food, so long the cause of social unrest and revolutions, is a good example to see how climate change intersects with other vulnerable globalised markets. As Chapter 8 explores in more detail, climate change is already impacting on agriculture. In 2012, as four-fifths of the United States as well as parts of Russia and Africa experienced drought, global food production fell by 2.6 per cent.[15] The 'Arab Spring' in 2011, while catalysed by a range of factors – long-standing political grievances, rampant inequality, rocketing unemployment, state repression and lack of basic social services – was also triggered by persistently record-high food prices.[16]

The impacts of drought are made worse by the way the current globalised food system interconnects with other markets, such as the energy markets. As much as 10 per cent of energy consumed annually in the US, for instance, is used by the food industry. Every major point in industrial food production – on-site machinery, production and synthesis of artificial fertilisers, processing, packaging, transport and storage – is heavily dependent on fossil fuels. Forty per cent of energy in the food system is used to produce fertilisers and pesticides.[17] Another 14 per cent goes to food transport, 16 per cent to processing, 7 per cent to packaging, 4 per cent to food retailing, 7 per cent to restaurants and caterers, and 32 per cent to home refrigeration and preparation.[18] This has made the global industrial food system inherently vulnerable to volatility in oil markets.

The six-fold rise in oil prices between 2003 and mid-2008 therefore had direct and severe consequences for food production, by impacting on farmers' fuel, fertiliser, pesticide, and transportation costs. As science journalist Julian Cribbs notes, while 'financial pain was high' in developed countries, in the less developed world – from where the developed countries import much of their food – 'farmers simply could not afford to buy fertilizer, and crop yields began to slip.'[19]

So as oil becomes more expensive, this will place massive strain on industrial food production – and the poor will suffer the hardest. The problem is that the best evidence suggests that the age of cheap oil is over. Although prices dropped in 2014–15, the cost of production remains very high, with global markets reflecting Saudi Arabia's desire to undermine its competitors and sustain high levels of supply despite weak demand. Most serious oil-industry observers agree that the long-term trend for oil prices, despite the recent slump, will be upwards.[20]

Canadian academic Homer-Dixon argues that 'negative synergy' between major 'stressors' such as food and oil prices is exacerbated by the 'multiplier', that is, the inter-connectivity of the global system. On the one hand, 'greater connectivity and speed often make economies and societies more resilient to shock because they can respond faster and draw from their larger networks a wider range of skills, resources, capital and goods and services.' Yet simultaneously, the very same connectivity means that a failure of one element of a tightly coupled system can propagate disturbances across large distances to other elements of the system, creating negative synergy between multiple stressors. Resources deployed to solve particular problems often fail to resolve the underlying causes, and therefore end up weakening the system in the long term, as those problems continue to escalate. This, in turn, can potentially overwhelm the capacity of the system to respond effectively, ultimately leading to 'synchronous failure', when the system is no longer able to respond, leading to systemic breakdown – or in Homer-Dixon's words, 'an abrupt breakdown in our vital social and technological systems'.[21] This can manifest in many different ways: the 2008 banking crisis and the Arab Spring, for instance, can both be seen as examples of synchronous failure. In both cases, many commentators note that even the current fixes have failed to tackle the problems at source and are therefore storing up bigger crises in the future.

Concerns about systemic failure are not just coming from academia or conspiracy theorists: even people like the former UK Government Chief Scientist John Beddington are warning of a 'perfect storm' of converging food, water and energy crises increasingly generating a swathe of complex emergencies as states struggle, and in many cases increasingly fail, to retain control and deliver goods and services.[22] Conventional modelling techniques (which view these crises in isolation) project the era of the 'perfect storm' to emerge by 2030; however, it is also suggested that we had already entered this era as of the year 2008 – when the world became subjected to complex synergies driving escalating oil and food prices, which interconnected with long-standing debt-based financial and economic vulnerabilities.[23]

What this crisis means for capitalism and social justice in the face of unchecked emissions growth and the threat of runaway global warming is *the* question of our times. While the Left can be relied upon to pronounce the end of capitalism at every opportunity – and did so with understandable relish when the financial system teetered on the brink following the collapse of Lehman Brothers – these proclamations almost always underestimate the resilience of those invested in the status quo to maintain their hegemony even amidst crisis. Rather than simply assuming that climate change means that the writing is on the wall for capitalism, or that the ongoing global depression makes 'post-capitalism' inevitable, we should be concerned with the way in which the elites are responding to the rise of complex emergencies and the growing vulnerability of certain populations. Unfortunately, the evidence suggests that rather than address the underlying causes, or take measures to protect the most vulnerable, governments appear to be focused on preparing crisis measures that militarise emergencies and undermine human rights.

Crisis management

'Crisis management' is shorthand for the way in which states deal with major events that cause or threaten to cause significant harm to the public. It is also used by businesses and other organisations to plan for events that threaten business continuity and other types of damage. There is certainly nothing new about crisis management; societies have had to respond to 'natural disasters' and man-made harms since the dawn of the time. Nor is there anything particularly unique in the preparation and response to extreme weather events as compared to other types of potential crisis such as pandemics or technological hazards (nuclear accidents, chemical spills, and so on).

What has changed is the complexity of what planners call the 'crisis cycle'. Traditionally, this envisaged three broad stages covering actions taken before, during and after the crisis: preparation, management and evaluation. Today, inspired first by the 'homeland security' strategies devised in the wake of 9/11 – which forced states to 'think the unthinkable' in terms of not just terrorist but chemical, biological, radiological, nuclear and most recently cyber-attacks – and then by the climate-security strategies described in Chapter 2, the crisis cycle has widened significantly. At the same time, the powers adopted in the name of emergency preparedness and management have become more coercive, with a much greater role envisaged for the military and private-security actors.

This was superbly documented in Naomi Klein's *Shock Doctrine*, which linked the tendency to respond militarily to disasters with the attempts of powerful corporations and interests to use disasters to make short-term profits and lay the ground for structural changes that will benefit elites in the long-term. Klein tells the stories of how this played out in Hurricane Katrina, the 2004 Asian Tsunami, Iraq's post-invasion 'reconstruction' and other places where disaster struck and neoliberalism profited.

Retelling the shameful story of Iraq's destruction by militarism and privatisation, Naomi Klein comments:

> Iraq under [the senior US administrator Paul] Bremer was the logical conclusion of Chicago School theory: a public sector reduced to a minimal number of employees, mostly contract workers, living in a Halliburton city state, tasked with signing corporate friendly laws drafted by KPMG and handing out duffle bags of cash to Western contractors protected by mercenary soldiers, themselves shielded by full legal immunity. All around them were furious people, increasingly turning to religious fundamentalism because it's the only source of power in a hollowed-out state. Like Russia's gangsterism and Bush's cronyism, contemporary Iraq is a creation of the fifty-year crusade to privatize the world. Rather than being disowned by its creators, it deserves to be seen as the purest incarnation yet of the ideology that gave it birth.[24]

Contemporary capitalism has then become increasingly predatory, seeking out disasters in order to impose neoliberalism and maximise profits for a nexus of private investors and contractors, many with close relationships to government.[25] What has happened in the decade since the publication of the *Shock Doctrine* is that the disaster-capitalism industry has exploded, fuelled by a globalisation of the US's 'homeland security' approach to terrorism.[26] The proliferation of complex emergency thinking has merely added fuel to the fire and led to growing securitisation of transnational 'critical infrastructure' itself.

The EU defines critical infrastructure as 'an asset or system which is essential for the maintenance of vital societal functions';[27] the US's definition is synonymous.[28] The EU therefore concludes that any 'damage to a critical infrastructure, its destruction or disruption by natural disasters, terrorism, criminal activity or malicious behaviour, may have a significant negative impact for the security of the EU and the well-being of its citizens.' In turn, the transport system, supply chains, the means of production, information and communications technologies, water and energy systems, and food distribution are becoming securitised in the quest to protect against 'all hazards'.

But securitisation alone is of little use if the root causes of potential hazards are not addressed as well. In Brazil, in the summer of 2015, authorities have been making military preparations in the megacity of São Paulo to defend water infrastructure amid an ongoing drought. Although water supplies have been dwindling for many years, current low levels are unprecedented. In response, the Brazilian authorities instructed the army to prepare for riots and attacks on the local water utility. Absent credible plans to save water, journalists reported that approximately seventy soldiers were involved in exercises to prepare the utility for an uprising, with thirty men with machine guns stationed in the facility's canteen.[29]

Thinking the unthinkable: the search for all risks

Preparing for crises used to mean a degree of internal planning on the part of states and organisations for particular scenarios and emergencies, including simulations and training. Now it means 'thinking the unthinkable' and developing appropriate risk analysis, threat assessment and mitigation strategies.[30] In the UK, for example, galvanised by the 9/11 terrorist attacks and the London bombings of 7 July 2005, crisis management has been catapulted up the political agenda over the past 15 years. The symbolism of preparedness – exercises involving first responders in radiation suits – have become a powerful sign of the times.

The UK's approach is founded on 'Integrated Emergency Management' (IEM), an approach to preventing and managing emergencies that entails six key steps: anticipation, assessment, prevention, preparation, response, and recovery. The possible emergencies that the UK may face are identified in the government's National Risk Assessment (NRA), a confidential assessment conducted each year, drawing on the expertise of a wide range of government departments and agencies. It focuses on three broad categories of risk: natural events, major accidents and malicious attacks.

The National Risk Register (NRR) is the public version of the NRA. First published in 2008, it provides businesses and the public with information regarding how they should

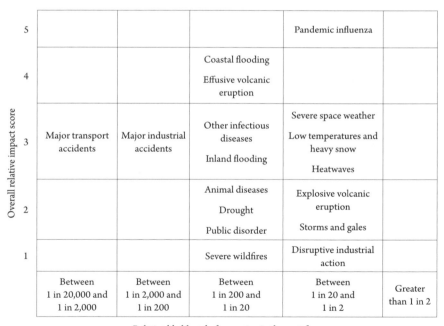

Overall relative impact score	Between 1 in 20,000 and 1 in 2,000	Between 1 in 2,000 and 1 in 200	Between 1 in 200 and 1 in 20	Between 1 in 20 and 1 in 2	Greater than 1 in 2
5				Pandemic influenza	
4			Coastal flooding Effusive volcanic eruption		
3	Major transport accidents	Major industrial accidents	Other infectious diseases Inland flooding	Severe space weather Low temperatures and heavy snow Heatwaves	
2			Animal diseases Drought Public disorder	Explosive volcanic eruption Storms and gales	
1			Severe wildfires	Disruptive industrial action	

Relative likelihood of occurring in the next five years

Figure 4.1   NRR Risk matrix – 'Other risks' – excluding terrorism and other malicious attacks

Source: National Risk Register of Civil Emergencies, 2013 edn.

prepare for civil emergencies. The risks posed to national security and human welfare by longer-term trends, such as technological advances and climate change, remains hidden in the classified National Security Risk Assessment.

According to the NRR, the highest priority risks facing the UK – based on both likelihood and impact – are pandemic influenza, coastal flooding, catastrophic terrorist attacks, and severe effusive (gas-rich) volcanic eruptions abroad. Other risks deemed less severe include inland flooding, new and emerging infectious diseases, severe weather, severe space weather, wildfires, explosive volcanic eruption styles emitting mainly ash, animal diseases, major industrial and transport accidents, disruptive industrial action, malicious attacks and public disorder (see Figure 4.1).

Despite the hype around the risks, a study of the impact of major civil security crises in the UK for period 2000–12 showed that during the 13-year period there were only 787 documented deaths – equivalent to 60 per year. The vast majority of these deaths (84 per cent) were the result of the heatwave in 2003 (301 deaths) and the 'Swine Flu' pandemic in 2009 (362).[31] By way of comparison, there were some 36,606 road accident fatalities in the UK over the same period – or 46 times the number of security crisis deaths.[32] But security planners are at least as concerned with economic disruption as death tolls, and by this measure, the most significant UK crisis events during the study period were the 2001 foot-and-mouth disease outbreak, the 2007 floods and the 2010 volcanic ash cloud.

A 2013 peer review of the UK's crisis management framework criticised government policy for focusing too much on emergency preparedness and failing to address longer-term vulnerabilities, finding that

> … risks with potentially large impacts and high likelihoods, especially when these are growing, could be better managed through vulnerability reduction than through preparing and responding to the event. Floods and droughts are examples of the types of risks that may require more long-term, whole-of-society approaches to their reduction, as climate change may have an impact on those in the future.[33]

A review of the crisis management arrangements in the 28 EU member states and five neighbouring non-EU states suggest that broadly the same preoccupations – that is, short-term emergency management rather than long-term vulnerabilities – prevail across the continent.[34]

Risk management and critical infrastructure

The UK National Security Strategy states that one of the government's key tasks is to improve the resilience of the infrastructure most critical to keeping the country running in the face of attacks, damage or destruction. Accordingly, Cabinet Office guidance promotes the building of a more 'resilient' society that is better prepared for and more able to recover from emergencies. It emphasises the collective nature of this endeavour: 'This responsibility needs to be shared between central and local government and the emergency services, the private sector (particularly those providing essential services to the public), civil society and communities.'[35]

The National Resilience Capabilities Programme is the core framework through which the government seeks to build resilience across all parts of the UK. It identifies challenges and monitors progress in 22 different 'workstreams', each overseen by a lead ministry, with the government's Civil Contingencies Secretariat (CCS) responsible for the overall management.[36] The 'essential services' workstream assesses resilience of six 'key sectors': health, food and water, transport, energy, telecommunications and postal services, and financial services. An additional Infrastructure and Corporate Resilience Programme established in 2011, supports public and private sector organisations to improve the resilience of their infrastructure, supply and distribution systems against potential disruption.[37]

The EU's Programme for Critical Infrastructure Protection (CIP) shares the same objectives of reducing vulnerability and increasing resilience against 'terrorism, criminal activities, natural disasters and other causes of accidents' through 'an all-hazards cross-sectoral approach'. To this end, the EU adopted a Directive in 2008 on 'European Critical Infrastructures' (ECIs) in the fields of energy and transport, requiring EU states to identify those infrastructures whose disruption would adversely affect other member states and prepare security and business continuity plans.[38] However, by 2012, a year after the Directive entered into force, only 14 ECIs had been identified.[39] At issue was not so much a lack of transnational critical infrastructure, but apparently the belief in most member states that they were already adequately designated and protected at the national level.[40] Given the lack of interest in the EU Directive, the European Commission is now focusing its CIP efforts on European rather than transnational infrastructure: the EU's electricity transmission grid, the EU's gas transmission network, the EU's Air Traffic Management system (EUROCONTROL) and the European programme for global satellite navigation (GALILEO).[41]

What is interesting about the rapid development of CIP programmes, as we shall see in the next section, is not so much the way that they are managed but, the nature of the investments designed to 'secure' the infrastructure. While the EU guidelines on this topic remain classified, the EU established various programmes to assist the owners and operators of critical infrastructure, including a European Reference Network for CIP,[42] a Critical Infrastructure Preparedness and Resilience Research Network,[43] and funding for more than a hundred projects under the Prevention, Preparedness and Consequence Management of Terrorism and other Security-related Risks programme.[44] This investment matters because, as Lancaster University Professor Michael Dillon explains, 'Ordinarily risk is something to be avoided in security politics because it is associated with danger. But risk is not simply the occasion of danger. Risk is also the occasion of profit.'[45]

Risk management as industry

Dillon is concerned that the understandable desire of policy makers to maintain the flows of goods, services, capital and people that underpin our social and material lives is not a rational response to their systemic vulnerability, but a reflection of the 'profit and invention extracted from the radical contingency of complex global circulations'. Indeed, whereas the modernist project aspired to security, neoliberalism embraces uncertainty and risk as a 'creative opportunity' necessary to capitalism, and to freedom itself.[46] We will see this clearly in Chapter 7, which shows how companies like Raytheon, one of the world's largest defence contractors, have pursued 'expanded business opportunities' arising from 'security concerns and their possible consequences', due to the 'effects of climate change' in the form of 'storms, droughts, and floods'.[47]

According to a 2015 market research report, the global market for security technologies that support Critical Infrastructure Protection is expected to grow from $72.3 billion in 2014 to $114.8 billion in 2019, representing year-on-year growth of almost 10 per cent.[49] But it is not just that CIP policies are providing new opportunities for security contractors, it is the type of security that this market growth is delivering, and the places that are being 'securitised'. Much of the physical controls and surveillance technology developed for the border (see Chapter 5) is now being deployed to protect public and private infrastructure, such as transport hubs, power stations and 'sensitive infrastructures' such as 'stadiums, holy places, defence establishments, IT and communication, BFSI and government facilities, chemical and manufacturing'. As Chapter 2 explored, the rapid deployment of these technologies can have a profound impact on civil liberties – particularly those of 'suspect communities'.

It is also worth pointing out, as then UK Prime Minister Tony Blair did in the wake of the '7/7' bombings in Britain, that 'all the surveillance in the world' could not have prevented the attacks. Nor of course will it prove much use in the face of rising sea levels, temperatures, or systemic shocks. This is not to say that all critical infrastructure protection is simply a ruse to line the pockets of the security industry – though a lack of research into where the money is actually going means we wouldn't bet against it – but it is certainly an extremely narrow and potentially unhelpful way of addressing the vulnerabilities that created the industry in the first place.

Perhaps more importantly, since the resilience industry needs a vulnerable subject to thrive, it has to constantly re-produce that vulnerable subject – a relationship that security scholars suggest is 'robbing human subjects of political options, especially options of resistance'.[50] This has particularly profound implications for the Global South, where, an already problematic 'development-security' nexus is being transformed by the contemporary obsession with 'resilience'. As Jens Stilhoff Sörensen and Fredrik Söderbaum have explained, development and security already constitute the world's largest business.[51] But the idea of achieving security through material development and the protection of the most vulnerable (once their *raison d'être*) has been usurped by a politics of 'resilience' and 'sustainable development' – a politics which requires 'constant global disaster management as well as intervention'.

These paradigm shifts also pose some uncomfortable questions for the humanitarian sector, which is seen to be retreating into defensive aid bunkers. While aid workers have genuine security concerns (and face increasing insurance premiums) as they operate in increasingly complex security environments, 'risk management within the civilian aid industry has been militarised', segregating aid workers from the communities they work with and at times forcing them into difficult and politically compromised alliances with oppressive security forces.[52] Similarly, in its report 'Aiding Surveillance', the campaign group Privacy International explains how information technology transfer is an increasingly crucial element of development and humanitarian aid initiatives, but warn that the unprecedented collection and use of personal information in these initiatives is subject to few legal safeguards:

> Social protection programmes are incorporating digitised Management Information Systems and electronic transfers, registration and electoral systems are deploying biometric technologies, the proliferation of mobile phones is facilitating access to increased amounts of data, and technologies are being transferred to support security and rule of law efforts. Many of these programmes and technologies involve the surveillance of individuals, groups, and entire populations.[53]

Emergencies and 'emergency powers'

When we had the idea for this book, back in 2010, and began to flesh out the contributions, we were concerned that the heavy-handed and racist response to Hurricane Katrina by the US government was not only a manifestation of Bush's militarised Homeland Security programme, but the shape of things to come for disaster management the world over. There is good reason to suppose that this is still the case because, in the wake of 9/11 and other high-profile emergencies, governments across the world have updated their emergency powers to enable similar responses. We also saw some of the same heavy-handed military responses to the earthquake in Haiti in 2010 and the typhoon in The Philippines in 2013 that we had seen after Katrina.

However, emergency planning is also about 'lessons learned', and like the American public, the whole world was, as US journalist and author Susan Faludi put it, 'forced to look at what lay behind the veneer of chest-beating [and] saw the consequences of having terrible government leadership'.[54] Does this mean that future crisis management will be less coercive? This of course depends upon the nature of the crisis, but states certainly appear to be accruing all of the coercive powers they might need.

The UK's emergency legislation is typical. Following a series of emergencies, including the fuel crisis and severe flooding in late 2000 and the outbreak of foot-and-mouth disease in 2001, the UK government initiated a review of its emergency planning regulations, including the 1920 Emergency Powers Act. The review was also strongly influenced by the terrorist attacks of 9/11, following which the UK government declared a 'state of emergency' which allowed it to opt out of the provisions in the European Convention on Human Rights prohibiting detention without trial. This enabled the government to reintroduce the internment of terrorist suspects, though this policy was ultimately declared unlawful by the British courts in 2004.

The emergency powers review resulted in the Civil Contingencies Act 2004, under which the government can declare a state of emergency without a parliamentary vote, and potentially without even publicly declaring a state of emergency. The term 'emergency' is defined broadly as an 'event or situation' which 'threatens serious damage to human welfare' or 'to the environment' of 'a place in the UK', or 'war, or terrorism, which threatens serious damage to the security of the UK'.[55]

Having invoked an emergency, ministers can – 'if it is necessary to make provision urgently in order to prevent, control or mitigate an aspect or effect of the emergency when existing powers are insufficient'[56] – introduce 'emergency regulations' under the Royal Prerogative without recourse to Parliament; such regulations can 'give directions or orders' of virtually unlimited scope, including the destruction of property, prohibiting assemblies, banning travel and outlawing 'other specified activities.' Failure to comply with the regulations would become a criminal offence punishable by up to three months in jail. The armed services can be deployed without parliamentary notification or approval, and emergency regulations 'protecting or restoring activities of Her Majesty's Government' may be passed.[57]

The UK emergency powers review – and many elements of the subsequent legislation – were mirrored in Australia and Canada. There are also striking similarities between the UK's and the US's emergency powers statutes. In the US, Section 1042 of the 2007 National Defense Authorization Act (NDAA), 'Use of the Armed Forces in Major Public Emergencies,' authorises the president to activate the military in response to 'a natural disaster, a disease outbreak, a terrorist attack or any other condition in which the President determines that domestic violence has occurred to the extent that state officials cannot maintain public order.'[58]

Whereas in the UK crisis management is of a civilian nature, with military involvement sought only in extreme cases, some European states have a longer tradition of deploying paramilitary and military units in emergency situations (and have agreed to provide troops to one another in certain circumstances). Almost all have followed the Anglo-Saxon trend of revising their statutes to take into account new threats.[59] In France, for example, the Presidential Defence White Paper of 2013 declares that 'The engagement of the armed forces to support homeland security and civil security in the event of a major crisis could involve up to 10,000 personnel from the land forces, together with appropriate resources provided by the navy and the air force.'[60] The White Paper also determines the National Gendarmerie, as an armed force under the operational control of the Ministry of Interior, to be able to 'respond rapidly to crisis situations or natural disasters, and it can therefore be deployed alongside the armed forces.'[61] Even Germany, where the deployment of the armed forces is tightly regulated by the Constitution, has recently determined that troops could be deployed domestically if Germany faced an emergency of 'catastrophic proportions'. It has however upheld the prohibition on the potential use of the army to control demonstrations.[62]

The geographer Ben Anderson has explained how, over the second half of the twentieth century, 'emergency' has shifted from being a term applied to a limited number of events to a term that can be used in relation to almost any event. But 'emergency' is still a selective concept. Many people consider the 'migrant crisis' at Calais that hit the headlines over the summer of 2015 to be a humanitarian emergency, as several thousand refugees seeking to travel to Britain are living in terrible conditions. The UN High Commission for Refugees (UNHCR) has described the number of people there as 'easily manageable', and the conditions they are living in as 'appalling', but Britain and France instead responded with more fences, dogs and gendarmes – and argued that the only genuine emergency is the porousness of Europe's borders. Meanwhile, the job of providing humanitarian assistance to the refugees has to date been taken on by charities and activists from both countries, who are appalled by the response of their own governments. As the number of refugees from North Africa and the Middle East continues to grow, the humanitarian crisis at Calais is being replicated at locations across Europe.

Outside of the most prosperous nations on earth, states of emergency are no less politicised. In Ecuador, the government declared a state of emergency in August 2015 using the pretext of a volcanic eruption in order to repress massive protests against extractive industries. In India, the Armed Forces (Special Powers) Acts – introduced first by the British in an attempt to quash the Quit India movement and maintained by the Indian government to deal with movements for autonomy and independence – remains in force in parts of the North-east and Jammu and Kashmir, granting the military extraordinary powers to break up protests and shoot-to-kill law breakers. In Tunisia, the state of emergency introduced after the 2015 attacks on tourists at the Mediterranean resort of Port El Kantaoui remained in force three months later, while new anti-terrorism legislation re-introduces the death penalty, allows suspects to be detained for 15 days without access to a lawyer, and fails to properly distinguish between protests and terrorist acts. Obviously if the state powers introduced *after* emergencies are almost always 'draconian', more 'emergencies' the world over do not bode well for civil liberties and fundamental rights.

Predicting the worst: When national security meets social unrest

What kinds of scenarios emerge when national security planners start to try to predict complex emergencies and social unrest? As this and other chapters explore, through the lens of the national security apparatus, crises like climate change and energy depletion are seen not as systemic problems requiring systemic transformation, but instead are externalised as 'threats out there' that therefore trigger reactionary 'containment' responses.

One particularly dangerous development of this approach is the conflation of protests against inequality and social injustice with new crisis-management paradigms. In other words, activism and protest become signs, not of a need for a change of policy, but of security threats that must be pre-empted, neutralised, or obstructed. As writer Rebecca Solnit observes, the real violence in a world of climate change is not that caused by riots, it is the violence inflicted by fossil-fuel barons that is causing climate change and destroying people's lives as a result:

> Climate change is not suddenly bringing about an era of equitable distribution. I suspect people will be revolting in the coming future against what they revolted against in the past: the injustices of the system. They should revolt, and we should be glad they do, if not so glad that they need to.[63]

It is a worrying feature then that government risk assessments frequently cite public disquiet and resistance as a major security threat, rather than a sign of a failing system. The UK National Risk Register (illustrated above), for example, lists 'public disorder' and 'disruptive industrial action' as among the most severe and likely security threats facing the UK.

It is also instructive to look closely at the kinds of security research the US government is now funding, as it suggests how the security community is increasingly seeking to build its understanding of activism and social unrest in order to combat it. The most significant programme underway is the 'Minerva Research Initiative', set up by the US Department of Defense (DoD) in 2008, which has been funding universities to model the dynamics, risks and tipping points for large-scale civil unrest across the world, under the supervision of various US military agencies.

Some of the research is clearly of understandable merit to social scientists and of broad public interest. For example, the Minerva's call for research tracking 'the factors that affect societal resilience to external "shock" events and corresponding tipping points' in order to better anticipate 'potential areas of unrest, instability, and conflict'. But it is important to remember the underlying goals of the programme, which even using their own language is designed to develop immediate and long-term 'warfighter-relevant insights' for senior officials and decision makers in 'the defense policy community', and to inform policy implemented by 'combatant commands'.[64] In this context, a project grant awarded in 2014 to the University of Washington which 'seeks to uncover the conditions under which political movements aimed at large-scale political and economic change originate', along with their 'characteristics and consequences', looks less innocent and more an attempt to prevent these often necessary movements for change from flourishing. After all, one study does not only ask 'where organized violence is likely to erupt, what factors might explain its spread', but also 'how one might circumvent its dissemination'. The focus here might be on violence, but given that most social unrest and indeed most liberation and civil rights struggles of the last century have followed the pattern of combined violent and nonviolent resistance, the end result is the repression of both.

Several other projects have looked closely at protestors' behaviour and the dynamics of political dissent. The Pentagon asks for proposals investigating underlying mechanisms for social and political mobilisation; as well as factors that 'foster or inhibit' an individual moving from passive support of 'fringe' social movements to what the Pentagon calls 'active political mobilization'. That also includes mining deep into the very structure and make-up of 'change-driven organizations' of any kind. The Pentagon wants researchers to analyse their 'topology, power structure, productivity', how and why they merge and splinter with other groups, and their overall resilience. The research has included developing advanced data-mining tools that can automatically categorise activist groups and rank them on a threat-scale to US interests. One such tool, called 'Looking Glass', can identify and locate individuals, and even rank their alleged propensity for violence or terrorism, just by automatically tracking and analysing their social media posts.[65]

In the EU, a host of research into the use of social media for policing, emergency response, crisis management, security assessments and pro-active emergencies management is underway.[66] Although the research is not geared explicitly toward protests and activism, the tools and techniques being developed represent the same overarching desire to predict and manage unrest using surveillance and risk assessment. As we have seen following the revelations by Edward Snowden, once the technological genie is out of the bottle and in the hands of the state, it is very difficult to put it back in again.

Resistance – The real resilience

The current state-corporate obsession with emergencies and new techniques for crisis management capitalises on public fears by promising resilience against disasters. But as this chapter has shown, the maximum security paradigm on which it is based can easily undermine societal resilience by facilitating state repression or providing cover for the militarised policing of vulnerable communities. This problem appears particularly acute when we consider its relationship to the repression of popular movements seeking to challenge the prevailing crisis-prone order. Here, the objective of new security policies is not just the maintenance of law and order but the outright pacification of vulnerable and restive populations.

The securitisation of disaster response is embedded in powerful, self-reinforcing logics in which more emergencies require better anticipation and more risk assessments; the more risks that are identified, the more protective and preparatory action that must be taken; the more emergencies, the greater the investment in response, and so forth. To be clear, we are not saying that states should not be better preparing for emergencies, or indeed that there is not a role for the private sector. But we are saying that so far it appears to have increased profiteering and militarisation in the face of too little critical scrutiny.

Orienting emergency preparedness around pacification also fundamentally misses the point about the kind of resilience that can withstand natural disasters and complex emergencies, which requires a reduction of the vulnerability that turns hazards into disasters. In the case of natural disasters, building resilience will involve providing better protection for vulnerable communities, and in the case of complex emergencies, it will involve addressing some of the systemic weaknesses in our globalised and corporate-dominated planet. This will require actions at local, national and international levels.

There are many examples of communities successfully building resilience, both in responding to disasters and supporting flourishing in the long term. The Huairou Commission, for example, a global membership and partnership organisation of grass-roots women's movements around the world, has developed a library of toolkits derived from concrete, real-world knowledge and experience. These toolkits are designed for both rural and urban communities. They show how to reduce vulnerability, deploy disaster-resistant technologies and enact post-disaster rehabilitation and rebuilding. The toolkits are continuously tested and improved through actual hands-on execution and improvement.[67] Meanwhile in San Francisco, a Neighbourhood Empowerment Network (NEN) empowers residents to identify neighbourhood goals relating to disaster preparedness and resilience collectively, and to then develop ways to achieve them through an inter-agency Resilient Action Plan. Every month, NEN convenes four working groups of children and their families; seniors and people with disabilities; immigrant communities; and local businesses and non-profits.

With or without such preparations, many communities have also displayed a remarkable response to disasters when they occur. In a detailed examination of five major disasters, such as the flooding of New Orleans in 2005, Rachel Solnit shows that amidst the suffering, crises often bring out the best evidence of altruism and solidarity in people. In disaster after disaster and often below the media radar, we see communities rally around, protect the vulnerable and mobilise support and assistance efficiently and effectively. This often contrasts with the inadequate or militarised responses by elites: 'Disaster often reveals what else the world could be like – reveals the strength of that hope, that generosity and that solidarity. It reveals mutual aid as a default operating principle and civil society as something waiting in the wings when it's absent from the stage.'[68] These inspiring experiences often also guide the rebuilding process. In Italy, for instance, the post-shock impact of the 2009 L'Aquila earthquake prompted local residents to dismiss the proposed neoliberal housing recovery solutions package, opting instead to construct earthquake-proof homes made of straw and wood. The 'eco-village' continues to exist today.[69]

At a national level, Cuba has shown that even a developing country with minimal resources can – with the right strategies – provide protection for its vulnerable communities. Between 1996 and 2002, for example, six major hurricanes hit Cuba, yet a total of only 16 people died. When Hurricane Sandy hit both Cuba and the US in 2012, only 11 people died in Cuba yet 157 died in the US. As a report by Oxfam explained, Cuba's success is based on a highly effective community mobilisation carried out by

Civil Defence Structures backed up by a pro-active state. Underlying it all, though, is a long-term foundation of a

> … socio-economic model that reduces vulnerability and invests in social capital through universal access to government services and promotion of social equity. The resulting high levels of literacy, developed infrastructure in rural areas and access to reliable health care and other created capital function as 'multiplier effects' for national efforts in disaster mitigation, preparation and response.

In other words, people in Cuba, despite their poverty, are educated about and prepared for disasters, live in houses built to regulated safety standards, have access to roads and electricity so can easily be alerted and supported, and most of all are organised in a way that enables solidarity with neighbours and facilitates rapid disaster relief.

Cuba's model points to the need for local actions to be bolstered by effective state and at times international action to provide real resilience. It also shows that long-term resilience requires a socio-economic model that reduces rather than exacerbates vulnerability. Without universal access to basic services, education for all, tackling of inequality and the creation of a culture of collaboration and solidarity rather than competition and individualism, it is very hard to build a truly resilient society.

This necessarily means redistribution of wealth at national and international levels in order for this to happen. The paltry resources the richest nations have promised to developing countries in climate finance are completely inadequate to the task. Rich countries pledged $100 billion in climate finance to help developing countries per year by 2020 but have so only succeeded in raising a third of that. Instead, they continue to spend more on subsidising fossil fuels which are worsening the climate crisis.[70] Money diverted from the current $1,776 billion spent worldwide on the military would be a good step towards a more solidarity-based response to the impacts of climate change.[71]

Beyond redistribution, we need fundamentally to start tackling the weak points that could enable what Homer-Dixon called 'synchronous failure', in other words, to tackle the root causes of complex emergencies. Michael Lewis and Pat Conaty suggest seven key characteristics that will make a community a 'resilient' one: diversity, social capital, healthy ecosystems, innovation, collaboration, regular systems for feedback, and modularity (the latter means designing a system where if one thing breaks, it doesn't affect everything else).[72] In some key respects, this is the antithesis of the systems and practices that underpin our current globalised economy, which has instead encouraged corporate monopolies, monocultures, the centralisation of power, environmental destruction and individualism. This in turn reinforces Naomi Klein's argument in *This Changes Everything*, that effective solutions to the climate crisis will necessarily involve wholesale changes to the current economic system.

Ultimately, however, the changes we need both to oppose militarised responses to crises and to advocate and develop alternatives will not happen without sustained pressure by social movements. The only certain way to prevent the steady erosion of civil liberties becoming a permanent state of emergency is to mobilise a permanent resistance – one that obstructs militarised responses and advances alternatives. Resistance is still the best form of resilience on offer.

Notes

1. *Food System Shock: The insurance impacts of acute disruption to global food supply* (Emerging Risk Report: Innovation Series, pp. 1–30, report). (2015). London: Lloyds. Retrieved from http://www.lloyds.com/~/media/files/news%20and%20insight/risk%20insight/2015/food%20system%20shock/food%20system%20shock_june%202015.pdf.
2. Worldwatch Institute. (2013). Natural disasters becoming more frequent. Retrieved from http://www.worldwatch.org/node/5825.
3. Patrick, S.M. (14 August 2012). Man-made cities and natural disasters: the growing threat, *The Internationalist*. Retrieved from http://blogs.cfr.org/patrick/2012/08/14/man-made-cities-and-natural-disasters-the-growing-threat/.
4. Anderson, J. and Bausch, C. (25 January 2006). *Climate change and natural disasters: Scientific evidence of a possible relation between natural disasters and climate change*, Policy Brief for the European Parliament Environment Committee (Institute for European Environmental Policy, p. 5. Retrieved from http://www.europarl.europa.eu/comparl/envi/pdf/externalexpertise/ieep_6leg/naturaldisasters.pdf.
5. Ibid., p. 2.
6. Hansen, J., Sato, M. and Ruedy, R. (6 August 2012). Perception of climate change, *Proceedings of the National Academy of Sciences of the United States of America* [*PNAS*] Retrieved from http://www.pnas.org/content/early/2012/07/30/1205276109. Also see Holpuch, A. (7 August 2012). Nasa scientist's study quantifies climate change link to extreme weather, *Guardian*. Retrieved from http://www.guardian.co.uk/environment/2012/aug/07/nasa-scientist-high-temperatures-climate-change.
7. Patrick, S.M (14 August 2012).
8. Nicholls, R. Hanson, S. et. al. (2007). Ranking of the world's cities most exposed to coastal flooding today and in the future. Paris: OECD Environment Working Paper. Retrieved from http://www.oecd.org/env/climatechange/39721444.pdf. Also see OECD press release (4 December 2007) retrieved from http://www.oecd.org/environment/climatechange/39729575.pdf.
9. Davis, M. (2006). *Planet of Slums*. London: Verso, p. 25.
10. The rising cost of catastrophes. *The Economist* (14 January 2012) Retrieved from http://www.economist.com/node/21542771.
11. Counting the cost of calamities, *The Economist* (14 January 2012) Retrieved from http://www.economist.com/node/21542755.
12. Giddens, A. (14 April 1999). Risk. Lecture presented at Runaway World, Hong Kong.
13. The globalization of security. Chatham House, 2005, p. 2–3 (ISP/NSC Briefing Paper 05/02), p. 3.
14. Duffield, M. (1994). Complex emergencies and the crisis of developmentism, *IDS Bulletin*. Brighton: Institute of Development Studies, 25(4). Retrieved from http://www.ids.ac.uk/files/dmfile/duffield254.pdf.

15. FAO Media Centre (4 October 2012). FAO Food Price Index up 1.4 per cent in September. Retrieved from http://www.fao.org/news/story/en/item/161602/icode/.

16. Ahmed, N.M. (February 2011). The Great Unravelling: Tunisia, Egypt and the protracted collapse of the American empire, *Le Monde diplomatique*. Retrieved from http://mondediplo. com/blogs/tunisia-egypt-and-the-protracted-collapse-of-the. Also see Ahmed, N.M. (2010). *A User's Guide to the Crisis of Civilisation: And how to save it*. London: Pluto, 2010.

17. Heller, M. and Keoleian, G. (2000). *Life Cycle-Based Sustainability Indicators for Assessment of the U.S. Food System*. Ann Arbor, MI: Center for Sustainable Systems, University of Michigan, p. 42. Retrieved from http://css.snre.umich.edu/css_doc/CSS00-04.pdf; Heinberg, R. (2005). Threats of peak to the global food supply. *Museletter*, July, No. 159. Retrieved from http://www.richardheinberg.com/museletter/159.

18. Murray, M. (9 May 2005). Oil and food: a rising security challenge. *Plan B Update*. Washington DC: Earth Policy Institute, No. 48. Retrieved from http://www.earth-policy.org/index.php?/ plan_b_updates/2005/update48.

19. Cribb, J. (2010). *The Coming Famine: The global food crisis and what we can do about it*. Berkeley, CA: University of California Press, pp. 6–7.

20. Rhodes, C. (2014, 20 February). Peak oil is not a myth. Retrieved from http://www.rsc.org/ chemistryworld/2014/02/peak-oil-not-myth-fracking.

21. Homer-Dixon, T. (2006). *The Upside of Down: Catastrophe, creativity and the renewal of civilisation*. London: Souvenir Press, pp. 11–13, 16.

22. Beddington, J. (2009). Food, energy, water and the climate: a perfect storm of global events?, *Department of Business, Innovation & Skills*. London: Government Office for Science. Retrieved from http://www.bis.gov.uk/assets/goscience/docs/p/perfect-storm-paper.pdf.

23. Ahmed, N. (2011). The international relations of crisis and the crisis of international relations: from the securitisation of scarcity to the militarisation of society. *Global Change, Peace & Security*, 23(3), October. Retrieved from http://www.tandfonline.com/doi/abs/10.1080/1 4781158.2011.601854.

24. Klein, N. (2007). *The Shock Doctrine: The rise of disaster capitalism*. New York: Metropolitan Books/Henry Holt, p. 359.

25. Gunewardena, N. (2008). *Capitalizing on Catastrophe: Neoliberal Strategies in Disaster Reconstruction*. London: AltaMira Press. Also see Broome, A. (2011). Negotiating crisis: The IMF and disaster capitalism in small states. *The Round Table: The Commonwealth Journal of International Affairs*, 100(413). Retrieved from http://www.tandfonline.com/doi/abs/10.10 80/00358533.2011.565627.

26. It is notable that Bremer, mentioned by Naomi Klein above, after leaving Iraq served as Chair of the board of GlobalSecure Corporation, whose stated goal was 'securing the homeland with integrated products and services for the critical incident response community worldwide'. See http://worldnews.nbcnews.com/_news/2013/03/19/17373886-iraq-war-10-years-later-where-are-they-now-paul-bremer-iraq-administrator?lite.

27. The Scandinavians invented the concept of 'societal security' and define them as a) management of government affairs; b) international activity; c) national military defence; d) internal security; e) functioning of the economy and infrastructure; f) the population's income security and capability to function, and g) psychological crisis tolerance. EU definition of 'critical infrastructure': retrieved from http://ec.europa.eu/dgs/home-affairs/what-we-do/ policies/crisis-and-terrorism/critical-infrastructure/index_en.htm.

28. US definition of 'critical infrastructure': retrieved from http://www.dhs.gov/what-critical-infrastructure.

29. Brazil's water crisis is so bad that the army is staging simulations of a mass uprising at the local water utility', *Business Insider*, 10 August 2015. Retrieved from http://www.businessinsider. com.au/the-brazilian-army-is-training-for-a-water-uprising-2015-8.

30. FOCUS – Crisis management cycle – Wiki. (n.d.). Retrieved from http://www.focusproject. eu/web/focus/wiki/-/wiki/ESG/Crisis+management+cycle;jsessionid=C1BE7F4BD0F10 F1F3108FBBAAF92668A.

31. Fanoulis, E., Kirchner, E. and Dorussen, H. (2014). ANVIL (Analysis of Civil Security Systems in Europe) Country Study: United Kingdom, February 2014. Retrieved from http://anvil-project.net/wp-content/uploads/2014/02/United-Kingdom_v1.1.pdf.

32. UK Department of Transport. (30 June 2011). *Annual Road Fatalities*. Retrieved from https:// www.gov.uk/government/publications/annual-road-fatalities.

33. Ibid.

34. DRIVER project (2015) *Crisis Management Policy and Legislation Report*. Retrieved from: http://driver-project.eu/sites/default/files/driver/files/content-files/deliverables/ D83%2011_CM_Policy_and_Legislation%20_report_v1.0.pdf.

35. UK Cabinet Office. (8 May 2015). *2010 to 2015 Government Policy: Emergency Response Planning*. Retrieved from https://www.gov.uk/government/policies/improving-the-uks-ability-to-absorb-respond-to-and-recover-from-emergencies/supporting-pages/ building-a-resilient-society.

36. UK Cabinet Office. (20 February 2013). *Preparation and Planning for Emergencies: The National Resilience Capabilities Programme*. Retrieved from https://www.gov.uk/preparation-and-planning-for-emergencies-the-capabilities-programme.

37. Individual plans are classified, but the Cabinet Office produces an annual summary of all departments' plans into one overall sector resilience plan for critical infrastructure. Sector resilience plans for the last four years can be viewed here: https://www.gov.uk/government/ collections/sector-resilience-plans. See further Cabinet Office guidance: UK Cabinet Office (October 2011) *Keeping the Country Running: Natural hazards and infrastructure*, p. 5. Retrieved from https://www.gov.uk/government/uploads/system/uploads/attachment_ data/file/61342/natural-hazards-infrastructure.pdf.

38. European Union, Council Directive. (8 December 2008). Council Directive 2008/114/EC. Retrieved from http://eur-lex.europa.eu/LexUriServ/LexUriServ.do?uri=OJ:L:2008:345:0 075:0082:en:pdf.

39. European Commission (22 June 2012). On the review of the European Programme for Critical Infrastructure Protection (EPCIP) (Commission staff working document). Retrieved from http://ec.europa.eu/dgs/home-affairs/pdf/policies/crisis_and_terrorism/epcip_ swd_2012_190_final.pdf.

40. European Commission (28 August 2013). On a new approach to the European Programme for Critical Infrastructure Protection: Making European Critical Infrastructures more secure (Commission staff working document). Retrieved from http://ec.europa.eu/dgs/ home-affairs/what-we-do/policies/crisis-and-terrorism/critical-infrastructure/docs/ swd_2013_318_on_epcip_en.pdf.

41. Ibid.

42. European Reference Network for Critical Infrastructure Protection website: https://erncip-project.jrc.ec.europa.eu/.

43. CIPRNET – Critical Infrastructure Preparedness and Resilience Research Network website: https://www.ciprnet.eu/summary.html.
44. European Commission. Terrorism and other Security-related Risks (CIPS). (n.d.). Retrieved from http://ec.europa.eu/dgs/home-affairs/financing/fundings/security-and-safeguarding-liberties/terrorism-and-other-risks/index_en.htm.
45. Dillon, M. (2005). Global security in the 21st century: Circulation, complexity and contingency, Chatham House ISP/NSC Briefing Paper 05/02.
46. Stilhoff, S. and Söderbaum, F. (2012). Introduction. *The End of the Development-Security Nexus?, Development Dialogue*, No. 58. Retrieved from http://globalstudies.gu.se/digitalAssets/1430/1430267_enddvlpmsecurity.pdf.
47. Schulman, J. (14 August 2013). Defense Contractor: Climate Change Could Create 'Business Opportunities'. Retrieved from http://www.motherjones.com/environment/2013/08/raytheon-climate-change-security.
49. Ibid.
50. Dunn Cavelty, M., Kaufmann, M. and Søby Kristensen, K. (2015). Resilience and (in)security: Practices, subjects, temporalities. *Security Dialogue*, 46(1), 3–14.
51. Stilhoff, S. and Söderbaum, F. (2012).
52. Duffield, M (2012). Risk management and the bunkering of the aid industry. *The End of the Development-Security Nexus? Development Dialogue*, No. 58. Retrieved from http://globalstudies.gu.se/digitalAssets/1430/1430096_riskmanagement1.pdf p. 10.
53. See website https://www.privacyinternational.org/?q=node/310.
54. Interview: Susan Faludi on 9/11 myths. (10 July 2007). *Newsweek*. Retrieved from http://www.newsweek.com/interview-susan-faludi-911-myths-103359.
55. Civil Contingencies Act 2004, Part 1, Article 1, Paragraph 1.
56. It should be noted that some 'emergency powers' exist in other statutory legislation, including the Control of Major Accident Hazards Regulations 1999 (as amended 2005 and 2008), the Pipelines Safety Regulations 1996, the Radiation Emergency Preparedness and Public Information Regulations, the Energy Act 1976, the Nuclear Installations Act 1965, the Ionising Radiations Regulations, the Energy Act (Carbon Capture and Storage) 2008, the Safety of Sports Grounds Act 1975, the Fire Safety and Safety of Places of Sport Act 1987, the Health and Safety at Work Act 1974, and the Flood and Water Management Act 2010.
57. Statewatch Briefing. (January 2004). Civil Contingencies Bill: Britain's Patriot Act – revised, and just as dangerous as before. Retrieved from http://www.statewatch.org/news/2004/jan/12uk-civil-contingencies-bill-revised.htm; Tyler, R. (21 January 2004). Britain prepares its own version of US patriot act. *WSWS*. Retrieved from http://www.wsws.org/articles/2004/jan2004/patri-j21.shtml.
58. Despite some of its worst provisions being repealed by Judge Katherine Forrest in 2012 as 'unconstitutional', three judges in the US Court of Appeals – all Obama appointees – overruled those repeals. Also in 2007, the White House issued National Security Presidential Directive 51 (NSPD-51) to ensure 'continuity of government' in the event of a 'catastrophic emergency', in which case the President alone is empowered to do whatever he deems necessary – including everything from cancelling elections to suspending the Constitution to launching a nuclear attack.
59. *Armed Forces' Support to Civilian Authorities: Study on Capabilities, Organisations, Policies, and Legislation (COPL) of using armed forces in crisis management and disaster response*, DRIVER. EU project, forthcoming.

60. *French White Paper on Defence and National Security.* (2013), p. 86. Retrieved from http://www. rpfrance-otan.org/White-Paper-on-defence-and.

61. Ibid., p. 92.

62. German army's crisis role widened. (17 August 2012). Retrieved from http://www.bbc.co.uk/ news/world-europe-19295351.

63. Solnit, R. (7 April 2014). Call climate change what it is: Violence. Retrieved from http://www. theguardian.com/commentisfree/2014/apr07/climate-change-violence-occupy-earth.

64. See http://minerva.dtic.mil/cois.html.

65. Ahmed, N. (19 February 2015). The bleak science bankrolled by the Pentagon. *VICE Motherboard.* Retrieved from http://motherboard.vice.com/read/the-science-of-the-pentagon.

66. See, respectively, the EU-funded projects at https://www.epoolice.eu/, http://www. westyorkshire.police.uk/athena, http://www.fp7-emergent.eu/, http://slandail.eu/, http:// isar.i112.eu/, http://www.cosmic-project.eu/, and http://super-fp7.eu/.

67. See http://huairou.org/resilience/community-resilience-toolkit.

68. Solnit, R. (2009). *A Paradise Built in Hell: The extraordinary communities that arise in disasters.* New York: Viking, p. 312.

69. Fois, F. and Forino, G. (October 2014). The self-built ecovillage in L'Aquila, Italy: community resilience as a grassroots response to environmental shock. *Disasters*, 38(4), 719–39.

70. *The Global Landscape of Climate Finance 2014* (report). (November 2014). Retrieved http:// climatepolicyinitiative.org/publication/global-landscape-of-climate-finance-2014/.

71. Perlo-Freeman, S. (13 April 2015). *Trends in World Military Expenditure* (report). Retrieved http://www.sipri.org/research/armaments/milex/recent-trends.

72. Lewis, M. and Conaty, P. (2012). *The Resilience Imperative: Cooperative transitions to a steady-state economy.* Gabriola, BC: New Society.

5

FROM REFUGEE PROTECTION TO MILITARISED EXCLUSION: WHAT FUTURE FOR 'CLIMATE REFUGEES'?

Ben Hayes, Steve Wright and April Humble

One of Britain's most senior military strategists has warned that the threat posed by migration to western civilisation is on a par with the barbarian invasions that destroyed the Roman empire. Rear Admiral Chris Parry likened modern immigration to the Goths and Vandals, saying that Europe could be subjected to 'reverse colonisation' over the next twelve years. Not since the days of Enoch Powell has such apocalyptic language been so acceptable, and its message so widely accepted. There is no recognition of responsibility for the refugees from the wars and anti-Muslim crusades of the Middle East, the resource wars of Africa, the fall-out wars born of the perverse boundaries of colonialism and the proxy wars against communism, those displaced by economic wars on the poor or by death squads. They, not the western policies and actions creating or contributing to their displacement, are seen by western European politicians and popular media as 'the problem'. To the image of locusts seeking to descend on the continent to strip it bare is superadded the label of criminal, justified by the necessary illegality of their travel, and now, after the twin towers, after Madrid and after 7/7 in London, they are potential terrorists too.

Frances Webber, 'Border wars and asylum crimes', 2006[1]

Introduction

In the spring of 2015, Europe's migration policy – or more accurately anti-immigration policy – was high on the EU agenda after two boats containing around 1,500 people sank in the Mediterranean in the space of a week. It was hard not to see the concern expressed by European officials as anything other than crocodile tears, given the decision by the EU to end financial support for Italy's *Mare Nostrum* search-and-rescue mission just six months earlier. Representatives of the UK and other powerful member states had argued that the rescue missions were simply encouraging more would-be refugees to try to make dangerous crossings from North Africa to Europe. This was nothing short of arguing that the best deterrent against unwanted migrants is mass death, and completely ignored the abject desperation that motivates people to leave their homes at huge cost and risk in the first place.

No one had outlined this policy option in 2008, when the EU's security and foreign policy chief had warned that climate change, droughts, poor harvests and food shortages – already tentatively linked to conflict and migration from Syria and Eritrea, currently the countries of origin of the two largest groups of refugees bound for Europe – would lead to 'substantially increased migratory pressure' from North Africa and the Middle East by 2020.[2] But rather than contributing to the amelioration of the appalling conditions that underpin this kind of emigration, or improving the opportunities and mechanisms for refugee protection in Europe, the EU has simply ratcheted up the security rhetoric by sending in the army to go after the people traffickers and destroy their boats. The United Nations High Commissioner for Refugees and *Amnesty International* have warned that this will likely worsen the plight of refugees. Gone is the EU's moral authority to tell South East Asian nations faced with boatloads of Rohingya fleeing ethnic cleansing in Burma to do the right thing by the refugees.

The growing awareness of climate change as a factor in inducing migration has led many in the environmental justice movement to call on the international community to extend the Geneva Conventions to recognise the rights of 'climate refugees'. We are concerned that this obscures three trends in migration policy that long pre-date debates about the relationship between climate change and migration or its potential future scale.

First, the securitisation of migration policy over the past thirty years or so has seen many rich countries long stop admitting refugees in significant numbers, while re-casting migrants and asylum-seekers as 'illegal', 'bogus' and a security threat to be countered with the full force of the state. Central to this process has been a 'tightening' of all migration controls and diminishing refugee protection as measured in both qualitative and quantitative terms.

Second, and intimately connected to the first trend, is the militarisation of border controls: the development and implementation of high-tech, highly militarised means of preventing unauthorised entry. Border zones have become the destination for extremely coercive means of surveillance and control developed on the battlefield – and a lucrative market for the security and defence contractors who supply them. We can now speak of a burgeoning border security-industrial complex selling everything from security fences to surveillance technology, from visa-processing services to detention centres.

Third, with the active support of the governments of the Global North, the legal and physical controls developed to prevent unwanted migration have increasingly been exported to developing countries and client states in the South. In the name of 'migration management', wealthier states – particularly those in the EU – have implemented migration controls in poorer Third World countries to prevent the transit of migrants and refugees and allow the expeditious return of those declared 'illegal'. The levers of aid and trade are frequently employed to achieve this. 'Technical assistance', 'export credit guarantees' and even aid and development funding have been used to fund the transfer of migration-control systems, boosting the coffers of the defence sector yet further.

Without challenging the overall direction of migration policy, it is clear that most political responses will not only fail to properly address the needs of environmental refugees, but will likely see an intensification of controls and physical infrastructure, forcing refugees to seek protection in, or close to, their countries of origin, or to take even more dangerous risks in an attempt to migrate. The worst-case scenarios could see states panicked into emergency measures and draconian restrictions on freedom of movement.

Where does all of this leave people who care about social justice and universal human rights – what should we do or advocate? What are the parameters in which debates about 'climate-induced migration' take place? What does this say about the utility and viability of expanding international law to recognise and accommodate 'climate refugees', or will a securitisation narrative out-trump all legal obligations? And how best can we resist these disturbing developments?

'Climate refugees' in context

Migrants and refugees occupy a central place in the discourse on climate change as a 'threat multiplier' and security issue in its own right – with the 'threat' of uncontrolled international migration identified as a core climate-security concern (see Chapter 2). The hypothesis is that climate change will exacerbate existing problems in poor and under-developed countries, leading to increased conflict and migratory pressure that will ultimately have to be addressed by richer countries, which will be the destination of choice for 'climate refugees'.

And it's not just the military strategists and the securocrats who make this argument. In their 2007 report *Human Tide*, Christian Aid warned that

> The danger is that this new forced migration will fuel existing conflicts and generate new ones in the areas of the world – the poorest – where resources are most scarce. Movement on this scale has the potential to de-stabilize whole regions where increasingly desperate populations compete for dwindling food and water.[3]

They also predicted that 'on current trends, a further 1 billion people will be forced from their homes between now and 2050.'

Context is everything and although Christian Aid was widely mis- (or selectively) quoted as having argued that climate change (and not all of the other things already resulting in forced migration) would produce the additional billion refugees, it suffered a barrage of criticism from commentators and academics for being overly alarmist, lacking a clear methodology and using language (that is, 'Human Tide') that contributes to existing and overwhelmingly negative public discourse about the 'threat' of migration.[4]

The furore surrounding Christian Aid's self-declared attempt to spark an important debate has introduced some nuance into the discussion about the likely relationship between climate change and international migration, but this debate has not yet filtered into the regular updates from the military and security threat assessors. For example, in its fifth edition of *Global Strategic Trends – Out to 2045*, published in June 2014, the UK Ministry of Defence maintains that 'Severe food shortages could lead to sudden mass migration of populations across national borders, triggering widespread social unrest.'[5]

Catastrophic predictions notwithstanding, recent scholarly debate about 'climate-induced migration' recognises that crediting climate change as a *primary* causal factor of migration is difficult, if not impossible, due to the prevalence of other contributing factors. As a Foresight Report on 'Migration and Global Environmental Change' published by the UK government in 2011 noted, while extreme weather events such as storms will likely cause displacement, it is gradual environmental degradation that will ultimately cause migration in the longer term.[6] This may be compounded by an array of other social, economic and political factors including water scarcity, salinisation of irrigated lands, deforestation, ineffective government responses, ethnic disputes and economic problems, amongst others. This complex interplay of factors, described as 'disaggregated causality', makes the 'climate-induced migrant' a somewhat intangible figure, and more importantly, makes it very difficult to create legal definitions of what is a 'climate refugee' and in turn develop effective frameworks for recognition and protection of their asylum rights.[7]

The issue is made more complex due to the traditional adaptation and coping mechanisms that many migrants already use to deal with climate variations, such as temporary and circular migration (basically, people moving for employment or subsistence).[8] This is important because the research that has been conducted to date suggests that most climate-linked migration is likely to be internal rather than cross-border.[9] Moreover, the migration-as-adaptation agenda is seen by its proponents as far more progressive and more focused on the needs of migrants: instead of seeing migrants as security threats or objects of pity, they are seen as agents who can adapt to climate change by moving.[10] This is not to say that such migration is unproblematic. On the contrary, newly arrived internal migrants often face discrimination and poverty when moving from rural areas to urban centres. They may also be subject to 'return migration' initiatives, where governments try to move people back to the countryside.

Climate change might also make people less able, rather than more likely to move. Migration usually requires resources, and as people's livelihoods are undermined (for example, by drought or desertification), they become less able to move, even though they might want to. While some people will be able to move, but prevented from doing so by borders, other people will be completely unable to move and trapped in worsening conditions. Conversely, not all movement linked to climate change is or will be refugee-like, in so far as people must move to survive, so the distinction between forced and voluntary migration will remain as important as ever. Many people who move in the context of climate change will have some choice about where and when they move, and will look more like the so-called 'economic migrants' of today, seeking work in pastures new as climate change erodes their existing livelihoods.

As the Intergovernmental Panel on Climate Change (IPCC) noted in 2007, 'estimates of the number of people who may become environmental migrants are, at best, guesswork.'[11] But while the level, extent and speed of climate change and its local impact on internal conflict and migration remains highly contested, this is largely immaterial to those tasked with defending the borders of the rich world against the 'human tide' from the poor. This is because security-resource expenditure and prioritisation is neither based, nor ranked, on an objective calculus of relative risk. Put another way: whereas activist and scientific communities may rationalise and promote rights-based solutions to future refugee crises, the exploitation of migration politics by populist decision makers ultimately serves to meet the demands of 'securocrats' for new powers while undermining paradigms predicated on notions of human security, such as the freedom to move.

Open societies or global apartheid?

All modern states now have well-oiled systems for controlling migration and preventing unauthorised entry and residence. These are highly securitised apparatuses in which concerns about illegal migration, crime and terrorism have converged to create a powerful populist narrative that is demanding of ever stricter controls. Indeed, migration control is now firmly established as a top political issue in many wealthy countries – and alongside hyped-up fears about 'Islamist terrorism', is inexorably linked to the current resurgence of the far right across Europe.

This has long meant that members of minority communities are frequently subjected to enhanced scrutiny at borders coupled with state-security prejudice and paranoia that invoke ethnicity and religion to determine risk and status. There is nothing novel in this. As Sri Lankan activist A. Sivanandan wrote of the then European Economic Community in 1988: immigration policies were producing a 'common market racism' that 'cannot tell one black from another, a citizen from an immigrant, an immigrant from a refugee – and classes all Third World peoples as immigrants and refugees and all immigrants and refugees as terrorists and drug dealers'.[12]

In security discourse, the reasons why people migrate have thus become much less important than the threat they are perceived to represent. Blind to social justice or cost, travelling for profit is encouraged, while travelling for survival is condemned.[13] Contemporary borders have become sprawling security checkpoints where all human traffic is viewed as a potential threat.[14] The bona fide are distinguished from the suspect and the illegitimate; irregular migrants and refugees are caught in a 'continuum of insecurity'.[15]

Borders thus reiterate (even reify) the distinction between the 'civilised' First World and the 'barbaric' Third World, or what Zygmunt Bauman called the 'global frontier land',[16] institutionalising racist state practice and fuelling racist attitudes. Joseph Nevins and other critics of contemporary border controls have adopted the term 'global apartheid' to capture the distinctive role of immigration controls in maintaining race and class disparities across the world.[17]

Against this backdrop, according to the UN, global migration as a whole has been increasing in recent years, to an unprecedented 232 million people in 2013 (up from 175 million in 2000, and 154 million in 1990).[18] Of this total, 136 million migrants lived in the Global North, while 96 million resided in the South, where international migration has been increasing more rapidly since the turn of the century.

Numbers of refugees have also grown significantly in recent years. According to the United Nations High Commissioner for Refugees (UNHCR), global displacement has risen to an unparalleled 50 million people, with the world's poorest nations hosting the vast majority (86 per cent of the world's refugees in 2013). Some 5.5 million people became refugees or internally displaced in the first half of 2014 alone.[19] Some of this movement is already being tentatively linked to climate change. As noted elsewhere in this book, some analysts have linked the outbreak of hostilities in Syria to food prices and drought.[20] There is some tentative evidence linking the crisis in the Horn of Africa to drought and climate change.[21]

Yet as these crises increase, rich countries are shouldering less and less of the human 'burden', not least because proportionately fewer refugees are able to reach those countries because of the coercive measures they have imposed (this is compounded by declining recognition rates for refugees able to lodge asylum applications). The overwhelming preference is to fund refugee assistance programmes instead of hosting refugees. One only has to consider the current Syria refugee crisis, the worst since the Second World War, with around 4 million people – half of them children – having fled the country to Turkey, Lebanon, Jordan, Iraq and Egypt by December 2014. The rest of the international community, meanwhile, had taken just 1.7 per cent of the total number of refugees.[22] These numbers are no accident – they reflect precisely the policy objectives that the EU and other states in the MENA (Middle East North Africa) region have pursued over the past decade and more.

Migration management and the warehousing of refugees

The 'Pacific solution' pursued by successive Conservative Australian governments since 2001, whereby asylum seekers are prevented from landing on the Australian mainland and transported and detained on Pacific islands, is the flag-bearer of rich countries' restrictive approaches to unauthorised immigration. It effectively paid hundreds of millions of dollars in aid to Pacific island states to outsource Australia's refugee protection obligations.

The policy was suspended for a short period by Kevin Rudd's intervening Labour administration, which brokered an immigration control deal with Indonesia, before being re-introduced in 2012, and supplemented by a 'Regional Resettlement Arrangement' with Papua New Guinea in 2013. This spelt out the purpose of Australian refugee policy in no uncertain terms:

> From now on, any asylum seeker who arrives in Australia by boat will have no chance of being settled in Australia as refugees. Asylum seekers taken to Christmas Island will be sent to Manus and elsewhere in Papua New Guinea for assessment of their refugee status. If they are found to be genuine refugees, they will be resettled in Papua New Guinea … If they are found not to be genuine refugees, they may be repatriated to their country of origin or be sent to a safe third country other than Australia.[23]

The Labour administration also reopened Australia's off-shore refugee processing centre on the island of Nauru. At the time of writing this chapter (2015), the centre is the subject of substantive investigations into allegations of widespread sexual and physical assault of detainees. 'Things happen', said current Prime Minister Tony Abbot of the revelations.[24] Indeed, the same things appear to be happening in immigration detention centres across the world.

Australia's 'Pacific Solution' won many admirers and in 2004 Tony Blair's government proposed that the EU adopt a similar off-shore processing and 'protection in the region' policy for refugees bound for Europe. Although off-shore processing was a bridge too far for many EU member states, the European Commission began developing policy on 'regional protection plans' that would provide funding for governments of third states that were hosting refugee camps, with the prospect of resettlement to Europe for a token few.[25]

By this time, the UNHCR was already lamenting what it called the 'warehousing' of refugees. Host states were 'containing refugees in isolated and insecure refugee camps, typically in border regions and far from the governing regime', with governments increasingly requiring the majority of refugees to live in these camps and prohibiting them leaving to seek employment or education.[26] 'To envisage such a plan [the warehousing of refugees] is to imagine ghettos created by the world's most peaceful and richest countries in some of the world's poorest and most unstable regions', wrote Raekha Prassad of the UK proposals.[27]

Indeed, since the late 1990s, the EU has – like Australia – pursued a policy of soliciting the cooperation of countries of origin and transit of migrants and refugees with the objective of creating immigration buffer zones. This was initially achieved in the countries of Central and Eastern Europe, who were offered the carrot of EU membership, then extended to encompass a 'European neighbourhood' that stretches from West Africa to Central Asia.

Although not formally adopted until 2005, the EU's 'Global Approach to Migration' dates back to 1997 and the arrival in Italy and Greece of thousands of Kurdish refugees from Iraq, who had travelled by sea from Turkey. This prompted the EU to draft a 46-point Action Plan to ensure that this kind of 'mass influx' did not recur. The Iraq plan was followed by an Austrian Presidency strategy paper on migration, which suggested explicitly that a

> ... model of concentric circles of migration policy could replace that of 'fortress Europe' ... the Schengen states currently lay down the most intensive control measures. Their neighbours should gradually be linked into a similar system ... particularly with regard to visa control and readmission policies. A third circle of states (CIS area, Turkey, and North Africa) will then concentrate primarily on transit checks and combating facilitator networks, and a fourth circle (Middle East, China, black Africa) on eliminating push factors.[28]

The Austrian strategy paper was widely condemned by migrant and refugee organisations and officially disowned by the EU, but the principles it contained were embodied in a 2002 EU Action Plan on illegal immigration. The plan provided EU funding for migration controls in the countries of origin of migrants and refugees, including border-management equipment and expertise, asylum-processing infrastructures, public registration structures (that is, biometrics/databases), reception centres for illegal immigrants in transit countries, and 'awareness-raising campaigns' for would-be 'illegal' émigrés. The Action Plan also called for the introduction of 'migration-management' clauses in EU agreements with third states, using the 'levers' of aid-and-trade to ensure cooperation. The European Commission began funding 'preparatory actions on cooperation with third countries in the field of migration' from the EC development budget, and taking an increasing interest in 'South-South migration' – all with the underlying objective of preventing people trying to reach the EU. In addition to tighter and more heavily fortified border controls, which we discuss further below, making refugees stay where they are, or as close to their countries of origin as possible, required a plethora of further EU initiatives including the criminalisation of illegal entry and residence (which saw ships' captains prosecuted for rescuing boat people), the adoption of the 'safe third-country rule' (meaning that any refugee who has transited through a country where they could have sought asylum en route to the EU can be sent back there), and readmission agreements with those countries to facilitate their return.

While this has made it more difficult for refugees to enter the EU in order to lodge an asylum claim, it hasn't stopped them attempting to come. On the contrary, all it has done is force them into ever more perilous journeys and the hands of people traffickers, who give little priority to safety and at times have acted ruthlessly to protect a booming trade. A political economy of migration management and coercion has duly emerged, with black-market profiteers creating ever more lucrative and dangerous flights of passage and a legitimate commercial sector increasingly cashing in on processing those who get caught. It is important to remember that as easy and convenient as it is to blame organised crime, the 'trafficker' is no more responsible for irregular migration than the travel agent is for tourism.[29]

For a very short time, the EU's migration-management policy appeared to work quite well thanks to the cooperation of strongmen like Libya's Colonel Gaddafi and Tunisia's Ben Ali, who secured a raft of political and financial concessions from EU member states in return for policing their borders for illegal emigrants and readmitting people expelled from Europe. Never mind that they meted out appalling treatment to migrants and refugees in Europe's name. The events of the so-called 'Arab Spring' – and in particular the NATO intervention in Libya and the war in Syria – put an end to these cosy relations, deposing the EU's friendly dictators, increasing insecurity across the region, and producing millions of new refugees. The number of EU asylum claims has been steadily rising ever since, topping 400,000 in 2013, and reaching 600,000 in 2014, helped also by the conflicts in Russia, Ukraine, Somalia, Eritrea and Sudan.[30] The number of *documented* deaths of people trying to reach the EU has also risen, to over 3,500 in 2014 alone.[31] The sinking of a packed fishing boat just half-a-mile off the coast of the Italian island of Lampedusa, in which 366 out of 518 people on board drowned (they had paid the trip's organisers approximately $1,000 each), galvanised the Italian government into launching a standing search-and-rescue operation, 'Mare Nostrum', which plucked more than 100,000 migrants and refugees from unsafe boats before it was canned twelve months later as outlined in the introduction. Its replacement, 'Operation Triton', coordinated by the EU border-management agency, FRONTEX, is primarily concerned with surveillance (rather than search-and-rescue), and limited to 30 miles off Italy's coast.

In 2015, the idea of outsourcing the processing refugees bound for the EU is back on the agenda, with Niger, Tunisia, Egypt, Morocco and Turkey in the frame as possible locations.[32] If the Australian experience is anything to go by, these proposed centres could signal the beginning of the end of asylum protection in the EU. In this scenario, those seeking refuge in Europe from 'climate-induced migration' in Africa would indeed be hemmed into refugee camps in the borderlands of countries that lack the means and resources to support them, dependent on international aid that is already woefully inadequate in the context of the existing refugee crisis (as shown by the repeated appeals by aid agencies supporting Syrian refugees in neighbouring countries).

Border controls as social controls: A world of red zones and green zones

Such fears are compounded by an acceleration in pace of states building hi-tech boundary fences along critical borders. So much so, that the politics of exclusion, now form a backdrop to contemporary culture. In September 2013, the *Guardian* asked 'Are you hemmed in by a fence or a separation wall?'[33] Hollywood has also envisioned the dispossessed being left in an inhospitable sprawl back on planet Earth, whilst the elite get to enjoy the bliss of an extra-terrestrial luxury gated community in its film *Elysium*.

Border controls have undergone significant changes over the past two decades. From sprawling physical barriers manned by sentries and typified by constructions like the Berlin Wall, security fences and border zones have been a testing ground for new surveillance technologies and control systems initially developed for the military. These developments are by no means limited to inter/national borders, and have instead come to characterise myriad elements of contemporary security planning – from 'smart cities', to 'megavents' like the Olympics and soccer's World Cup, to the protection of elite population enclaves, crowd control and crisis management.

Examining these developments, Stephen Graham at Newcastle University says we are witnessing the emergence of a much more brutalised and militarised urban policing to enforce apartheid-scale inequalities, such as that witnessed in places like the occupied territories of Palestine. What has already emerged, according to Graham, is an ideology of a militarised urban battle-space.[34] The demands to police this space and the border in particular – in the context of rapid technological developments in political control – has benefited a small group of multinational military conglomerates or 'primes', who see an extraordinarily lucrative market opportunity for diversification into security walls and weaponry. The border-exclusion technologies deployed against unauthorised migrants include concrete walls, virtual walls, monitoring and sniper towers, cameras, land radars and wireless telecommunication infrared surveillance, carbon-dioxide probes, information technology, identification systems and immigration databases. These technologies reinforce a massive proliferation of global fence building in recent years, particularly in the period since 9/11.

Figure 5.1 represents empirical information on 54 border security fences. The security capacity and stage of development vary greatly, as does the permeability of the borders. The map includes four categories of border fences, from the most robust land (shown as a consistent line) and maritime (diagonal dashes) security with multi-dimensional technologies and surveillance, to the use of enhanced but incomplete fences (dots), to the least robust (long dashes) where the border remains relatively porous. The map shows that the highest intensity of border securitisation is largely clustered around Europe, America, the Middle-East and southern Asia. Territories with similar developments include North Africa, Central Asia and Russia; other isolated cases exist elsewhere.

The borders of America are becoming increasingly fortified, with the US–Mexico border having multiple layers of security. A virtual wall of surveillance is being constructed along the Canadian border and the maritime area between the South East and the Caribbean is strongly guarded. 'Fortress Europe' has long characterised the EU's approach to border control, with recent investment focusing on the maritime borders to the South. The Greece–Turkish land border is believed to be the route taken by many undocumented migrants' entering Europe, and Greece has begun to construct a fence along a portion of the crossing. To the North West, barriers also exist intermittently along outer European borders with Russia.

In North and West Africa, Morocco has increasingly guarded borders with Algeria and so does Mauritania with Mali. The Spanish enclaves of Cueta and Mellilla, where Europe has a land border with Morocco, are hemmed in by razor wire. Fifteen migrants drowned there in 2014 after Spanish police fired rubber bullets at a group of several hundred

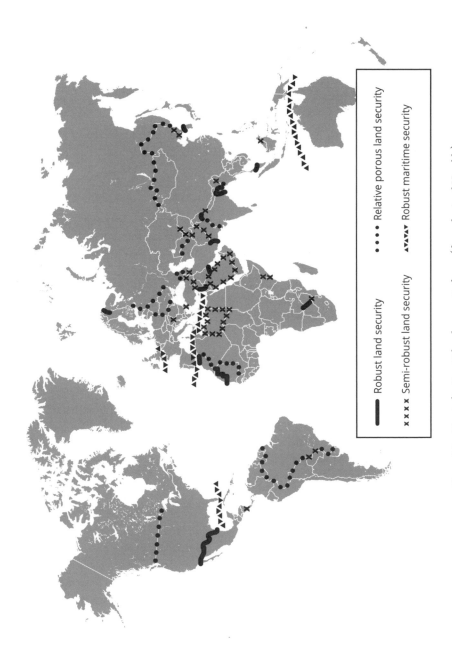

Figure 5.1 Map indicating 54 border security fences (drawn by April Humble)

Legend:
— Robust land security
x x x Semi-robust land security
•••• Relative porous land security
▲▼▲▼ Robust maritime security

people who had made a swim for it.[35] Morocco has its own 1,500-mile-long mixed sand and stone barrier lined with mines along the Western Sahara territory and, prior to the fall of Gaddafi, Libya had entered into a €300 million contract with Finmeccanica to secure its borders. In the South, electric and barbed-wire fences secure the Zimbabwe–Botswana border and the Zimbabwean–South Africa border respectively. The Middle East has a large number of highly secured borders, most notably between Israel and the Palestinian Territories. There is a highly secured barrier under construction between Oman and the United Arab Emirates and between Saudi Arabia and Yemen; in 2009, European Aeronautic Defence and Space Company (EADS) was contracted to securitise all of Saudi Arabia's borders.

The term 'Fortress India' has also been coined, following the construction of a heavily guarded 1,790-mile border fence around Bangladesh, parts of which are electrified. India is also deploying border securitisation across its borders with Pakistan, Tibet, Burma and the Kashmiri region. Pakistan meanwhile has considered proposals for a mine-lined fence with Afghanistan.

Central Asia also has some fortified border security zones, such as between Uzbekistan and Kyrgyzstan, and Uzbekistan and Afghanistan. Further east, Russia has an extensive low-security, barbed-wire fence along its borders with China and Mongolia. Both of North Korea's land borders are becoming increasingly secured; Brunei and Limbang, Malaysia and Thailand both have heightened border security between their respective shared borders.

Of course, this summary is a mere snapshot and more border fences have been erected since 2011, when our research was undertaken. And while there are well-founded fears that the spectre of 'climate refugees' is driving the border-securitisation agenda, it is too early to make strong claims about the extent to which this is happening, as 'illegal migration' still serves to justify most developments. However, it is worth noting that climate change is already being linked to attempted border crossings from Mexico to the US,[36] to migration in the Sahel,[37] and to the border between India and Bangladesh, whose vulnerability to sea-level rises is frequently cited in the climate-security strategies discussed in Chapter 2.[38] It is equally important to point out that the majority of borders in Africa, South America, Central America and South East Asia remain as yet without bolstered security deployments, allowing people to move between many states in the Global South with relative freedom. However, an absence of securitised border fences does not tell us anything about conditions in other borderland areas, which are often at the forefront of ethnic and religious tensions and outbreaks of violence, and/or attempts to create or impose ethnically or religiously defined 'homelands'. Today, many contested or prized border zones are subject to quasi-military rule, draconian security measures, widespread human rights abuses (by state and non-state actors) and limited prospects for democratic governance. Consider, for example, the current picture in central Africa, with conflicts dotted along the borders between countries from Mali to Yemen, the disputes along Russia's internal and external borders to the east and south, and the borderlands of Afghanistan and Pakistan, North East India and Southern China.

From borders that see to borders that bite

The 2011 study on which the above map is based showed that more than half of the 54 borders have developed enhanced security since 9/11, and that the total number of securitised borders has effectively tripled since this date. This suggests that the emergent, post-9/11 paradigm of border securitisation is not the end of the narrative, but the beginning.

We already live in an era of ubiquitous surveillance that is enveloping our urban settlements and critical infrastructures. Border zones are already some of the most intensely surveilled places on earth. Over the past decade, billions have been spent in upgrading capacities at borders to include everything from biometric identification systems (fingerprinting, face recognition, and so on) to cameras that can spot anomalous behaviour, to predator drones for wide area surveillance.

What is now being done in the name of border security may have a long-term bearing on how internally displaced migrants are treated, because national borders are simultaneously spreading inwards and outwards. Inwards through the development of biometric profiling, population registers and risk-profiling systems, and through operability with local policing systems (mobile fingerprint checks, for example). Outwards through the creation of external border zones, which allow states to impose surveillance and control on territories other than their own. Israel is very much the model, having established blanket surveillance systems over what remains of Palestine.

The US border with Mexico is policed by 21,000 guards, ten Predator drones, tower-mounted cameras and ground sensors that monitor land movements.[39] In Europe, the EU's new external border surveillance system, EUROSUR, which links national border-control agencies and coastal patrols with FRONTEX, the EU border management agency, envisages surveillance of the entire Mediterranean. To this end, EUROSUR is capable of integrating new surveillance technologies as they come online.[40] This will almost certainly include satellite surveillance and unmanned aerial vehicles (UAVs) or 'drones'. The EU has also already invested heavily in both areas, funding numerous border-surveillance projects.[41] The use of armed unmanned aerial vehicles (UAVs), commonly known as drones, for assassination missions by the US in Pakistan, Afghanistan, Somalia and Yemen has sparked enormous controversy. A crucial concern for NGOs, such as Human Rights Watch and the International Committee for Robot Arms Control (ICRAC), is the prospect of these systems becoming fully autonomous. We already have semi-autonomous precursor operations: so-called 'signature strikes' – where targets are chosen automatically because they resemble similar situations, where the use of lethal force could be justified.

R&D projects in military research institutes are pioneering new capacities to immobilise individuals and crowds, using weapons which cause pain, maim, or paralyse their targets – that could at some point be mobilised against refugees. This has not happened in a vacuum. Even before 9/11, the US military in particular was re-orientating towards a different type of warfare where unconventional opponents would be operating within urban terrain amongst ordinary civilians.

New military doctrines emerged to justify this reframing as part of the so-called 'Revolution in Military Affairs' (RMA), under which the United States would strive for 'full spectrum dominance' and hence military superiority over all potential adversaries. These doctrines incorporated new and autonomous targeting tactics, as well as high-tech weaponry designed to be used against both combatants and civilians. This was promoted by the likes of Col. John Alexander, who advocated the notion of a non-lethal set of alternatives for twenty-first-century warfare. With sci-fi writers Janet and Chris Morris and Alvin and Heidi Toffler, Alexander managed to persuade the US DoD to set up a new programme of work exploring this new form of warfare – the Joint Non-Lethal Weapons Directorate (JNLWD) – of which he became the first director in 1996. Post 9/11, the JNLWD, based at the Marine Corp HQ at Quantico, has become the engine of soliciting and approving new sub-lethal technologies, border protection and exclusion systems. Some of these using direct energy sound like science fiction,[42] but there has in fact been a relentless search for technologies which can bridge the gap between 'shout and shoot' over several hundred metres.

Critics of such alleged 'non-lethality' raise their potential for torture and mass human rights violation. Landmine Action was one of the first NGOs to report on potential con-figurations of some of these weapons for mass exclusion and perimeter protection, as new weapons were researched for replacing antipersonnel land mines, in the wake of the Ottawa Treaty Ban.[43] The Raytheon pain-beam based on a millimetre-wave device, which heats up humans to over 130 degrees, has been championed by the JNLWD and prototypes have been fielded, but without operational use yet because of understand-able controversy.[44] Such powerful directed-energy systems capable of shocking would-be migrants, from very long distances away, are already now beyond prototype stage. Raytheon recently advertised related devices like the Silent Guardian, which are based on notions of 'tuneable lethality', but promoted as harmless.[45]

So-called 'Non-Lethal' Weapons (NLW) technologies have subsequently globalised and form part of the new arsenals of military, police and special forces as their various roles and tactics converge.[46] Their key role is to provide enhanced coercion without the public opprobrium that might accompany any state use of lethal force. Amnesty Inter-national has identified their deployment with many human rights violations including torture.[47] Increasingly, such weapons are used in conjunction with other coercive tactics, including small arms. In 2014, JNLWD was testing robotic ships for intercepting other vessels in maritime security operations, as well as promoting new research to incapacitate vessels and their contents via aircraft- and ship-mounted directed-energy weapons.[48]

Other less 'intelligent' killing systems are more autonomous. For example, the lethal 'self-healing' minefield uses neural networks to reposition mines if a border zone is breached.[49] Another variant, which can be either lethal or sub-lethal, is Metal Storm's virtual minefield, which designates where 'mines' are on a virtual map held by a surveillance system which could be anything from an UAV or even a satellite. Cameras react to any physical breach by launching multiple mortar strikes to the designated spot.[50] In 2013, *New Scientist* reported on drone systems which could tag those found in unauthorised spaces – again setting off unsavoury images of tracking and hunting down un-cooperative humans. Again, we have inklings of future configurations. Currently, drones within the US can only be used for surveillance, but the Electronic Frontier Foundation shows that at least one US agency explored arming them with less-lethal weapons.[51] The security vulnerabilities of long interstate borders or critical infrastructures are used to justify 24/7 surveillance – a thankless and relentlessly dull task, which will always be presented as ripe for automation, either by ground-based or UAV robotic system with either surveillance, or guns, or both. Put another way: as long as we have fortified borders, they will remain a testing ground for new technologies of surveillance and control.

The kind of 'terminator' scenarios outlined above may sound like science fiction, but the rapid justification and escalating deployment of the US drone-led assassination strategy, shows how quickly things can change. South Korea has already fielded the armed Samsung SGR-1 robot on its border, the demilitarised zone with North Korea.[52] Whilst the SGR-1 has autonomous surveillance functions, it needs human permission to open fire on live targets. More established democracies have the same intent. The Pentagon made a call for contractors to provide a 'multi-robot pursuit system' that will let a pack of robots 'search for and detect a non-co-operative human'. What we have here are the beginnings of something designed to enable robots to hunt down humans like a pack of dogs. Once the software is perfected we can reasonably anticipate that they will become autonomous and become armed.[53] What will happen when such means end up policing border regimes of countries that have little or no respect for human life or the rule of law?

Secure borders, secure profits

The process of proliferation is being accelerated by specialist arms fairs such as the Border Security Expo. The industry itself is learning how to network more effectively to secure the massive security contracts now on offer, such as the multi-billion, multi-year, multi-partner contract to provide Saudi Arabia with a new border fence led by EADS,[54] or the transnational upscaling of southern Arizona's border with Mexico by Israeli security company Elbit Systems, seeking to benefit from a $40 billion 'Security treasure trove'.[55] As Chapter 7 explores, it is primarily large multinational defence contractors, or 'primes', that service this market. In Europe, the five big mega-defence conglomerates are EADS, BAE Systems, Finmeccanica, SAFRAN and Thales. In the US, the huge military systems corporations are Lockheed-Martin, Boeing, Northrop Grumman, Raytheon and General Dynamics. Given the growing importance of biometric borders, IT conglomerates such as L3 Communications, Hewlett Packard, Dell, Verizon and IBM in the US, and Eriksson, Indra, Siemens Diehl and Sagem in Europe have all become key players in many recent initiatives. Few other corporations could manage the enormity of the security contracts implemented post 9/11.

Inevitably, the highly lucrative security-industry complex holds a strong vested interest in the intensification and expansion of border securitisation and in a 'paradigm shift' towards states militarising borders. Within this context, researchers have only just started to map the rapidly emerging industry which seeks to profit from every aspect of migration management, including surveillance, interdiction, detention and deportation. The Transnational Institute (TNI)'s *NeoConOpticon* report in 2009 was an early attempt to get a handle on the reframing of border-security architecture now emerging and the significance of 'inter-operability' in creating flexible systems of security capability sets.[56] TNI's follow-up report, *Eurodrones Inc.*, showed how drone manufacturers had captured the EU policy development process. In each report, the 'primes' are shown to be setting the security research and development agenda, securing generous research subsidies and then pushing for policies that depend on the procurement of their wares.[57]

Martin Lemberg-Petersen has also provided significant insight into this business by identifying the actors and dynamics in the European 'borderscapes' and performing an analysis of what is financing the political economy of private security borderscaping. He too highlights the rise of aggressively lobbying private security companies such as G4S, Finmeccanica and Thales, to which lucrative border security and immigration control contracts are outsourced. Through a complex web of procurement and collusion with banks and policy makers via obscure and secretive EU security policy-making forums, these companies have become an integral part of accelerating hi-tech-based border policy making.

It is important to note that, despite the constant propaganda about perfect technological solutions to social problems, the high-tech border-control industry has also had its fair share of setbacks. In 2011, the US pulled the plug on its attempt to create a virtual border fence along its southern border with Mexico. The 'SBInet project', which began in 2006, was beset by missed deadlines and cost overruns and the Department of Homeland Security ultimately acknowledged that the project, led by Boeing, had cost over $1 billion to cover just 53 miles of Arizonan desert.[58] But one failed technology contract does not a change in policy make, even if the evidence as to the utility, cost-effectiveness and secondary impacts of the technology is damning.[59] The virtual fence has been replaced by only slightly less ambitious but no less costly initiatives using similar technology supplied by different contractors. As migration management becomes increasingly globalised, so the supra-national reach of such mega-security conglomerates has grown to the point that it can confidently seek to extract profits regardless of human rights considerations, because the services and products on offer have already been rolled out in democratic countries. And while migration management is currently focused on national borders, the mobile, scalable and deployable solutions that are being developed may not be limited to control of our external borders in the future.

Resisting containment

A dystopian future that sees refugees failed by governments and crammed into camps and border zones owes as much to the (lack of) vision of western security establishments and the laboratories of their defence research institutes than any evidence-based assessment of the likely impact of climate change on migration.

As immigration and refugee policies become harsher, and the border-control industry consolidates its influence over national policy and procurement, it is hard enough to imagine a just solution for the world's 50 million existing refugees, never mind the 1 billion predicted by Christian Aid in years to come.

In this context, advocating for the rights of 'climate refugees' in isolation – that is, ignoring wider developments in contemporary migration control (and the treatment meted out to other categories of refugee and migrant) – may have limited impact in the future. This is because international law is no longer the principal driving force for national refugee policies; it is nationalism, populism and militarisation, coupled with the tightening high-tech border controls (and its export from Global North to Global South), that is shaping contemporary policy. Scholars and activists are documenting these developments – the deaths, the detention centres, the policies, the new technologies and the corporate profiteering – but this work is currently at the margins of social and environmental justice movements.

In the short-term, it is clear we need countries to work together and through international organisations like the EU and UN to respond to refugee and humanitarian crises – whether it's search-and-rescue in the Mediterranean or support for the admission of Syrian refugees. These initiatives need proper resources, and they need to evolve into more durable solutions.

It should be scandalous that the international community, and the richest countries in the world in particular, are not doing more for refugees; yet the narrative of the European Right is that they are already doing too much. And if countries that gave us the Geneva Conventions are no longer willing to follow the letter and spirit of those laws, do they really expect countries that are less well-equipped to do so?

We also need to think about ways to prevent the application-by-application development of the most dystopian border-security technologies described above. This includes checks on technological development with clear red lines (for example, those demanded by the campaign Stop Killer Robots) and global restrictions on the trade in security and law-enforcement equipment. Those invested in the business of homeland security will never willingly accept this, but the process of education and persuasion can lead to unexpected breakthroughs, as we saw through the Landmines convention, which started when six NGOs decided to work together towards the common goal of ending the use, production and trade in landmines and cluster munitions. But given the difficulty of putting the technological genie back in the proverbial bottle, we also have to think about how to use new technologies of surveillance and location tracking to help people – not just to keep them where they are. With the political will, EUROSUR, the

EU border-surveillance system, could for example easily be developed from an exclusory system to one predicated on saving lives at sea.

This opens the space to look at much more radical policy reforms. Matt Carr, author of *Fortress Europe: Dispatches from a Gated Continent* suggests that if Europe wants to welcome the living and not the dead, it 'needs to abandon an essentially repressive and exclusory approach to border enforcement' which in effect 'accepts migrant deaths as collateral damage'.[60] Refugees receive our pity when what they really need is our solidarity. Yet in rich countries, the frequent appeals and hunger strikes by refugee groups rarely make the news; it is only mass death that commands periodic coverage. If solidarity begins with the recognition and support of other people's demands, then solidarity with refugees and asylum seekers begins with a defence of the right of *all* people to migrate, in support of free movement for survival as well as profit. This can only come about if we end our acquiescence to detention centres, dispersal programmes, off-shore processing, and the forced repatriation of migrants and refugees.

We need alternatives to the emerging paradigm of global apartheid that can trigger a reversal of restrictive policies in Europe and elsewhere. This will only be achieved if immigration policy can be de-coupled from the toxic populist rhetoric and reclaimed from the 'securocrats' of the post-9/11 policing and security revolution. From here, it may be hoped that a positive, alternative agenda around climate-induced migration that looks beyond restrictive migration controls could emerge.

We might take inspiration from Scotland, where in stark contrast to the rest of the UK, and indeed much of the EU, a political party swept to power in May 2015 on a broadly pro-immigration ticket. Greece and Spain are also witnessing pro-immigration parties gaining in popularity. Germany is now leading by example.

This, however, still begs the question of who is allowed to migrate, and why, in our current exclusory migration system. Fundamentally, migration management isn't only about governments keeping people out or militarising their borders against people they see as a risk. It's also about letting the 'right' people in – and in doing so providing businesses with a continued supply of cheap labour. Borders continue to be entirely porous for elites, and malleable for the people that they need to keep profits flowing.

In supporting and building movements that stand up for migrants and refugees we should also consign the idea that climate change will inevitably cause migration – and more importantly the premise that all 'climate refugees' are powerless actors who pose a threat to their neighbours' way of life – to the dustbin. But unless we manage to open the doors for people who need to migrate to actually do so, we will remain complicit in their entrapment in dangerous places.

Notes

1. Webber, F. (2006). Border wars and asylum crimes. *Statewatch*, 3. Retrieved from http://www.statewatch.org/analyses/border-wars-and-asylum-crimes.pdf.

2. High Representative and the European Commission to the European Council. (2008). *Climate Change and International Security*. Retrieved from http://www.consilium.europa.eu/ueDocs/cms_Data/docs/pressdata/EN/reports/99387.pdf.

3. Christian Aid. (2007). *Human Tide: The real migration crisis*. Retrieved from http://www.christianaid.org.uk/Images/human-tide.pdf

4. Su, Y.Y. (2014). The one billion 'climate refugees' that never was: INGOs and the human rights perspective to climate change – induced displacement. *Oxford Monitor of Forced Migration*, 4(1), 19. Retrieved from http://oxmofm.com/wp-content/uploads/2014/05/OxMo-Vol.-4-No.-1-Final.pdf.

5. Ministry of Defence. (2014). *Global Strategic Trends – out to 2045*. Retrieved from https://www.gov.uk/government/uploads/system/uploads/attachment_data/file/348164/20140821_DCDC_GST_5_Web_Secured.pdf

6. The Government Office for Science. (2011). *Foresight: Migration and Global Environmental Change: Final project report*. Retrieved from https://www.gov.uk/government/uploads/system/uploads/attachment_data/file/287717/11-1116-migration-and-global-environmental-change.pdf.

7. Zetter, R. (2008). Legal and normative frameworks. *Forced Migration Review*, 31, 62–3.

8. Jakobeit, C. and Methmann, C. (2012). 'Climate refugees' as dawning catastrophe? A critique of the dominant quest For numbers, in: Scheffran, J., Brzoska, M., Brauch, H.G., Link, P.M. and Schilling, J., eds. *Climate Change, Human Security and Violent Conflict: Challenges for societal stability*. Berlin: Springer.

9. White, G. (2011). *Climate Change and Migration: Security and borders in a warming world*. Oxford: Oxford University Press.

10. Tacoli, C. (2009). *Crisis or adaptation? Migration and Climate Change in a Context of High Mobility*. Retrieved from http://www.unisdr.org/files/12831_popdynamicsclimatechange1.pdf#page=115; Black, R., Bennett, S. R., Thomas, S.M. and Beddington, J.R. (27 October 2011 27). Climate change: Migration as adaptation. Retrieved from http://www.nature.com/nature/journal/v478/n7370/abs/478477a.html.

11. Bettini, G. (8 November 2012). Climate barbarians at the gate? A critique of apocalyptic narratives on 'climate refugees'. Retrieved from http://www.academia.edu/4865081/Climate_Barbarians_at_the_Gate_A_critique_of_apocalyptic_narratives_on_climate_refugees_.

12. Sivanandan, A. (1988). The new racism. *New Statesman and Society*, 1(22), 8–9.

13. Bauman, Z. (2002). *Society Under Siege*. Oxford: Polity Press, p. 84.

14. Heinrich Böll Foundation. (2012, July 16). Borderline – The EU's new border surveillance initiatives. Retrieved from https://www.boell.de/en/content/borderline-eus-new-border-surveillance-initiatives.

15. Bigo, D. (2002). Security and Immigration: Toward a Critique of the Governmentality of Unease. *Alternatives: Global, Local, Political*, 27 (Special Issue), 63–92.

16. Bauman, Z. (2002), p. 90.

17. Nevins, J. (2002). *Operation Gatekeeper: The rise of the 'illegal alien' and the making of the U.S.-Mexico boundary*. New York: Routledge; Nevins, J. (7 July 2006). Boundary enforcement and national security in an age of global apartheid. Speech presented at A fundraiser for La Coalición de Derechos Humanos, Tucson, AZ.

18. Population Division of the United Nations Department of Economic and Social Affairs. (2013). Population facts. *UN Population*, 2013(2). Retrieved from http://esa.un.org/unmigration/documents/The_number_of_international_migrants.pdf.

19. UNHCR. (7 January 2015). UNHCR report shows world's poorest countries host most refugees. Retrieved from http://www.unhcr-centraleurope.org/en/news/2015/unhcr-report-shows-worlds-poorest-countries-host-most-refugees.html.

20. Trombetta, M.J. (28 August 2014). Linking climate-induced migration and security within the EU: Insights from the securitization debate. Retrieved from http://www.tandfonline.com/doi/abs/10.1080/21624887.2014.923699.

21. Oxfam International Secretariat. (2011). Briefing on the Horn of Africa drought: Climate change and future impacts on food security. Retrieved from http://www.preventionweb.net/english/professional/publications/v.php?id=21118.

22. Sherwood, H. (7 December 2014). Take in Syrian refugees, aid agencies tell rich countries. *Guardian*. Retrieved from http://www.theguardian.com/world/2014/dec/08/take-in-syrian-refugees-rich-countries.

23. Transcript of Joint Press Conference. Commonwealth of Australia. 19 July 2013. Retrieved from http://parlinfo.aph.gov.au/parlInfo/search/display/display.w3p;query=Id%3A%22media%2Fpressrel%2F2611766%22.

24. Hurst, D. (20 March 2015). 'Things happen': Tony Abbott on sexual assault allegations in offshore detention. *Guardian*. Retrieved from http://www.theguardian.com/australia-news/2015/mar/20/things-happen-tony-abbott-on-sexual-assault-allegations-in-offshore-detention.

25. Commission to the Council and the European Parliament. (4 June 2004). Communication from the Commission to the Council and the European Parliament on the managed entry in the EU of persons in need of international protection and the enhancement of the protection capacity of the regions of origin 'improving access to durable solutions'. Retrieved from http://eur-lex.europa.eu/legal-content/EN/TXT/?uri=CELEX:52004DC0410.

26. United Nations High Commission on Refugees. (2006). *The State of the World's Refugees 2006: Human displacement in the new millennium.* Oxford: Oxford University Press, pp. 114–15.

27. Prasad, R. (10 February 2013). Refugee camps don't work. *Guardian*. Retrieved from http://www.theguardian.com/uk/2003/feb/10/immigration.raekhaprasad.

28. Strategy paper on immigration and asylum policy. EU Council document 9809/98, 1 July 1998. Retrieved from http://database.statewatch.org/e-library/1998-9809-strategypaper-immigrationasylum.pdf.

29. Green, P. and Grewcock, M. (2002). The war against illegal immigration. *Current Issues in Criminal Justice*, 14(1).

30. European Parliamentary Research Service. (March 2015). Asylum in the EU: Facts and Figures. Retrieved from http://epthinktank.eu/tag/eprs-briefings/.

31. Fargues, P. and Di Bartolomeo, A. (2015). *Drowned Europe* (report). Migration Policy Centre, European University Institute. Retrieved from http://cadmus.eui.eu/bitstream/handle/1814/35557/MPC_2015_05_PB.pdf?sequence=1.

32. Traynor, I. (6 March 2015). EU plan to set up migrant centers in counties outside EU borders, *Guardian*, p. 29.

33. GuardianWitness. (September 2013). Are you hemmed in by a separation wall or security fence? *Guardian*. Retrieved from https://witness.theguardian.com/assignment/51f7a7c5e4b0472f65d02668?INTCMP=mic_2781.

34. Graham, S. (2009). The urban 'battlespace. *Theory, Culture & Society*, 26(7–8), 278–88. Retrieved from doi:10.1177/0263276409349280.

35. BBC. (10 March 2014). Spain admits use of rubber bullets on migrants was wrong. Retrieved from http://www.bbc.co.uk/news/world-europe-26516703.

36. Feng, S., Krueger, A.B. and Oppenheimer, M. (2010). Linkages among climate change, crop yields and Mexico-US cross-border migration. *Proceedings of the National Academy of Sciences*, 107(32), 14257–62. Retrieved from doi:10.1073/pnas.1002632107

37. Hamro-Drotz, D. (2014). Conflict-sensitive adaptation to climate change in Africa, *Livelihood Security: Climate change, migration and conflict in the Sahel*, p. 195. Retrieved from http://postconflict.unep.ch/publications/UNEP_Sahel_EN.pdf.

38. Panda, A. (n.d.). Climate induced migration from Bangladesh to India: Issues and challenges. *SSRN Electronic Journal*. Retrieved from doi:10.2139/ssrn.2186397.

39. Secure enough. *The Economist* (22 June 2013). Retrieved from http://www.economist.com/news/united-states/21579828-spending-billions-more-fences-and-drones-will-do-more-harm-good-secure-enough.

40. Hayes, B. and Vermeulen, M. (2012). *Borderline: the EU's new border surveillance initiatives*. Heinrich Böll Foundation. Retrieved from www.statewatch.org/news/2012/jun/borderline.pdf.

41. Hayes, B., Jones, C. and Toepfer, E. (5 February 2014). *Eurodrones, Inc.* Amsterdam: Transnational Institute. Retrieved from http://www.tni.org/eurodrones.

42. Their official wish-list included: lasers and heat beams designed to disperse crowds; nausea-inducing sound waves targeted at scuba divers; the Impulse Swimmer Gun, described as being able to 'suppress underwater swimmers and divers'; system designed to move people through an area by emitting a 'heat sensation' causing 'involuntary movement'; electro-muscular pulses which 'substantially increase' the time a hostile person can be incapacitated; a portable system which emits high-powered microwaves capable of stalling a car engine at a distance, and an unmanned, airborne vessel equipped with a microwave-emitting device capable of preventing a ship's propulsion by causing 'electrical system malfunction'.

43. Doucet, I. and Lloyd, R. (2001). *Alternative Anti-personnel Mines: The next generations*. Landmine Action.

44. Arthur, C. and Wright, S. (5 October 2006). Targeting the pain business. *Guardian*. Retrieved from http://www.theguardian.com/technology/2006/oct/05/guardianweeklytechnologysection.

45. Raytheon. (n.d.). *Silent Guardian® SG-R50: Point Defense Short-Range Deterrent*. Retrieved from http://www.atmarine.fi/ckfinder/userfiles/files/Silent%20Guardian%20SG-R50.pdf.

46. Davison, N. (2009). *'Non-Lethal' Weapons*. London: Palgrave.

47. Amnesty International (2003) The Pain Merchants – Security equipment and its use in torture and other ill treatment. Retrieved from http://www.amnesty.org/en/documents/ACT40/008/2003/en/.

48. US Department of Defense Non-Lethal Weapons Program. (June 2012). Newsletter. Retrieved from http://jnlwp.defense.gov/Portals/50/Documents/Press_Room/Newsletters/Newsletter_053112.pdf.

49. Vance, A. (11 April 2003). The self-healing, self-hopping landmine. *Register*. Retrieved from http://www.theregister.co.uk/2003/04/11/the_selfhealing_selfhopping_landmine/.

50. Metal Storm's virtual minefield gets a patent. *Gizmag*. (26 January 2010). Retrieved from http://www.ideaconnection.com/newinventions/metal-storm-virtual-minefield-03248.html.

51. U.S. Border Agency has considered weaponizing domestic drones to 'immobilize' people. *Slate*. (3 July 2013). Retrieved from http://www.slate.com/blogs/future_tense/2013/07/03/documents_show_customs_and_border_protection_considered_weaponized_domestic.html.

52. Korean machine-gun robots start DMZ duty. *Cnet.com*. (14 July 2010). Retrieved http://news. cnet.com/8301-17938_105-20010533-1.html.

53. Packs of robots will hunt down uncooperative humans. *New Scientist*. (22 October 2008). Retrieved from http://www.newscientist.com/blogs/shortsharpscience/2008/10/packs-of-robots-will-hunt-down.html

54. Saudi Arabia Securing its Borders with Sensors and Software. *National Defense Magazine*. (December 2009). Retrieved from http://www.nationaldefensemagazine.org/archive/2009/December/Pages/SaudiArabiaSecuringitsBorderswithSensorsandSoftware.aspx.

55. Tomgram: Miller and Schivone, bringing the battlefield to the border. *TomDispatch.com*. (25 January 2015). Retrieved from http://www.tomdispatch.com/blog/175947/tomgram%3A_miller_and_schivone,_bringing_the_battlefield_to_the_border/.

56. Hayes, B. (2009).

57. Hayes, B., Jones, C. and Toepfer, E. (5 February 2014).

58. Pelofsky, J. (15 January 2011). Administration giving up on full 'virtual fence' on border. *Washington Post*. Retrieved from http://www.washingtonpost.com/wp-dyn/content/article/2011/01/14/AR2011011406893.html.

59. Webber, F. (2012). *Borderline Justice: The fight for refugee and migrant rights*. London: Pluto. See also Secure enough. *The Economist*. (22 June 2013).

60. Carr, M. (2014). 'We want to welcome the living, not the dead': Borders, deaths and resistance. *Statewatch Journal*, 23(3/4), February. Retrieved from http://www.statewatch.org/subscriber/protected/statewatch-journal-vol23n34.pdf.

6

THE FIX IS IN: (GEO)ENGINEERING OUR WAY OUT OF THE CLIMATE CRISIS?

Kathy Jo Wetter and Silvia Ribeiro, ETC Group

David Keith: '... you could actually spray sulphuric acid in the stratosphere 20 kilometers over our head and use that to stop the planet warming ... You put, say, 20,000 tons of sulphuric acid into the stratosphere every year and each year you have to put a little more ... so people are terrified about talking about this because they're scared that it will prevent us cutting emissions.'

Stephen Colbert: 'Right, and also that it is sulphuric acid.'

Harvard Professor David Keith promoting his book, A Case for Climate Engineering, *on The Colbert Report, 9 December 2013*

Introduction

When the Intergovernmental Panel on Climate Change's (IPCC) published the first instalment of its latest Assessment Report in September 2013, the final paragraph of its *Summary for Policymakers* invoked geoengineering – defined in the report as proposals that 'aim to deliberately alter the climate system to counter climate change'.[1]

The IPCC's inclusion of geoengineering was a watershed moment. The IPCC represents the consensus position of the international scientific community and this marked the first time the data-driven group mentioned speculative, climate-altering technologies in an Assessment Report.[2] The paragraph alluded to geoengineering's associated uncertainties and risks and fell far short of an endorsement; it pointed out that geoengineering schemes 'carry side effects and long-term consequences on a global scale'.[3] But the fact that the IPCC gave the last word to an unproven technofix reveals both the dismal state of efforts to curb climate change and a willingness to contemplate a formerly taboo climate change response. Ken Caldeira, a geoengineering proponent and climate researcher at the Carnegie Institution for Science, told *Nature* that he understood the inclusion of geoengineering in the report as 'a reflection of growing governmental interest in these ideas'.[4] The author of the article in which Caldeira's quote appeared presented the IPCC's hat-tip to geoengineering as a sign that 'the controversial area is now firmly on the scientific agenda.'[5]

The proof of principle – that cumulative, local interventions in ecosystems can bring about planetary-level effects – is beyond dispute. That was demonstrated by the Industrial Revolution and why we have human-induced climate change. None the less, as we approach so-called climate 'tipping points', the notion of intentionally changing the climate is gaining ground: the idea that we can apply new technologies as an emergency measure to purposefully intervene and correct the inadvertent but serious harm we've done to the planet.

But geoengineering's implications go beyond a risky (and speculative) corrective to climate change. Geoengineering offers the possibility of bringing together corporate and military aspirations in an unprecedented way: not just *owning nature* but also *controlling nature*. While weather-as-weapon is not a new idea, the spectre of (theoretical) climate control in the midst of intensified state-resource grabs (including food-related land and water grabs) and corporate profit seeking raises serious concerns related to global (climate) justice, in addition to the serious risks to environment and health. That geo-engineering is being contemplated as a potentially unavoidable 'Plan B' by some 'liberal' policy makers, scientists and academics – while at the same time, it is being embraced by neoconservatives as an end-of-pipe innovation that will enable unrestricted economic growth – increases the likelihood that geoengineering will be pursued; and this increases the urgent need for vigilant resistance.

(Re)defining geoengineering

A wide range of approaches to alter the earth's systems has been variously placed under the geoengineering umbrella, most commonly divided (by governments and academics) into two categories: technologies that deflect sunlight away from the earth and technologies that remove, capture and/or store carbon dioxide (CO_2).[6] A third category of 'weather-modification' techniques, some of which have been practiced since the mid-twentieth century (for example, 'cloud seeding'), is sometimes included in discussions of geoengineering. Whether or not weather modification is included depends largely on who's talking. Geoengineering advocates who exclude (or, more commonly, ignore) weather modification often base the exclusion on definitional parameters related to scale or temporality,[7] but weather modification's dubious efficacy and historical use as a clandestine weapon of war may also help explain the reluctance of geoengineering advocates to claim weather modification as a cohort of the climate-engineering project.[8] Especially given the interdependent relationship between weather and climate ('climate is an average pattern of weather for a particular region', according to NASA[9]), the argument that weather modification should be excluded from geoengineer-ing discussions is not persuasive.

Harvard physicist and geoengineering advocate David Keith has described geoengineering in the context of climate change as 'a countervailing measure, one that uses additional technology to counteract unwanted side effects without eliminating their root cause, "a technical fix".[10]

However, as geoengineering is discussed in more contexts and its circumscription becomes more consequential – with possible legal and public-relations implications – there are attempts to fix a definition, which sometimes means getting away from the term 'geoengineering' altogether. The scientists who gathered in 2010 for an international conference in Asilomar, California, to consider 'voluntary guidelines' for research, for example, not only studiously avoided the term 'geoengineering', but they also sought to re-brand 'solar radiation management' as 'climate intervention' and carbon-dioxide removal as 'carbon remediation'. The statement made by the Scientific Organizing Committee at the close of the meeting did not make mention of geoengineering (or, for that matter, the voluntary standards the meeting was explicitly convened to develop).[11]

While different governments, academic institutions and multilateral bodies may end up circumscribing geoengineering differently, there is general agreement on geoengineering's defining features. First, geoengineering is deliberate (even if it has unintended impacts). Unintentional harm to the global environment from other activities (for example, agriculture, industrial processes) is thus (far) excluded. Second, geoengineering will have global, or at least 'large-scale', effects, even if deployment/application is 'local'. And third, geoengineering is understood to be a high-technology approach involving unknown risk to the environment: changing consumption patterns or adopting agro-ecological practices, for example, do not qualify, even though either could have a significant impact on the environment.

These general definitional characteristics are useful; however, it is important to recognise their problematic imprecisions. It is also likely that if geoengineering techniques are realised, their deployment will not be limited to instances of so-called 'climate emergencies'. Geoengineering schemes could be deployed to 'manage' other earth systems, such as the hydrological or nitrogen cycles, or even to 'improve' conditions for food production.[12] While it may be useful to refer to climate impacts for descriptive purposes, it would be shortsighted to think that climate-change mitigation will be the sole deployment context.

It is also crucial to recognise that defining geoengineering is more than describing the scope and features of earth-altering techniques; it is a political act and a reflection of a particular worldview. Geoengineering contrasts sharply with the notion of stewardship: Geoengineers see ecosystems as resources to be improved, optimised, or 'fixed' rather than systems to be protected and restored. Ecologist-activist Vandana Shiva has suggested that geoengineering reflects the 'paradigm that created the fossil fuel age that gave us climate change'.[13] Shiva argues, 'To now offer that same mindset as a solution is to not take seriously what Einstein said: that you can't solve the problems by using the same mindset that caused them.'[14] The ETC Group has referred to geoengineering as 'geopiracy' to underline our position that in the absence of global governance – implying informed consent by the world's peoples – geoengineering is both illegal and immoral.

A brief history of 'climate engineering'

The idea that geoengineering could be a potential response to anthropogenic climate change isn't new. As early as 1965, the US President's Science Advisory Committee warned in a report, *Restoring the Quality of Our Environment*, that CO_2 pollution was modifying the earth's heat balance.[15] That report, regarded as the first high-level acknowledgment of climate change, went on to recommend – instead of emissions reductions – a suite of geoengineering options. The authors of the report asserted, 'The possibilities of deliberately bringing about countervailing climatic changes ... need to be thoroughly explored.'[16] They suggested reflective particles could be dispersed on tropical seas (at an annual cost of around $500 million), which might also inhibit hurricane formation. The Committee also speculated about using clouds to counteract warming. As James Fleming, a leading historian of weather modification, wryly notes, the first-ever official report on ways to address climate change 'failed to mention the most obvious option: reducing fossil fuel use'.[17] Another report published in 1965, the US National Science Foundation's (NSF) *Weather and Climate Modification*, emphasised the 'exciting', long-range aspects of 'man's achieving the ability to modify the atmospheric environment'.[18]

The mid-1970s' revelations of clandestine acts of weather warfare during the Vietnam War (leading to the ENMOD treaty) dampened enthusiasm for weather and climate modification,[19] but the reality of climate change helped revive it around the turn of the millennium. In 2002, Paul J. Crutzen – who won a Nobel Prize for pioneering work on the ozone layer and is a professor at the Max Planck Institute for Chemistry in Mainz, Germany – offered grudging support for geoengineering in the journal *Nature*. Since we are living in the 'Anthropocene' – the era in which humans are increasingly affecting the climate – Crutzen suggested our future 'may well involve internationally accepted, large-scale geoengineering projects'.[20] The same year, *Science* published its own article that argued for geoengineering as a legitimate approach to combating climate change.[21]

Three years later in 2005, and forty years after the release of the Science Advisory Committee and NSF reports, everybody – including the sitting US president George W. Bush – was talking about global warming, as scientists warned that the temperature rise on the Arctic ice cap and Siberian permafrost could 'tip' the planet into an environmental tailspin.

The failure to reach a meaningful multilateral consensus on emissions reduction at the UN Framework Climate on Climate Change's 15th Conference of the Parties in Copenhagen in 2009 – despite the largest mobilisation for climate justice to date – offered geoengineers a more popular public platform. As delegates were heading to the airport to catch their flights home, entrepreneur and geoengineering advocate Nathan Myhrvold gave a 30-minute interview to CNN, extolling the virtues of putting sulphate particles into the stratosphere as a solution to global warming. He explained how a 25-kilometre hose held up by balloons could deliver the particles to the right place to reflect sunlight away from the earth.[22]

Myhrvold, a former chief technology officer at Microsoft, is founder and CEO of Intellectual Ventures Management, LLC, which holds patents on geoengineering technologies. Ken Caldeira and John Latham of the National Center for Atmospheric Research in the US are listed among the firm's senior inventors, whom Intellectual Ventures supports with funding and business expertise. The firm files hundreds of patent applications annually. Caldeira and Harvard's David Keith jointly manage the Fund for Innovative Climate and Energy Research (FICER), bankrolled by Bill Gates's personal funds. Since 2007, FICER has given out $4.6 million in research grants, but recent information on its activities is scarce. (David Keith's 2013 book, *A Case for Climate Engineering*, merited a back-cover endorsement blurb from Gates, who claims that Keith's book lays out 'a compelling argument about the need for serious research on geo-engineering and for a robust policy discussion on its possible use'.)

The UK's Royal Society and the National Academy of Sciences in the US have both already spent money and time bringing experts together to speculate about geoengineering's prospects and have found, thus far, no sufficiently compelling reasons to take geoengineering 'off the table'.[23] A handful of dedicated geoengineering research projects are known to be currently funded by governments, and government-supported governance initiatives, such as the Solar Radiation Management Research Governance Initiative (SRMGI), largely funded by the UK's Royal Society; also the Gates-funded FICER, and the Climate Geoengineering Governance project, supported by two UK Research Councils, are up and running. (See below for a discussion of geoengineering governance.)

Just as its inclusion in the IPCC report was seen to confer scientific legitimacy on geoengineering, gatherings of august national science bodies and the establishment of university-based research programmes focused on geoengineering produce a similarly legitimising effect. (It appears, however, that the effect of the involvement of the US 'intelligence community' in a project to evaluate the technical merits of geoengineering proposals is less soothing for media commentators.[24])

Climate sceptics and profit prophets: Geoengineering in the service of capitalism

One striking effect of geoengineering's ascendency has been an alignment of positions that were previously diametrically opposed. While some long-time climate scientists such as Crutzen and Caldeira claim to have only gradually and reluctantly embraced geoengineering out of a fear of global warming's devastating effects, a new and powerful lobby for geoengineering has emerged in recent years, made up of people whose motivation has never been concern for the planet or its poorest inhabitants.

In June 2008, Newt Gingrich, former Speaker of the House in the US Congress, sent a letter to hundreds of thousands of Americans, urging them to oppose proposed legislation to address global warming through emissions reductions. Gingrich argued for geoengineering the atmosphere with sulphates as a better option to fight climate change. 'Geoengineering holds forth the promise of addressing global warming concerns for just a few billion dollars a year', wrote Gingrich. 'Instead of penalizing ordinary Americans, we would have an option to address global warming by rewarding scientific innovation … Bring on the American Ingenuity. Stop the green pig.'[25]

Gingrich, author of *Drill Here, Drill Now, Pay Less* and senior fellow at the American Enterprise Institute (AEI), a neoconservative think tank promoting free enterprise and limited government, was closely associated with the George W. Bush administration. AEI had its own geoengineering project led by Lee Lane, an advisor to the Bush administration, now at the Hudson Institute, another neoconservative think tank. In 2009, Lane and co-author J. Eric Bickel published *An Analysis of Climate Engineering as a Response to Climate Change*, a report advocating the addition of geoengineering to existing responses to climate change on the basis of a cost-benefit analysis. Lane and Bickel claimed spraying seawater into clouds could fix climate change and thereby add $20 trillion to the global economy.

The report was published and widely broadcast by Bjørn Lomborg's Copenhagen Consensus Center (CCC).[26] Lomborg is best known as the self-styled and controversial 'Skeptical Environmentalist' who has consistently downplayed the seriousness of climate change. Lomborg is now using his CCC and prominent media profile to push for geoengineering not as 'Plan B', but as 'Plan A' – the preferred route to cooling the planet.

The 'Lomborg manoeuvre' – switching from opposing action on climate change to supporting the most extreme action on climate change – is now seemingly de rigueur among industrial apologists and former climate-change sceptics, especially in the United States. Besides the Hudson Institute and AEI, political operators at the Cato Institute, the Thomas Jefferson Institute, the Hoover Institution, the Competitive Enterprise Institute, the International Policy Network and elsewhere have professed their faith in the geoengineering gospel. Geoengineering has been a mainstay of discussion for several years now at the International Conference on Climate Change, an annual jamboree for climate deniers organised by the Heartland Institute, dubbed by the *New York Times* 'the primary American organization pushing climate change skepticism'.[27]

For those who previously doubted (or still do doubt) the science of anthropogenic global warming, the geoengineering approach shifts the discussion from reducing emissions to end-of-pipe 'solutions'. Once geoengineering is an option, there is less need to bicker about who put the CO_2 in the atmosphere (and less need to ask them to stop). If we have the means to suck up greenhouse gases or turn down the thermostat, emitters can, in principle, continue unabated.

'Owning the weather': Intellectual property and geoengineering

Adding to the controversy surrounding geoengineering are the critical issues of ownership and control. An early survey of geoengineering patenting concludes that patents are broad, increasing in number, and concentrated in a small number of owners.[28]

In multilateral fora, intellectual property (IP) is almost always a contentious issue: governments from the Global South generally advocate for enabling greater transfer of useful technologies, including significant financing from developed countries, arguing that existing IP regimes are a barrier to accessing the technologies necessary to mitigate and adapt to climate change. The North advocates – and generally gets – strong protection of intellectual property, arguing that high profits derived from IP drives innovation and, eventually, the transfer of technologies. If geoengineering techniques move toward deployment, the existence of patents held by individuals and private companies could mean that decisions over the climate-commons will be effectively handed over to the private sector. Indeed, some geoengineers are already claiming that their patents give them extended commercial rights over the commons in which they operate. One of several patents assigned to Ian S.F. Jones, founder and CEO of Ocean Nourishment Corporation and professor at the University of Sydney, for example, explains how the described method of ocean fertilisation will increase fish populations; the patent claims ownership of the fish subsequently harvested from a fertilised patch of ocean.[29]

Some geoengineering patents also effectively privatise indigenous and traditional knowledge, most clearly demonstrable in the area of biochar. The technique of burying charcoal in soil was widely practiced by communities throughout the Amazonian Basin before the turn of the first millennium, where it was known as *Terra Preta*. This technology is now the subject of several patent applications.[30]

As other technology innovators have done (in software, biotechnology, robotics), some geoengineers are considering forgoing their intellectual property claims in order to speed up development of the technology. David Keith has filed for patents on carbon-capture technologies and heads a start-up company called Carbon Engineering, but has said more recently that he believes that 'core' geoengineering technologies should remain in the public domain.[31]

Governing Gaia?

Looking into the future to the time when field experiments with weather or climate modification are expanded in scope and number and involve actual attempts to introduce changes in the atmosphere, some form of international collaboration will be essential in the planning and execution of projects that may have an effect not only upon the immediate localities but on areas in other countries and even upon other continents distant from the scene of work ... Steps should be taken by the United States, in concert with other nations, to explore the international institutional mechanisms that may be appropriate to foster international cooperation and cope with the problems which may be anticipated in the field of weather and climate modification. The United Nations and its specialized agencies (e.g., the World Meteorological Organization) is suggested as a possible intergovernmental framework.

US National Science Foundation, Report of the Special Commission on
Weather Modification, Weather and Climate Modification, 1965, pp. 26, 28.

The political context of climate manipulation has shifted in the fifty years since the NSF's Special Commission published its report. While the 'energy crisis' of the 1970s and later, the spectre of 'peak oil', provided the early impetus for developing alternative energy and 'renewables', the debate has moved beyond how much fossil fuel remains to how much greenhouse gas our planet and its inhabitants can tolerate – and what happens to some very big economies and corporations if fossil fuels stay in the ground and can no longer be tallied as assets. States in the Global North – the countries responsible for most of the historic greenhouse-gas emissions and which have either denied climate change or prevaricated for decades – have fuelled geoengineering's recent momentum.

Geoengineering's (re)emergence as a proposed solution to the climate crisis comes in the context of growing public unease and increasingly devastating climate-change impacts, where OECD (Organisation for Economic Cooperation and Development) member countries, in particular, are feeling pressure to adopt policies to dramatically cut fossil-fuel consumption and concomitant GHG emissions. This is where geoengineering technologies, 'unconventional energy' technologies to increase reserves (for example, fracking, methane hydrate extraction), the interests of the 'supermajors' (the world's biggest oil companies), and the interests of the world's biggest greenhouse-gas emitters come together. If technologies are able to capture the carbon and lower the thermostat as well as 'enhance' oil recovery, then there is no need to shake up the global economic status quo or to inconvenience the electorate by asking citizens to change how they live their lives. As Clive Hamilton of Charles Sturt University, Canberra, puts it, the political appeal of technofixes such as geoengineering is that they offer hope of solving a problem 'that would otherwise require social change'.[32] At the same time, geoengineering could offer a lifeline to the major private- and state-sector players – the 'old guard geoengineers' – that profited from the climate-changing industries of the twentieth century. These are the geopolitical realities that cannot be set aside in discussions of the development, deployment and governance of geoengineering.

Gaia is complicated, and despite decades of modelling, we are still unlikely to predict next month's best picnic day. From stratospheric currents to undersea methane hydrates – and from plankton to palm tree emissions and sequestrations – quantifying and qualifying planetary systems is challenging and continually under revision. But we need to know – accurately – what life on earth will be like (in every place on earth) at higher levels of GHG concentrations. The IPCC can offer us scenarios, but not certainty. We also need to know – accurately – who's reducing emissions and who's effectively cooking the books, as the US did when it reported significantly lower emissions but exported its coal-related emissions by selling surplus coal supplies to Asia.[33] Without that knowledge, how could we decide that it's time to deploy geoengineering technologies? In other words, how will we come to agreement that a 'climate emergency' is imminent, or even already underway?

Reducing GHG emissions is complicated. Not reducing emissions is bound to prove more complicated. Moving perhaps a billion people from coastal plains to higher ground will be extremely difficult. Sorting out correctly which crops can grow where will be hugely critical and equally complex. Responding to extreme hydrothermal events (for example, floods, droughts, typhoons) will be excruciating – and costly. That all of these challenges will also be political compounds the problem, even though every government will claim 'sound science' as their basis for decision making. Now, by advancing geoengineering as a postponement of climate change or even as part of a solution, scientists are compounding the complexity by several orders of magnitude and rendering the politics of climate governance still more opaque.

Geoengineering may appear a prudent Plan B until we acknowledge how it compounds complexity, and how experimental manipulations of earth systems could change everything for everybody, even those living 'distant from the scene of work', as was understood fifty years ago by the authors of NSF's report on climate modification but seems to have been forgotten in the intervening decades. Similarly, attempts to work out geoengineering governance frameworks may appear prudent and even lamentably inchoate until we acknowledge how audaciously premature those discussions are, given the uncertainties and risks.

Who has the right to deploy geoengineering technologies in the global commons (seas, space, stratosphere)? Will there be liability for unintended transboundary effects? How could those effects be proven? What are the implications of one country, corporation, or even one extremely rich person deciding unilaterally – or as part of a 'coalition of the willing' – to pursue deployment of geoengineering technologies?

Morally and politically, climate engineering requires global governance.

The United Nations Convention on Biological Diversity (CBD) was the first multilateral body to begin tackling the issue of global geoengineering governance. Rather than establishing a framework to facilitate possible deployment, the CBD, in 2008, adopted a moratorium on one geoengineering technique: ocean fertilisation. At its 10th Conference of the Parties in 2010 in Nagoya, Japan, the CBD's 193 Parties agreed to expand that moratorium to cover all geoengineering technologies, marking geoengineering's 'definite coming of age', according to *The Economist*.[34] While carving out an exemption for small-scale scientific experiments in controlled settings within national jurisdiction, the CBD decision invoked the precautionary approach to prohibit geoengineering activities until social, economic and environmental impacts have been properly considered and a regulatory mechanism is in place.[35] (The CBD has almost universal state membership; however, the United States, along with Andorra, the Vatican and South Sudan, have not ratified the treaty. Significantly, the CBD has a mandate to not only consider biodiversity, but also to involve local communities and indigenous peoples in its processes.)

The likelihood of the UN's members agreeing that the deployment of geoengineering is in the best interest of all Parties is vanishingly minuscule, but in the absence of global agreement, geoengineering is indefensible. Would governments, then, act unilaterally? Today's climate-change 'Hot War' could come to resemble the 'Cold War' that dominated global politics after the Second World War. During that period, countries, including the United States, Russia, China, the UK, France, India, Israel and Pakistan, felt morally qualified to unilaterally jeopardise planetary security and risk nuclear war by exploding 459 nuclear bombs (most above international waters) that were ultimately shown to damage the health and well-being of not only their own citizens but of the world.[36] The political/scientific complex initially denied the dangers of atmospheric nuclear testing and then tried to underplay the dangers until forced into – decades later – a nuclear test ban treaty.

Similarly, unilateral geoengineering initiatives represent a direct threat to global security and invite – almost require – responses from other governments. Ocean and SRM interventions, in particular, would likely spur an escalation of meteorological experimentation that could quickly spin out of control. Before that happens, it's time for a geoengineering test ban.

Conclusion

In April 2010, the World Peoples' Conference on Climate Change and the Rights of Mother Earth, held in Cochabamba, Bolivia, brought together more than 25,000 *campesinos*, teachers, students, engineers, activists, diplomats, elders and ordinary folk to discuss how best to minimise the impacts of global warming and to respond to the failure of negotiations at the UN Framework Climate on Climate Change to bring about reductions in global GHG emissions. Seventeen working groups contributed to a Peoples' Agreement, which explicitly rejected geoengineering as a solution to climate change.[37] From Cochabamba, the Hands Off Mother Earth (HOME) campaign to oppose geoengineering experiments was launched.[38]

In the meantime, a small but influential group of researchers has increased calls for governments to support geoengineering experiments as part of developing a 'Plan B'[39] in the event of a 'climate emergency'[40] – despite the adoption of the decision to restrict geo-engineering activities by the UN's Convention on Biological Diversity in October 2010.

Governments are being persuaded: As this chapter was in press, the US's National Academies, 'Advisers to the Nation on Science, Engineering and Medicine', released two reports: one on CDR and one on SRM (the latter is referred to by the authors using the term 'albedo modification').[41] The reports recommend government investment in dedicated research and development programs for both CDR and SRM. Not all authors agreed, however; one author, a professor of geophysical sciences at the University of Chicago who contributed to the report's technical evaluation, warned: 'Developing albedo-modification technology would be like giving a loaded gun to a child.'[42]

From some perspectives, it may seem responsible to keep all climate-change response options and a 'Plan B' on the table, and support for geoengineering research has been promoted as a prudent, practical and even precautionary 'insurance policy'.[43] But geo-engineering's prudence will not be universally obvious. If you are one of the members of the G8 that launched the Industrial Revolution responsible for anthropogenic climate change and your GHG emissions keep going up instead of down, it may be easier to appreciate the attraction of a technofix. But for poor communities in the South, further tampering with the climate by unaccountable elites is, not surprisingly, seen differently. As Professor Simon Dalby has argued, 'old-fashioned geopolitics' may bring about 'temporary violent fixes to some of the symptoms of climate change. But by no stretch of the imagination will such geopolitics be climate security in any sense that matters either for the poorer parts of humanity in this generation or for future generations.'[44] For Dalby, 'the key point now is not what climate change will do for geopolitics, but what geopolitics does to climate change', which 'now has to be about sharing a crowded world rather than trying to dominate a divided one'.[45]

A reasoned rejection of geoengineering's technofix on precautionary, political, technical and/or moral grounds does not imply a denial that science and technology have important roles to play in dealing with climate change. It is urgent and important that the scientific community work with national as well as local governments to monitor, accurately relay and address the climate threats ahead. This collaborative effort will require a lot of investment and focused energy. The practical responses to climate change must change with the latitudes, altitudes and ecosystems. However, once we acknowledge the current geopolitical realities of climate change, the 'temporary violent fixes' that geoengineering offers are specious at best; at worst, they are *geopiracy* and a threat to us all.

ANNEX: OVERVIEW OF GEOENGINEERING TECHNOLOGIES AND THEIR POSSIBLE EFFECTS

It cannot be over-emphasised that 1) geoengineering is untested and its technologies remain largely in the realm of the theoretical, with some notable exceptions (see below), and 2) the effects of geoengineered climate interventions are not known. Techniques that alter the composition of the stratosphere or the chemistry of the oceans are expected to have unequal impacts on both ecosystems and societies around the world.[46] Some anticipated effects are described below. Geoengineering will surely have unintended consequences, as well, due to any number of factors, including inadequate understanding of ecosystems, biodiversity and the earth's climate; unforeseen natural phenomena; mechanical failure; human error, irreversibility and/or funding lapses.

Solar radiation management

So-called solar radiation management (SRM) technologies aim to counter the earth-warming effect of greenhouse gases (GHGs) by increasing the radiation of sunlight back into space. SRM encompasses a variety of proposed techniques, including blasting particles in the stratosphere to reflect the sun's rays, blocking incoming sunlight with 'space shades', covering deserts with reflective plastic and genetically engineering crops so their leaves might reflect more sunlight. None of these technologies lowers concentrations of GHGs in the atmosphere; the intention is only to counter some of the unwanted effects of high concentrations of GHGs.

Despite SRM's growing presence in both scientific literature and popular culture,[47] it remains a theoretical climate-change response. And despite a range of proposed ways to 'manage' solar radiation (see Box 6.1, below), the ascendant vision is also the most radical: to continuously disperse particles of sulphur dioxide (or sulphuric acid vapour) into the stratosphere to scatter sunlight – in effect, to mimic the effects of a volcanic eruption, which is known to produce a cooling effect.

Proponents have said so often that SRM would be easy and inexpensive to deploy that the question of mechanics and cost have, for the moment, been largely set aside.[48] An exception is the so-called SPICE (Stratospheric Particle Injection for Climate Engineering) experiment, a major research project involving four UK universities, three of the UK's research councils, and the Marshall Aerospace and Defence Group, which began in 2011 to investigate the feasibility of putting particles into the stratosphere. One of the project's streams of work included an outdoor trial of a mini-version of a proposed SRM deployment mechanism, which involved a reinforced garden hose – 1 kilometre long – tethered to a balloon. (The trial would have dispersed water instead of reflective particles, and the hose was one-twentieth the length that actual stratospheric injection would require.)

However, the 'test bed' portion of SPICE never got off the ground; it was cancelled amid controversy, which included an open letter signed by seventy organisations from around the world, expressing opposition and dubbing the experiment the 'Trojan Hose'.[49] Opponents considered the experiment politically damaging to the UK government with respect to ongoing multilateral climate negotiations, as well as a dangerous distraction from the need to cut GHG emissions – immediately and deeply – in order to curb climate change.

Even proponents of SRM largely acknowledge that, as currently envisioned, SRM has the potential to cause environmental harm, including changing weather patterns and reducing rainfall, damaging the ozone layer, diminishing biodiversity, reducing the effectiveness of solar cells and/or causing sudden and dramatic climatic changes if deployment is stopped, either intentionally or unintentionally.[50] SRM might be able to keep temperatures from rising – though this is not a certainty – but it will definitely not address the problem of ocean acidification or atmospheric GHGs, both of which would likely increase in a solar-managed world.[51]

Artificial 'volcanic eruptions':
Continuously spraying particles (for example, sulphur, titanium dioxide) into the stratosphere to increase reflection of incoming solar radiation; particles could be injected into the stratosphere by, for example, airplanes, artillery, hoses held aloft by giant balloons.

Desert blankets:
Covering large expanses of desert with reflective material.

Space sunshades:
One suggestion describes launching trillions of small, free-flying spacecraft a million miles above the Earth to form a cylindrical cloud 60,000 miles long to divert about 10 percent of sunlight away from the planet.

Arctic ice covering:
Covering snowpack or glaciers in the Arctic with insulating material or a nanoscale film to reflect sunlight and prevent melting.

'Climate-ready' crops:
Includes genetically engineering plants to increase reflectivity, as well as plans to engineer crops and trees to be drought, heat, or saline resistant.

Space mirrors:
Putting a superfine reflective mesh of aluminium between the earth and the sun.

Large-scale land-use change/rainwater harvesting:
Engineering large-scale changes in water movements in order to provoke cloud formation to reflect sunlight.

Carbon dioxide removal, carbon capture and storage, bioenergy with carbon capture and storage

In its *Summary for Policymakers* in 2013, the IPCC was unequivocal: 'A large fraction of anthropogenic climate change resulting from CO_2 emissions is irreversible on a multi-century to millennial time scale, except in the case of a large net removal of CO_2 from the atmosphere over a sustained period.'[52] That large net removal refers to still largely theoretical and/or problematic carbon dioxide removal (CDR) technologies that include biological means (such as biomass-based energy with carbon storage and ocean fertilisation) and mechanical/chemical means (such as direct air capture with carbon storage) (see Box 6.2). While the *Summary* document does not assess the likelihood of a successful and 'large' net removal of CO_2, the full report (over 1,500 pages long) dims the prospects considerably by detailing the ways CDR is both speculative and risky. According to the IPCC, most CDR methods

... cannot be scaled up indefinitely and are necessarily limited by various physical or environmental constraints, such as competing demands for land ... Direct air capture methods could in principle operate much more rapidly, but may be limited by large-scale implementation, including energy use and environmental constraints.[53]

The IPCC also notes that the biggest uncertainty is the storage capacity and the permanence of stored carbon; this is true for both so-called biological carbon sinks, such as forests, and for carbon that is mechanically injected into the earth or dumped into oceans. Permanent carbon removal and storage by CDR would decrease climate warming in the long term. However, non-permanent storage strategies would allow CO_2 to return to the atmosphere, where it would once again contribute to warming.

The report also acknowledges that CDR could also have climatic and environmental side-effects:

For instance, enhanced vegetation productivity may increase emissions of nitrous oxide (N_2O), which is a more potent greenhouse gas than carbon dioxide (CO_2). A large-scale increase in vegetation coverage, for instance through afforestation

---

Box 6.2   Geoengineering technologies involving CO_2 removal and capture/storage

Ocean fertilization with iron or nitrogen:
Adding nutrients to ocean water to stimulate the growth of phytoplankton with the aim of promoting long-term, deep-sea carbon storage.

Biochar:
Burning biomass through pyrolysis (that is, low-oxygen environments so carbon is not released) and burying the concentrated carbon in soil.

Carbon-sucking machines or air capture, and mineral sequestration or synthetic trees:
Extracting CO_2 from the air by using liquid sodium hydroxide, which is converted to sodium carbonate, then extracting the CO_2 in solid form to be buried.

Modifying ocean upwelling or downwelling:
Using pipes to bring up nutrient-rich seawater to the surface to cool surface waters and enhance ocean sequestration of CO_2.

'Enhanced weathering' (ocean):
Increasing ocean alkalinity in order to increase carbon uptake.

'Enhanced weathering' (terrestrial):
Controlling levels of atmospheric CO_2 by spreading fine-powdered olivine (magnesium iron silicate) on farmland or forestland.

Crop Residue Ocean Permanent Sequestration (CROPS):
Storing carbon by dumping tree logs or other biomass into seawater.

Genetically engineered algae and marine microbes:
Engineering communities of synthetic microorganisms to sequester higher levels of CO_2 (in ocean communities or in closed ponds, or even to cover buildings).

---

or energy crops, could alter surface characteristics, such as surface reflectivity and turbulent fluxes .... Ocean-based CDR methods that rely on biological production (i.e., ocean fertilisation) would have numerous side effects on ocean ecosystems and ocean acidity and may produce emissions of non-CO_2 greenhouse gases.[54]

The IPCC reveals the state of uncertainty in a 'synthesis' section at the end of the chapter: 'The level of *confidence* on the effects of both CDR and SRM methods on carbon and other biogeochemical cycles is *very low*.'[55] While the prospect of CCS as a future climate-change response may provide some optimism when one considers the likely state of the planet at the turn of the next century, a hard look at the reality of CCS – and its role in protracting an unsustainable status quo – has led some scientists to conclude that CCS is specious and a dead end: 'a large, expensive, and unnecessary fossil-fuel subsidy with an extremely low probability of eventual societal benefit'.[56]

Weather modification

The idea that humans can intentionally control the weather has a long history and is the conceptual ancestor of the geoengineering project.[57] Since the 1830s, governments and private companies have attempted to apply technological know-how to increase or decrease precipitation or to restrain storms by altering landforms, burning forests and dropping chemicals into clouds – both for military and non-military purposes. Weather warfare by the US government during the Vietnam War (dubbed Operation POPEYE) included 2,600 cloud-seeding missions over the Ho Chi Minh Trail, with the aim to make it impassable. While the efficacy of the covert operation couldn't be verified, its eventual exposure did precipitate the UN Convention on the Prohibition of Military or Any Other Hostile Use of Environmental Modification Techniques (ENMOD) of 1977, which the United States immediately signed, hat in hand.

Predicting the weather is difficult; proving the efficacy of weather interventions is even more difficult. However, as climate change brings more frequent and extreme weather events, ranging from drought to tropical storms, interest in weather control is on the rise. If interventions such as altering the course of hurricanes become possible, it is

---

Box 6.3   Geoengineering technologies involving weather modification

Cloud seeding to increase precipitation:
Spraying chemicals (usually silver iodide) into clouds to precipitate rain or snow – already practiced on a large scale in the United States and China, despite scepticism about effectiveness.

Storm modification (for example, redirecting or suppressing hurricanes):
Attempting to prevent the formation of storms or affect their pathways.

---

easy to imagine weather modification deployed in 'self-defence' being viewed as a hostile act by neighbours who find themselves in the eye of the storm. Weather modification is a classic 'end-of-pipe' response that has been considered, since the 1960s, as an adaptation technology to cope with climatic changes (see Box 6.3).

Notes

1. IPCC. (27 September 2013). *Climate Change: The physical science basis* (Summary for policymakers) (report). Retrieved from Intergovernmental Panel on Climate Change (IPCC) website: http://www.climatechange2013.org/spm.
2. The September 2013 publication is not, however, the first evidence of the Intergovernmental Panel on Climate Change's (IPCC) consideration of geoengineering: The IPCC held an expert meeting on geoengineering in 2011, which included all three of its Working Groups. In response to that meeting, 160 civil-society organisations sent an Open Letter to the IPCC questioning the meeting's purpose and asking the Panel not to stray from its mandate (that is, to 'provide policy-relevant but not policy-prescriptive information'). As the IPCC's role is to provide scientific and technical information to the UN Framework Convention on Climate Change, it appears likely that the presence of geoengineering in AR5 will soon result in the official appearance of geoengineering in negotiating texts at the Convention. Open Letter's text is at http://www.etcgroup.org/content/open-letter-ipcc-geoengineering.
3. IPCC. (2013), p. 21.
4. Cressey, D. (2 October 2013). Climate report puts geoengineering in the spotlight. *Nature*. Retrieved from http://www.nature.com/news/climate-report-puts-geoengineering-in-the-spotlight-1.13871.
5. Ibid.
6. Whether or not to include carbon capture and storage or weather modification under the rubric of geoengineering, for example, is hotly disputed. At the same time, as governments and multilateral organisations begin to articulate positions on technological developments, they require more precise definitions. Anyone who has participated in international negotiations knows the long and tedious hours spent wrangling over definitions that can have far-reaching consequences when they are incorporated into international law or multilateral agreements.
7. See, for example, the record of the debate: *The regulation of geoengineering*. (18 March 2010). In UK House of Commons 2010 Science and Technology Committee. Retrieved from http://www.publications.parliament.uk/pa/cm200910/cmselect/cmsctech/221/22105.htm.
8. For more, see Fleming, J.R. (2010). *Fixing the Sky: The checkered history of weather and climate control*. New York: Columbia University Press.
9. Dunbar, B. (1 February 2005). What's the difference between weather and climate? Retrieved from http://www.nasa.gov/mission_pages/noaa-n/climate/climate_weather.html. See also memorandum on cloud seeding: Lee, J. (18 March 2010). House of Commons – Science and Technology Committee – Minutes of evidence. Retrieved from http://www.publications.parliament.uk/pa/cm200910/cmselect/cmsctech/221/10011310.htm.
10. Keith, D. (2010). Engineering the planet, in *Climate Change Science and Policy*. Washington, DC: Island Press, p. 294.

11. Asilomar Scientific Organizing Committee. (November 2010). *The Asilomar Conference Recommendations on Principles of Research into Climate Engineering Techniques* (report), p. 28. Retrieved from http://www.climateresponsefund.org/images/Conference/finalfinalreport. pdf.

12. See documentation related to an ocean fertilisation deployment off the coast of British Columbia: http://www.etcgroup.org/tags/hsrc-geoengineering-russ-george-haida-gwaii-ocean-fertilization The ostensible reason for the iron dump was to increase the salmon population for the financial benefit of the local fisher community.

13. Goodman, A. and Gonzalez, J. (producers). (8 July 2010). A debate on geoengineering: Vandana Shiva vs. Gwynne Dyer (television series episode). *Democracy Now!* New York. Retrieved from http://www.democracynow.org/2010/7/8/a_debate_on_geoengineering_vandana_shiva.

14. Terra futura 2013: Interview with Vandana Shiva about geoengineering (interview by M. Heibel and No Geoingegneria). (9 July 2013). Retrieved from http://www.nogeoingegneria.com/interviste/terra-futura-2013-interview-with-vandana-shiva-about-geoengineering/.

15. [United States] President's Scientific Advisory Committee (PSAC). (1965). Restoring the Quality of our Environment, Environmental Pollution Panel, 1965, pp. 121–4.

16. Ibid., p. 127.

17. Fleming, J.R. (2010), p. 27.

18. National Science Foundation. (1965). *Report of the Special Commission on Weather Modification, Weather and Climate Modification*, pp. 27, 119.

19. Fleming, J.R. (2007). The climate engineers. *Wilson Quarterly*, Spring, pp. 56–8.

20. Crutzen, P.J. (3 January 2002). Geology of mankind. *Nature*, vol. 415.

21. Hoffert, M.I. et al. (1 November 2002). Advanced technology paths to global climate stability: Energy for a greenhouse planet. *Science*, 298(5595), 981–7.

22. GPS Podcast (20 December 2009), Fareed Zakaria interviews Nathan Myhrvold, (online). Retrieved from http://www.cnn.com/video/#/video/podcasts/fareedzakaria/site/2009/12/20/gps.podcast.12.20.cnn.

23. For example, John Holdren, US Senior Science Advisor, quoted in Borenstein, S. (8 April 2009). Obama looks at climate engineering. *Associated Press*: '[Geoengineering's] got to be looked at. We don't have the luxury of taking any approach off the table.'

24. Liebelson, D. and Mooney, C. (17 July 2013). Climate Intelligence Agency. *Slate*. Retrieved from http://www.slate.com/articles/technology/future_tense/2013/07/cia_funds_nas_study_into_geoengineering_and_climate_change.html. For more details, see the US National Academies website: http://www8.nationalacademies.org/cp/projectview.aspx?key=49540.

25. Gingrich, N. (3 June 2008). Can geoengineering address concerns about global warming?. *Human Events*. Retrieved from: http://www.humanevents.com/2008/06/03/stop-the-green-pig-defeat-the-boxerwarnerlieberman-green-pork-bill-capping-american-jobs-and-trading-americas-future/.

26. See http://www.copenhagenconsensus.com/publication/fix-climate-climate-engineering.

27. Gillis, J. (30 April 2012). Clouds' effect on climate change is last bastion for dissenters. *New York Times*. Retrieved from http://www.nytimes.com/2012/05/01/science/earth/clouds-effect-on-climate-change-is-last-bastion-for-dissenters.html?_r=0.

28. Parthasarathy, S., Avery, C., Hedberg, N., Mannisto, J. and Maguire, M. (22 September 2010). A public good? Geoengineering and intellectual property. *Science, Technology and Public Policy Working Paper*, pp. 10–11.

29. Jones, I.S.F. (2008). Method for attracting and concentrating fish, World Intellectual Property Organization, WO2008131485A1 (Patent Application), claim 15.

30. There are several examples provided in ETC Group's *Geopiracy: The case against geoengineering*, 2010, Communique No. 103, pp. 31–2. Retrieved from www.etcgroup.org/content/geopiracy-case-against-geoengineering.

31. Mulkern, A.C. (18 April 2012). Researcher: Ban patents on geoengineering technology. ClimateWire, *Scientific American*. Retrieved from http://www.scientificamerican.com/article. cfm?id=researcher-ban-patents-on-geoengineering-technology.

32. Hamilton, C. (2013). *Earthmasters: The dawn of the age of climate engineering*. New Haven, CT: Yale University Press, p. 120.

33. Marshall, M. (25 August 2012). Lowest US carbon emissions won't slow climate change. *New Scientist*.

34. Anon. (4 November 2010). Geoengineering: Lift-off. *The Economist*. Retrieved from http:// www.economist.com/node/17414216.

35. The text of the decision is available online: http://www.cbd.int/climate/geoengineering/.

36. Higuchi, T. (2010). Atmospheric nuclear weapons testing and the debate on risk knowledge in Cold War America, 1945–1963, in McNeill, R. and Unger, C.R., eds. *Environmental Histories of the Cold War*. New York: Cambridge University Press, pp. 301–22.

37. The Peoples' Agreement is available online: http://pwccc.wordpress.com/support/.

38. ETC Group is a founding member of the HOME campaign: www.handsoffmotherearth.org.

39. For 'Plan B', see John Shepherd, quoted in Connor, S. (2 September 2009). Man-made eruptions – 'Plan B' in the battle for the planet. *The Independent*. Retrieved from http://www. independent.co.uk/environment/climate-change/manmade-eruptions-ndash-plan-b-in-the-battle-for-the-planet-1780268.html.

40. For 'Climate Emergency', see Caldeira, K. and Keith, D.W. (2010). The need for climate engineering research. *Issues in Science and Technology*. Retrieved from http://www.issues. org/27.1/caldeira.html.

41. The two reports are: National Academies. (2015). *Committee on Geoengineering Climate: Technical Evaluation and Discussion of Impacts; Board on Atmospheric Sciences and Climate; Ocean Studies Board; Division on Earth and Life Studies; National Research Council, Climate Intervention: Reflecting Sunlight to Cool Earth*. Washington, DC: National Academies Press, and, by the same authors, *Climate Intervention: Carbon Dioxide Removal and Reliable Sequestration*, also 2015. Pre-publication copies of both reports are available online: http://www.nap.edu/ catalog/18988/climate-intervention-reflecting-sunlight-to-cool-earth. The report calls SRM 'albedo modification'.

42. Pierrehumbert, R.T. (15 February 2015). Climate hacking is barking mad. *Slate*. Retrieved from http://www.slate.com/articles/health_and_science/science/2015/02/nrc_ geoengineering_report_climate_hacking_is_dangerous_and_barking_mad.single.html.

43. Plan B: John Shepherd, quoted in Connor, S. (2009); Insurance Policy: John Shepherd, quoted in Alleyne, R. (1 September 2009). Geo-engineering should be developed as insurance against dangerous climate change. *The Telegraph*. Retrieved from http://www.telegraph.co.uk/ science/6122322/Geo-engineering-should-be-developed-as-insurance-against-dangerous-climate-change.html.

44. Dalby, S. (25 October 2013). Rethinking geopolitics: Climate security in the Anthropocene. *Global Policy*. Retrieved from http://onlinelibrary.wiley.com/doi/10.1111/1758-5899.12074/full.

45. Ibid.

46. Shepard, J.G. (9 September 2009). *Geoengineering the Climate: Opportunities and uncertainties* (report). Newport Pagnell: The Royal Society, p. 52.

47. For example, David Keith's appearance on Stephen Colbert's late-night talk show, *The Colbert Report*, 10 December 2013.

48. For example, Keith, D.W. (2013). *A Case for Climate Engineering*. Cambridge, MA: MIT Press: 'Deployment is neither hard nor expensive.' Geoengineering boosters Lee Lane and Eric Bickell argue that 'the potential benefit of [solar radiation management] is so obvious that one hardly needs a formal economic assessment to prove that researching its merits could pay large dividends.' None the less, they 'roughly estimate' that the benefit-to-cost ratio of researching SRM technologies is 'on the order of 1000 to 1': Lane, L. and Bickel, E. (May 2012). Climate change: Climate engineering R&D [Challenge paper]. In Third Copenhagen Consensus: Copenhagen Consensus Center, pp. 2–3. Retrieved from http://www.copenhagenconsensus.com/sites/default/files/climatechangeengineeringr26d.pdf.

49. The Open Letter is available online: http://www.etcgroup.org/fr/node/5282.

50. Jones, A. et al. (2013). The impact of abrupt suspension of solar radiation management (termination effect) in experiment G2 of the Geoengineering Model Intercomparison Project (GeoMIP). *Journal of Geophysical Research: Atmospheres*, 118(17), 9743–52. Retrieved from doi:10.1002/jgrd.50762.

51. Stocker, T.F. et al., eds. (2013). *Climate Change 2013: The Physical Science Basis, Working Group I Contribution to the Fifth Assessment Report of the Intergovernmental Panel on Climate Change*, pp. 632–4. Retrieved from www.climatechange2013.org/report/full-report/.

52. Intergovernmental Panel on Climate Change (IPCC). (2013), p. 28.

53. Stocker, T.F. et al., eds. (2013), p. 633.

54. Ibid., p. 633.

55. Ibid., p. 552, emphasis added.

56. Stephens, J.C. (20 December 2013). Time to stop investing in carbon capture and storage and reduce government subsidies of fossil-fuels. *Wiley Interdisciplinary Reviews (WIREs): Climate Change*. Retrieved from http://onlinelibrary.wiley.com/doi/10.1002/wcc.266/full.

57. Fleming, J.R. (2010), pp. 165–88.

7

GREENWASHING DEATH: CLIMATE CHANGE AND THE ARMS TRADE

Mark Akkerman

I think [climate change] is a real opportunity for the [aerospace and defence] industry.
Lord Drayson, then UK Minister of State for Science and Innovation
and Minister of State for Strategic Defence Acquisition Reform, in 2009[1]

Introduction

'The military takes on climate change deniers', read a headline in *BusinessWeek* in October 2014. The article told of the US military's unlikely confrontation with some of its most outspoken supporters, Republican representatives, over the issue of climate change. With climate-change admission seen as heresy by a Tea Party-dominated Republican party, even the military top brass have faced an uphill struggle. In May 2014, Republicans had passed an amendment to the annual National Defense Authorization Act forbidding the Defense Department from spending money on any climate-related initiatives – an action denounced by Defense Secretary Chuck Hagel as 'ideology getting in the way of sound planning'.[2]

So, has the military all of a sudden turned into an unlikely environmental campaign group? In recent years, the US military has certainly emerged as the most unlikely ally of environmentalists. Not only is it calling for political action, but it is also apparently walking the walk, switching to alternative fuels and looking to address the impacts of climate change. But a closer look shows that the motivations of the military differ greatly from environmentalists or even the general public.

The military's primary strategic interest is less about climate change itself and more about the adjacent problems of energy scarcity, seeking to safeguard fuel transit routes and reducing the military's oil dependency. Second, it is also looking ahead to protect its infrastructure and military assets from climate impacts. In other words, the military is looking for ways to keep itself running, mainly by trying to switch to alternative fuels. Its third focus is an attempt to identify perceived security threats caused by the impact of climate instability – from increased humanitarian disasters to the possible rise of conflict, migration and disruption – that the military believes it will need to respond to. Fourth, the military's interest in the new field of environmental security is strongly driven by commercial interests and the defence industry, which has a very poor record on issues of sustainability and thrives on fuelling insecurity rather than resolving it.

This chapter focuses on the intersections between the military, green technologies and the defence industry. I suggest that the 'greening' of the military is actually a 'greenwashing' exercise; in other words, the military spins positive communication about the environment in order to obscure poor environmental performance. Alternative fuels and other 'green' measures not only ensure that the military remains operational, they also create new markets for the defence industry. The greenwashing also projects the military as a suitable partner for tackling climate-change impacts, justifying an increased role and budgets. Altogether, they serve to cast an environmentally friendly image over an otherwise toxic brand in the eyes of much of the public.

The military and alternative energy

The most touted evidence of the military's new-found commitment to the environment is its increasing use of alternative fuels. Traditionally, armies are known for their high-energy use – especially fossil fuels. The US military spends about $22 billion a year on energy and is the world's single-largest user of petrol.[3] Military operations account for about 80 per cent of the total US federal government's energy use.[4]

The dependency on oil causes problems in two ways. First, fuel transported through war zones is vulnerable to attacks. Battlefield experiences in Afghanistan and Iraq caused military commanders to sound the alarm about the high number of casualties connected to such attacks. The US Department of Defense *Operational Energy Strategy: Implementation Plan* (2012) warns that 'the security of energy supply infrastructure for critical missions at fixed installations is not always robust.'[5]

On the other hand, looming energy scarcity and volatility in oil prices will mean a drastic rise in costs for fossil fuels, at a time when militaries already face ballooning budgets. This might cause new security problems around obtaining oil and protecting supply routes. Deputy Secretary of Defense William Lynn said at a Pentagon briefing, 'Our adversaries are increasingly employing asymmetric tactics, and energy can be a soft target.' He mentioned improvised explosive device (IED) attacks on supply convoys in operational zones and cyber attacks on homeland energy infrastructure as primary examples.[6]

'The armed forces recognize that their dependence on energy is a strategic and operational vulnerability that must be addressed', wrote UK Rear Admiral Neil Morisetti, the UK's climate and energy security envoy, and Amanda Dory, US Deputy Assistant Secretary of Defense for Strategy.[7] The UK Ministry of Defence Climate Change Strategy 2010 takes this issue further: 'Not only does the reduction of emissions across all business areas reduce costs and our vulnerability to energy price spikes, but reduction in fuel use at the front line has a direct benefit in reducing the logistical costs and risks of getting it to theatre.'[8] And its Sustainable Development Strategy (2011–30) lists as one of its objectives: 'To have significantly reduced the Armed Forces reliance on fossil fuels to provide operational energy, thereby mitigating operational and financial risk'.[9]

The concern is not just about supply routes and fuel insecurity but also the challenges posed by global temperature increases. As one spokesperson for the UK Ministry of Defence put it: 'One key concern is ensuring that our equipment is robust enough to deal with the range of temperature extremes. We now demand this when placing contracts with industry'.[10]

Tad Davis, the US Army's Deputy Assistant Secretary for Environment, Safety and Occupational Health, boasted, 'In essence, the Army is building green, buying green and going green.'[11] Measures taken or to be taken by the US military include the use of all kind of stand-alone solar- and wind-power equipment on bases, the acquisition of electric vehicles, tents that trap warm and cool air and solar-powered water-purification systems.

All parts of the armed forces are involved. In August 2012, the US Army opened bids to buy $7 billion in renewable energy for domestic bases.[12] Tests by the US Air Force suggested that airplanes could fly further with less fuel when using agrofuels.[13] And in September 2014, the US Department of Defense awarded three companies contracts to construct and commission agro-refineries capable of producing agrofuels to meet the transportation needs of the Navy.[14]

The Department of Defense is required to produce or procure 25 per cent of its total facility energy use from renewable sources from 2025 on.[15] However, it is questionable whether this goal will be reached. The military failed to meet the goal of sourcing at least 5 per cent of their energy consumption from renewables in 2012.[16]

The most ambitious plan in progress might be the so-called US 'Great Green Fleet', which was expected to be operational in 2016. 'The Great Green Fleet will signal to the world America's continued naval supremacy, unleashed from the tether of foreign oil,' wrote Secretary of the Navy Ray Mabus.[17] The Great Green Fleet is made up of planes, submarines and ships powered entirely by agrofuels and nuclear power. A demonstration in 2012 showed off ships and aircraft powered by nuclear power or advanced agrofuel blends and using energy-efficiency measures, including LEDs.[18]

While the military is promoting nuclear power as more sustainable, to call it 'green' is highly dubious, since huge amounts of energy (mostly fossil fuels) are needed in some parts of its generation process, apart from the unsolvable problems dealing with nuclear waste and the safety and health risks involved in the nuclear cycle.

In the UK, where the Ministry of Defence is responsible for about 1 per cent of the total UK CO_2 emissions (5.6 megatonnes a year), the focus lies on buying 'equipment and infrastructure that can operate in a wide variety of climatic and environmental conditions, and to reduce our reliance on hydrocarbon fuels and other finite resources'.[19] One example is the effort to 'green' forward operating bases with the aim of making them self-sustainable, including installing solar panels on smaller bases in southern Afghanistan. A number of contractors were invited to put forward ideas about how bases could switch to alternative energy sources, to 'remove the logistics burden of transporting fuel to the base.'[20]

The US and the UK are regarded as forerunners in adapting their militaries to climate change. Michael Brzoska, Professor of Political Science at the University of Hamburg, concludes that, for example, 'Both the Russian and the Chinese military seem to have only paid minor attention to the consequences of climate change for their future activities.'[21] Militaries in some other countries are trying to clean up their act. The Bundeswehr, for example, has reduced its emissions of carbon dioxide by 70 per cent since 1991, by switching to less polluting fuels.[22] It also conducted a breakthrough study on oil, warning 'peak oil is unavoidable' and it's 'necessary and sensible to prepare for' it.[23] But in general, most efforts seem to be aimed at educating individual soldiers about issues such as energy saving and waste separation.

US Navy Secretary Ray Mabus is honest about the real purpose of 'greening' the military: 'We are moving toward alternative fuels in the Navy and Marine Corps for one main reason, and that is to make us better fighters.'[24] Lower carbon emissions are only 'a byproduct', according to Mabus; so much a byproduct that the US even exempted US military operations from the 1998 Kyoto Agreement, which lays out binding commitments to reduce 'greenhouse-gas' emissions.

Greenwashing and the military: Fossil-fuel nexus

What the turn to alternative energies obscures is how entwined the military is with the fossil-fuel industry. Not only is the military the largest single user of fossil fuels, its primary purpose in recent decades has been to secure the supply and transport of fossil fuels – and to a lesser extent ensure the smooth operation of a consumer-based, high-carbon-emitting globalised economy. This also puts the 'green' efforts of the military in perspective as more propaganda than a real change, because 'energy security emerges as the primary focus for innovation and investment to combat geopolitical concerns around the reliance on foreign oil and the threat to military personnel in the field.'[25]

It is the toxic military-oil nexus that has turned the Middle East into a cauldron of conflict, and which governs military intervention and rising tension (and subsequent booming arms sales) in every corner of the globe. It is a nexus that completely overrides ethical or human rights considerations – let alone concern for environmental sustainability.

For the US, the Middle East has traditionally been the most important region for oil supplies. Since the 1960s, this has culminated in constant intervention to control resources, support of autocratic regimes (for example, Saudi Arabia and Iraq in the 1980s) – including a steady flow of arms deliveries, and a large military presence in the region. In his 1980 State of the Union address, then-president Jimmy Carter proclaimed his so-called Carter Doctrine with the words: 'Let our position be absolutely clear: An attempt by any outside force to gain control of the Persian Gulf region will be regarded as an assault on the vital interests of the United States of America, and such an assault will be repelled by any means necessary, including military force.'[26]

In line with this, the wars against Iraq in the 1990s and the 2000s have been, to an arguable extent, motivated by oil dependency.

In recent times, the central role of the Middle East for US energy security has been somewhat in decline and the focus has spread out to include other regions. Newly discovered oil reserves have turned the attention of the US, as well as other players such as Russia, Canada and Norway, to the Arctic. Obama's 'Pivot to Asia' also has a lot to do with keeping open oil-supply routes. The same goes for international anti-piracy missions, which conceal a competition – mainly between the US and China – for control over supply lines.

China is just as implicated. Throughout Latin America and Africa, it provides arms-for-oil exports. China came heavily under fire for its arms exports to Sudan during the Darfur war, accompanied as they were by rapidly growing Sudanese oil exports to China. China built similar, though less overt, relations based on oil and arms with Venezuela. The Venezuelan government used weapons purchased in China in confrontations with street protesters in early 2014.[27]

Britain's largest ever arms deal also uses oil as currency. The so-called 'Al-Yamamah arms deal', agreed in 1985, is a still-ongoing series of arms sales from the UK to the autocratic regime of Saudi Arabia, largely consisting of aircraft and missiles. In turn, Saudi Arabia has delivered up to 600,000 barrels of crude oil *per day* to the British government.[28] The UK's main contractor, BAE Systems, has earned tens of billions of pounds from these sales, which helps to subsidise the UK's own arms purchases. The deal has been surrounded by allegations of fraud, with the UK Serious Fraud Office controversially ending its investigation into this, citing 'the public interest' as the reason.[29]

France, for its part, started 'oil for arms' deals in the 1970s, in a bid to finance its rapidly growing dependence on oil imports. This included substantial arms deals with Saudi Arabia and Abu Dhabi. Even when there wasn't a direct exchange of oil for arms, French arms sales have paid for a substantial percentage of its oil imports. There is a high correlation in the countries concerned between arms exports and oil imports: Important oil suppliers such as Nigeria, Iraq and Saudi Arabia are also important clients of the French military industry.

The most well-known prolonged internal conflict that centres on oil is probably the conflict in the Niger Delta in Nigeria. In May 2011, Human Rights Watch (HRW) wrote, 'The ruling elite has squandered and siphoned off the nation's tremendous oil revenues, while neglecting basic health and education services for the vast majority of ordinary citizens.'[30] While calling on Nigeria's then-president Goodluck Jonathan to take action, HRW declared, 'Government security forces are widely implicated in serious abuses, including extrajudicial killings and torture.'[31]

All this didn't stop Dutch company TP Marine from building a close relationship with the Nigerian Navy, including the 2009 sale of twenty high-speed troop-carrying catamarans for €4.8 million. Security expert Daniel Volman wrote that the catamarans were acquired to 'transport soldiers up the creeks and small rivers of the Delta region'.[32] In response to parliamentary questions, the Dutch government shamelessly named the protection of the interests of Shell in Nigeria as one of the main reasons for allowing the controversial export.[33]

Green bullets

The military's supposed environmental concerns have quickly extended into the arms industry – where its absurdity has become ever more apparent. In 2006, BAE Systems was one of the first major arms-producing companies to promote a whole new series of 'environmentally friendly weapons', including reduced-lead bullets, rockets with fewer toxins and armoured vehicles with lower carbon emissions. The BAE spokesperson said: 'Weapons are going to be used and when they are, we try to make them as safe for the user as possible, to limit the collateral damage and to impact as little as possible on the environment.'[34]

A response from Symon Hill from Campaign Against Arms Trade (CAAT) expressed the scorn of many: 'BAE is determined to try to make itself look ethical, but they make weapons to kill people and it's utterly ridiculous to suggest they are environmentally friendly.'[35]

Nevertheless, other companies followed the lead of BAE, mostly in the area of alternative-fuel use. Boeing developed an agrofuel-powered fighter jet, the 'Green Hornet', first tested by the US Navy in April 2010. General Dynamics is developing a 'green' jet engine for the US Air Force.[36] Raytheon is partnering with Cyclone Power Technologies in the development of an all-fuel engine, which can run on algae fuel and waste oil and will have lower carbon emissions. And EADS (now called Airbus Group) modified a Diamond Aircraft DA42 Twin to fly on pure algae fuel.[37]

In general, the burgeoning American agrofuels industry is very dependent on military demand: '... the value chain of the nascent biofuels industry in response to ... military targets will create thousands of jobs and billions of dollars in new revenue, especially in states or regions with biorefineries.'[38] And the military is a willing partner: in 2010, the US Department of Defense's Defense Logistics Agency and the US Department of Agriculture signed a strategic alliance with the goal of creating 'a demand signal for the biofuels industry, for venture capital, for all those people standing up for the biofuel industry'.[39]

The green arms race is also on in the sector of unmanned aerial vehicles (UAVs), or drones, with the idea of developing drones that can use solar power or other alternative fuels, in order to stay in the air for extended periods. In 2010, Boeing won a $89 million contract from the Pentagon to develop the so-called 'SolarEagle' drone, with QinetiQ and the Centre for Advanced Electrical Drives from Newcastle University in the UK to build the actual plane.[40] India's Defence Research and Development Organisation is also planning to develop solar-powered UAVs, for use by the Indian armed forces and para-militaries on counter-insurgency missions.[41]

There is even now a greener way to die at the hands of a soldier. In 2003, the US Department of Defense awarded Alliant Techsystems a $5 million contract to develop lead-free combat bullets. US Army spokesperson Bob DiMichele said, 'We want [Alliant] to develop one lead-free bullet that will work all the time. One that can kill you or that you can shoot a target with and that's not an environmental hazard. We are talking about green ammunition for pistols, rifles and machine guns.'[42]

Since then the US Army has adopted these new bullets with a copper core instead of a lead one as its standard combat ammunition.

Despite its absurdity, the penchant for greening all sectors of economy is still hard to resist for politicians and businesspeople. In 1999, the late Dutch GreenLeft MP Ab Harrewijn asked the Ministry of Defence to do some calculations on the possibility of equipping battle tanks with solar panels. It turned out that this could be done – with a solar panel as large as two soccer fields. According to then-Defence Minister De Grave, 'because of practical and tactical considerations, there remained a preference for the use of fossil fuels.'[43]

Greenwashing the military-industrial complex

Explaining the military embrace of all things green also requires an understanding of the purpose of the military-industrial complex and how it has successfully adapted itself to new challenges and situations and continued to grow – despite the end of the Cold War and the clear failure of military interventions in Afghanistan and Iraq.

The term 'military-industrial complex' describes

> … coalitions of vested interests within the state and industry, which could lead to decisions being made which were in the interest of the coalition members and not necessarily in the interests of national security. These coalitions could include some members of the armed services, of the civilian defence bureaucracy, of the legislature, of the arms manufacturers and of their workers.[44]

The military-industrial complex revolves around the often-close relationships between the military and government in general on one side, and (large) military producers on the other side. The term was famously used by US President Eisenhower in his farewell speech in 1961, in which he warned of the growing influence of the complex in promoting and shaping certain policies.

Military thinking centres on the use of force or the threat of the use of force as a 'deterrence' to defend something or to attain certain goals. To be able to reach those goals, one needs to have more power than the enemy. Moreover, the ability to use external and internal force is the basis of the modern state; it guarantees the continuing of the current order and of the power of the elites. President Obama stated it this way in May 2014, saying that the US should always lead on the world stage, explaining: 'The military ... is, and always will be, the backbone of that leadership.'[45]

Apart from manpower and the capacity to form coalitions, military power is largely based on the weapons arsenal a state has, in terms of numbers and how advanced the equipment is. This is where the arms industry steps in. In order to make ever increasing profits, this industry needs to sell as many weapons as possible. In 2014, world military spending reached the dizzying heights of $1,776 billion, or about 2.3 per cent of the global GDP. The US alone is responsible for $610 billion of this – a third of total world military spending.[46]

This seemingly unstoppable race is partly spurred by the notion that a country needs to have more and better equipment than its potential enemies (such as we saw in the US–USSR arms race during the Cold War), but it is also driven by the international arms trade, which over the years has become more and more a supply-driven market. The arms industry offers so-called 'solutions' for threats nations haven't even identified or up until now haven't regarded as security-related problems.

To fend off talk of the peace dividend after the Berlin Wall fell, the military-industrial complex first turned to the idea of humanitarian interventionism, and then through the War on Terror justified a perpetual military campaign. Rising tensions between the NATO alliance and Russia, and growing unrest in the Middle East, have resulted in calls for more defence spending within NATO.

The impact of these interventions and other military operations caused immense human suffering, large numbers of refugees and environmental destruction; yet, sadly, this is exactly what is needed to keep the military-industrial complex – which feeds on war and chaos – going, and even broaden its scope of work into new areas. British arms giant BAE Systems was surprisingly open about this in its Annual Report in 2005: 'New threats and conflict arenas are placing unprecedented demands on military forces and presenting BAE Systems with new challenges and opportunities.'[47]

The military thrives on insecurity and perceptions of insecurity – and climate change and its consequences fit perfectly into this pattern. US Secretary of Defense Chuck Hagel, in a speech in November 2013, listed as possible security-related consequences, 'Food and water shortages, pandemic disease, disputes over refugees and resources, more severe natural disasters'.[48] The Department of Defense further elaborated upon these threats in its October 2014 'Climate Change Adaptation Roadmap', which focuses on adaptation and mitigation.[49]

The military is already being called upon more often to respond to disasters – which are likely to increase in magnitude and regularity as a result of climate change. In March 2014, Admiral Samuel J. Locklear, then commander of US Pacific Command (PACOM), noted that:

If you look at my AOR [area of responsibility] this year how many people lost their lives or got hurt by any event, it wasn't through any kind of military activity, it was through natural disaster ... I mean, if there's one thing I tell everybody that comes to work for me – every commander – I said 'While you're here, you may not have a conflict with another military, but you will have a natural disaster that you have to either assist in, or be prepared to manage the consequences on the other side. And that has been true every year.'[50]

The arms industry is, not surprisingly, keen to promote itself as providing the solutions to deal with these consequences. In an advertorial, Airbus Military, part of the Airbus Group (formerly known as EADS), promotes its versatile military aircraft, claiming that it will bring 'hope for 375 million people worldwide', who need urgent aid because of human conflict, natural disasters or 'unstable borders'.[51] They refer to a report by Oxfam that indicates that by 2015, on average 375 million people a year will be affected by climatic disasters.[52] This does not suggest that Oxfam endorses governments to spend more on the military; however, Airbus sees no obstacle in abusing Oxfam's report to portray itself with a humanitarian face.

Another area that has prompted increased military involvement has been border security, which has become more and more militarised, leading to a boom in profits for the security industry (see Chapter 5). As researcher Emily Gilbert writes, 'Militarism encourages the use of force against foreigners, with barriers erected to exclude those who bear the immediate impact of climate change, even though they are usually the least responsible for climate change.'[53]

Anticipated new markets related to climate change are causing some excitement in the defence industry. In 2011, the second Energy Environmental Defence and Security (E2DS) conference in Washington, DC, was certainly jubilant about the potential business opportunity of expanding the defence industry into environmental markets:

> The defence market worldwide is worth a trillion dollars annually. The energy and environmental market is worth at least eight times this amount. The former is set to contract as governments address the economic realities of the coming decade; the latter is set to expand exponentially, especially in the renewables arena. Far from being excluded from this opportunity, the aerospace, defence and security sector is gearing up to address what looks set to become its most significant adjacent market since the strong emergence of the civil/homeland security business almost a decade ago.[54]

This conference was followed by another one, called E3DS, in November 2012 in London, with speakers from the arms industry, several militaries and NATO. The conference was sponsored by large arms-producing companies, such as Raytheon, Lockheed Martin, Saab, Finmeccanica, EADS, Thales and Northrop Grumman. Lockheed Martin trumpeted its expansion into the alternative-energy market, providing energy-efficiency programmes and developing ocean-thermal and solar plants.

Perhaps the most promising new market for defence companies lies in satellite observations, monitoring, data collecting and analysis. One example of this is the

European initiative Global Monitoring for Environment and Security (GMES), renamed Copernicus in December 2012.[55] This satellite system was set up in 1998 to monitor the earth and provide data for preparing legislation on environmental matters. Shortly thereafter (1999), its mission broadened to include security issues, such as maritime surveillance and border control. This clearly shows how certain technology, used initially for civilian purposes, can soon take on a strong security and militaristic tone.

This is not to discount that some high-tech and other inventions by the defence industry may be useful to address some aspects of climate change and its consequences, particularly if the research and skills are transferred to civilian use (see accompanying online chapter by Wainwright and Cock[56]). Many high-skilled workers in the arms industry could deploy many of their skills in the green sector; similarly government-supported arms-conversion plans could boost investments in renewable energy.[57]

However, this should not distract attention and resources away from the real solution to worsening climate change: a radical change in our carbon and globalised economy. Nor should it hide the fact that the military has more potential to thrive from our failure to do this than from our success. According to journalist David Cronin, the defence industry 'could be one of the few beneficiaries from ecological catastrophes' by 'turning an environmental question into a security issue' and be propelled by the impacts of 'global warming expected to increase competition between nations over energy sources'.[58]

Author David Sirota adds:

> … the military's message is designed to have us believe that the Pentagon can somehow continue the energy-expensive environmentally destructive policy of permanent war while conserving energy. It's as fantastical a notion as an oil company saying it aims to help reduce carbon emissions by producing more oil, but the propaganda has a goal: making war that much more acceptable to a frugal public.[59]

Strange bed companions? Environmentalists, the military and the arms industry

While the military is mostly clear that security-related matters – with some greenwashing efforts on the side – drive its transition to sustainable energy, some parts of the environmentalist movement none the less embrace it as a forerunner in the struggle against climate change. Curious as this may seem, they apparently are either fooled by the military's 'green' propaganda or feel that having the military on their side may be one of the few ways to swing reluctant or resistant conservatives into embracing climate action, particularly in the US. It is also a result of a tunnel vision amongst some environmentalists that focuses on certain aspects of environmentalism (mainly nature conservation) without keeping the broader environmental and/or social contexts in sight. In some cases, it is sadly fuelled by the expectation that their environmental charity might even gain from such alliances in terms of both funding and profile. Whatever the reason, it has led to some unlikely and morally dubious alliances.

As early as 1993, retired General Schwarzkopf joined the national board of The Nature Conservancy, the largest US environmental organisation, saying: 'Anyone who doesn't think the military is environmentally involved doesn't know the military.'[60] His statement focused on landscape maintenance on military bases and practice areas, ignoring the enormous environmental damage caused by the military. The Nature Conservancy still lists the Department of Defense as one of its 'Partners in Conservation'.

The National Resources Defense Council (NRDC) is also 'partnering with the Department of Defense to help expedite the siting process for renewable energy projects near DOD [Department of Defense] facilities and ensure that both environmental and military considerations are taken into account'.[61] Executive Director Peter Lehner knows exactly why the military is going 'green': 'The military services know they must embrace clean energy – not because it is cutting-edge or politically correct but because it makes sense for our troops and our country's security.'[62] It raises serious questions why an NGO describing itself as a grassroots environmental action group with a 'purpose to safeguard the earth' thinks along with the militarist mindset of one of the major polluters in the world.

Conservation International goes further, embracing many arms industries – including highly controversial ones such as defence giants Northrop Grumman and United Technologies – in greenwashing their image.

John Stauber from the Center for Media and Democracy argues, 'It is obscene for anyone to laud the military for being green. The US military possesses thousands of nuclear bombs and prides itself on obeying any order to use them. It is stupid to greenwash history's most lethal and destructive organization.'[63]

Friends of the Earth Brisbane, which protested a US-Australian military exercise in 2010, also denounced the greenwashing of the military: '... despite the greenwashing, the U.S. and Australian militaries are not clean and green. They leave a legacy of toxic munitions pollution, physical damage to the landscape, flora and fauna, and frequently impinge upon the human rights of those who live near their operational areas.'[64]

Not all greenwash attempts go smoothly. The announcement of a partnership to work on clean-energy projects with Lockheed Martin by the US city of Burlington, Vermont, caused an uproar amongst the large environmentalist and peace community, culminating in Lockheed Martin pulling out of the partnership agreement. A video by two journalists using a hidden camera that showed Conservation International employees willingly supporting the idea of greenwashing horrific weaponry by Lockheed Martin similarly cast a bad light (see Box 7.1).

Fight back

There are no military strategies that focus on the root causes of climate change and what should be done to change these, because the military's primary objective is to secure the current world order, no matter how unjust or unsustainable it is. The military's only

When two journalists from the British magazine *Don't Panic* approached Conservation International, posing as representatives of Lockheed Martin – and secretly filmed the encounter – the environmental organisation gladly offered the company ways to polish up its green image, including assisting its green PR efforts and associating it with conservation activities – all in return for large sponsorship fees.

While the fake Lockheed Martin representatives made it very clear that they were only interested in a greener image, Conservation International didn't question their disastrous activities at all. Heydon Prowse from *Don't Panic* recounted, 'We told them that one of our key environmental strategies was to recycle bomb shrapnel from battle zones to use again in new bombs and that we were adapting our cluster bomb technology to drop seeds so as to re-forest remote regions. We waited for them to be outraged … they never were.'[65]

Instead of at least pushing Lockheed Martin to clean up its act, Conservation International merely suggested the company become part of its Business & Sustainability Council, where for $37,500 a year it could join companies such as Shell, Monsanto and fellow arms producer Northrop Grumman. Other suggestions for Lockheed Martin included buying a forest in Mozambique and adopting the endangered Middle East vulture as a mascot.

Absurd as this all may seem, according to former Conservation International media manager Christine MacDonald, it is common practice: 'I found it rather odd that the filmmakers presented the idea of C.I. taking money from Lockheed Martin as utterly shocking. The Nature Conservancy, after all, has already taken money from Lockheed. And C.I. has funding ties to B-2 bomber maker, Northrop Grumman.'[66]

goal is to adapt to a changing security situation, with the aim of maintaining its own power and influence as well as defending the interests of those who have been the main actors causing the climate crisis. As a consequence, the military, defence and security industries, rather than being a solution to climate change, are part of the problem. It is the dominance of military power on our planet that bolsters a systematic failure to tackle the root causes of climate change.

It is therefore critical that environmental, peace and international justice activists join forces to challenge this problem at the crossroads of their distinct areas of work. The first step is to develop a common vision of how to unmask the so-called 'green' efforts of the military and the arms trade and to strategise on how to communicate this to the broader public.

Most campaigns against certain aspects of the arms trade tend to focus on either so-called 'controversial' weapons, such as land mines, cluster bombs, or nuclear weapons, or arms sales to areas of conflict, developing countries, or regimes known for human rights abuses. In those cases, the urgency of action is clear, with images of the consequences of arms exports clearly visible. The ways arms companies profit from climate change are more insidious, with long-lasting effects, and they cannot be pinpointed to a certain point in time or related to a specific weapon or arms deal. Nevertheless, the process needs to be unveiled.

The second step is to mobilise broad support to fight climate change, militarism and the arms trade. This support should be translated into action that builds the needed pressure on governments and companies. How this can best be done differs greatly from country to country, but a mix of activities aimed at informing the public, broadening public support and engaging in radical but nonviolent direct action against strategic targets has the greatest chance of success.

There are some examples of crossover activism, such as the above-mentioned successful joint effort by environmentalists and peace activists to get Lockheed Martin out of a partnership with the city of Burlington. In 2014, the UK's Campaign Against Arms Trade (CAAT) launched a call for trade unionists to get involved in its 'Arms to Renewables' campaign,[67] stating:

> Large scale military procurement and arms exports only reinforce a militaristic approach to international problems. Real security requires tackling the negative effects of climate change, with its associated food and water shortages, as well as developing a reliable and clean energy supply ... arms trade makes the world a more dangerous place, whereas renewable energy is vital for a fairer, safer world. Shifting resources would help tackle problems rather than create them.[68]

To counter trade unions' fears of losing jobs, CAAT argues that government needs to shift financial support to the renewable energy industry: 'Many of the workers [in the arms industry] are highly skilled engineers. These are much needed to tackle problems such as climate change.'[69]

Such initiatives are rare, however. Many activists tend to focus very much on their own particular issue, leaving little time and resources to connect with other movements. Yet strengthening each other's struggles in a broader context will give more power to each movement. And we have no choice but to build a stronger counterpower in order to confront and overcome the tremendous power of the military-industrial complex and its devastating effect on the earth and humanity.

Notes

1. Cook, N. (2009). Engaging the challenges ahead, E2DI. *The Journal, Dynamixx*, 2 (Autumn/ Winter).

2. Hertsgaard, M. (23 October 2014). The military takes on climate change deniers. *Businessweek*. Retrieved from http://www.bloomberg.com/bw/articles/2014-10-23/the-military-takes-on-climate-change-deniers.

3. Bennet, J.R. (14 February 2011). The mean green military machine, *ISN Insights*; US Department of Defense. (April 2013). *Defense Budget Priorities and Choices – Fiscal year 2014*. Retrieved from www.isn.ethz.ch/Digital-Library/Publications/Detail/?lang=en&id ... .

4. Peck, L. (8 December 2010). New mission for U.S. military: breaking its dependence on oil. *Yale Environment*, 360.

5. US Department of Defense. (2-12). *Operational Energy Strategy: Implementation Plan, March 2012*. Retrieved from http://energy.defense.gov/Portals/25/Documents/Reports/20120306_OE_Strategy_Implementation_Plan.pdf.

6. William J. Lynn, Remarks at the Department of Defense Operational Energy Strategy Rollout, Pentagon Briefing Room, 14 June 2011.

7. Morisetti, UK Rear Adm. N. and Dory, A. (29 March 2010). The climate variable: world militaries grapple with new security calculus. *DefenseNews*.

8. UK Ministry of Defence. (April 2010). *MOD Climate Change Strategy 2010*.

9. UK Ministry of Defence. (1 May 2011). *Sustainable Development Strategy: A sub-strategy of the Strategy for Defence (2011–2030)*.

10. Moss, T. (22 April 2009). Climate of war. *Jane's Defence Weekly*.

11. Sheftick, G. (4 June 2010). Army building, buying, going 'green'. Retrieved from http://www.army.mil/article/40399/.

12. Brewin, B. (7 August 2012). Army kicks off $7 billion renewable energy procurement. *Nextgov.com*.

13. Lane, J. (13 April 2014). Can warplanes fly farther, carry more weapons, with advanced agrofuels? More new data. *Agrofuels Digest*.

14. US Department of the Navy. (19 September 2014). Departments of the Navy, Energy and Agriculture invest in construction of three biorefineries to produce drop-in agrofuel for military [press release].

15. US Department of Defense. 10 USC 2911: Energy performance goals and master plan for the Department of Defense. Retrieved from uscode.house.gov/quicksearch/get.plx?title=10&section=2911.

16. Danko, P. (27 June 2013). US military faces trio of renewable energy goals. *EarthTechling*.

17. Mabus, R. (2012). Seeking alternative energy sources key to Navy mission. *Currents: the Navy's energy & environmental magazine*, Summer.

18. http://greenfleet.dodlive.mil/energy/great-green-fleet/.

19. Ministry of Defence, MOD Climate Change Strategy 2010, April 2010.

20. Marsden, S. (6 February 2011). Green energy plan at military bases. *The Independent*.

21. Brzoska, M. (16 March 2012). Climate change and the military. *E-International Relations*.

22. Bundeswehr. (31 July 2014). Bundeswehr und Umweltschutz – die unbekannte Partnerschaft.

23. Bundeswehr Transformation Centre – Future Analysis Branch. (2010). *Armed Forces, Capabilities and Technologies in the 21st Century: Environmental dimensions of security – Sub-study 1: Peak Oil – Security policy implications of scarce resources*, November.

24. Ray Mabus, Remarks, Center for National Policy, Washington, DC, 12 May 2010.

25. Gilbert, E. (2012). The militarization of climate change. *ACME: An International E-Journal for Critical Geographies*, 11(1).

26. Jimmy Carter, The State of the Union address delivered before a Joint Session of the Congress, 23 January 1980.

27. Fisher Jr., R.D. (27 February 2014). Chinese systems get 'combat experience' in Venezuela. *Jane's Defence Weekly*.

28. BBC News. (25 February 1999). Arms sales fuel BAe's profits.

29. Vranckx, A., ed. (2010). *Rhetoric or Restraint?: Trade in military equipment under the EU transfer control system – A Report to the EU Presidency*, Ghent: Academia Press, November.

30. Human Rights Watch. (28 May 2011). Nigeria: president should make rights a priority [press release].

31. BBC News. (23 October 2012). Stolen Nigerian oil 'goes to Balkans and Singapore'.
32. Volman, D. (13 September 2009). Nigeria: govt gears up for another offensive in the Delta. *Inter Press Service*.
33. Tweede Kamer (25 January 2010). Wapenexportbeleid – lijst van vragen en antwoorden, 22054 – no. 157.
34. Haines, L. (18 September 2006). Arms manufacturer loads lead-free bullets. *The Register*.
35. Ungoed-Thomas, J. (17 September 2006). Watch out, sarge!: it's environmentally friendly fire. *Sunday Times*.
36. Vogelaar, R. (23 April 2010). US Navy tests biofuel-powered 'Green Hornet'. *Aviationnews.eu*.
37. Pew, G. (9 June 2010). EADS: algae-fueled DA42 a 'world's first' (and better). *AVweb*.
38. Environmental Entrepreneurs (E2). (10 November 2012). The economic benefits of military agrofuel programs; Woody, T. (24 September 2012). The U.S. military's great green gamble spurs agrofuel startups. *Forbes*.
39. *Agrofuels Digest*. (16 December 2010). Military signals advanced agrofuels demand: 336 million gallons per year by 2020.
40. QinetiQ and the Centre for Advanced Electrical Drives were earlier 'successful' in collaborating on the Zephyr, the UAV with the longest unmanned aerial flight to date (336 hours).
41. *DefenceNow*. (24 August 2011). DRDO to develop solar-powered drones for armed forces.
42. Buncombe, A. (5 September 2009). Pentagon spends millions seeking environmentally friendly bullets. *The Independent*.
43. Tweede Kamer (15 November 1999). Verslag houdende een lijst van vragen en antwoorden, 26800X – no. 12.
44. Dunne, J.P. and Sköns, E. (2010). The military industrial complex, in Tan, A., ed. *The Global Arms Trade*. London and New York: Routledge.
45. The White House, Remarks by the President at the United States Military Academy Commencement Ceremony, West Point, New York, 28 May 2014.
46. Perlo-Freeman, S., Wezeman, S., Weizman, P. and Fleurant, A. (13 April 2015). Trends in world military expenditure [fact sheet]. Retrieved from http://books.sipri.org/files/FS/SIPRIFS1504.pdf.
47. BAE Systems. *Annual Report 2005: Delivering real advantage*. Retrieved from investors. baesystems.com/~/media/Files/B/BAE-Systems…/ar-2005.pdf.
48. Parrish, K. (22 November 2013). Hagel announces DOD's Arctic strategy. *American Forces Press Service*.
49. US Department of Defense. (2014). *2014 Climate Change Adaptation Roadmap* [report]. Retrieved from doi:http://www.acq.osd.mil/ie/download/CCARprint_wForeword_c.pdf.
50. Discussion at Atlantic Council's Brent Scowcroft Center on International Security, 6 March 2014: https://www.youtube.com/watch?v=V0y83FE_cJc.
51. Slijper, F. (4 April 2011). Airbus military manipulates Oxfam figure to bolster arm sales. *Campagne tegen Wapenhandel*.
52. Oxfam. (2009). *The Right to Survive – The humanitarian challenge for the twenty-first century*, April.
53. Gilbert, E. (2012).
54. http://home.janes.com/events/conferences/e2ds2011/.
55. http://www.un-spider.org/about-us/news/en/6357/2013-01-08t075900/gmes-renamed-copernicus.

56. See www.climatesecurityagenda.org.

57. Schofield, S. (2008). Making arms, wasting skills: alternatives to militarism and arms production, *Campaign Against Arms Trade*, April.

58. Cronin, D. (16 February 2010). Arms lobby licks its lips over climate change. *The Samosa.*

59. Sirota, D. (23 May 2011). The Pentagon's attempt to greenwash the military. *Salon.*

60. Loughlin, S. (12 April 1993). Environmentalists find ally in military. *Times Daily.*

61. http://switchboard.nrdc.org/blogs/plehner/the_department_of_defense_know.html.

62. Lehner, P. (11 October 2011). Military top brass support clean energy development: It's a matter of national security, NRDC Staff blog.

63. http://desmogblog.com/pentagon-back-tried-and-true-pr-tactic-greenwashing.

64. http://indymedia.org.au/2010/12/10/friends-of-the-earth-respond-to-military-greenwashing-of-us-aust-joint-war-games.

65. *The Ecologist.* (11 May 2011). Conservation International 'agreed to greenwash arms company'.

66. See http://www.huffingtonpost.com/2011/05/17/conservation-international-lockheed-martin-video_n_863205.html.

67. See website https://arms-to-renewables.org.uk.

68. CAAT. (2014). Arms to renewables: Trade union info sheet. Retrieved from https://www.caat.org.uk/issues/jobs-economy/resources/trade-union-infosheet.pdf.

69. CAAT. (29 July 2014). Get involved: Trade unionists.

PART III

ACQUISITION THROUGH DISPOSSESSION

8

SOWING INSECURITY: FOOD AND AGRICULTURE IN A TIME OF CLIMATE CRISIS

Nick Buxton, Zoe W. Brent and Annie Shattuck[1]

Agroecology is political; it requires us to challenge and transform structures of power in society. We need to put the control of seeds, biodiversity, land and territories, waters, knowledge, culture and the commons in the hands of the peoples who feed the world.

Declaration of the International Forum for Agroecology, Nyéléni, Mali, 27 February 2015

Introduction

'The food-pocalypse is already upon us', blared a headline in the *Guardian* in March 2014,[2] as it warned of how food price increases, changing climate and increased demand were harbingers of hunger and anger that would increasingly explode onto the world stage. The article drew on the 2014 Intergovernmental Panel on Climate Change's report released the same month that warned of predicted temperature increases of 7.2 degrees Fahrenheit or more by the end of the century that 'would pose large risks to food security globally and regionally.'[3]

Food prices and political conflict have a long, intertwined history. Think of the French Revolution: the guillotines came out after wheat prices shot up 88 per cent following two failed harvests. But food and conflict seems to have become a particularly hot issue in the last decade. Two events in particular sparked the renewed interest. The first was the food crisis in 2007–08, when the price of basic foods spiked, fuelling a new wave of large-scale land deals, or 'land grabs', as corporations, the financial sector and new state players sought to secure land.[4] The second was the wave of revolutions that unfurled with the Arab Spring, along with food riots elsewhere in the world, both prompted by rising food prices.[5] Scientific predictions of looming, devastating climate-change impacts that will compound these pressures have added to the fears that our food supply, and hence our very political systems, are more fragile than we think.

The trouble, as this chapter explores and documents, is that the proposed cure for a food system viewed in this way can be worse than the disease. The narrative of food scarcity and impending conflict is gathering steam in policy circles, emphasising a 'need' to dramatically increase food supply by expanding the industrial model of agriculture.

Stepping back, the conventional framework for explaining the relationship between hunger, land and climate change is anchored around a common, singular notion of 'security': that pursuing large-scale investments in land and agribusiness can lead to food security, and the best way to do this is to put in place governance instruments that would guarantee security to investors. The drive for this security – including secure profit streams capitalising on volatile, high food prices and increased commodities demand – has led to land grabs and dispossession across wide swathes of the world, with disastrous implications for the security of human lives and dignity. Meanwhile, important questions are not being addressed: who will carry out this new production, who will consume it, and who will control the land and resources needed to do so?

Current consensus on the impacts of climate change on agriculture

The Intergovernmental Panel on Climate Change (IPCC) Working Group II report is unequivocal on the negative impacts of climate change on agriculture and food. The report warns that 'All aspects of food security are potentially affected by climate change, including food access, utilization, and price stability.'[6] It predicts declines of up to 25 per cent for major crops (wheat, rice and maize) in tropical and temperate regions. The report finds that rising sea levels and increased salinisation are destroying agricultural land on vulnerable islands and in important food-rich deltas. And it warns that coastal areas and nations dependent upon fishing for food and revenue are likely to suffer, too, as warming and increasingly acidic seas cause species to die out or move to different parts of the ocean. Analysts, from the international aid community to the US military, have paired these dire predictions with fears of rising food prices and resulting global unrest.[7] The figure opposite, for example, from a report on democracy in the Middle East, warns of more Arab Spring-like political unrest and food rebellions if food supplies are not secured.

Climate scientists agree that the effects of climate change will impact some communities more than others. Projections vary across studies, however. In their survey of global studies carried out over the past twenty years, Tim Wheeler and Joachim van Braun find one consistent pattern: 'Crop yields are more negatively affected across most tropical areas than at higher latitudes, and ... climate change will exacerbate food insecurity in areas that already currently have a high prevalence of hunger and undernutrition.'[8] This is echoed by the IPCC and the World Bank, which highlight how the effects of climate change will be uneven and will impact tropical countries of the Global South most negatively. This includes the six countries – India, China, Bangladesh,

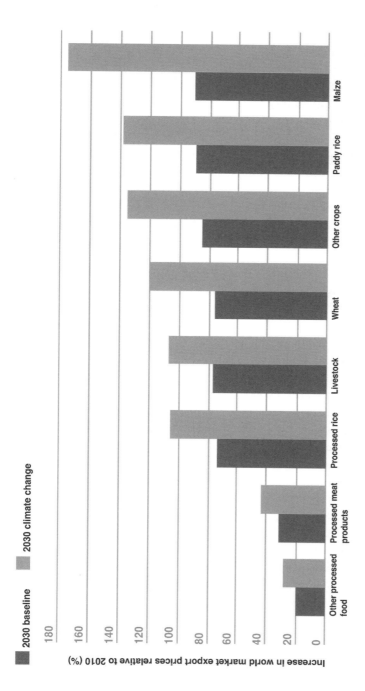

Figure 8.1 Food price increase projections due to climate change over the next twenty years

Source: 'Exploring Food Price Scenarios towards 2030 with a Global Multi-Region Model', Oxfam Research Reports, June 2011.

Indonesia, Pakistan and Ethiopia – in which, according to FAO, over half of the world's food-insecure people live.[9]

This uneven impact is already playing out in countless communities across the globe. In Pakistan, for example, extreme flooding in 2010 led to income losses of up to 50 per cent among three-fifths of affected households, particularly those in rural areas.[10] In Kirabati, the community of Tebunginako has already been forced to relocate because of seawater intrusion destroying coconut and taro trees; with Kiribati's 33 coral atolls and islands standing at an average of just two meters above sea level, there is only so far they can go.

Increased extreme weather conditions can also affect vulnerable developing countries, no matter where on the globe they take place, due to outsized dependence in some countries on global food markets. Research published in *Nature* revealed how drought in Russia and Ukraine in 2010 reduced their harvests by 32.7 per cent and 19.3 per cent, respectively, prompting a doubling in global wheat prices in eight months.[11] This had a major impact on wheat-importing countries, particularly in North Africa. As poor people spend a higher proportion of their income on food, they are particularly affected by price increases.

Very poor farmers may also be affected disproportionately by the kinds of climate disturbances that never make headlines. To a farmer on marginal soils, with little access to credit or capital, even a two-week delay in the rainy season can spell disaster. Resource-poor farmers, the urban poor, those in water-stretched areas where natural resources have been depleted and those with little access to political power are more vulnerable than others, even when exposed to the same events.

The emerging scientific consensus on the uneven impacts of climate change is pushing adaptation efforts toward the lower-income tropical areas identified as most vulnerable, especially in Africa. In the words of the UN's Food and Agriculture Organization (FAO), 'Agriculture in developing countries must undergo a significant transformation in order to meet the related challenges of food security and climate change.'[12]

Policy makers unfortunately focus less on the role of agricultural systems in industrialised countries and give less weight to the conclusion in the IPCC Working Group II report that warns against becoming over-distracted by climate-change impacts to the extent that we lose the overall picture of how world agriculture and food systems operate. It saliently notes: 'At the same time, it is likely that socio-economic and technological trends, including changes in institutions and policies, will remain a relatively stronger driver of food security over the next few decades than climate change.'[13] Those trends include the deep historical roots of the vulnerability to swings in global food prices. It is to these roots we briefly turn.

Global food regimes and food security

Flooding the global market with cheap food is not the only way to prevent the kinds of food riots and hunger that people fear. In fact, the history of these kinds of cheap food policies have a lot to do with why people are so vulnerable to swings in the global market today. To understand global *food security*, it is useful to look at the recent history of the global *food regime* and its implications for land use and control.

A food regime analysis looks at how food is produced, distributed and consumed in the context of an international political economy and presided over by a constellation of power holders. Harriet Friedmann and Philip McMichael use the term 'food regime' to highlight the formal and informal rules in specific periods that governed the production, distribution and consumption of food globally.[14] The first food regime was anchored by the British Empire, starting in the 1870s and lasting until the eve of the First World War, based on colonial and settler economies producing cheap grains and meat through extensive agriculture in order to export them to the centres of capital and working-class populations in Europe. In the second food regime, which lasted from the 1930s until the early 1970s, power shifted from the UK to the US, where large-scale, chemical-based, mechanised and heavily subsidised agriculture began producing massive food surpluses, which were often dumped in developing countries via food aid.

Transnational corporations (TNCs) are the presiding power in what McMichael categorises as the third, corporate, food regime that emerged in tandem with neoliberalism.[15] Structural adjustment policies in the 1980s and 1990s bankrupted national agricultural research programs, and free-trade agreements unleashed a flood of cheap commodities, which put millions of producers in the Global South out of business. By the early 2000s, many low-income countries were left with a strong trade deficit in food and vulnerable to global market swings.

Part of the newly emerging reality involves a reconfiguration of key hubs of global capital, with a whole new set of players emerging and vying for power and influence in reshaping the international rules that govern the production, distribution and consumption of food and other closely related commodities. The new actors include the BRICS countries (Brazil, Russia, India, China and South Africa), some MICs (middle-income countries) and the Gulf States. Many of these countries have moved from being only big food importers/consumers to also becoming important producers of key commodities; others are seeking to ensure food supplies to their national populations, as did European countries a century ago.

This does not mean that the emergence of challengers to the traditionally North Atlantic-based food regime has marginalised the conventional power holders: Europe and the US still remain key players in the global food system and in the dynamics of regime rule making. The top ten food producers globally, measured by income, assets, turnover, or market capitalisation, are all corporations based in the US or Europe.[16] This dominance is still especially true with respect to the financialisation of agricultural production, in which North Atlantic-based finance capital has played a growing role in land deals.[17]

The fluid, still-unfolding transition to a more polycentric global food regime nevertheless marks a further expansion of agribusiness in both the Global North and South, in which farmland itself has become a globalised asset, altering the livelihoods of millions of people.

Expansion of industrial agriculture deepens the climate crisis

The rising dominance of this agro-industrial global economy means that agriculture and land conversion for agricultural expansion are currently responsible for a significant portion of greenhouse-gas emissions.[18] The data presented below in Figure 8.2 breaks down all emissions by sector. However, it is important to note the way industrial agriculture is tied into emissions of other sectors as well. Land use, for example, refers to emissions from deforestation and forestry practices, which may be fuelled by agricultural expansion or monoculture tree plantations. Power refers to energy supply which, as the agrofuels boom has shown, is increasingly intertwined with agriculture. Agricultural production, of course, relies on transportation to reach markets, generates waste and requires building infrastructure, so agriculture's contribution to greenhouse-gas emissions goes well beyond the 13.5 per cent attributed to farming in Figure 8.2.

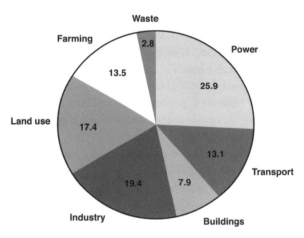

Figure 8.2 Greenhouse-gas emissions and agriculture[19]

Source: IAASTD/IPCC, 2009.

Changing global diets driving the growth of livestock production is also having serious impacts on our climate. Not only is livestock the largest producer of methane and N_2O (GHGs that are more potent than CO_2), much of the feed given to animals also uses nutritional energy less efficiently than if it was used directly by humans. This means more and more land is required as meat consumption rises, leading to what Tony Weis calls:

> ... an expanding 'ecological hoofprint.' This involves the loss of forests, grasslands and wetlands, which in turn has a major impact on the carbon cycle, both in the release of carbon as diverse ecosystems are converted to agriculture, and in the diminished capacity for carbon sequestration.[20]

Moreover, as author Michael Pollan points out, there is also a geopolitical externality, as this system is ultimately 'defended by the US military, another never-counted cost of cheap food', given that 'one-fifth of America's petroleum consumption goes to producing and transporting our food.'[21] Any strategies for addressing climate change and its impacts that do not address the reality of military involvement in securing food and its related oil resources will therefore come up short both in terms of effectiveness and justice.

Food distribution and access: The missing pieces of the climate puzzle

Even so, scarcity and supply remain the dominant themes of climate discourse, ignoring the fact that hunger is a symptom of a deeper lack – a lack of income, equality and political power – rather than an issue of material scarcity.[22] As Eric Holt-Giménez and colleagues explain: 'The world already produces enough food to feed 10 billion people. But the people making less than $2 a day – most of whom are resource-poor farmers cultivating un-viably small plots of land – cannot afford to buy this food.'[23]

The problem of global hunger is *not* that there is not enough food to go around, or due to a failure to close the 'yield gap' between observed yields and potential yields (which, it is argued, can only be resolved with the help of increased agricultural technology).[24] Helping small farmers increase their incomes – not just their yields – is a political, rather than technical, challenge.

Highlighting this contradiction between rising yields and hunger, the FAO reported that world cereal output in 2013 broke records, reaching a new high of around 2,500 million tonnes, even while it warned that food security in the Sahel, Central Africa, Southern Africa, parts of the Middle East and the Philippines is deteriorating due to instability and/or drought, other types of severe weather and land degradation.[25] Dominant TNC players – usually in alliance with national states – generated huge profits producing industrial food during the 2008–12 years of global high prices and food scares. The 'ABCD' of agribusiness – ADM, Bunge, Cargill and Louis Dreyfus – control 75–90 per cent of the global grain trade;[26] in 2014, ADM reported a 25 per cent profit increase on net sales of over $81 billion, while in the same year, Cargill's profits had fallen in comparison to the previous year but the company still generated sales and revenue of over $134 billion.[27]

A focus on supply also ignores the role of other factors in fuelling food price increases, notably agrofuel production and the increased speculation in food commodities by the financial sector. At the peak of the 2008 financial crisis, *Euromoney* declared: 'Farmland is the new gold: There are not many markets left in which it would be safe to invest, but agriculture should be a safe bet.'[28] Seen as a perfect inflation hedge, speculation in food commodities exploded between 2004 and 2014, as the commodities sector was steadily deregulated, particularly after the US approval of the Commodity Futures Modernization Act (CFMA) in 2000. Speculation on food commodities increased tenfold between 2000 and 2011.[29] While there remains some debate about the exact contribution of financialisation to food price increases, researchers have shown how futures markets do impact actual commodity prices by shaping expectations by private actors.[30] Moreover, financialisation in every part of the industrial-agricultural supply chain has clearly played a role in strengthening the most powerful actors – in particular, food retailers – and consistently discriminated-against small-scale farmers.[31]

One of the resulting problems of the structural organisation of our current food regime is waste – or in the words of the FAO food security definition: 'utilisation'. Between 30 and 50 per cent of the food produced globally – about 1.2–2 billion tonnes of food, and 550 billion cubic meters of water – is wasted, according to a 2013 study by the UK's Institution of Mechanical Engineers.[32] The global food system, dominated by supermarkets and agro-industries, has a major role in generating such waste.

The FAO recognises that improved distribution, utilisation and access are critical to food security, but there has been much less focus on these factors. In one study of peer-reviewed journal articles on food security and climate change since the first Inter-governmental Panel on Climate Change (IPCC) report in 1990, the authors found that 70 per cent of the papers focused on food availability, while only 11.9 per cent dealt with food access.[33]

Proposed solutions: Climate-smart agriculture

With demand projections rising, climate change threatens the bottom line of the companies seeking to fill that demand as well as nation states facing geopolitical instability due to rising prices. In September 2014, the Obama administration announced the new Global Alliance for Climate-Smart Agriculture at the UN Climate Summit in New York. The alliance includes the governments of 14 countries, the Consultative Group for International Agriculture Research (CGIAR) institutions, UN agencies, private corporations – including Mosaic Fertilizer – and major conservation organisations such as the Nature Conservancy and the International Union for Conservation of Nature (IUCN). Offering a 'triple win', 'Climate-smart agriculture' (CSA) rests on three pillars: increasing productivity, strengthening farmers' resilience and reducing agriculture's greenhouse-gas emissions.[34] CSA is about both adapting to and mitigating climate change. The adaptation strategy involves increasing investment and technical assistance in order to maintain productivity at a time of rising temperatures and less predictable weather. The mitigation strategy promotes linking agriculture to carbon markets such as REDD (Reducing Emissions from Deforestation and Forest Degradation), REDD+, or a proposed soil-carbon market, so that farmers in Africa and elsewhere can sell their carbon offsets to polluters in the North.

'Climate-smart agriculture' is an umbrella term that includes everything from efforts to genetically engineer drought tolerance into maize and other staple crops, private investment in agribusiness supply chains, efforts to increase productivity per unit-area, new index-based crop insurance products, improved weather data delivered by mobile phone, more energy-efficient machinery, incorporating livestock into small-scale farms and intercropping with nitrogen-fixing 'fertiliser' tree species. So far, many commitments to action are vague. An African Union project, for example, aims to make 'CSA practices and technologies' more accessible and strengthen 'evidence-based policy' on the continent.[35]

There is potentially a significant amount of money for initiatives that fall under the CSA umbrella – and that umbrella seems to be expanding. The World Bank Group pledged $5 billion over the next four years to 'mainstream' CSA in its development projects, making sure all of its agricultural investments adhere to a rubric of productivity, resilience and emissions reductions. In 2012, the International Fund for Agricultural Development requested $350 million to 'mainstream' its CSA work, including trainings, participatory risk management and making land-management practices more resilient. The Feed the Future initiative, begun in 2009, with a $3.5 billion commitment from the Obama administration, is now part of the Alliance for Climate-Smart Agriculture, focusing on efforts to improve agricultural productivity.[36] Major food corporations are coming on board as well: Kellogg's, for example, has promised an undisclosed sum to help small-scale farmers in their supply chain adapt to climate change, improve their agronomic practices and upgrade their business skills. To start, Kellogg's will target rice farmers in Bangladesh, India, South Africa, Thailand and Vietnam.[37] What all these initiatives have in common is a strong focus on the sustainability of the private sector.

Not everyone is excited about these new initiatives, however. For Simon Mwamba of the East and Southern African Small-Scale Farmers Forum (ESAFF), 'Climate Smart Agriculture is being presented as sustainable agriculture, but the term is so broad that we fear it is a front for promoting industrial, green revolution agriculture too, which traps farmers into cycles of debt and poverty.'[38] Calls by Kofi Anan for a 'uniquely African Green Revolution'[39] seem to have learned nothing from the growing body of research on the negative social and environmental impacts of the first Green Revolution. As Nick Cullather notes in his book *The Hungry World*, a cutting critique of the Green Revolution myth:

... the green revolution epicenters – Pakistan, India, Sri Lanka, Bangladesh, Mexico, the Philippines, and Indonesia – are all among the most undernourished nations, each with higher rates of adult and childhood malnutrition and deficiency diseases ... than most Sub-Saharan countries.[40]

Similarly, Climate-smart agriculture also proposes to mitigate climate change by linking agriculture to carbon markets and providing a 'potential source of finance for improved agriculture in the future.'[41] However, with transaction costs high, a history of abuse, and fraud in offset programmes, and with voluntary carbon markets lagging behind expectations and the EU carbon markets currently in turmoil, it is difficult to imagine that small-scale farmers will receive a carbon windfall. Tosi Mpanu-Mpanu, chair of the African Group on Climate Change Negotiations, argues it is unlikely the promise of carbon credits from soil-carbon sequestration will actually benefit African farmers, most of whom have less than two hectares of land, 'which is not enough to sequester an amount of carbon that would be meaningful to sell. We're very suspicious that offset schemes will lead to a perversion of African agriculture with farmers farming what is incentivized, and giving up traditional crops.'[42]

Small-farmers' organisations and social movements have been largely excluded from international planning on climate-change adaptation. Instead, climate-smart agriculture is consistently framed as a way that foreign investors can help farmers deal with the problem of climate change. The buzzword is 'sustainable intensification' – one of the techniques that fall under the big tent of CSA, which seeks to use inputs more efficiently, produce more per unit-area and thereby reduce emissions by avoiding deforestation of new land for agriculture. The Obama administration's Feed the Future initiative backs this strategy with agricultural aid in twenty developing countries. It actively promotes genetically modified (GM) crops (with 28 per cent of its research funding), the integration of small farmers into commercial markets, and public/private partnerships with agribusiness giants such as DuPont and Syngenta, which plan to expand business in Africa to $1 billion between 2015 and 2025.[43]

An FAO report argues, 'Investing in climate-smart agriculture at a landscape scale will have a large price tag.' To meet rising global demand, the FAO estimates it will take $83 billion of investment per year in developing countries, the majority of which will 'need to come from private investors.'[44] Yet meeting the demand for agricultural commodities is clearly not the same as building food systems that will continue to serve the poor under an increasingly unstable climate. The estimate is about growing agribusiness, not adapting to climate change.

There is ample evidence that it is not just how much food is produced, but who controls the resources needed to produce food that makes a difference when it comes to combating hunger. Calls for investments in climate-smart agriculture could include a wealth of agroecological practices, local infrastructure improvements and institutional arrangements that benefit small-scale farmers and provide resilience to extreme weather. But many of these are not profitable enough to draw private-sector support. Public financing is being used instead to create enabling conditions for investors, monitor and verify soil-carbon stocks, develop GM crops and invest in infrastructure for export agriculture. These all come with a significant opportunity cost. And they come with a potentially powerful discourse that justifies the consolidation of land and territory, which undermines food security.

The land question: Investment, land grabs and security narratives

The call for food security, powered by the underlying myth of impending global food scarcity, plays a key role in justifying the contemporary cycle of land grabbing – and on the pretext of tackling climate change may even exacerbate it. The global phenomenon of land grabbing was initially reported with alarm by nongovernmental organisations (NGOs) and the media, but it is persistently being reframed as 'land investment' by those seeking to profit from it.

The case of climate-smart agriculture, for example, demonstrates this dark irony. Proposed climate-mitigation strategies in the arena of agriculture have themselves become key drivers in land grabbing. This has been the case with the promotion of agrofuels that received significant state subsidies and support worldwide and were painted as a solution to both the energy crisis and climate change. This trend must be understood in the context of the rise of what Saturnino Borras and colleagues call 'flex crops and commodities' – one offshoot of the recent convergence of multiple crises (food, energy, climate and finance).[45]

Flex crops and commodities have multiple uses (food, feed, fuel and industrial material) that can be easily and flexibly interchanged: soya (feed, food and biodiesel), sugarcane (food and ethanol), palm oil (food, biodiesel and commercial/industrial uses), corn (food, feed and ethanol) and now carbon sequestration. It has resolved one difficult challenge in agriculture, that of fluctuating prices: diversified product portfolios avoid devastating price shocks, meaning more security to capital investments. The fact that key crops and commodities can 'flex' undermines the argument that the main motive behind agricultural land expansion is specifically *food* security while exposing the main motivation, which is to *secure profits*.

With the emergence of relevant markets (including financialised speculative ones) and the development and availability of technology (for example, flexible mills) that allows multiple and flexible uses of these crops, diversification of products has certainly been achieved, but only within a single crop sector. When sugarcane prices are high, sell sugarcane; when ethanol prices are high, sell ethanol. When the actual market for biodiesel is not there yet, sell palm oil for cooking oil, while waiting (or speculating) for a more lucrative biodiesel market to emerge. Yet, as we know now, rather than reducing use of fuel or avoiding deforestation and forest degradation in order to curb runaway GHG emissions, agrofuels ended up contributing GHG emissions, especially through massive forest clearing.[46]

Tree plantations are another sector where global land grabbing is implicated. It is in many ways a kind of 'flex commodity' – these are trees and forests with multiple and flexible uses, the emergence of which is traceable to the same changes in the global political economy that ushered in the rise of flex crops. Tree plantations can be used for timber extraction for industrial purposes and for the growing paper and pulp industry (for example, for packaging), largely for export. But the same plantation can be anticipated for possible rise in wood chip-based energy complex, while at the same time it can be used to speculate on carbon-offset schemes such as REDD+. During the past decade, this sector has had a rising impact on land use.[47]

Widespread concern about the negative impacts on local communities has led many advocates of land investment, such as Hernando de Soto and the World Bank, to argue that Western-style property rights will shield poor people from land grabbing and by implication prevent abuses under the banner of 'climate-smart agriculture'. This has led to the development of a number of codes and standards, notably the 'principles of responsible agricultural investments' (RAI principles) put forward by the World Bank, and the Code of Conduct initially proposed by the International Food Policy Research Institute (IFPRI).[48] Yet efforts to codify Western-style property rights and make them more transparent have not turned the tide against land grabbing.[49] Unfortunately, even 'good transparent deals' can still end up involving grabbing, because what is being 'grabbed' is not just the actual physical resource itself but, more profoundly, the *political control over it*: in other words, the very power to decide how it will be used and for what purposes – and not just now, but into the future, as well. Land grabbing does not always or automatically mean the expulsion of communities from their lands; it can also mean their incorporation – for good, or for ill, or both – into new economic arrangements through lease, labour and growing contracts. Justifying a deal with the argument that relevant authorities were 'consulted' ignores the weak political position of poor people that enter into land-deal negotiations, as well as the dangers and insecurity created by the privatisation and commoditisation of land that can quickly lead to dispossession.[50]

From 'security' to 'sovereignty'; agro-industry to agroecology

The singular focus on production eclipses the power and politics that cause hunger today. As the former UN Special Rapporteur on the Right to Food reminds us:

> ... investments that increase food production will not make significant progress in combating hunger and malnutrition if not combined with higher incomes and improved livelihoods for the poorest – particularly small-scale farmers in developing countries. And short-term gains will be offset by long-term losses if they lead to further degradation of ecosystems, thereby threatening our future ability to maintain current levels of production. The question therefore is not simply how much, but also how. Pouring money into agriculture will not be sufficient. We need to take steps that facilitate the transition towards a low-carbon, resource-preserving type of agriculture that benefits the poorest farmers.[51]

At the heart of the new (and still evolving) debate over land grabbing is an old question: which agricultural model can produce more food (or energy) – small-scale, less-mechanised, non-industrial, localised and diversified farming, or monocrop, large-scale industrial, mechanised, fossil-fuel-based farming? This time, however, the question must be asked within a changed context: that is, in the era of climate change. Which system is best able to adapt to and mitigate the impacts of climate change? Which agriculture and food system is more resilient?

Farmers' movements are already advancing resilient alternatives based on agroecology.[52] Agroecology seeks to adapt agriculture to the ecosystem in which it operates, minimises off-farm inputs and maximises the system's own resilience and diversity in order to reduce pests, improve soils and harvest water. It also integrates forestry, aquaculture and livestock into farming systems.[53]

Peasant-based agroecology systems may be more ecologically resilient to climate stress, if not to the ravages of the market. In an extensive comparison of more than 150 studies[54] that examined agroecological systems and industrial agriculture, Brenda Lin and colleagues show that not only is large-scale, fossil-fuel-based industrial agriculture more likely to rely on practices that emit GHGs, it is also far less effective at sequestering carbon than agroecological methods. Agroecological functions, such as nutrient cycling, micro-climate control, soil-moisture retention and pest management have also been proved to help an agroecosystem maintain vital services – such as yield – even if challenged by a disturbance, such as a severe drought.[55] Genetic diversity can also buffer against risk. In an oft-cited study of heterogeneous rice plantings in Yunnan, China, Zhu found that disease-susceptible rice varieties planted in mixtures with resistant varieties had 89 per cent greater yield, and incidence of disease was 94 per cent less severe than when grown in monoculture.[56]

The study corroborates recent empirical experiences of increased resilience in diversified agroecosystems. Peter Michael Rosset and Braulio Machín-Sosa describe the experience of one of Cuba's Credit and Service Cooperatives (CCS) after Hurricane Ike tore through the region in 2008. The authors ranked and grouped individual farms on their levels of agroecological integration, which includes diversification, and estimated both the percentage of damage (resistance) and the time to recovery (resilience) of the farms. After 30 days, farms that showed the highest degree of agroecological integration – a measure that includes diversification and on-farm production of inputs – were an estimated 80 per cent recovered from the disaster. Those with the lowest level of integration had recovered by 60 per cent. But this recovery was also aided not just by agricultural diversity, but also by the concerted efforts of social movements and the Cuban state.[57] Another study of a thousand farms in Central America in the aftermath of Hurricane Mitch found that farmers using the agroecological agricultural methods had 30–40 per cent more topsoil, half as many landslides, much less erosion and, most importantly, had fewer economic losses after the hurricane.[58]

Meanwhile, proposed technical solutions promoted by biotechnology giants – such as the use of genetic modification to create drought-tolerant seeds – have proved to be overblown. The US Department of Agriculture's (USDA) analysis of Monsanto's trumpeted DroughtGuard™ corn (using the engineered gene *cspB*), for example, showed very modest results – and only under moderate drought conditions. It predicted that, at most, its use would increase productivity by about 1 per cent.[59]

Perhaps more important than yields and techniques at a time of climate crisis is the role agroecology plays in protecting the environmental conditions required for community health and survival. Small-scale farmers – who already provide 70 per cent of the food we eat – more efficiently use water, light and nutrients, which will be critical in regions where these resources become scarce.

This awareness that agroecology offers a better path at a time of climate crisis than agroindustry is gaining increasing traction, although not without a strong backlash from the powerful corporate interests that seek to profit from crisis. In 2008, the International Assessment of Agriculture Science and Development (IAASTD), a three-year process sponsored by the UN Environment Programme (UNEP), the UN Food and Agriculture Organisation (FAO), the World Bank and other institutions, and involving over four hundred experts from over eighty countries, made a surprisingly bold call for a radical transformation of the world's food and agriculture system. The IAASTD report concluded that chemical-intensive industrial agriculture had degraded our environment and threatened water, energy and climate; it warned against reliance on unproved technological fixes and it critiqued transnational agribusiness's influence over public policy and their responsibility for unjust global trade policies that leave millions undernourished.[60]

In place of chemical-intensive industrial agriculture, the IAASTD report called for investment in agroecology, such as supporting agroecological research and education and providing incentives for resource-conserving practices. It argued for more support for small-scale farmers – particularly women – by investing in infrastructure and supporting community-based organisations that produce and process food. It called for more equitable regional and global trade policies to support communities and developing countries in meeting their own food and livelihood security needs. The IAASTD's bold conclusions unsurprisingly rankled some of the participants: biotechnology corporations walked out, and three governments (the US, Australia and the UK) refused to endorse the texts. Even so, 58 governments voiced their support.

Growing climate impacts on agriculture and food will clearly put a test on any food system. Turning around an agroindustrial juggernaut is also no easy task. Organic agriculture in the US, for example, comprises a mere 0.52 per cent of total crop acreage and receives only 1 per cent of USDA research funds.[61] But the growing climate crisis is a warning that rather than deepening an unsustainable land, agriculture and food system, we need a radical transformation that returns power to farmers and communities and reintegrates ecology into the way we grow food.

One term that encapsulates that vision for transformation is the call for 'food sovereignty', made originally by the international peasant movement La Via Campesina in the early 1990s. Food sovereignty is broadly defined as the right of peoples to produce, distribute and consume safe, healthy and culturally appropriate food in sustainable ways in and near their territory – all issues ignored by the term 'food security'.[62] Food sovereignty addresses the issue of 'distancing' (producer-consumer, geographic distance, rural-urban) that is a hallmark of industrial agriculture and a major cause of greenhouse-gas emissions. The food sovereignty alternative emphasises 'localisation' of the food systems, (although this concept is not without its own problems), essentially taking the control away from industrial corporations and putting it back in the hands of local communities.

As agrarian scholars Saturnino Borras, Jennifer Franco and Sofia Monsalve have argued,[63] food sovereignty needs to be accompanied by 'land sovereignty': supporting the demand for land by rural working peoples. The term connotes 'belongingness': the land belongs to the people who work it, care for it and live on it. Conversely, the people belong to a particular land as a people. Land sovereignty also reminds us that individual and collective plots of land are part of larger, socially constructed landscapes and waterscapes in which we must strive for a renewed relationship with land – one that supports workers' rights, bolsters and strengthens communities and engages consumers, all within ecological boundaries.

Ultimately, the growing demand for sovereignty over our land and food is a resounding call to ditch security narratives that focus only on securing food supplies and not on securing dignified livelihoods and fighting hunger. This demand is only becoming more urgent as corporate actors propose false solutions in the face of growing climate-change-induced stress in our agricultural systems.

Notes

1. Thank you to Jenny Franco and Saturnino 'Jun' Borras who worked on earlier drafts and informed much of the land-based work in this chapter.
2. Schiffman, R. (31 March 2014). Think the new climate report is scary? The food-pocalypse is already upon us. *The Guardian*. Retrieved from http://www.theguardian.com/commentisfree/2014/mar/31/new-climate-report-food-prices-already-here.
3. Intergovernmental Panel on Climate Change (IPCC). (2014). Summary for policymakers (p. 18). In *Climate Change 2014: Impacts, adaptation, and vulnerability. Working group contribution to the Fifth Assessment Report.* Cambridge and New York: Cambridge University Press.
4. Holt-Giménez, E., Patel, R. and Shattuck, A. (2009). *Food Rebellions! Crisis and the hunger for justice.* Oakland: Food First Books; Bello, W. (2009). *The Food Wars.* London: Verso.
5. Mabey, N. et al. (2013). *Underpinning the MENA Democratic Transition: Delivering climate, energy and resource security.* London, Berlin, Brussels and Washington, DC: Third Generation Environmentalism Ltd. (E3G).
6. Porter, J.R., Xie, L., Challinor, A.J., Cochrane, K., Howden, S.M., Iqbal, M.M., Lobell, D.B., and Travasso, M.I. (2014). Food security and food production systems, in Field, C.B. et al., eds. *Climate Change 2014: Impacts, adaptation, and vulnerability. Part A: Global and sectoral aspects. Contribution of Working Group II to the Fifth Assessment Report of the Intergovernmental Panel on Climate Change.* Cambridge and New York: Cambridge University Press, pp. 485–533.
7. CNA Military Advisory Board. (2014). *National Security and the Accelerating Risks of Climate Change.* Alexandria, VA: CNA Corporation. Retrieved from http://www.cna.org/sites/default/files/MAB_2014.pdf.
8. Wheeler, T. and von Braun, J. (2013). Climate change impacts on global food security. *Science.* 134, p. 508.
9. Food and Agriculture Organization, International Fund for Agricultural Development, and World Food Programme. (2014). *The State of Food Insecurity in the World 2014: Strengthening the enabling environment for food security and nutrition.* Rome: Food and Agriculture Organization of the United Nations.

10. World Food Programme. (2010). *Pakistan Flood Assessment*. Rome: World Food Programme. Retrieved from http://home.wfp.org/stellent/groups/public/documents/ena/wfp225987. pdf.

11. Sternberg, T. (2011). Regional drought has a global impact. *Nature*, 472, p. 169.

12. FAO (2014). *The Post-2015 Development Agenda and the Millennium Development Goals. Climate change*. Rome: Food and Agriculture Organization of the United Nations. Retrieved from http://www.fao.org/post-2015-mdg/14-themes/climate-change/en/.

13. IPCC WG II (2014). *Climate Change 2014 – Impacts, Adaptation and Vulnerability: Global and sectoral aspects*. Working group II Contribution to the Fifth Assessment of the Intergovernmental Panel on Climate Change, p. 513. New York: Cambridge University Press.

14. Friedmann, H. (1982). The political economy of food: The rise and fall of the postwar international food order. *American Journal of Sociology*, 88, pp. 248–86; McMichael, P. (2009). A food regime genealogy. *Journal of Peasant Studies*, 36(1).

15. McMichael, P. (2012). The land grab and corporate food regime restructuring. *Journal of Peasant Studies*, 39, 681–701.

16. *Financial Times*. (2013). FT 500 – 2013: Nestlé, Archer Daniels Midland, Unilever, Mondelez International, Danone, Monsanto, Kraft, General Mills, Kellogg, and HJ Heinz. Retrieved from http://www.ft.com/indepth/ft500.

17. For extended discussions of financialisation of the food system, see Isakson, S.R. (2014). Food and finance: the financial transformation of agro-food supply chains; Clapp, J. (2014). Financialization, distance and global food politics, and Fairbairn, M. (2014). 'Like gold with yield': Evolving intersections between farmland and finance, all in *Journal of Peasant Studies*, 41(5).

18. International Assessment of Agricultural Knowledge, Science and Technology for Development (IAASTD). (2010). *Synthesis Report: A synthesis of the Global and Sub-Global IAASTD Reports*. Washington, D.C.: Independent Evaluation Group, World Bank Group.

19. International Assessment of Agricultural Knowledge, Science and Technology for Development (IAASTD). (2009). *Synthesis Report: A synthesis of the Global and Sub-Global IAASTD Reports*. Washington, DC: Island Press.

20. Weis, T. (July 2010). The accelerating biophysical contradictions of industrial capitalist agriculture. *Journal of Agrarian Change*, 10(3), 317.

21. Pollan, M. (2006). *The Omnivore's Dilemma: A natural history of four meals*. New York: Penguin Press, p. 83.

22. Watts, M. and H. Bohle. (1993). The space of vulnerability: the causal structure of hunger and famine. *Progress in Human Geography*, 17(1), 43–67.

23. Holt-Giménez, E., Shattuck, A., Altieri, M., Herren, H. and Gliessman, S. (2012). We already produce enough food for 10 billion people ... and we still can't end hunger. *Journal of Sustainable Agriculture*, 36(6).

24. Lobell, D. and Burke, M. (2010). Climate effects on food security: An overview, in Lobell, D. and Burke, M., eds. *Climate Change and Food Security; Adapting Agriculture to a Warmer World, Advances in Global Change Research* 37. Dordrecht, Heidelberg, London, New York: Springer, p. 19.

25. See http://www.fao.org/worldfoodsituation/csdb/en/.

26. Holt-Giménez, E. and Shattuck, A. (2011). Food crises, food regimes and food movements: Rumblings of reform or tides of transformation? *Journal of Peasant Studies*, 38(1).

27. ADM Facts, ADM website. Retrieved on 30 April 2015 from http://www.adm.com/en-US/company/Facts/Pages/default.aspx; Cargill. (2015). *Annual report 2014*. Retrieved from http://www.cargill.com/wcm/groups/internal/@ccom/documents/document/na31674913.pdf.

28. Avery, H. (28 July 2014). Agriculture: Farmland is the new gold. *Euromoney Magazine*. Retrieved from http://www.euromoney.com/Article/2059838/Agriculture-Farmland-is-the-new-gold.html.

29. Spratt, S. (2013). Food price volatility and financial speculation. Future Agricultures Consortium, Working Paper 047.

30. Ghosh, J., Heintz, J. and Pollin, R. (2012). Speculation on commodities futures markets and destabilization of global food prices: exploring the connections. *International Journal of Health Sciences*, 42(3), 465–83.

31. Isakson, S.R. (2013). *The Financialization of Food: A political economy of the transformation of agro-food supply chains*, ICAS Review Paper Series No. 5.

32. *Global Food: Waste not want not* [report]. (2013). London: Institute of Mechanical Engineers. Retrieved from doi:http://www.imeche.org/docs/default-source/reports/Global_Food_Report.pdf?sfvrsn=0.

33. Wheeler, T. and von Braun, J. (2013). Climate change impacts on global food security. *Science*, 134(508).

34. World Bank. (2011). *Climate Smart Agriculture: A call to action*. Washington, DC: World Bank.

35. See UN Climate Summit. (2014) Global Alliance for Climate Smart Agriculture Action Plan Agriculture Annex. Retrieved from http://www.un.org/climatechange/summit/wp-content/uploads/sites/2/2014/09/AGRICULTURE-annex.pdf.

36. Feed the Future Initiative Overview Fact Sheet. (October 2012). Retrieved from http://feedthefuture.gov/sites/default/files/resource/files/ftf_overview_factsheet_oct2012.pdf.

37. UN Climate Summit. (2014).

38. Anderson, T. (16 December 2011). Farming carbon credits a con for Africa: The many faces of climate smart agriculture. The Gaia Foundation. Retrieved from http://www.gaiafoundation.org/blog/farming-carbon-credits-a-con-for-africa-the-many-faces-of-climate-smart-agriculture.

39. World Bank (2011).

40. Cullather, N. (2010). *The Hungry World: America's Cold War battle against poverty in Asia*. Cambridge, MA: Harvard University Press.

41. Climate Focus Inc., IIASA, and UNIQUE Forestry Consultants. (n.d.)., Carbon Market and Climate Finance for Climate-Smart Agriculture in Developing Countries, DFID Climate Change, Agriculture and Food Security Policy Research Program, Agriculture and Carbon Market Assessment, p. 10. Retrieved from r4d.dfid.gov.uk/Output/190534/.

42. Anderson, T. (16 December 2011).

43. Collins, E.D. and K. Chandrasekaran. (2012). *Wolf in Sheep's Clothing? An Analysis of the Sustainable Intensification of Agriculture*. Amsterdam: Friends of the Earth International.

44. Schmidhuber, J., Bruinsma, J. and Boedeker, G. (2009). Capital requirements for agriculture in developing countries to 2050 [conference paper]. Expert Meeting on How to Feed the World in 2050. 24–26 June 2009. Rome: Food and Agriculture Organization of the United Nations Economic and Social Development Department. Retrieved from http://www.fao.org/3/a-ak542e/ak542e09.pdf.

45. Borras Jr., S.M., Franco, J.C., Isakson, R., Levidow, L. and Vervest, P. (2014). *Towards Understanding the Politics of Flex Crops and Commodities: Implications for research and policy advocacy*. Think Piece Series of Flex Crops and Commodities. No. 1 Amsterdam: Transnational Institute (TNI).

46. Searchinger, T. (2008). Use of US croplands for biofuels increases greenhouse gases through emissions from land-use change. *Science*, 319 (5867), 1238–40.

47. Kroger, M. (2012). Global Tree Plantation Expansion: a review. *ICAS Review Paper Series No.3*. Amsterdam: Transnational Institute.

48. Borras Jr., S. and J. Franco. (2010). From threat to opportunity? Problems with the idea of a 'code of conduct' for land-grabbing. *Yale Human Rights and Development Law Journal*, 13, 507–23.

49. Dwyer, M. (2013). The formalization fix? Land titling, state land concessions, and the politics of geographical transparency in contemporary Cambodia. Land Deal Politics Initiative (LDPI) Working Paper 37.

50. Vermeulen, S. and Cotula, L. (2010). Over the heads of local people: Consultation, consent, and recompense in large-scale land deals for biofuels projects in Africa. *Journal of Peasant Studies*, 37(4).

51. FIAN. (2011). *Right to Food Quarterly*, 6(1), p. 2.

52. Agroecology is the science and practice of applying ecological concepts and principles to the study, design and management of sustainable agroecosystems. It shares some common elements with organic agriculture but is not wedded to a particular practice or code, nor does it necessarily rule out technological inputs. Rather, it assesses everything from a holistic perspective: it includes social, political, cultural and economic dimensions and integrates state-of-the-art formal science with traditional and community-based knowledge, local food-system experiences, and innovations that are low-cost, readily adaptable by small- and medium-scale farmers and likely to advance social equity while conserving biodiversity, natural resources and ecosystem function.

53. Altieri, M.A. and Toledo, V. (2011). The agroecological revolution in Latin America: rescuing nature, ensuring food sovereignty and empowering peasants. *Journal of Peasant Studies*, 38(3).

54. Lin, B. et al. (2011). Effects of industrial agriculture on climate change and the mitigation potential of small-scale agro-ecological farms. *CAB Reviews: Perspectives in Agriculture, Veterinary Science, Nutrition and Natural Resources*, 6(20).

55. Gattinger, A., Muller, A., Haeni, M., Skinner, C., Fliessbach, A., Buchmann, N., and Niggli, U. (2012). Enhanced top soil carbon stocks under organic farming. *Proceedings of the National Academy of Sciences of the United States of America*, 109(44): 18226–31.

56. Zhu Y.H., Chen, J., Fan, Y., Wang, Y., Li, J., Chen, J., Fan, S., Yang, L., Hu, H., Leung, T.W., Mew, P.S., Teng, Z., Wang, C. and Mundt, C. (2000). Genetic diversity and disease control in rice. *Nature*, 406(6797), 718–22. Research also shows that it can also increase yields: one of the largest studies carried out that analyzed 286 projects in 57 countries showed 64 per cent increases in yields over four years: Pretty, J. (2006). *Agroecological Approaches to Agricultural Development*. Washington, DC: World Bank. Retrieved from https://openknowledge.worldbank.org/handle/10986/9044.

57. Rosset, P., Machín Sosa, B., Roque Jaime, A.M. and Ávila Lozano, D.R. (2011). The campesino-to-campesino agroecology movement of ANAP in Cuba: Social process methodology in the construction of sustainable peasant agriculture and food sovereignty. *Journal of Peasant Studies*, 38(1), 161–91.

58. Gimenez, E.H. (2002). Measuring farmers' agroecological resistance after Hurricane Mitch in Nicaragua: A case study in participatory, sustainable land management impact monitoring. *Agriculture, Ecosystems & Environment*, 93(1–3), 87–105. Retrieved from doi:10.1016/S0167-8809(02)00006-3.

59. Gurian-Sherman, D. (2012). *High and Dry: Why genetic engineering is not solving agriculture's drought problem in a thirsty world*. Union of Concerned Scientists. Retrieved from http://www.ucsusa.org/food_and_agriculture/our-failing-food-system/genetic-engineering/high-and-dry.html.

60. International Assessment of Agricultural Knowledge, Science and Technology for Development: IAASTD. (2010). *Synthesis Report; A Synthesis of the Global and Sub-Global IAASTD Reports*.

61. Miles, A. and Carlisle, L. (2013). Strengthening the US agricultural research system, in *Five Perspectives on Improving the U.S. Public Research, Extension, and Education System*. Washington DC: AGree, pp. 64–77. Retrieved from http://www.foodandagpolicy.org/sites/default/files/AGree%20REE%20report%20June2013.pdf.

62. Martínez-Torres, M.E. and Rosset, P.M. (2010). La Vía Campesina: The birth and evolution of a transnational social movement. *Journal of Peasant Studies*, 37(1), 149–75.

63. Borras, S., Franco, J. and Monsalve, S. (2015). Land and food sovereignty, *Third World Quarterly*, 36(3).

9

IN DEEP WATER: CONFRONTING THE CLIMATE AND WATER CRISES

Mary Ann Manahan

What we do to water, we do to ourselves and the ones we love.

Popol Vuh, *ancient Mayan text*

Introduction

As the lifeblood of the earth, the hydrological cycle is the primary link between the climate system, human society, the environment, food, and economic development. Any changes to the water cycle will affect the natural, socio-cultural, political and economic systems of the world. But at the same time, the reverse is true. Our management of water resources can have as great an impact on watersheds and biodiversity as on cities and people. What ecological sciences and hydrology teach is that any interruption in these interlinked and overlapping systems will have a domino effect. Removing trees, for example, reduces the water-absorptive capacity of landscapes, leading either to loss of rainfall and reduced capacity of the soil to sequester carbon or to water run-offs, soil erosion and landslides that can wipe out communities.

The growing impacts of climate change on water are looming, while the world has failed to ensure access to clean water for hundreds of millions of people. This is not because of a lack of resources, nor necessarily of political will, but, as this chapter explores, due to an overriding determination to treat water as a commodity and a resource to be exploited and secured, rather than considering water as a fluid, holistic, integrated and dynamic system of life in which humans should play only a small role. The impacts of climate change offer the chance to re-establish an ethic of water use based on the principles of human rights, public trust and commons, but this will only happen if dominant state and corporate actors end their agenda of resource capture and control for the few, and marginalisation and insecurity for the many.

Water, water everywhere, not a drop to drink?

The global supply of fresh water is limited. Only 2.41 per cent of the world's total water resources is fresh water, the majority of which (about 26.32 million cubic meters or

1.88 per cent of total water resources) is trapped in polar ice caps and glaciers. The remaining resources are found in groundwater, soil moisture and surface water, such as rivers and lakes. There is still enough fresh water on the planet for everyone to share, but it is unevenly distributed and too much of it has become polluted and is unsustainably managed, exploited and wasted. In short, water scarcity is both human made and natural, or, as scholar Lyla Mehta puts it, 'scarcity is both "real" and 'constructed.'[1]

A fundamental reason why it is 'real' is the fact that the supply of fresh water cannot be increased, despite human ingenuity and innovation. The fresh-water supply can be replenished by nature, as in the case of groundwater and aquifers, but it will take centuries or even thousands of years before these can achieve full capacity again. Annual global water withdrawal is expected to grow by about 10–12 per cent each decade through 2025, which is 1.38 times greater than in 1995.[2] Further estimates predict, that by 2040, water demand will outstrip current supply by 40 per cent.[3]

According to UN estimates, 783 million people are living without improved access to safe drinking water,[4] and 2.5 billion people live without basic access to sanitation: Every 20 seconds a child dies from preventable diseases, such as diarrhoea, dysentery and cholera, due to the lack of proper hygiene and safe drinking water, particularly in the mega-cities of the South.

Climate change is compounding this already fragile situation. The Intergovernmental Panel on Climate Change (IPCC) projects a decrease in water availability of 10–30 per cent in dry regions in low and mid-latitudes. Meanwhile, current projections suggest that water demand is likely to double by 2050.

The result today is that many regions are already experiencing water shortages – the Middle East, Central Asia, the Americas (the midwestern US, Mexico and the Andes), Pakistan, eastern Australia, Spain, southern India and northern China. The UN argues that water scarcity[5] will affect over 1.8 billion people by 2025,[6] with major impacts on agricultural production, health, urban settlements and people's livelihoods.

Other regions are expected to experience increased flooding, while rising sea levels threaten many coastal communities. Climate change does not just affect supply. It impacts the variation of stream flow and groundwater recharge, and consequently water quality and seasonal water availability. It also increases the intensity and frequency of storms during the monsoon season and drought during the summer. Sea-level rise also causes saltwater intrusion into surface and groundwater, affecting the amount and quality of water supplies.

These climatic changes interconnect with human-caused environmental impacts, such as industrial pollution, overuse and deforestation. The latter, for example, leads to soil erosion and siltation or sedimentation of rivers and lakes, which obstructs waterways and affects the water quality and can lead to increased run-off, causing flash floods in mountainous areas.

These are all very serious threats to people and the environment; however, it is important to look more deeply at how scarcity is defined. The dominant narrative of

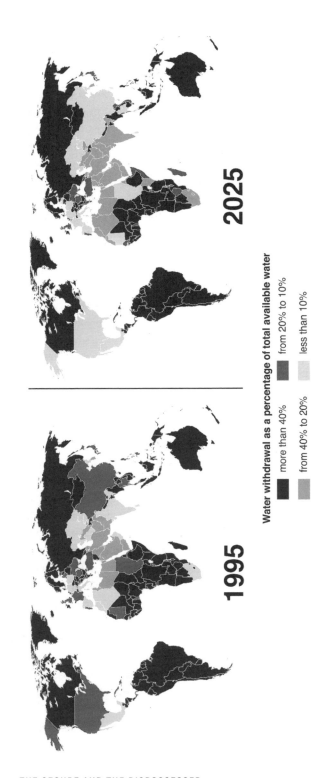

Figure 9.1   Increasing global water stress

Source: United Nations Environmental Programme. (2008). *Vital statistics: An overview of the state of the world's fresh and marine waters* (2nd edn).

scarcity is skewed towards physical, natural and economic forces rather than focused on 'human-induced land and water use practices and at socio-political considerations'.[7]

The demands on this limited resource are very much driven by man-made systems, particularly industrial and irrigated agriculture, affluent lifestyles, extractive industries, and population increase. Agriculture accounts for nearly 70 per cent of global water consumption (some estimates are as high as 85 per cent),[8] with 10 per cent going to domestic use and 20 per cent to industrial production. While there are major regional differences, calculations suggest 50 per cent of water use in developed countries goes to industry, and agriculture accounts for 80 per cent of water use in developing countries. The interconnections between agriculture, water and urbanisation are playing out, for example, in 2014 and 2015 in the severe drought in São Paulo, one of Brazil's fastest growing cities. Studies suggest the drought has been partly caused by massive deforestation in the Amazon due to agribusiness expansion – soya and cattle breeding. Not only does agribusiness account for nearly 70 per cent of the country's water consumption, but the resulting deforestation also contributes to rainfall decrease.[9]

Lyla Mehta argues, through her case-study on the semi-arid region of Kutch in Gujarat, India, that the language of water scarcity too often is used by corporations and governments to justify increases in supply for water-intensive development projects, such as the Narmada Water Project, that often end up worsening scarcity for marginalised groups while enriching a few rich farmers and industries. Meanwhile, traditional and more effective grassroots water-security projects, such as rain harvesting, are neglected and underfunded. Mehta declares, 'The story of declining rainfall obscures the fact that water has been misused and regulations constantly circumvented. The power of the water lords remains unquestioned and their greed is exonerated.'[10]

Larry Swatuk, a professor at the University of Waterloo, also questions the basis on which most scarcity is measured:

The dominant 'freshwater availability' maps that one finds around the world turn on our accepting the fact that if a country has less than 1700 cubic metres per capita per year of water, then it suffers serious water issues. However, this measures only blue water availability (i.e., groundwater recharge and runoff availability) relative to population. Yet, of the water that we individually consume, about 80–90 per cent of that is in our food, most of which derives from rain-fed agriculture, which is green water – i.e., transpired rainfall. So the dominant scarcity indicator is in fact a fiction. If you cast the narrative not as one of scarcity due to population divided by freshwater availability, but one of resource capture by the few and ecological marginalization of the many, you see that we have lots of water but, in Mehta's terms 'socially constructed the scarcity'.[11]

The language of scarcity hides how water is currently distributed and is also wasted. Water scarcity is both a poverty and equity issue. Not only do one in five people in the developing world lack access to clean water, but daily per capita use of water varies dramatically too, from 10–20 litres in residential areas of sub-Saharan Africa, compared to 200–600 litres in Japan, the US, and developed countries in Europe. The poor also tend to pay as much as five to ten times more in slum communities of developing countries than people who have access to piped water.[12]

Wealthier communities also tend to use more water, because it is less expensive for them. The historic drought in California of 2013–15 showed how, even in the US, per capita consumption of water differed wildly between rich and poor neighbourhoods and between residential and industrial areas. Affluent residential Hillsborough has the highest per capita water use, at an average 334 gallons a day, compared to the 79 gallons a day used by residents in working-class East Palo Alto, which is just 14 miles away. Golf courses are also known to be large gulpers of water, and in Palm Springs, a shocking 736 gallons a day per person are used and wasted to maintain vast lawns.[13]

This inequality also of course affects how scarcity is experienced. For poor and marginalised people who rely on these resources for their livelihood, sustenance and way of life, water scarcity is devastating and has already caused many to migrate to cities that increasingly face their own pressures to deliver water to all their citizens. There are also real, physical changes in communities' landscapes when floods ravage a whole town or when rivers dry up.

The scramble for water security

The language of water scarcity and climate change-induced related conflicts is nevertheless shaping how many prominent actors are approaching the future. Swatuk writes: 'Securitizing water through a scarcity and conflict narrative, however, allows for the usual suspects to creep in and capture water – not only the resource but also the ways and means of thinking and acting in the name of water scarcity.'[14] One such 'suspect' is the US intelligence sector.

According to the US Intelligence Community Assessment, *Global Water Security*, released in February 2012:

> … during the next 10 years, water problems will contribute to instability in states important to U.S. national security interests. Water shortages, poor water quality, and floods by themselves are unlikely to result in state failure. However, water problems – when combined with poverty, social tensions, environmental degradation, ineffectual leadership, and weak political institutions – contribute to social disruptions that can result in state failure … we judge that as water shortages become more acute beyond the next 10 years, water in shared basins will increasingly be used as leverage; the use of water as a weapon or to further terrorist objectives also will become more likely beyond 10 years.

Water has long been tied to security issues and attributed as the source of conflicts. The Pacific Institute has documented more than 300 water-related conflicts and instances of violence since 3000 BCE.[15] They argue that disputes over access to water have been a constant feature of many ancient and modern societies. The risks of these conflicts are growing with the increase of population, demand for resources and economic and environmental pressures on water. For example, battles over water took centre stage in the annexation of territories and the occupation of the West Bank, Golan Heights and Gaza Strip by Israel in 1967. More recently, analysis of the 2012 Syrian uprising suggests that drought played a significant role in the country's upheaval.[16]

Asia, in particular, is considered to be at the forefront of hot spots for 'water wars'. In 2010, Pakistan sued India at the International Court of Arbitration over the latter's Kishanganga hydropower project on the contested area of the Neelum River in Kashmir, saying it violates the Indus Treaty of 1960. Nepal and India are also in similar disputes over the governance of the Kosi River. Control of Tibet's glaciers and plateau lies at the heart of many of these conflicts, as it is the source of the world's greatest river systems and thus a lifeline or source of water for China, India, Bangladesh, Nepal, Cambodia, Pakistan, Laos, Thailand, Vietnam and Myanmar – countries that together account for 47 per cent of the world's population.

These conflicts add fuel to the common adage that the next world war will be about water, rather than oil or ideology. However, a closer analysis of history suggests that water issues have more often than not been grounds for cooperation, rather than conflict. Irina Bokova, director-general of UNESCO, points out that nearly '450 agreements on international waters were signed between 1820 and 2007.'[17] Similarly, a seminal paper published in 1998 by Professor Aaron Wolf of Oregon State University notes that during the twentieth century, 'only seven minor skirmishes' occurred and 'no war has ever been fought over water … while 145 water-related treaties were signed in the same period.'[18]

'A lot of times we believe that scarcity drives conflict,' says Wolf, when in fact, 'scarcity is not the sole driver of conflict; it's not even the primary driver of conflict.'[19] His studies show that conflicts arose primarily when rapid change overwhelmed the existing institutional capacity to absorb that change. In practice, this means that conflict (and avoiding it) has more to do with governance mechanisms than geography.

The likelihood of conflict increases, however, when powerful countries such as India and China have tried to exploit their riparian position and dominance, and treated water security as a zero-sum game. Prime Minister Wen Jibao's statement that 'water scarcity threatens the very "survival of the Chinese nation"' is telling in this regard, and it is reflected in China's emphasis on sovereign control of Tibet.[20] However, it is also expressed in China's massive and extensive efforts to dam its rivers to solve its own water crises and energy demands brought about by the spread of intensive farming, export-oriented agriculture, water-intensive industries such as mining, a burgeoning middle class that wants high water-consuming comforts such as washing machines, rapidly increasing household consumption and growing cities.

The growing nationalism, self-interest and narrowly technical approaches to water management – in the context of climate-change impacts – are already creating a scenario in which regional players justify a more aggressive foreign policy. Indeed, even hegemonic nations outside the region are seeking to use the divisions to intervene. Former US Secretary of State Hillary Clinton justified increased US involvement in the strategic region as an 'expert in water management'[21] that can provide legal and institutional arrangements for water-dispute resolution, especially for seven major river basins, including the Nile and Mekong. Of course, it is no coincidence that the US interest in this area emerges at the same time as its 'pivot to Asia', in an attempt to counteract growing Chinese power.

Corporate water grabbing

While governments seek to both confront and take advantage of water insecurity, global financial capital – private investors, hedge funds and other speculators – seek to profit. Corporate leaders for some time have argued that water, as the single most important resource, is the new oil of the twenty-first century. This means that investing in this 'blue or liquid gold' is a no-brainer (even if in practice many private companies have found that delivering water services is not as easy or publicly palatable as they had initially hoped). Still, water remains the 'perfect commodity': it is inflation proof, it can be sold any time, everyone needs it, and demand will continue to grow, especially as populous countries and emerging markets like China and India experience water stress.

The 'scarcity card' is used as a pretext to justify the corporate scramble to secure water. One glaring example is how corporate investors in agriculture are often as keen to secure water resources as land, given the importance of water to agriculture. Behind the recent surge in land grabbing lays an even more significant expansion of water grabbing. Environmental scientists peg that water grabbing by corporations worldwide amounts to 454 billion cubic metres annually, which is about 5 per cent of global water use per year.[22] In many cases, corporations have received backing from nation states such as China, and Middle Eastern and Gulf countries, as well as the US and EU member states, which through leases in other countries both obscure and outsource their lack of water sustainability to other countries. The water needs of local communities, from where water is grabbed, are all too often ignored or forgotten.

This was the case, for example, in Mozambique, where a 30,000-hectare sugarcane plantation for ethanol was set up by the ProCana corporation for the British company Bioenergy Africa and the Mozambican government. The land is near the Massingir Dam, which presently generates electricity for export; however, the Mozambican government earlier granted ProCana extensive rights for irrigation waters from the dam.[23] According to research group FIAN, such

> … [re]allocation of water resources undermines the autonomy and capacity of adjacent local communities to produce food. Moreover the project would affect the pastoralists by disrupting spaces for livestock grazing and pastoralist routes. There is a

great risk that these communities would lose their lands and livelihoods against their will and without being properly reallocated and compensated.[24]

Agrofuel production is in fact one of the key drivers for the surge in land and water grabbing. Agrofuel production is very water intensive. Estimates suggest the amount of water required for producing one litre of ethanol in the US can range from 5 litres up to 2,138 litres, depending on regional irrigation practices.[25] Water consumption and agrochemical use during agrofuel production also adversely impacts both the availability and quality of water.

Wherever it happens, water grabbing has grave human and ecological costs; when companies pollute rivers by mismanaging water resources, the entire water flow is affected, as well as the lives of all those that rely on them. In the US Midwest, agrofuel production has contributed to significant contamination of the Mississippi River and oxygen depletion in the Gulf of Mexico, which have caused high levels of fish kill and loss of marine diversity. In Ethiopia's Gambela region, a Saudi billionaire acquired a plantation and diverted water from the Alwero River, which is the source of livelihood for thousands of people, mostly relying on fishing and farming.[26]

Water profiteers

The spectre of water shortages and high demand has led to a new kind of water profiteer. PICO Holdings, a US private company which has business interests in water resources and storage, agribusiness and real estate, spotted the potential gap and has acquired more than 54 hectares (134,130 acres) of water rights in Nevada, Arizona and Colorado.[27] With an average value of $3,500 per acre,[28] the company can earn as much as $469 million – turning water into money. Similarly, legendary US-based oil investor T. Boone Pickens spent $100 million to buy up water rights in Texas and build a 250-mile pipeline to the city of Dallas, where he hopes to sell water. Pickens owns more water rights than any other individual in the US, having acquired the right to drain over 65 billion gallons of water per year from the Ogallala Aquifer.[29] Royal Dutch Shell is reportedly buying rights to Colorado's groundwater, as the corporation plans to extract oil from the shale deposits there[30] through hydraulic fracturing, or fracking.[31]

The confluence of interests in oil/energy and water has emerged as a permanent nexus among investors, because they are inextricably linked. On the one hand, energy and power production requires water for thermoelectric cooling, hydropower, mining and extractive industries, and fossil-fuel production and use. On the other hand, production of potable water requires electricity for extraction, transportation and delivery.

In fact, all corporations that use large of quantities of water are seeking to secure their supplies, expecting climate-induced scarcity. Some of the active buyers of land and water rights in the US include multinational investors Nile Trading and Development, BHP Billiton, Unitech and media magnate Ted Turner.[32]

The result is a booming private water industry and a growing trade in water rights and water-related investments. According to Marc Robert of Water Asset Management, a New York hedge fund, 'climate change for us is a driver.'[33] Already, the hedge fund is cashing in on drought, with about $400 million allocated for the purchase of water rights, creating private equity and making stock market investments in water-treatment companies. For investors, water is a 'natural growth market', as demands for technology, infrastructure and ways to provide water continue to rise steadily, along with water prices. With the market fast maturing and still largely unregulated, the water industry is expected to grow annually from 5 to 7 per cent; its value set to grow from $425 billion to $1 trillion within five years.

Roughly three hundred global water companies from the US, Europe and Japan that dominate the water-industry market are the major beneficiaries of this speculative boom.[34] The big players include the UK's private utilities, Suez Environment and France's Veolia, as well as bottling companies such as Coca-Cola. Manufacturers and infrastructure-service providers such as Swiss-based Pentair Ltd, Texas-based Flowserve Corporation, New York-based Xylem, Japan-based Kurita Water Industries, Ltd and Hong Kong-based China Everbright International are also expected to cash in.[35] These companies have carved out a special niche in water efficiency, recycling and treatment, by providing supply engineering and technology, including desalination, filtration, conservation and waste management. Their growth rates may be even higher than those of water utilities. The Calvert Global Water Fund, for instance, has holdings in infrastructure stocks to the tune of $197 million.

The investment boom has created an increasingly financialised water sector. Specialised water-targeted investment funds (exchange-traded water funds, hedge funds and water certificates) are already being offered by major investment banks in stock markets. These include subsidiaries of Netherland's Rabobank's SAM Sustainable Water Fund and Sarasin Sustainable Water Fund, Pictet Water Fund, Swisscanto Equity Fund Water, and Tareno Waterfund.

According to the American ecological planner and engineer Jo Shing Yang:

> ... the real story of the global water sector is a convoluted one involving 'interlocking globalized capital': Wall Street and global investment firms, banks, and other elite private-equity firms – often transcending national boundaries to partner with each other, with banks and hedge funds, with technology corporations and insurance giants, with regional public-sector pension funds, and with sovereign wealth funds – are moving rapidly into the water sector to buy up not only water rights and water-treatment technologies, but also to privatize public water utilities and infrastructure.[36]

There is much reason to worry about the corporate profiteering and control of water. The water demands of agribusiness out-compete the needs of other users, such as small and family farmers. Mining and other extractive industries are not only water intensive, they also pollute and poison lands and water sources and threaten the lives and livelihoods of rural communities, especially indigenous peoples. In Latin America, mining operations are in constant conflict with local indigenous communities. In Ecuador, for example, Chevron Oil has been fined $18 billion for contaminating water resources. In the Philippines, more than half of the ancestral domains of indigenous peoples are affected by mining operations, 72 per cent of which operate without securing prior and informed consent (FPIC).[37]

Furthermore, the largest corporate users of water, such as Nestlé and Coca-Cola, have been embroiled in a number of conflicts around extraction of water at the expense of local communities. In drought-stricken California, Nestlé is under attack for draining the state's aquifer and then selling bottled water back to the public at a steep profit. The company reported that in 2014, it used 705 million gallons – enough to fill 1,068 Olympic-size swimming pools.[38] Coca-Cola meanwhile had its recent application to operate in Varanasi, North India, rejected in 2014 by local authorities due to massive protests by local activists and NGOs. Yet we can expect many more such struggles and conflict, since the company has aggressive plans to grow in India and other developing nations, as its markets in the US decline due to increasing public health concerns.

Green water grabbing

The intricate web of water profiteers is able to thrive in part because of its success in recent years in remaking international water governance. First, a series of international declarations declared water an economic good, including the 1992 Dublin Statement on Water and Sustainable Development, reinforced in Agenda 21, and the ministerial declarations of the World Water Forum[39] in The Hague and Kyoto. Now, under a new framework called the 'green economy', promoted heavily at the United Nations Conference on Sustainable Development in 2012 (Rio+20), water and the whole of nature are now deemed capital.

Under the rubric of the 'green economy', water and other environmental services are treated as an economic asset, in which a price is put on *all* the dimensions, services and functions of water. Proponents argue that the instruments of the market are powerful tools for conserving water, improving water quality, ensuring efficient water use and protecting water itself. However, putting a price on nature goes beyond the privatisation and commodification of water as a public good and service; it sets the stage for the creation of markets where water and its ecosystem functions (for example, water purification by pristine watersheds or carbon sequestration by forests and oceans) can be traded, while people's rights and common interests are ignored.

The result has been a major fillip to water-rights trading, a property-rights approach encouraged by the World Bank as a cornerstone of water management for both solving water scarcity and encouraging private-sector investment. Virtual platforms, such as Ecosystem Marketplace,[40] provide the latest updates and investment possibilities for carbon, water and diversity markets, enabling the corporate private sector and speculators to profit from ecological crises.

The agriculture sector in particular is being eyed for water-rights trading. Australia currently has one of the most developed water-rights systems in the world. According to water broker Waterfind, temporary and permanent water-rights trading across specialised exchanges in the country totalled $1.3 billion in 2010, and it is expected to grow by 20 per cent per year.[41] However, this approach in practice has discriminated against small farmers and indigenous communities who depend on these resources for their livelihoods. A 2013 report by the Institute of Agriculture and Trade Policy, penned by Shiney Varghese, who also serves on the UN Committee on Food Security's High Level Panel of Experts (CFS-HLPE), notes that the experience for local agricultural water users and family farmers has been that 'the costs of conveyance facilities for water transfers are to be borne by the public while the benefits accrue to those engaged in water trading. To them, this process appears to be a private appropriation of public resources.'[42]

Global water trading for financial gains is still in its infancy, and it is part of a broader move towards using market mechanisms to tackle ecological crises. Carbon trading is the most infamous. While there are still no global water-offset markets, as water is still publicly owned in most countries, proposals are underway to establish trading schemes that will separate land ownership and entitlements to water resources to allow for their transfer to private parties. Supply and demand can then determine the market price.

The nearest example of a water-offset market is the so-called mitigation banking or wetland savings account in the US, which was established through the 2004 Federal Clean Water Act and the Endangered Species Act. Under the Clean Water Act, anyone who plans to dredge a wetland that nurtures other water bodies is mandated to find a way to avoid their destruction, that is, 'establish, enhance, restore or preserve' an amount of wetland equal to or greater than what will be dredged, usually within the same watershed. The goal of mitigation banks is to generate credits that can be sold to developers later as offsets.[43]

However, whose interests would such a system serve? Critics of carbon trading point out that the big polluters – corporations and powerful governments – can best afford credits while doing nothing to change their damaging practices. With water, similar actors would profit with the same negative consequences.

Adaptation for whom?

Under the dominant corporate mindset, it doesn't take long before technical and infrastructure solutions are sought for issues of water distribution. As far back as 1825, vainglorious engineers proposed capturing icebergs and moving them to places without water.[44] In 2008, such madcap proposals came a little closer to reality, when the Canadian hedge fund Sextant reportedly bought 95-year water rights to three glaciers in northern Europe. According to the hedge fund, one glacier would be used to create bottled water and the other two would provide bulk water transported to customers in 24,000-litre containers or super tankers. The proposal was eventually exposed as a Ponzi scheme, as it became clear that the costs would be too high to be economically feasible (transporting water costs more than expensive desalination processes). However, the scheme still lives on, this time as a website offering bottled glacier water (drinksnowater.com).[45]

Expensive waterworks have been the staple solution for decades for countries wishing to have water where it isn't to be found. In the mid-nineteenth century, they were pioneered by Sir Arthur Cotton, an irrigation engineer, who by the time of Indian Independence had bequeathed a legacy of 100,000 kilometres of irrigation canals in both India and Pakistan. During the New Deal years, California built a conduit of dams and canals to divert the Colorado River to a prominent agricultural region, the Imperial Valley. This was followed in 1960 with the world's largest water-conveyance system – the State Water Project – which transports water from northern California to meet the needs of the more populous and water-scarce south.

Most of these canals have relied on dams. In the twentieth century, a dam became the symbol of development, and they continue to be built today, notably in China and Brazil, as governments seek to stock, harvest and funnel an even greater share of rainwater towards irrigation, electricity, domestic and other uses.[46] Meanwhile in the Persian Gulf, where options for transporting water are less feasible, close to three hundred desalination plants have been constructed, the majority of which are located in Saudi Arabia.[47]

These engineering marvels have not been without their costs. The iconic Colorado River, for example, now tops the 2013 list of the US's ten most endangered rivers. It has become so dry that the river no longer enters the Gulf of Mexico. In Pakistan, irrigation schemes have left a legacy of waterlogging and salination that affects more than 3 million hectares in the Indus Basin, and leads to many farmers abandoning salt-encrusted farmland each year.[48] Meanwhile, the most extensive evaluation of dams by the World Commission on Dams concluded that, while dams have brought benefits for human development, 'in too many cases an unacceptable and often unnecessary price has been paid to secure those benefits, especially in social and environmental terms, by people displaced, by communities downstream, by taxpayers and by the natural environment.'[49]

In the context of climate change, reliance on infrastructure to resolve water distribution has further uncertainties. As the UN warns, 'Large-scale structural measures, for example, often require accurate information regarding flows, sediment loads, extreme event frequencies and other hydrological characteristics' that no longer exist. It notes that approaches that are smaller in scale, locally controlled and rely on natural systems, such as the 'absorptive capacity of riparian and wetland areas, may be more resilient under highly variable conditions.'[50]

Nevertheless, some companies are gearing up for some of the infrastructure and technology that is predicted to be applied to adapting to climate change, particularly in the field of flood control. Dutch engineering firm Arcadis is one such company, and its revenues have grown dramatically – increasing by 26 per cent in 2012 to $3.25 billion, thanks partly to Superstorm Sandy.[51] The company has bagged contracts in New York

City, New Orleans and San Francisco to deal with flood protection and rising sea levels and has secured more than $3 billion in revenues in 2014. In California, engineering giant CHM2 Hill is gearing up to benefit from the $15 billion expected to be spent on building a new water-conveyance infrastructure, designed in part to address climate-change impacts.

Bluewashing

The corporate takeover of the climate-adaptation agenda is coupled with a good dose of corporate greenwashing, perhaps more accurately called 'bluewashing'. Much of this takes the form of corporations' promising to reduce their 'water footprint',[52] that is, the total volume of water directly or indirectly consumed/used in the production of a product or service. Multi-billion-dollar food giant Nestlé, for example, claims it is reducing its water footprint throughout its supply chain. Yet, as the world's leading distributor of bottled water, Nestlé is built on a model of making profit out of scarce resources, and by promoting bottled water, it undermines the public provision of water for all.

Moreover, these efforts to reduce rarely provide long-term solutions to the over-extraction of water in regions where many plants operate. In India, 9 out of 34 PepsiCo bottling plants operate in areas officially designated as water-stressed ('over-exploited', 'critical', or 'semi-critical').[53] More often than not, corporations seek to pay other producers, such as peasant farmers in India, to conserve water rather than make radical reductions themselves. The voluntary nature of these initiatives also means there is little scope for independent verification of company claims.

These corporations use their showcase efforts (insignificant compared to their overall impact) to justify their broader involvement in water policy. One such institution is the 2030 Water Resources Group (WRG), a public-private platform established under the World Bank's private-sector arm, the International Finance Corporation (IFC). The companies most involved in the water industry dominate the group: beverages, mining, engineering and service companies. Chaired by Nestlé's Peter Brabeck-Lethmathe, who is on record as saying that water should be treated like any other commodity, the WRG provides technical and analytical assistance to governments to 'transform' their water policy by privileging economically productive uses and linking them with corporate partners. It has established active partnerships with the governments of South Africa, India, Jordan, Mongolia, Peru and Mexico. Their central message, argued in most of their reports, is that water scarcity will need to be resolved through water efficiency, clearer water rights and, of course, corporations' involvement in institutional decision making.

Corporations argue that they share the risks from water scarcity and therefore have a vested interest, along with other actors, in protecting water. What they fail to mention is that the 'shared risk' they face looks very different from the perspective of a community losing access to clean water due to a bottling plant or a shale-gas plant.

As explored in a special issue of the journal *Water Alternatives* in 2012, increased corporate involvement in water policy opens up a 'Pandora's box' of problems. These include *conflicting interests* that pit the public good against companies' legal obligations to distant shareholders. But they also include a) policy and regulatory capture where corporations have the resources and know-how to steer policy in their favour; b) inequities in decision making, due to corporate access, knowledge and power that invariably sideline the most vulnerable and marginalised, and c) a tendency to displace and undermine local sustainable solutions in favour of corporate solutions that do not always have benign effects and usually end up allocating water based on its highest economic value rather than its optimal value.[54]

Climate justice = water justice

As many activists under the banner of 'Climate Justice' have advocated, addressing climate change in a socially just way will require 'system change', and nowhere more so than in the world of water politics. Many of the alternatives already exist: from applying agroecological methods in agriculture, to harvesting and conserving water, to changing wasteful practices (bottled-water bans, grey-water systems utilising recycled household waste water for toilet flushing) in urban areas, to ending the extraction of fossil fuels and other non-renewable resources that lead to the overuse and contamination of water. These alternatives can both mitigate the impacts of climate change as well as build the resilience to respond to its impacts. The key will be re-engineering the economy and public policy to allow these approaches to flourish, and being prepared to tackle the vested powers that seek to sustain an unsustainable system.

It requires a public model of water management that is more able to address issues of distribution, justice and functioning ecosystems than a private-sector model that seeks to maximise capital.[55] In many cases, it will defer to local decision making: climate adaptation is best done at the local level, where the impacts of both climate change and water stresses are felt, and where more flexible and appropriate responses to water management can emerge. In the wake of Super Typhoon Haiyan (local name Yolanda) in the province of Leyte in the Philippines, two public water utilities – the Baybay City Water District and Leyte Metro Water District – were able to restore service and undertake rationing within 24 hours of the storm. According to on-the-ground reports, the management's foresight and leadership became decisive, while the workers' determination also helped restore crucial municipal services despite them being victims of the typhoon themselves.[56]

Ensuring real popular participation is essential to empowering and assisting communities with drought and flood planning, as well as disaster management. At the same time, it will be important to link local decision making with international solidarity, which will become ever-more critical to responding to the uneven impacts of climate change.

Fortunately, the existing practice of public and community allocation and management of water services and resources has already created alternative models. One of these options is Public-Public Partnerships (PuPs): not-for-profit, mutually beneficial partnerships between public-sector water operators, local communities, trade unions and other social-economic groups. PuPs aim 'to link up public water operators on a nonprofit basis to strengthen management and technical capacity'. As opposed to Public-*Private* Partnerships (PPPs), which look to marry private gain with public guarantees, PuPs are about sharing good practices and ideas, going beyond efficiency to look at issues of reaching excluded water users, respecting workers' rights and building popular and democratic participation in water services. A number of PuPs are geared towards healthy watershed-protection programmes and climate-adaptation plans.

Another innovative model that has particular relevance for adapting to climate change is the example of public utilities seeking to protect their whole watershed, bridging urban and rural communities. In the Philippines, public utilities in the Visayas and Mindanao invest in agroecological farming practices and in community livelihoods, with the philosophy that 'a good environment will produce good water.'

Meanwhile in Thailand, the Ping River Basin Committee brought together various upstream and downstream water users, along with farmers and indigenous people relying on the river for livelihood and sustenance. The group agreed to work to a mutually agreed goal of an ecologically sustainable and equitable system of water allocation for all.[57] Their example of 'river diplomacy' shows the potential for resolving transboundary water conflicts during a time of climate change, as parties realise that a situation of cooperation can ensure water for all much better than a zero-sum game.

Community collaboration has also proved highly effective in protecting watersheds and sources of water in water-scarce regions. In New Mexico, in the US, an ancient system of communal irrigation called *acequias* has sustained agriculture in an erstwhile arid region and has respected nature at the same time for the last four centuries. The system was introduced by the Moors in southern Spain, which was then brought to the New World by the Spanish colonisers. The *acequias* included

> ... specific governance over water distribution, water scarcity plans, and all other matters pertaining to what was viewed as a communal resource. The *mayordomo*, or watermaster, of the acequia made decisions about water distribution among community members, with the consent and advice of the acequia members.[58]

To this day, this ancient system thrives, even in the US's hyper-individualised capitalist society.

New water vision

Such models and examples promote a new vision for water management,[59] one that re-establishes water as commons and prioritises social and ecological justice and democratisation within water governance. They draw on a set of principles for water governance, that consider:

- Water is a public good, a shared commons and a human right. It brings life, is a gift of nature, and its nurture remains the responsibility of everyone.
- Ecosystems are interconnected, which necessitates breaking down the false division between urban and rural water systems.
- Water as part of nature has its own logic, which means that the laws of nature and the integrity of the water cycle must be maintained.
- Water citizenship in the management and governance of water or the act of stewardship and protection of water is critical and must involve active popular participation.
- Social justice and just distribution must be central to any water resource management policies.
- A conservation-first approach must take precedence over 'return on investment' approaches.
- The state, or at least public utilities (whether local, regional or national), have a critical role in ensuring the right to water and sanitation.
- Public funding is needed to invest in public systems and institutions in order to cope with the additional pressures of climate change on water systems.
- The power of corporations over water resources and water governance – especially that wielded by transnational water companies and extractive industry companies – must be rolled back.[60]

Adopting these principles will mean that it is possible to achieve water justice even at a time of additional stress. But there is still much to be done in terms of implementing progressive models of water management and governance as a strategy in shaping a progressive adaptation to climate change. Learning from the past and thinking of creative ways to achieve 'the future we want' will be necessary.

As this chapter stated at the outset, the nature of water has a lot to teach us as we face the growing challenge of climate change. Water connects everyone, from the farmer upstream to the city dweller downstream. It ignores all political boundaries and separations. Its pollution or over-extraction in one region will affect people, animals and plants in another region. And it is likely to become the visual symbol of ever increasing climate change, as countries face unprecedented droughts in some regions and devastating floods elsewhere. The good news is that, despite the doom-laden warnings of 'water wars', our history has shown that water is more often a cause for cooperation than conflict. In the words of Aaron T. Wolf, water 'offers a vehicle for bringing those who share it together and, since it touches all we do and experience, it suggests a language by which we may discuss our common future.'[61]

Notes

1. Mehta, L. (2003). Contexts and constructions of scarcity. *Economic and Political Weekly*, 38(48). Retrieved from doi:10.2307/4414344.

2. United Nations Environmental Programme. (2008). Water withdrawal and consumption: The big gap, in S. Diop and P. Rekacewicz, eds. *Vital Statistics: An overview of the state of the world's fresh and marine waters* (2nd edn). Nairobi, Kenya: UNEP. Retrieved from http://www.unep.org/dewa/vitalwater/article42.html.

3. Office of the Director of National Intelligence. (2012). *The Intelligence Community Assessment (ICA): Global water security*. Retrieved from http://www.dni.gov/files/documents/Newsroom/Press%20Releases/ICA_Global%20Water%20Security.pdf.

4. The Joint Monitoring Program for Water Supply and Sanitation of the World Health Organisation and the United Nations Children's Fund defines an improved drinking-water source as 'one that, by nature of its construction or through active intervention, is protected from outside contamination, in particular from contamination with faecal matter'. Improved drinking-water sources include pipes on premises, protected springs, public taps or standpipes, protected dug wells or boreholes, and rainwater collection. Retrieved from http://www.wssinfo.org/definitions-methods/

5. The parameters widely adopted in development policy circles, including the UN Environmental Programme, is Malin Falkenmark's 'water stress index', calculated on the basis of annual resources and population. This definition proposes a threshold of 1,700 cubic meters (m^3) per person per year, below which countries are categorised as water stressed; absolute scarcity is less than 50 cubic meters per person per year.

6. United Nations. (n.d.). *Water Scarcity*. Retrieved from http://www.un.org/waterforlifedecade/scarcity.shtml.

7. Mehta, L. (2005).

8. United Nations – Water. (2014). *Statistics*. Retrieved from http://www.unwater.org/statistics.

9. Vigna, A. (2015 April). When Sao Paulo's water ran out. *Le Monde diplomatique*, English edition, April. Retrieved from http://mondediplo.com/2015/04/10saopaulo.

10. Mehta, L. (2003). Contexts and constructions of water scarcity. *Economic and Political Weekly*, 5066–72.

11. Swatuk, L. (September 2014). Correspondence with author. For details, see Swatuk, L.A., McMorris, M., Leung, C. and Zu, Y. (2015). Seeing 'invisible water': Challenging conceptions of water for food, agriculture and human security. *Canadian Journal of Development Studies*, 36(1), 24–37.

12. UN – Water and Food and Agriculture Organization of the United Nations. (2007). *Coping with Water Scarcity: Challenge of the twenty-first century*. Retrieved from http://www.fao.org/nr/water/docs/escarcity.pdf.

13. California Drought: Database shows big difference between water guzzlers and sippers. (7 February 2014). *Mercury News*. Retrieved from http://www.mercurynews.com/science/ci_25090363/california-drought-water-use-varies-widely-around-state.

14. Swatuk, L. (September 2014).

15. Pacific Institute. (n.d.). *Issues We work On: Water and conflict*. Retrieved from http://pacinst.org/issues/water-and-conflict/.

16. Mohtadi, S. (16 August 2012). Climate change and the Syrian uprising. *Bulletin of the Atomic Scientists*. Retrieved from http://thebulletin.org/climate-change-and-syrian-uprising.

17. Deen, T. (2 September 2013). Water scarcity could drive conflict or cooperation. *Inter Press Service News Agency*. Retrieved from http://www.ipsnews.net/2013/09/water-scarcity-could-drive-conflict-or-cooperation/.

18. Wolf, A.T. (1998). Conflict and cooperation along international waterways. *Water Policy*, 1(2), 251–65. Retrieved from http://www.transboundarywaters.orst.edu/publications/conflict_coop/.

19. Jackson, M. (8 April 2014). USAID launches new water, conflict, and peacebuilding toolkit. *New Security Beat*. Retrieved from http://www.newsecuritybeat.org/2014/04/usaid-launches-water-conflict-peacebuilding-toolkit/#.U0gr-cYi5uZ.

20. Klare, M.T. (2013). Entering a resource-shock world: How resources scarcity and climate change produce a global explosion. *Tomdispatch*. Retrieved from http://www.tomdispatch.com/blog/175690/michale_klare_the_coming_global_explosion.

21. Biron, C.L. (9 May 2012). Water conflicts move up on US security agenda. *Inter Press Service News Agency*. Retrieved from http://www.ipsnews.net/2012/05/water-conflicts-move-up-on-us-security-agenda.

22. Rulli, M.C., Saviori, A. and D'Odorico, P. (2012). Global land and water grabbing. *Proceedings of the National Academy of Sciences of the United States of America*, 110(3), 892–7. Retrieved from http://www.pnas.org/content/110/3/892.full.

23. Due to protests and controversies hounding the bioethanol project, in 2009, the Mozambique government revoked the concession due to non-compliance of contractual obligations. The British investor, CAMEC also announced that it will shift its investment to mining instead.

24. Food First Information and Action Network. (2010). *Land Grabbing in Kenya and Mozambique: A report on two research missions – and a human rights analysis of land grabbing*. Germany: FIAN International Secretariat. Retrieved from https://www.inkota.de/fileadmin/user_upload/Themen_Kampagnen/Ernaehrung_und_Landwirtschaft/Land_Grabbing/Land_grabbing_in_Kenya_and_Mozambique_FIAN_EN.pdf.

25. Chiu, Yi-Wen, Brian Walseth, and Sangwon Suh (2009). 'Water Embodied in Bioethanol in the United States.' *Environmental Science and Technology* 43.8: 2688–692

26. GRAIN. (11 June 2012). *Squeezing Africa Dry: Behind every land grab is a water grab*. GRAIN Report. Retrieved from http://www.grain.org/article/entries/4516-squeezing-africa-dry-behind-every-land-grab-is-a-water-grab.

27. Dwinnell, T. (17 January 2007). T. Boone Pickens invests in water – should you? Retrieved from http://seekingalpha.com/article/24410-t-boone-pickens-invests-in-water-should-you. Also see, Rees-Mogg, J. (11 May 2007) How to profit from the world's water crisis. *Money Week*. Retrieved from http://moneyweek.com/how-to-profit-from-the-worlds-water-crisis/. For PICO Holdings, visit their website, http://www.picoholdings.com/index.html.

28. The value of land and water rights differs significantly between Nevada, Colorado and Arizona. The range is from $2,100 to as much as $7,500. Some analysts say that it can climb to as much as $10,000 due to the water crisis. In the US, senior water rights are more valuable and sought after.

29. Yang, J. (6 May 2014). Wall Street mega-banks are buying up the world's water. *Popular Resistance Daily Movement News and Resources*. Retrieved from http://www.popularresistance.org/wall-street-mega-banks-are-buying-up-the-worlds-water/.

30. Befield, S. (11 June 2008). There will be water. *Bloomberg Businessweek Magazine*. Retrieved from http://www.businessweek.com/stories/2008-06-11/there-will-be-water.

31. Fracking is the natural gas and oil extraction practice that pumps millions of gallons of water, sand and chemicals into the ground to break open shale formations to access the energy sources inside.

32. Bienkowski, B. (12 February 2013). Corporations, investors 'grabbing' land and water overseas. *Environmental Health News.* Retrieved from http://www.environmentalhealthnews.org/ehs/news/2013/land-grabbing.

33. Campbell, M. and Nicholson, C.V. (7 March 2013). Investors seek ways to profit from global warming. *Bloomberg Businessweek Markets & Finance.* Retrieved from http://www.businessweek.com/articles/2013-03-07/investors-seek-ways-to-profit-from-global-warming.

34. Water Fund. (2013). Turning water into gold. Retrieved from http://worldswaterfund.com/turning-water-into-gold.html.

35. Ibid.

36. Yang, J. (31 October 2008). Why big banks may be trying to buy up your public water system. *Alternet.* Retrieved from http://www.alternet.org/story/105083/why_big_banks_may_be_trying_to_buy_up_your_public_water_system.

37. Philippine Partnership for the Development of Human Resources in Rural Areas. (2008). *Philippine Asset Reform Report Card.* Quezon City: PhilDHRRA.

38. James, I. (8 March 2015). Bottling water without scrutiny. *The Desert Sun.* Retrieved April 8, 2015, from http://www.desertsun.com/story/news/2015/03/05/bottling-water-california-drought/24389417/.

39. Every three years, the World Water Council (WWC), a Marseilles-based policy think tank run by the World Bank, development aid agencies like the United Nations, the major water corporations such as Vivendi and Suez, water ministries of a number of Northern countries, and water experts and professionals, hosts the World Water Forum (WWF).

40. Visit http://www.ecosystemmarketplace.com/.

41. O'Connor, S. (23 July 2008). Thirsty markets eye water. *Financial Times.* Retrieved from http://www.ft.com/cms/s/0/ff3e5756-58c8-11dd-a093-000077b07658.html?siteedition=intl#axzz3YvfRlu7i.

42. Varghese, S. (March 2013). Water governance in the 21st century: Lessons from water trading in the US and Australia. *Institute for Agriculture and Trade Policy,* 7.

43. Kenny, A. (31 March 2008). New EPA wetland guidelines to boost mitigation banks. Retrieved from http://www.ecosystemmarketplace.com/pages/dynamic/article.page.php?page_id=5706&section=home&eod=1.

44. Merton, T. (1825). *The Literary Magnet of the Belles Lettres, Science, and the Fine Arts.* London: W.C. Wright.

45. McKenzie, F. (14 June 2013). Glaciers for sale. *The Investigative Fund.* Retrieved from http://www.theinvestigativefund.org/investigations/envirohealth/1806/glaciers_for_sale.

46. Everard, M. (2013). *Hydropolitics of Dams: Engineering or ecosystems?* New York: Zed Books.

47. Ahmed Zain Aidrous, I. (18 August 2008). How to overcome the fresh water crisis in the Gulf. *Russian International Affairs Council: Middle East Analysis.* Retrieved from http://russiancouncil.ru/en/inner/?id_4=4190#top.

48. Qureshi, A.S., McCornick, P.G., Qadir, M.M. and Aslam, Z.Z. (2008). Managing salinity and waterlogging in the Indus Basin of Pakistan. *Agricultural Water Management,* 95(1), 1–10.

49. World Commission on Dams. (2000). *Dams and Development: A new framework for decision-making.* London: Earthscan.

50. United Nations Economic Commission for Europe. (2009). *Guidance on Water and Adaptation to Climate Change.* New York: United Nations.

51. See Arcadis website: www.arcadis.com.

52. This term was coined by Professor Arjen Y. Hoekstra of the Netherlands. He further states that water problems are connected with the structure of the global economy. For more reading materials about water footprint, see http://www.waterfootprint.org.

53. Hall, D. and Lobina, E. (2012). Conflicts, companies, human rights and water: A critical review of local corporate practices and global corporate initiatives. Retrieved from http://www.world-psi.org/sites/default/files/documents/research/psiru_conflicts_human_rights_and_water.pdf.

54. Hepworth, N.D. (2012). Open for business or opening Pandora's box? A constructive critique of corporate engagement in water policy: An introduction. *Water Alternatives,* 5(3), 543–62.

55. Schlosberg, D. (2013). Political challenges of the climate-changed society. *PS: Political Science & Politics,* 46, 13–17.

56. Manahan, M.A. (30 June 2014). Philippines' public water systems in the face of disasters and climate change. *Municipal Services Project Exploring Alternatives to Privatization.* Retrieved from http://www.municipalservicesproject.org/blog/philippines-public-water-systems-face-disasters-and-climate-change#sthash.MsNoNZr8.dpuf.

57. Dargantes, B.B., Manahan, M.A. and Batistel, C. (2012). Springs of hope: Alternatives to commercialization of water resources and services in Asia, in McDonald, D.A. and Ruiters, G., eds. *Alternatives to Privatization Public Options for Essential Services in the Global South.* London: Routledge: Routledge Studies in Development and Society Series.

58. Sandoval, A. (May 2010). Ancient traditions keep desert waters flowing. *Yes Magazine.* Retrieved from http://www.yesmagazine.org/issues/water-solutions/ancient-traditions-keep-desert-waters-flowing.

59. For more examples, read Dargantes, B., Manahan, M.A., Moss, D. and Suresh, V. (2012). *Water Commons, Water Citizenship and Water Security.* Retrieved from http://www.focusweb.org/content/water-commons-water-citizenship-and-water-security, or http://www.ourwatercommons.org/water-commons-citizenship-security.

60. Manahan, M.A. (June 2010). *Alternative Models for Water Governance and Management: The people's challenge to 'green economy'.* Retrieved from http://focusweb.org/content/alternative-models-water-governance-and-management-people%E2%80%99s-challenge-%E2%80%9Cgreen-economy%E2%80%9D.

61. Wolf, A.T. (2012). Spiritual understandings of conflict and transformation and their contribution to water dialogue. *Water Policy,* 14(S1), 73–88.

10

POWER TO THE PEOPLE: RETHINKING 'ENERGY SECURITY'

The Platform Collective[1]

> He who is firmly seated in authority soon learns to think security, and not progress, the highest lesson of statecraft.
>
> *James Russel Lowell, US diplomat, 1870*

In recent years, the concept of 'energy security' has come to dominate media and policy debates on the provision of heat, light and power. It has been adopted both by oil corporations and increasingly by non-governmental organisations (NGOs) as a way of talking about energy provision and futures. However, the term 'energy security' embraces a number of different – and often contradictory – elements depending on whether the discussion is about supplying the economy, consumers, or people. For some, it means having access to a warm home or the means to cook; for a government, it might mean producing more oil domestically or guaranteeing access to oil and gas fields; for an oil corporation, it could mean preserving a delicate balance between abundance and scarcity (that is, ensuring they have enough reserves to keep their share price high but not so much oil available that the price of oil starts to fall). The phrase has multifarious meanings that are grounded in different histories and promote different assumptions.

Energy companies and political elites have been successful in pushing energy security to the top of the political agenda, and maximising the term's ambiguity to advance their own interests.[2] The imprecise notion of energy security makes it easier for politicians and their advisers to push regressive, militaristic, social and environmental programmes by evoking an ill-defined threat to 'energy' and reinforcing a narrowly defined exclusionary type of security.

In this chapter, we look at examples of how energy security is used to further justify the aggressive expansion of 'unconventional' fossil fuels, the use of military resources to secure energy transport routes, the suppression of protests against further fossil fuel extraction with the threat that otherwise 'the lights will go out', and the expansion of renewable energy in a way that ignores concerns about human rights, democratic governance, or energy access. We consider whose interests are being evoked in discussions of energy security, which voices are granted credence and which are excluded – in other words, what is being secured and for whom?[3]

A history of energy security

An early and significant manifestation of energy security policy can be found in the run-up to the First World War, when strategic decisions by British military planners to fuel the British Navy with oil instead of coal set in motion a literal sea-change in thinking about energy sources. Foreign Secretary Lord Curzon, after the war, remarked that 'the Allies had floated to victory upon a wave of oil.' The government's strategic decision in favour of oil ensured that Anglo-Persian Oil – a forerunner of BP – was able to start extracting oil in volume.[4]

This shift to petroleum as a key source of energy for the industrialised West – and the need to acquire oil supplies from halfway across the globe, in contrast to relying on readily abundant domestic reserves of coal – set in motion a century of geopolitical turmoil, conflict and competition that has dominated world affairs ever since. The contention between Turkey and Britain in the early 1920s over Iraq's oil-rich Mosul, Imperial Japan's expansionist policy of the 1930s that led to a four-year war in the Pacific, Adolf Hitler's invasion of Russia, and America's repeated military interventions in the Middle East since 1945 – all were spurred on by an increasing dependence on oil, and a need to secure its supply.[5]

The first appearance of 'energy security' as a term in modern policy debates was during the 1970s energy crisis. Then, governments invoked now-familiar energy-security refrains as a response to OPEC-induced oil-price shocks abroad, and strikes by coal-mining unions at home. While some environmentalists at the time attempted to use energy-security arguments to advocate alternative energy strategies, such as using renewables and reducing fossil-fuel demand, the debate was driven by the policy establishment. The International Energy Agency (IEA), founded at the height of the 1974 oil crisis thanks in large part to the lobbying efforts of US Secretary of State Henry Kissinger, was set up to be an 'energy NATO'.[6] Energy security lay at its heart: in the words of Edward Morse, former US representative to the IEA, the founding member states sought to 'blunt the use of the oil weapon'.[7]

Energy security has resurfaced as a key concern of states and defence forces in the past few years because of the unprecedented oil price spikes of 2007–08 and the 'end of cheap oil'.[8] (Most analysts believe that the slump in oil prices in 2014–15 is likely to be temporary due to the continual rise in production costs and declining rates of extraction.) Security of supply is now an important goal of energy policy for many countries, and always supersedes looking at how energy is used and the damaging impacts of our current energy model. It is unthinkingly equated with well-being: as the European Commission *Energy 2020* puts it: 'Energy is the life blood of our society. The well-being of our people, industry and economy depends on safe, secure, sustainable and affordable energy.'[9] The EU is not alone in prioritising energy security over climate insecurity – the Obama administration in the US has done everything it can to increase petroleum production in US territory, including expansion into offshore areas that were long closed to drilling due to environmental concerns. This action has been taken to boost US domestic energy consumption and according to Tom Donilon, the president's senior adviser on national security, to 'afford us a stronger hand in pursuing and implementing our international security goals'.[10]

The current usage of energy security in public discourse reinforces three distinct logics that downplay concern about environmental threats – in particular climate change. These are a *nationalist* logic – 'that the energy needs of the nation can only be met at the expense of other peoples'; a *corporate* logic – 'that a private, marketised system where profit is the main goal is the best way of meeting our energy needs', and a *military* logic – 'that, the nation is in "competition" for a scarce resource and it is therefore necessary to militarise energy infrastructure.' Within these logics, the solution to energy provision is to secure more of it, rather than reduce consumption – energy is a *scarcity* which must be 'secured' by controlling it as much as possible.

From the start of the 'petroleum age', scarcity was built into the energy system. As oil began to replace coal as the key energy source, oil companies introduced delays and interruptions to limit the flow of energy and raise prices by ensuring a constant shortage of oil. Shortage was manufactured via government quotas and price controls, cartel arrangements to govern worldwide distribution, consortium agreements to slow the development of new oil discoveries in the Middle East and sometimes deliberate acts of sabotage.[11] Another method of preventing energy abundance involved the rapid construction of lifestyles in the United States that were dependent on the increasing consumption of extraordinary quantities of energy.

The concept of energy security arose at a time when energy was relatively abundant, but extraction rates were deliberately reduced. Now the scenario is different: oil extraction rates are rapidly declining. The finite nature of fossil fuels is becoming increasingly apparent: to keep oil reserves (and share prices) at a stable level, oil companies are attempting to extract oil from increasingly risky and dangerous places.

Entwined with the idea of scarcity, is the seemingly contradictory, but in practice complementary, concept of abundance. The Industrial Revolution was described by one historian as an 'escape from the constraints of an organic economy',[12] that is, an escape from the limits of land, soil time and space. With the tapping of millions of years of 'fossilised sunshine', seasonal rhythms could be disregarded. As energy became unlimited, mass production and consumption became possible.

It is this mass consumption (consumption which played a fundamental part in creating energy scarcity) without limits that policy makers are attempting to keep 'secure'. Energy security hence becomes not about meeting the basic needs of people, but rather creating and responding to the expansion of a consumer society.

Energy security and climate change

The current energy system brings with it a plethora of insecurities, yet debates on energy security tend to focus on just one: how the continued supply of oil, gas and coal to the market will be achieved. This obsessive focus ensures that the largest threat to human existence – the climate crisis – is ignored. The devastation of a changing climate has been created by a network of powerful institutions formed of both fossil-fuel corporations and an array of legal, cultural, financial and government organisations that provide crucial support to oil companies. This vast carbon web prevents democratic decision making about societies' systems of energy provision and their responses to climate change.

Decisions about energy are made behind closed doors in corporation headquarters, at parliamentary bars and during $2,000-a-ticket conferences that lock us all into decades of fossil-fuel use. Individuals and wealth flow through the revolving doors between the state, oil and finance. To entrench themselves further, oil companies actively set about influencing and shaping our values and politics, placing themselves at the heart of both the establishment and our cultural consciousness – for example, through their sponsorship of cultural institutions – all with the intention of making the needed urgent transition to a low-carbon economy seem impractical or impossible.

Faced with a crisis that threatens the continuation of human life, Western countries are not only continuing but actually increasing their investments in an energy model that created the threat in the first place. In 2013, global carbon-dioxide emissions were 61 per cent higher than they were in 1990, when negotiations towards a climate treaty began.[13] Why are Northern countries utterly failing in the face of this crisis? Precisely because the dominant elite will do anything to keep our current energy systems intact, despite these systems' role in causing climate change.

Our current energy systems give us neither the means to stop climate change, nor to adapt to its impacts. European decision makers are investing in a rapidly expanding web of import pipelines to 'diversify' energy supplies and suck gas from across the globe to the continent.[14] Such an infrastructure would lock Europe into high-carbon dependency for the next fifty years. The blinding short-sightedness of such policies is staggering, yet also utterly predictable. Neoliberalism created the conditions under which our governments would be co-opted by corporations and therefore is wedded to short-term strategies of profit seeking that cannot deliver a fair, efficient, or peaceful response to the devastating impacts of climate change.

Re-telling energy stories

The words and images we use have an impact on the world around us. Decision makers, corporate spokespeople, community representatives and NGOs are all part of a day-to-day struggle over language. Humans have become adept at promoting arguments that win support and legitimacy. But are we as adept at considering the full implications of how arguments about key resources are framed? In order to do so, there are a number of questions we should ask ourselves: how has this story been told and why was it told this way? How could it have been told differently? How does the dominant framing of this issue impact on public understanding?

We can consider these questions in relation to debates about energy security. In 2014, Russia's invasion of Crimea renewed the debate about where Europe gets its gas from, prompting a dominant narrative that we (Europe) are too reliant on Russian gas and that this reliance makes us energy insecure. A typical article appeared in the British newspaper, *The Times* in April 2014 titled 'West seeks to end Putin stranglehold over energy'. The article, written by journalist Ben Webster, states that 'Britain is to lead an international effort to stop Russia from using its vast natural energy supplies to hold the world to ransom.' Here Webster is drawing on a frame that dates back to the Cold War, evoking the idea that Russia is implacably pitted in battle against the 'West', that it has a significant weapon (be it a nuclear arsenal or a gas pipe tap) and that the West must stand up to this unaccountable power to ensure its own survival.

Webster isn't alone in using this frame. Webster's article quotes Energy and Climate Change Minister Ed Davey, who says the UK government's action shows 'Russia we mean business by improving our energy security and resilience'. Davey makes it apparent whose energy security he is concerned with by adding 'because of Russian action, EU gas prices go up, that affects consumers and businesses here very quickly.' It is the private, individual concerns of consumers and businesses that matter for Davey – those with spending power, while those struggling to purchase energy and food are overlooked.

It is worth considering alternative frames that could be used. Despite constant references to the EU's over-dependence on Russian gas, there has not been a rise in overall dependence on Russian gas over the past decade. What has changed is that Russia has altered the conditions under which it supplies countries of the former Soviet Union. Gas is no longer sold at subsidised rates, but instead at higher and more variable market prices.[15] An alternative frame could therefore be the inadequacy of the gas market to provide people with affordable energy.

It would have been possible for Webster to offer a positive rebuttal of the Cold War narrative – emphasising that relations between Europe and Russia have fundamentally changed since that period – the headline might have read 'Putin threatens European and Russian energy co-operation'. Alternatively, the article could have looked at Western oil companies' cooperation with the Russian oil sector, emphasising that BP, for example, owns 20 per cent of Rosneft and is therefore concerned with any drop in share price as a result of punitive measures against Russia. In this case, the headline might have been 'Oil companies' collusion with Putin undermines European energy sovereignty'.

The US sanctions designed to hit 'Putin's inner circle' notably excluded Russian heads of oil companies, and in May 2014, BP signed a shale-oil deal with Russia. BP CEO Bob Dudley would attend a meeting with Putin and afterwards state that: 'We have a responsibility to stand with our partners in difficult times.' The close relations and overlapping interests of 'our' energy companies and 'Russian' energy companies complicates the idea that Russia is 'holding us to ransom' over energy, and is therefore often excluded from the discussion of European energy security.

This example highlights how stories about energy can be framed in ways that highlight certain elements and exclude others. In this case, the concept of energy security is used to privilege national, private and military interests in ways that exclude the discussion of complexity and collaboration.

Energy security and foreign policy

Overemphasis of energy security imperatives by most countries has led to policies and initiatives designed to influence and control the extraction and flow of energy resources abroad and to directly benefit their own companies involved in the energy sector. Take Britain, for example. The equation of British corporate interests with the wider 'national interest' is such a central tenet of UK foreign policy (and of many other nation states) that it is almost universally unquestioned. For as long as there has been a Foreign Office in Britain, there has been an automatic assumption that 'British corporations' represent British 'national interests'. In 1840, Foreign Secretary Lord Palmerston was unequivocal on this point: 'It is the business of the Government to open and secure the roads for the merchant.'[16] Over 150 years later, in 2007, Foreign Secretary Margaret Beckett reiterated this premise: 'It is the Government's core responsibility to make sure that the rest of the world was safe and well-disposed for our businesses.'[17]

Related to 'energy security', this approach includes pressuring oil-producing countries to allow foreign control over their resources, supporting British companies in gaining long-term oil and gas contracts and asserting military and diplomatic dominance over resource-rich areas and 'energy corridors'. British civil servants and ministers intervene geopolitically in pursuit of their perceived 'energy interests', alongside allies in Europe and the US.

This not only ensures that resources flow towards Britain's power plants and refineries. Crucially, the foreign energy policy apparatus also seeks to guarantee high profits for its fossil-fuel companies and configures the physical, legal, political and financial infrastructure to ensure fossil fuels are pumped onto the 'open market'. The supply of fossil fuels to open markets ensures that resources aren't just delivered to where there is a gap in demand, but instead to where they will be must profitable. Supply must be carefully controlled to ensure there is not an 'over-supply' of fuel, which would deflate the market value. As the Platform Collective observed in the book *The Oil Road*:

> The mass relocation of great volumes of fossil fuels requires constant coordination of logistical and financial resources. Analysts in Geneva and London assess and counter-assess the profitability of particular shipments, aiming to maximise their return. Some deliveries are based on long-term commitments, but many others are short-term contracts betting on swings in the global oil price.[18]

As long as energy resources are mobilised within market structures, the world's most powerful economies will be able to maintain energy dominance, as they can ultimately afford to pay more. Hence the pressure for greater 'market opening' in both producing and transit countries, as expressed in policy documents prepared by the G8, the EU Commission and the UK Department for Energy and Climate Change.[19]

As in other countries, UK energy-security policy tends to create perceived threats and privilege militarisation as a solution, sparking and exacerbating conflict in many countries.[20] Its pursuit can mean using armed force to guard oil pipelines and tankers from guerrilla or pirate attacks, or even invading countries to ensure energy flows. Human rights and environmental safeguards are comparatively low on the list of priorities, while the importance placed on maintaining oil, gas and coal supply ensures continued dependence on fossil fuels and delays in transition to low-carbon lifestyles and communities.

Pushing back the fossil-fuel frontier

Reserves of traditional fossil fuels are becoming more and more challenging to reach, and as a result, international oil companies and many governments are increasingly investing financially and politically in 'unconventional' oil and gas. This encompasses both tar-sands extraction and operations in ever more inaccessible and inhospitable locations (such as the Arctic, or ever deeper offshore sites). Unconventional oil and gas sources tend to be more polluting and cause greater impacts on local communities and ecosystems. For instance, extracting tar sands *in situ* requires large amounts of gas and water to steam the bitumen out of the ground, while drilling in the Arctic carries a greater risk of pollution impacts due to its inaccessibility for clean-up operations. It also locks us into a high-carbon future by creating infrastructure that will keep us dependent on fossil fuels for decades to come, and undermining serious investment in renewables.

'Energy security' is routinely rolled out to legitimise these extreme operations and override popular concerns. Public and political anxiety in the US around oil imports from the Middle East and Venezuela has been used to make fuel sources closer to home more attractive, such as the vast reserves of tar sands in Alberta or US shale gas. Energy security has come to be viewed as synonymous with a greater degree of energy independence.

Mary Landrieu, the Democrat Senator for Louisiana, is typical of many defending the expansion of offshore oil drilling:

> I mean the gallons [resulting from spills] are so minuscule compared to the benefits of US strength and security, the benefits of job creation and energy security. So while there are risks associated with everything, I think you understand that they are quite, quite minimal.[21]

Similarly, Shell downplays the severe environmental risks of Arctic drilling, for both oil and gas, due to inaccessibility and reduced efficacy of spill control techniques. In the opening paragraph for their Arctic drilling webpage, Shell writes: it is 'essential to securing energy supplies for the future, but it will mean balancing economic, environmental and social challenges.'[22] So energy supply is essential, while environmental damage is a 'challenge' to be overcome rather than a serious concern which must be addressed before drilling commences.

Debates about energy security in relation to Arctic drilling are premised around national security. The Arctic states of Canada, Russia, Denmark, Norway and the United States share their claim to Arctic territory and have enjoyed a relatively peaceful relationship for many years. The discovery of fossil-fuel resources beneath the melting tundra, as a result of climate change, though, has prompted an escalation of militarisation in the region.[23]

In 2009, the Harper government in Canada published its *Northern Strategy*, calling for the construction of six to eight Arctic offshore vessels, expansion of the Arctic Rangers programme, building a large Arctic-capable icebreaker, developing indigenous surveillance capabilities, creating a Northern Reserve Unit based in the Arctic, constructing a deepwater resupply port in Nanisivik, and developing an Arctic training base in Resolute, Nunavut. Not all of these proposals have come to fruition, but the emphasis was clearly on conflict preparation rather than coordination with other Arctic countries.[24] Other Arctic states are making similar preparations. Norway defended its building of five combat naval vessels – its most expensive single defence project ever:

> Norway's position as a significant energy exporter and as a country responsible for the administration of important natural resources extending over large sea areas has an important bearing on security policy. We must be able to uphold our sovereignty and our sovereign rights.[25]

Militarising the seas

Since the ship *Sirius Star*, carrying two million barrels of Saudi oil, was captured in November 2008 by Somalis and held for a $3 million ransom, a spate of kidnappings led the north-western Indian Ocean to become another militarised region in the name of 'energy security'. A vast triangle of open sea between India, Madagascar and Djibouti is now heavily patrolled by warships and scoured by Reaper spy-drones. A European Union naval presence, a NATO task force and the US Fifth Fleet deploying out of Bahrain have been empowered by the UN to use 'all necessary means' to eliminate piracy.[26]

The anti-piracy mission is run out of Northwood HQ, an underground military complex in leafy north-west London. Many storeys deep, behind steel blast doors, navy officers use charts and screens to constantly co-ordinate tanker and trade traffic with nearby warships. Ships are advised to travel in groups and at night: 'this enables military forces to "sanitise" the area ahead of the merchant ships.'[27]

While piracy does present a danger to both cargo and crew, the militarised reaction seems disproportionate given that most vessels and crew were released unharmed once a ransom was paid, and that less than 1 per cent of tankers travelling through the Gulf of Aden have ever been hijacked. Yet international shipping describes itself as a 'system under attack'. Jan Kopernicki, in his former role as president of the British Chamber of Shipping, did the rounds of political and military leaders in Britain and the EU, exaggerating the danger to European energy supplies: 'I don't want to be alarmist but I provide transport for essential oil and gas for this country and I want to be sure that the lights are on in Birmingham, my home city.' The fact that Birmingham's lights have no dependence on oil was conveniently ignored.

Kopernicki, also vice-president of Shell's shipping arm, gave a further fillip to the arms industry, saying there was a 'gaping hole in the UK's defence strategy', demanding an increase in naval spending and to bring forward the acquisition of a new generation of warships currently scheduled for 2020.[28] Kopernicki's intervention came in November 2010, in a context of public austerity cuts hitting millions of people, and yet he found a sympathetic ear in the debating chambers of British politics. In thinking reminiscent of the Suez war, Liberal Democrat Baron John Burnett argued, 'Should we not now be thinking that it is a legitimate security interest for us to consider the trade routes as far as the Gulf of Aden as part of our national concern?'[29]

Alongside an increasing militarisation of the seas, some countries have even begun renting out their military personnel to private corporations. Since 2012, the Dutch government has been providing units to escort ships. Total costs for the Dutch teams are estimated at US$29 million, but the shipping companies are only expected to pay half of this, leaving the Dutch government to make up the US$14.5 million shortfall.[30]

Hiring out navy personnel to private companies at a reduced fee, or even for free, means the public taxpayer is subsidising corporations' security costs. Companies' private use of military personnel also raises a range of legal and political questions. As James Brown, military fellow of the Lowry Institute, observes, putting national military personnel under the control of a commercial ship captain 'essentially makes a commercial vessel a warship'.[31]

Although the use of marines on commercial ships is fairly new, there has already been one incident demonstrating the potential dangers. In February 2012, two Italian marines were placed on board the oil tanker MV *Enrica Lexie*. While serving on the tanker, they shot and killed two Indian fishermen that they incorrectly suspected of piracy. The incident sparked a diplomatic row between India and Italy. Both of the Italian marines were arrested by the Indian police and in early 2015 were still awaiting trial for murder.[32]

Suppressing dissent to 'keep the lights on'

Repression of civil dissent runs in tandem to increased militarisation, with energy security promoted as its alibi. In the summer of 2008, a quiet corner of Kent was transformed into one of the most contested sites of energy politics in Britain. An existing coal-fired plant owned by energy giant E.ON was due to be decommissioned by 2015, but E.ON controversially announced plans to construct Britain's first new coal-fired plant for over thirty years at the site.

The plans were met with widespread resistance by climate activists in the country, ranging from NGOs to faith groups and grass-roots activists. The Camp for Climate Action hosted a week-long protest camp near the proposed site at Kingsnorth in August 2008.

'Energy security' was given as a justification for the draconian policing of the Climate Camp that cost £5 million, amid claims that the police were protecting the electricity supply to millions of homes. Protesters had more than 2,000 possessions confiscated including soap, board games and a clown costume, and were subject to over 8,000 indiscriminate stop-and-searches, some of which were later successfully challenged in court.[33]

A subsequent Freedom of Information Act request made by David Howarth MP revealed that the police, E.ON and Department for Business, Enterprise and Regulatory Reform (BERR) shared intelligence about the movements of protesters and their meetings in the run-up to the camp. The UK newspaper, the *Guardian* concluded that 'it is as though BERR was treating the police as an extension of E.ON's private security operation.'[34]

A spokeswoman for BERR argued that 'given the potential threats to the security of energy supplies posed by the protests, it is only right that the government liaised with the police and the owner of the power station to exchange factual information and discuss contingency plans.'[35] Documents later obtained by the *Guardian* showed that officials privately knew that it was 'unlikely that disruption at any of the power stations in the area in this week would cause a national electrical power supply problem', because demand was low and power stations had good stocks.[36]

Association of Chief Police Officers (ACPO) spokesperson Jon Murphy has also justified the use of undercover surveillance such as the case of Mark Kennedy (who spent seven years infiltrating environmental groups in the UK):

Unfortunately ... there are a small number of people who are intent on causing harm, committing crime and on occasions disabling parts of the national critical infrastructure. That has the potential to deny utilities to hospitals, schools, businesses and your granny.[37]

The cry of energy security is also used to silence protests in the Global South. The open-pit Phulbari coal project in north-west Bangladesh is one example. The project, proposed by Asia Energy, a subsidiary of GCM resources, will take up almost 6,000 hectares of land (60 sq. km) and, will physically and economically displace 50,000–220,000 people. Over 80 per cent of the land taken for this project will be fertile, agricultural land, leaving farmers dependent on the land with few options for employment.[38] The mine will also deplete the water table, leading to water scarcity and likely significant contamination of rivers and land for communities around the mine. In addition, it may lead to the degradation of the Sundarbans, a UNESCO-protected mangrove forest, because the coal will be transported through this area in barges.

A determined grass-roots resistance campaign against the mine mobilised tens of thousands for marches, general strikes and highway blockades. The government and company response to such large and sustained protest was vicious. In August 2006, the Bangladesh Rifles, a paramilitary force, opened fire on 50,000 peaceful protesters – at least three people were killed, including a 14-year-old boy, and over a hundred people were wounded. In February 2007, Mr S.M. Nuruzzaman, one of the protest leaders, was falsely arrested and subsequently tortured; his arrest was reportedly requested by officials of Asia Energy.[39]

GCM refuses to comment on the perpetrated human rights abuses, instead saying, 'The Project will make a significant contribution to the country's energy security by providing reliable supplies of good quality coal to new power stations.'[40] Despite the project's grand claims, only 20 per cent of the coal extracted is for domestic energy consumption – 80 per cent is destined for foreign markets.[41] Serving international markets rather than providing Bangladesh with reliable energy is GCM's real priority.

Renewables as 'energy security' – Prioritising Europe's energy wishes over everyone else

Energy security isn't only being used to justify fossil-fuel projects – it is also mobilised to argue in favour of unjust and environmentally damaging renewable projects. Even though renewable energy has significantly less carbon impact than fossil-fuel development, it is still important to ask whose interests are being served and whose rights are being denied by large-scale, renewable energy projects.

A case in point is Desertec, an ambitious plan to build large, concentrated solar thermal power plants in the North African desert and direct the electricity northwards across the Mediterranean via High Voltage Direct Current transmission line. The Sahara offers proximity to Europe, a sparsely populated area and intense sunlight. Originally estimated to cost €400 billion, the project involved major shareholders including German power companies E.ON and RWE, the international insurance company Munich Re, Siemens engineering and Unicredit bank (as of October 2014, the project has been scaled down due to the majority of shareholders pulling out – of the above list only RWE remain in the consortium).

The corporations behind the project repeatedly described it as 'a comprehensive concept, combining energy security and climate protection'.[42] The Desertec Industrial Initiative aimed to provide 15 per cent of Europe's electricity by 2050. The proposal was touted by some as the great solution to Europe's 'energy needs', or perhaps more honestly, to sustain our current levels of consumption.

Just days before the Tunisian revolt began in February 2011, German Prime Minister Angela Merkel met autocratic Algerian President Abdelaziz Bouteflika in Berlin to discuss

Desertec's future. As uprisings spread across North Africa, company executives were questioned about how their project would relate to the repression and lack of democracy in their target countries. Their response was framed in the language of ensuring security, stability and control: 'The project planners emphasize the importance of their energy concept to the long-term stabilization of the region of North Africa ... Desertec planners are now more than ever convinced that they can shape the political upheaval in Egypt and Tunisia.'[43]

The project's supporters cite the creation of local jobs and export earnings, as well as inexpensive electricity and the use of extra energy to desalinate sea water in its defence,[44] but as with fossil-fuel projects, avoid the underlying issue of power imbalances.

On many levels, the project was founded on questionable approaches to resource sovereignty, land use and energy consumption. The use of African land and energy resources for European consumption and profit reinforces traditional exploitative ties between Europe and its former colonies. Renewable energy is a resource that can equally be enclosed, privatised, controlled and profited from. There are currently 600 million people in Africa without access to electricity; the International Energy Agency predicts that number will rise to 645 million people by 2030.[45] Yet in the discussion of Desertec, it was the energy security of European consumers that was prioritised.

Desertec is just one example of a large-scale renewable-energy project that involves Northern countries extracting further resources from Southern ones. Other examples include agrofuel plantations in South America,[46] huge hydroelectric dams in the Democratic Republic of Congo,[47] or large-scale wind farms in Mexico.[48]

A failed energy model

The predominant focus of the energy-security debate on providing security for corporations and nation states has obscured the failure of current systems of energy provision to provide affordable, sustainable energy for people to heat their homes, cook their food, or light their rooms.

In Southern countries, infrastructure is developed primarily for industry – it often bypasses the people who live there. In Nigeria, 72 per cent of the population are forced to use wood for cooking, while their country exports 950 billion cubic feet of gas every year. In India, 45 per cent of households do not have electricity – only 11 per cent of households consume more than 100kwh per month, while at the other end of the scale the US average consumption is 900 kwh.[49] Inefficient centralised infrastructure serves producers rather than consumers. Decentralised models of energy provision would be far more resilient and effective, particularly at a time of increasing climate-change impacts, but instead energy is provided through large grids, owned often by private monopolies (who have no interest in empowering households).

In Northern countries, energy systems are also failing. When UK civil society group Platform brought Niger Delta activist Celestine AkpoBari to London, he was astounded to hear that Britain suffers the worst levels of fuel poverty in Western Europe – in 2010, one in five households were classified as in fuel poverty, and in 2012, one person died of cold every six seconds during the winter – as energy bills continue to rise.[50]

The current problems will only be exacerbated by the growing financialisation of energy infrastructure, as traders and speculators look towards pipelines, oil rigs, gas wells and wind turbines as a source of profit. Key decisions relating to infrastructure investment are increasingly being made by a tiny elite of fund managers from about 120–150 private institutions. That severely biases energy investment against projects which benefit the poor, are sensitive to local needs, and are less carbon intensive.[51]

Currently, Northern countries consume, on average, around 8000W per person per year.[52] The energy 'needs' of such consumption-saturated countries are enormous. Yet when policy makers consider how we might transition to a low-carbon economy, they almost invariably assume that there must be enough energy available for 'life as usual to continue'. While increased energy efficiency is accepted as a way of reducing energy consumption, changes that would have a larger impact, such as altering the way our lives are organised, are firmly off the table.

Individuals in both the North and the South are still encouraged to buy as many products and use as much energy as they can afford. In many countries, it is the norm to drive your own car (despite the hundreds of others making the same journey), to buy individually packaged items, and to 'upgrade' your mobile phone every two years (even if your old one is still working).

Societies are structured so that people consume massive amounts of energy every single day without even noticing. Plans for low-carbon transitions too often assume that our lives are unchangeable. They are based on the premise that societies need to secure large amounts of energy to meet current consumption patterns. Of course, it is not possible to change cultures, structures and habits overnight, but by uncritically bolstering the idea that our societies need large amounts of energy, we are ensuring energy continues to be scarce – a resource of which we can never have enough.

Energy alternatives

The above examples show how the concept of 'energy security' is used to prioritise corporate, national and military interests above international cooperation and the needs of people. It is clear that social-justice activists need new narratives to talk about energy futures – narratives that frame energy as a common resource and a basic right, that put the environment and people at the centre of debates, and that de-link energy from the corporate, national and military contexts they are currently embedded in. We need this, not just to prevent worsening climate change, but also to build an energy model that works, as the stresses of climate change hit home.

New narratives will not spring up ready-formed, but will emerge out of the grass-roots movements and communities currently organising around energy – groups that stand in opposition to the corporate monopolisation of energy. The following few case studies provide just a partial picture of these alternatives, but they are nevertheless instructive – they suggest it is possible to create a very different relationship between people and energy, wresting back control from profit-motivated monopolies, asking very different questions about energy provision, and creating new narratives with which to discuss energy futures.

Taking back control

A growing number of communities are demanding control over energy resources and taking back ownership from private companies. In some countries, community control of energy is nothing new. Denmark has had remarkable success at ending dependence on imported fuel, which has in large part been replaced with local renewables. Denmark's wind-power revolution has been described as 'a grassroots, community-based initiative, underpinned by decentralised, cooperative and municipal ownership alongside small-scale private ownership'.[53] This came about after an intense political struggle in the late 1970s, when a coalition of leftists, greens and conservative rural interests united against proposals based on centralised forms of energy (oil and nuclear-based). Instead they promoted an alternative vision of a more localised non-nuclear future based on renewables and more radical democratic practices. And they achieved remarkable success. Within twenty years, the country went from dependence on oil imports for 90 per cent of its energy demand to self-sufficiency in energy. Crucially, 80 per cent of wind turbines in Denmark are owned by co-operatives or families. Ownership of the electricity-distribution system is also decentralised in Denmark, with 55 per cent of the grid owned by user-run co-ops, 12 per cent by municipalities and 26 per cent by Denmark's state oil company. The state played an enabling role by setting targets, rules around ownership, and prices.

Germany's energy economy is currently being transformed by its policy of *Energiewende* (Energy transition), supported by both main political parties. Germany is witnessing a mass movement towards community- and city-controlled renewables. In September 2013, Germany's second biggest city, Hamburg, voted to take over the electricity, gas and district heating networks that had been sold to Vattenfall and German energy company E.ON a decade earlier.[54] Hamburg is just one of 170 municipalities in Germany that have taken back control of their energy services from private companies,[55] which has changed the relationship between people and energy from being passive consumers to collective owners.

Energy is not the only resource that communities are demanding return to public control: there are now over 235 cases of water re-municipalisation in over 37 countries[56]

These examples point to a practical and discursive shift from a model driven by corporate and individual purchases of resources such as of energy and water to a collective model of resource ownership where profit is not the key concern. As re-municipalisation struggles link up across national borders, they also challenge the notion of national competition for energy – instead, the competition is between communities and corporations.

Alternatives forged out of resistance

Many examples of collective energy ownership arise directly out of struggles against corporate- or national-controlled infrastructure. Nepal has the largest hydroelectric potential of almost any country, with 6,000 or so rivers. But hydroelectric development has, until recently, consisted of building large dams, not as a rational assessment of what would best serve the needs of poorer groups, but as the result of decisions by government departments and international financial institutions whose economic, bureaucratic and political interests are intimately bound up with the large dam industry and its chief industrial clients.[57] Popular opposition to one of the largest dams planned in Nepal, Arun III, coupled with the restoration of multi-party democracy in 1990, led to the energy sector being opened up to small producers, resulting in numerous villages introducing their own mini-hydro schemes, some run collectively, some privately. The outcome was to produce almost one-third more electricity at close to half the cost and half the time of the proposed Arun III project.

In the UK, villagers in Balcombe resisting energy firm Caudrilla's attempts to frack their backyards, started to think about the current structures of energy provision and then set up a locally owned renewable-energy scheme. Similarly, communities in Puglia, in southern Italy resisting the Euro-Caspian Mega Pipeline – a destructive piece of gas infrastructure that will harm Puglia's world heritage coastline and its people's livelihoods – are working to create a community-owned co-op that can produce enough electricity for the town through wind turbines and solar panels.[58]

Energy justice not security

Confronting the reality of hundreds of thousands of UK households unable to pay for heating or light, fuel-poverty campaigners in the UK have focused on unfair distribution of energy according to wealth, rather than engaging in nationalist discourses around security of energy supply. They have juxtaposed energy-company monopolies and their rising profits with the reality for the 25 per cent of UK households in fuel poverty, and the thousands who die each winter because they can't afford to heat their homes. In 2014, Fuel Poverty Action launched their 'Energy Bill of Rights' – declaring that 'We all have the right to affordable energy to meet our basic needs. Everyone should be able to cook food and keep warm when it's cold.'[59] The commonly touted concept of energy security for consumers is replaced with energy justice for people. Fuel Poverty Action back up their actions with practical case work – supporting individuals and community groups to challenge the instalment of pre-payment meters – used by companies as a way of cutting poor people off from energy.

Conclusion

Our energy system is in crisis. Each year, more and more energy is generated and yet 1.6 billion people, 20 per cent of the world's population, do not have regular access to electricity.[60] In the coming years, a significant increase in fossil-fuel use is projected – this will make our ability to control global warming almost impossible. It is clear that when policy makers talk about energy security, they do not mean ensuring the basic needs of people are met, or averting climate disaster. Instead they are obsessed with one issue – how the continued supply of oil, gas and coal to the market will be achieved.

As this chapter has explored, the history of how energy security has been used – to bolster particular geopolitical relationships, defend militarisation and national security, and advance increasingly 'unconventional' fossil-fuel extraction – means it is time for concerned citizens to ditch the term. Calling for 'energy security' is most likely to justify exactly the kinds of unsustainable, undemocratic and unjust energy practices that concerned citizens are working to abolish. A survivable and just energy future means breaking the grip of elite interests on our energy systems, ending dependency, increasing autonomy, building diverse power structures through which we can hold one another to account, and leaving fossil fuels in the ground.

In the last two years, the term 'energy democracy' has gained increasing popularity – arising out of climate-justice movements, it is a concept that is capable of integrating energy and climate debates to consider both the needs of people and the planet. The nature of democracy is diversity: there is not one blueprint that applies to all situations, but that is also its strength. A resilient energy future will be composed of diverse energy commons, solidarities, practices and ideas. It is also a critical step in a creative re-imagining of our current society, one that challenges a neoliberal order which is concerned with 'securing' frontiers and resources for the most powerful, and instead seeks collectively to meet the needs of all.

Platform (www.platformlondon.org), a UK collective of artists and activists working on social and environmental issues, has participated in energy debates for a long time. This chapter was conceived by progressive activists, researchers and academics working on issues related to energy policy and practice.

Notes

1. See the Platform Collective's website www.platformlondon.org.
2. Labban, M. (2011). The geopolitics of energy security and the war on terror: The case for market expansion and the militarization of global space, in Peet, R., Robbins, P. and Watts, M., eds. *Global Political Ecology*. London: Routledge, pp. 325–44.

3. Hildyard, N., Lohmann, L. and Sexton, S. (16 February 2012). Energy security for whom? For what? Retrieved from http://www.thecornerhouse.org.uk/resource/energy-security-whom-what.

4. Longhurst, H. (1959). *Adventure in Oil: The story of British Petroleum.* London: Sidgwick & Jackson.

5. For a more detailed account of the drive to secure oil resources in these conflicts, see: Yergin, D. (1992). *The Prize: The epic quest for oil, money, and power.* New York: Simon & Schuster.

6. Shaffer, B. (2008). *Energy Politics.* Philadelphia: University of Pennsylvania Press.

7. Ibid.

8. A phrase originally coined in Campbell, C.J. and Laherrère, J.H. (1998). The end of cheap oil. *Scientific American*, 278(3), 78–83. Retrieved from doi:10.1038/scientificamerican0398-78.

9. Commission to the European Parliament, the Council, the European Economic and Social Committee and the Committee of the Regions. (10 November 2010). Energy 2020 A strategy for competitive, sustainable and secure energy. Retrieved from http://eur-lex.europa.eu/legal-content/EN/TXT/?uri=celex:52010DC0639.

10. Henderson, J. (2011). Domestic gas prices in Russia – Towards export netback? *Oxford Institute for Energy Studies*, 57. Retrieved from http://www.oxfordenergy.org/wpcms/wp-content/uploads/2011/11/NG_57.pdf.

11. Mitchell, T. (2013). *Carbon Democracy: Political power in the age of oil.* London: Verso.

12. Wrigley, E.A. (2010). *Energy and the English Industrial Revolution.* Cambridge: Cambridge University Press.

13. Klein, N. (2014). *This Changes Everything: Capitalism vs. the climate.* New York: Simon & Schuster.

14. European Commission. (n.d.). Projects of common interest – Energy – European Commission. Retrieved from http://ec.europa.eu/energy/en/topics/infrastructure/projects-common-interest.

15. Henderson, J. (2011).

16. Platt, D.C. (1968). The imperialism of free trade: Some reservations. *Economic History Review*, 21(2), 296–306. Retrieved from doi:10.1111/j.1468-0289.1968.tb01768.x.

17. Uk watch (07 May 07). The Future of British Foreign Policy. *New Left Project* http://www.newleftproject.org/index.php/site/article_comments/the_future_of_british_foreign_policy.

18. Marriott, J. and Minio-Paluello, M. (2012). *The Oil Road: Journeys from the Caspian Sea to the City of London.* London: Verso.

19. Global Energy Security. (16 July 2006). Retrieved from http://www.mofa.go.jp/policy/economy/summit/2006/energy.html; Commission to the European Parliament, The Council, & The European Economic and Social Committee and the Committee of the Regions. (September 2011). The EU energy policy: Engaging with partners beyond our borders. Retrieved from http://eur-lex.europa.eu/legal-content/EN/TXT/?uri=CELEX:52011DC0539; Wicks, M. and Department of Energy and Climate Change. (August 2009). Energy security: A national challenge in a changing world. Retrieved May 4, 2015, from https://books.google.com/books?id=E43yMgEACAAJ&dq=%22Energy%2BSecurity%3A%2BA%2Bnational%2Bchallenge%2Bin%2Ba%2Bchanging%2Bworld%22%2BDECC&hl=en&sa=X&ei=JGVIVae9Co_GogT--oAo&ved=0CCwQ6AEwAA.

20. Florini, A. (2010). Global governance and energy, in Pascual, C. and Elkind, J. eds. *Energy Security: Economics, politics, strategies, and implications.* Washington, DC: Brookings Institution Press, pp. 149–84.

21. Obama biggest recipient of BP cash. (5 May 2010). Reuters. Retrieved from http://www.reuters.com/article/2010/05/05/us-politico-obama-bp-idUSTRE64420A20100505.

22. Shell in the Arctic. (n.d.). Retrieved from http://www.shell.com/global/future-energy/arctic.html.

23. Singh, A. (16 October 2013). The creeping militarization of the Arctic. Retrieved from http://thediplomat.com/2013/10/the-creeping-militarization-of-the-arctic/.

24. Government of Canada. (12 December 2012). Our north, our heritage, our future: Canada's northern strategy. Retrieved from http://www.northernstrategy.gc.ca/index-eng.asp.

25. Norwegian Government. (4 February 2007). The Soria Moria declaration on international policy. Retrieved from https://www.regjeringen.no/en/dokumenter/the-soria-moria-declaration-on-internati/id438515/.

26. Nincic, D.J. (19 February 2009). Maritime piracy: Implications for maritime energy security. *Journal of Energy Security.* Retrieved from http://www.ensec.org/index.php?option=com_content&view=article&id=180%3Amaritime-piracy-implications-for-maritime-energy-security&catid=92%3Aissuecontent&Itemid=341.

27. MSCHOA. (n.d.). The Maritime Security Centre – Horn of Africa (MSCHOA): Safeguarding trade through the high risk area. Retrieved from http://www.eunavfor.eu/about-us/mschoa/.

28. Jeory, T. and Giannangeli, M. (7 November 2010). Piracy will lead to power cuts. *Daily Express.* Retrieved from http://www.express.co.uk/news/uk/210035/Piracy-will-lead-to-power-cuts.

29. Strategic defence and security review — Motion to take note. (12 November 2010). Retrieved from http://www.theyworkforyou.com/lords/?id=2010-11-12a.393.2.

30. Hughes, E. and Minio-Paluello, M. (2012). A secret subsidy: Oil companies, the Navy & the response to piracy. *Platform London.* Retrieved from http://platformlondon.org/wp-content/uploads/2012/10/A-Secret-Subsidy-piracy.pdf.

31. Felton, R.Y. (16 September 2012). Here come the navies. Retrieved from http://www.somaliareport.com/index.php/post/3595/Here_Come_the_Navies.

32. AsiaNews. (17 February 2012). Kerala: The fishermen killed by Italian marines were Catholic. Retrieved from http://www.asianews.it/news-en/Kerala:-the-fishermen-killed-by-Italian-marines-were-Catholic-24008.html.

33. Evans, R. and Lewis, P. (12 January 2010). Police admit stop and searches on 11-year-olds at Kingsnorth protest. Retrieved from http://www.guardian.co.uk/uk/2010/jan/12/kingsnorth-stop-search-boys-illegal.

34. Taylor, M. and Lewis, P. (20 April 2009). Secret police intelligence was given to E.ON before planned demo. Retrieved from http://www.theguardian.com/uk/2009/apr/20/police-intelligence-e-on-berr.

35. Ibid.

36. Evans, R. and Lewis, P. (26 October 2009). Kingsnorth: How climate protesters were treated as threat to the country. Retrieved from http://www.theguardian.com/environment/2009/oct/26/kingsnorth-protests-climate-change-campaign.

37. BBC News. (20 January 2011). Acpo defends use of undercover officers amid new claims. Retrieved from http://www.bbc.co.uk/news/uk-12238445.

38. Banktrack. (n.d.). Phulbari coal mine, Bangladesh. Retrieved from http://www.banktrack. org/manage/ajax/ems_dodgydeals/createPDF/phulbari_coal_mine.

39. Dasgupta, G. (30 April 2011). Another time: Coming up – another occasion to displace people. Retrieved from http://refugeewatchonline.blogspot.co.uk/2011/04/another-time-coming-up-another-occasion.html.

40. Ibid.

41. Phulbari Coal Project. (2015, March 16). Retrieved from http://www.sourcewatch.org/ index.php/Phulbari_Coal_Project.

42. DESERTEC Foundation: Concept. (n.d.). Retrieved from http://www.desertec.org/en/ concept/.

43. Hädicke, G. and Werner K. (4 February 2011). Desertec soll Nordafrika stabilisieren. Retrieved from http://www.ftd.de/unternehmen/industrie/:unruhen-in-aegypten-desertec-soll-nordafrika-stabilisieren/60007469.html.

44. First steps to bring Saharan solar to Europe. (n.d.). Retrieved from http://www.euractiv.com/ energy/steps-bring-saharan-solar-europe/article-184274.

45. Organisation for Economic Co-operation and Development and International Energy Agency. (2011). *Energy for All: Financing access for the poor.* World Energy Outlook. Retrieved from http://www.iea.org/media/weowebsite/energydevelopment/weo2011_energy_for_ all.pdf.

46. Biofuel crops cultivated as a combustion fuel have been rejected by indigenous populations and local communities the world over due to the destruction of forests and land grabs of areas previously used for subsistence agriculture or small-scale farming. Numerous declarations rejecting biofuel projects have been signed by social movements from the Global South over the past decade.

47. Howden, D. (25 August 2009). The big question: Should Africa be generating much of Europe's power? Retrieved from http://www.independent.co.uk/news/world/africa/the-big-question-should-africa-be-generating-much-of-europes-power-1776802.html.

48. Altamirano-Jimenez, I. (17 April 2014). Indigenous land has never been modern. Retrieved from http://nationsrising.org/indigenous-land-has-never-been-modern/.

49. Bidwai, P. (3 October 2010). India is implementing active measures to combat its ever-growing rise in energy consumption. Retrieved from http://www.tni.org/article/india-implementing-active-measures-combat-its-ever-growing-rise-energy-consumption.

50. Institute of Health Equity. (2014). *Local Action on Health Inequalities: Fuel poverty and cold home-related health problems.* Retrieved from https://www.gov.uk/government/uploads/ system/uploads/attachment_data/file/355790/Briefing7_Fuel_poverty_health_ inequalities.pdf.

51. Lohmann, L. and Hildyard, N. (31 March 20141). Energy, work and finance. Retrieved from http://www.thecornerhouse.org.uk/resource/energy-work-and-finance.

52. Bardi, U. (30 May 2014). The transition to sustainable energy: How much will it cost? Retrieved from http://cassandralegacy.blogspot.co.uk/2014/05/the-transition-to-sustainable-energy. html.

53. Cumbers, A. (2012). *Reclaiming Public Ownership: Making space for economic democracy.* London: Zed Books.

54. Leidreiter, A. (8 October 2013). Hamburg citizens vote to buy back energy grid. Retrieved from http://energytransition.de/2013/10/hamburg-citizens-buy-back-energy-grid.

55. Ibid.

56. Kishimoto, S., Lobina, E. and Petitjean, O. (3 April 2015). Our public water future: The global experience with remunicipalisation. Retrieved from http://www.tni.org/briefing/our-public-water-future.

57. Gyawali, D. and Dixit, A. (2010). The construction and destruction of scarcity in development: Water and power experiences in Nepal, in Mehta, L., ed. *The limits to Scarcity: Contesting the politics of allocation.* London: Earthscan.

58. Platform. (19 February 2014). We don't want the oil companies – Italian community says no to pipeline. Retrieved from http://platformlondon.org/2014/02/19/we-dont-want-the-oil-companies-italian-community-says-no-to-pipeline/.

59. Fuel Poverty Action. (n.d.). Energy Bill of Rights. Retrieved from http://www.fuelpovertyaction.org.uk/home-alternative/energy-bill-of-rights-2/.

60. This is what energy democracy looks like. (n.d.). Retrieved from http://unionsforenergy democracy.org/.

CONCLUSION: FINDING SECURITY IN A CLIMATE-CHANGED WORLD

Nick Buxton and Ben Hayes

On 29 October 2012, Hurricane Sandy slammed into the New York metropolitan area. Built along a peninsula that narrows to almost a right angle, New York was at the end of a funnel into which 90-mile winds and 13-foot waves surged. Within minutes, large swathes of New York City were flooded with a mix of seawater and sewage. Water streamed into the subway system, a number of public hospitals were evacuated, and hundreds of thousands of residents lost their electricity. The famous Manhattan skyline was plunged into darkness. But one building continued to glow in defiance of the storm: 200 West Street, the headquarters of investment bank Goldman Sachs, shielded behind 25,000 sandbags and powered by a huge backup generator.[1]

Like Hurricane Katrina before it, Sandy exposed the deep inequality in US society. Again, it was the poorest districts that suffered the most – Hardscrabble, Red Hook, Coney Island, the Rockaways. A month after the disaster, thousands were still without power and heat; three months later, few had received the promised support and repairs to their damaged flats and houses.[2] Many also suffered long-term effects from contamination due to the flooding of nearby toxic industries, typically placed in the lowest-income areas. One year later, a study showed that the poorest residents affected by the hurricane were still enduring material hardship and an inability to meet their routine daily living expenses.[3]

New York State Governor Andrew Cuomo responded to the hurricane by sending in the military: 61,000 soldiers in total. Many of them backed up Federal Emergency Management Agency (FEMA) staff by clearing debris and distributing food and water. There was certainly no repeat of the violence and repression witnessed after Katrina in New Orleans, but the operation bore many of the same hallmarks, including an emphasis on crowd control, the protection of petrol stations, and conducting neighbourhood patrols to prevent looting.[4] The army's own internal evaluation found that the mission lacked coordination and clarity of purpose.[5]

Incredibly, the state's response was soon overshadowed by Occupy Sandy, an offshoot of the global Occupy movement that had started in New York City in September 2011.[6] Based out of ten hubs, at its peak 60,000 volunteers were running remarkably efficient centres across the city for people to donate and receive food and clothing. On one day, Michael Premo, one of the volunteers, estimated the effort included 2,500 volunteers, 15,000 meals and 120 carloads of supplies sent to recovery sites. Another volunteer, Ethan

Murphy, explained there wasn't any kind of official decision or declaration that 'occupiers' would now try to help with the hurricane aftermath: 'This is what we do already: build community, help neighbours, and create a world without the help of finance.'[7]

The story of Sandy prefigures many dimensions of our world's unfolding climate crisis. These kinds of extreme weather events are becoming more frequent as the climate changes. Extreme inequality dictates that corporations like Goldman Sachs are well protected, while the poor and marginalised are exposed. After a tweeted photo of the Goldman Sachs building's lights went viral, the bank turned on the PR, explaining that it had provided water for nearby residents and had set up a free mobile phone-charging station. This of course missed the point of the popular outrage. Having been bailed out with billions of taxpayer dollars a few years earlier, Goldman Sachs had abundant resources to protect itself, while local hospitals and the community apparently did not.

These inequalities were replicated across national borders. While the US government eventually spent $60 billion to help businesses and residents rebuild after the storm,[8] the UN was still scrambling a year later to raise $40 million to alleviate the hunger and malnutrition in impoverished Haiti that resulted from the impact of Hurricane Sandy.[9]

Back in New York, the most important part of the Sandy story is how an 'army' of volunteers self-organised a more effective response than many could have imagined possible. Their success was motivated by compassion, justice and solidarity, rather than self-interest and a 'security state confrontational mentality' that views the victims of climate change as a population to be 'carefully controlled'. In its own way, the Sandy story reminds us that our response to the climate crisis can and should have very different start and end points to the military-corporate-led approach exposed by this book.

A mirror on ourselves

'Climate change is a mirror in which we will all come to see the best and the worst of ourselves', says the UK's former climate-change negotiator John Ashton.[10] In looking at the mirror through the lens of the militarisation and the corporate capture of climate-change policy making, as this collection has, we certainly see the worst. The reflection is one of paranoid and overextended state-security apparatuses which lack the imagination and, more importantly, the mandate to envisage anything other than disaster and social unrest. Lurking in the background are those corporate elites who see only risks and opportunities, and use the language of climate change and fears about security to profit from both.

Security used to mean the ability of people to care for themselves and each other. In many senses it still does, with survey after survey showing that people are far more concerned about job security, or the security of having a long-term home, even climate change and environmental security, than they are worried about the threat of 'terrorism' and other supposed threats to the national security and the integrity of the state. But the promise of human security – freedom from want, freedom from fear – that was nurtured by the UN is being eclipsed by a state-corporate security that offers a catch-all for a range of dubious and immoral policies.

For the security/military-industrial complex, climate change is just the latest in a long line of threats constructed in such a way as to consolidate its grip on power and public finance. For corporations, the risk posed by climate change is also an opportunity for profit, and nowhere more so in a security industry that offers an endless supply of resilience- and disaster-related services. Whether it is written into a US defence manual, a retail giant's corporate risk strategy, or a World Bank agriculture proposal, security now provides a ubiquitous framework for policies that seek to consolidate the interests of the powerful. 'Water security', for example, becomes justification for a soft-drinks multinational to secure water supplies in drought-prone regions in India, even if it denies local villagers clean drinking water. For the powerful military giants, particularly of the US and EU, security means protecting shipping routes that allow the resources and profits of the world to continue to flow North, while militarising borders to ensure that impoverished people don't take the same route or often die in the trying. In the eyes of the elites, the communities and individuals that suffer the consequences have become disposable people: invisible or ignored, a minor footnote in media stories, regrettable perhaps, but ultimately not as important as the 'security' that is gained as a result. Through their lens, those people most vulnerable to climate change are more often identified as a potential threat to national security, by virtue of their vulnerable or failing states, rather than seen as priorities for assistance. Territories are being demarcated and divided by more and more borders, not just between countries but within them; corporate power is being given ever more control of our resources, with the support of state-sponsored violence and coercion if necessary.

None of these trends, of course, are new or exclusive to a time of climate crisis. Land and water grabbing was happening long before the 2008 food crisis put climate change in the frame. Repression and racism against migrants has been a troubling reality in most countries worldwide. In terms of dwindling reserves of fossil fuel, the 'race for what's left' would still be causing environmental and social havoc regardless of its impact on the climate. However, all of these conditions are being intensified. And in true Orwellian fashion, much of the modern-day structural violence is done in the name of tackling climate change and creating greater security for everyone.

Sometimes the rhetoric of environmentalists on climate change contributes to this problem. The idea that climate change is a threat to everyone, and therefore the shared responsibility of everyone to address it, can allow dissent about the problems of certain approaches to be dismissed, even in progressive circles. This also limits the space for talking about the way in which climate change affects different groups of people in markedly different ways depending on economic status, race, gender and location. Climate change interacts with existing systems of exploitation, and in turn our responses to the threat can also exacerbate class and race divides.[11] Brushing over these differences, to demand urgent action at all costs, can all too easily play into the hands of a militaristic Pentagon planner or a self-serving corporate executive.

One tangible result of the widespread adoption of 'security' as the approach to follow has been to further expand national security apparatuses that have grown to monstrous proportions in the name of keeping 'us' safe from 'them', be they poor people, refugees, or terrorists. This is a perverse and irrational response that promises to dismantle hard-won civil liberties, entrench existing inequality and stifle political debate, all the while helping to protect the current political and economic system from the meaningful, systemic changes that are necessary to overcome the challenges we face.

Adaptation or resilience as alternatives?

In looking for alternatives to a security-led approach, many concerned citizens have invested instead in efforts focused on climate adaptation and resilience. There is much to commend these approaches which offer an inherently more democratic and accountable response to the climate crisis. Adaptation is what people have been doing from time immemorial to cope with change, including variations in the climate. The climate-adaptation plans drawn up by many cities, for example, are rooted in the best traditions of devolved power and are making necessary preparations for climate impacts. Green buildings that can provide cooling during heat waves, reduce energy costs, and make cities more liveable are a good example of the sort of initiatives we need.[12]

However, the success of adaptation locally also highlights the main problem with the prevailing adaptation narrative, which is intrinsically related to scale. On the one hand, the impact of adaptation at the local level is de facto undermined by the behaviour of nation states and multinational corporations. On the other hand, the language of adaptation can favour acquiescence and a lack of resistance to precisely these drivers of climate change. The suggestion is that people – and never mind any other species on the planet – should 'adapt' to climate change, rather than arguing that it is the structures of power and processes that are creating climate change that have to change.

In the hands of the worst offenders, climate adaptation is even used as a reason *not* to take effective action against the causes of climate change, particularly by those climate sceptics and free market ideologues who, forced to admit that climate change exists, have quickly switched to arguing that it is cheaper to adapt to climate change or even 'fix' climate change with geo-engineering rather than to try to prevent it.[13]

Moreover, many communities worldwide lack the resources to make any meaningful preparations. Where adaptation policies are applied in the South, they can often end up reinforcing inequalities, as shown in the chapters on food, water and energy security. An EU research project in 2013 focused on the Mediterranean, the Middle East and the Sahel showed that poorly designed climate-adaptation policies (interconnected with systemic inequalities and lack of democratic accountability) were the prime cause of human insecurity in their 14 case studies.[14] Truly effective adaptation policies, such as building a strong social-welfare state or supporting traditional forms of community resilience are rarely mentioned, let alone prioritised.

Perhaps the most dangerous assumption is the idea that we can easily adapt to climate change, as if all that is required is small increases in sea-wall heights, the diversion of a road, or some new green kit. If, as Nafeez Ahmed and others warn, the triggering of feedback mechanisms within our atmosphere more dramatically disrupts intensely inter-connected systems for providing food, water and energy, such piecemeal measures will soon seem ridiculous.

A similar critique can be made of resilience. Again, there is much to commend the notional pursuit of resilience that enhances the 'ability of a system to absorb change while retaining essential function; to have the ability for self-organization; and to have the capacity to adapt and learn'.[15] But part of the reason that we face a climate crisis is due to the resilience of a global capitalist economic system, a carbon-based energy system and a compromised political system – that have all survived and persisted despite the global economic and ecological crisis and the growing distrust of corporate politicians. As environmental-security scholar David Schlosberg puts it: 'Power is incredibly resilient, ignorance is resilient, compromised politicians are resilient. Resilience is not, in itself, necessarily a redeemable feature.'[16]

Boldly tackling the underlying causes

The underlying causes of both the climate crisis and human insecurity are well-known, if still widely ignored. Capitalism, militarism and imperialism are disastrously intertwined with the fossil-fuel economy and are, in many places in the world, creating seemingly intractable security problems at every turn. A globalised economy predicated on growth at any social or environmental cost, carbon-dependent international trade, the limitless extraction of natural resources and a view of citizens as nothing more than consumers cannot be the basis for either tackling climate change, or for creating the kind of societies that can respond justly to the challenges climate change poses. Little wonder, then, that elites have nothing to offer beyond continued militarisation and trust in techno-fixes.

As environmental scholar Simon Dalby reflects:

The challenge facing those of us who struggle to rethink geopolitics in these novel times, and to make useful contributions to the discussions of transitions to a more sustainable world, is to facilitate shifting analysis from focusing on questions of dominance on a divided world to modes of sharing a crowded planet which is actively being transformed by human action ... Who we are is now irretrievably interlinked to what kind of a biosphere we are remaking; there is no nature out there for us to dominate.[17]

There is little point in downplaying the enormity of this task. The pursuit of off-shore capital and the satisfaction of the demands of corporations has become the priority of government.[18] Neoliberalism has done its utmost to replace moral values with commercial values, caring with indifference, altruism with selfishness, and generosity with greed.[19] The architects of the dystopian visions described in this book – the military, security and corporate strategists – represent a formidable alliance.

It is not surprising that some activists have felt the battle is not worth fighting. People like Paul Kingsnorth, a former environmental activist, now of the Dark Mountain Project, argue that it is time to 'withdraw' from the fight in order to reflect more deeply.[20] His arguments vividly capture some of the grief associated with environmental damage and the frequent hubris and arrogance in our (lack of) response, but withdrawal simply hands more power over our future to those who stand in the way of environmental justice.

Resistance is crucial – and it must be nonviolent, bold and confrontational. As the great Frederick Douglass, a former slave, observed in 1857:

> If there is no struggle there is no progress. Those who profess to favor freedom and yet deprecate agitation are men who want crops without plowing up the ground; they want rain without thunder and lightning. They want the ocean without the awful roar of its many waters. This struggle may be a moral one, or it may be a physical one, and it may be both moral and physical, but it must be a struggle. Power concedes nothing without a demand. It never did and it never will.[21]

Resistance also means being awake to the subtle shifts in military and corporate strategies that seek to make previously unacceptable policies seem increasingly natural and therefore acceptable. Environmental psychologists call this 'shifting baselines', which is the phenomenon that 'perception of changes in the social and psychological environment is never absolute but always relative to one's own observational standpoint.'[22] In other words, we assume that what we see around us is what has always been around us and is therefore natural – we forget or become blind to the fact that our local river was once filled with fish, or that people used to walk down city streets without cameras following them. Indeed, perhaps nowhere are the shifting baselines more terrifying than in the gradual legitimisation and acceptance of militarised policy and practices – in the gradual acceptance of the US programme of assassination by drone strike, or the EU's substitution of its legal and moral obligations toward refugees with a military blockade in the Mediterranean Sea. By its very nature, climate change promises to make the unimaginable tangible; in doing so, it also threatens to make the exceptional normal.

The frequently depressing nature of the material in this collection presents a constant intellectual struggle. Any reasoned assessment of the climate science, when coupled with contemporary power structures and the multiple sources of today's widespread insecurities point toward a frightening mid-term trajectory for the world. How can we respond in a way that puts the future firmly in our hands, yet properly acknowledges the challenges and structures of power we need to overcome? In working through some of these issues and thinking through their vulnerabilities and fault-lines, the first thing we would want to stress is how this doom and gloom is being socially constructed and cynically exploited and therefore needs to be challenged. As others who have grappled with this topic have explained:

> We can never escape fear. Neither can we escape language rhetoric or performance. These are currencies of life in the twenty-first century ... understanding fear and anxieties is one of the pressing political projects of our time. To develop and enact a progressive political agenda, we must unravel the dense thicket of ideology, politics, and economies that are imbricated in the dramas of fears and threats.[23]

We hope this book contributes to this task.

Secondly, as most of the chapters in this collection stress, it is clear that the key to resisting the future world we have attempted to reveal is embedded in the seeds of the resistance to current inequalities and injustice. While elites may consider people disposable, the fact is that people everywhere are refusing to be victims and are both actively resisting the power structures described in this book, and developing creative and empowering alternatives. They are the other reflection in the climate change mirror: the 'best of ourselves'. We should be amplifying their efforts, not overwhelming the spirit with fears about some nightmare future that doesn't yet exist.

With this in mind, we finish by outlining some practical principles based on the lessons and experiences we have drawn from the scholarship and advocacy in this book.

Stay focused on stopping the extraction and production of fossil fuels

Whereas the climate security and corporate strategists emphasised in this book tend to pay lip service to the need to prevent runaway climate change, some analysts are more circumspect. In its 2014 report 'The Gathering Storm: Climate Change, Security and Conflict', the Environmental Justice Foundation laments the way in which 'The potent significance of the fact that the world's major military powers and security institutions consistently and increasingly voice their concerns regarding the impacts of climate change jars with the simple fact that there has been a failure to act on the issue.' This 'collective failure', it suggested, 'is the defining global human rights issue of the 21st Century.'[24] Indeed, there can be no doubt that in terms of potential impact, the difference between global temperature rises of 1–2°C, let alone scenarios of 4°C, is huge. Put simply, the longer it takes to replace our carboniferous economy, the worse the impact is likely to be. The number one priority must be to leave as much oil, gas, and other carbon-based fossil fuels in the ground, and to do this as quickly as possible. This action can take many forms – taxes, regulation, direct action, and so on – but ultimately we must confront and dismantle the oil industry, usher in a planned reduction of fossil-fuel use, leave fossil fuels in the ground, and switch to alternative and renewable forms of energy.

Play no part in greenwashing

It is naive in the extreme for environmentalists to ally themselves with military and big corporate polluters on the grounds that we are all somehow pushing in the same direction. Too many times, we have seen that partnerships between civil society and corporations result in the greenwashing of corporate malpractice; at worst, they have strengthened corporate control over critical resources. We need look no further than carbon trading, which is supported by many large environmental organisations and has ended up providing cash windfalls for the dirtiest companies on the planet, while doing almost nothing to reduce emissions.[25] As to looking to the military to speak 'green' in order (unsuccessfully we might add) to bring on board right-wing climate sceptics, or to somehow scare their political masters into action: we should be absolutely clear that uncritical acceptance of this discourse has merely strengthened the emerging consensus that authoritarian policies will be needed to control populations at times of crisis. Environmental activist Tim DeChristopher is exactly right when he says:

> I don't care if the military is taking climate change seriously. But you can be sure they are not a group whose power I want to reinforce when things become ugly ... So in all our actions we need to look to overturn these power structures. We should not be asking major corporations like Walmart or institutions like the military to be kinder and gentler. We need to start working now on putting in place power structures that share our values as we enter difficult times. When things get ugly, and access to resources becomes difficult, we want to have trust that those making decisions will act justly, and not just favour the strong.[26]

At the same time we cannot be anti-everything. The outright rejection of scientific adventure, of innovation, of large-scale production, of 'security' – in favour of some kind of small-is-beautiful, organic localism – offers no challenge to the power structures we must confront (nor is it by any means a desirable state of affairs for the world's 7 billion inhabitants). By analogy, surveillance and corporate dominance of the Internet is not a reason for activists to stop using the Internet; it's a reason for them to take steps to protect their privacy and campaign for a freer Internet. The same is true for technology and the forces of production: it's a question of 'how best', not 'what else'. In another online chapter prepared for this collection,[27] two eminent scholars and labour-movement activists, Hilary Wainwright and Jacklyn Cock, focus on the transformative potential of labour and environmental activists working together, particularly when workers and unions shift from a narrow focus on workplace rights to advocate for worker-based solutions done in collaboration with other citizen groups. They cite, for example, the work done by the National Union of Metalworkers in South Africa (NUMSA), which has set up a whole range of worker-led Research and Development Groups exploring how to produce renewable-energy infrastructure and create climate jobs in South Africa.

Defend democracy and challenge authoritarianism

A just response to climate-change impacts will require a renewed emphasis on democracy, which has been hollowed out by transnational capital and neoliberalism, and is threatened further still by climate-security narratives. This book has focused on the suspension of democracy in the name of 'disaster' response, but the trend is also increasingly found in other areas of public life. At the international level, more and more important global-policy decisions are taken by thinly accountable multi-stakeholder forums. Projects like the Global Redesign Initiative, championed by the corporate-dominated World Economic Forum, have seen self-selected groups of elites, corporations and big NGOs start to dictate policy to the UN, circumventing what fragile democracy exists at that scale.[28]

It is also the case that many of the transnational security frameworks that are closing in on environmental activists and others who threaten the status quo have been devised and implemented in largely or completely undemocratic forums. This includes the international frameworks underpinning mass surveillance, counter-terrorism and global migration management.

This anti-democratic trend is also evidenced by the powerful and their media's disdain for democratic elections that deliver results elites don't want, whether it is Hamas in Gaza or Syriza in Greece.[29] The rise of one-party-state China on the global stage is only likely to deepen this trend. The 'threat' of climate change has even led scientists such as James Lovelock to argue that 'it may be necessary to put democracy on hold for a while', saying that we need 'a more authoritative world' where there are 'a few people with authority who you trust who are running it'.[30] The convergence of these threads – combined with fear of climate-change impacts – is creating a powerful trend towards authoritarian environmentalism, which could have dangerous consequences for democracy.

As Sussex academic Andy Stirling notes

> … the more assertive and apocalyptic the envisaged threat the more seemingly desperately necessary the Faustian pact with power … And neither history nor current affairs suggest any guarantee that such bargains will be delivered … time and again these actually reproduce the old incumbent structures in new forms, often being even more entrenched.[31]

Today's China – born of an agrarian revolution and now dispossessing peasants with an iron fist – is a modern-day example of this. Democracy is obviously messy and slow, and clearly needs invigorating and renewing through the engagement of social movements in order to counter its capture by elites and corporations, but it is the only way we have to counter authoritarian environmentalism.

There is clearly a role for reinvigorated forms of sovereignty here too. As the chapters on food, energy and water have demonstrated, marginalised communities worldwide are confronting powerful interests (which are using the language of climate security to justify resource grabs and repression) with their own calls for food, energy and water 'sovereignty'. What these communities are seeking is the power to take decisions over the use of these resources in the interests of the majority of those whose livelihoods depend on them. The global peasant farmers' federation, for example, defined food sovereignty in a way that could easily be extended to other resource domains:

> Food sovereignty is the right of peoples to healthy and culturally appropriate food produced through ecologically sound and sustainable methods, and their right to define their own food and agriculture systems. It puts those who produce, distribute and consume food at the heart of food systems and policies rather than the demands of markets and corporations. It defends the interests and inclusion of the next generation.[32]

In the context of climate change, resisting authoritarianism also means giving people a say in how they are policed, democratising those apparatuses involved in disaster preparedness and crisis management, and holding security forces to account. This is another area of activism that has for too long been at the margins of the concerns of social movements; in dangerous times, it is imperative that advocates of social justice step up their engagement with the coercive apparatuses of power.

Ensure that adaptation and resilience delivers for people, not profit

Previous chapters have shown how concepts like 'security', 'adaptation' and 'resilience' have joined the ranks of modern-day weasel-words: hollowed-out, appropriated and twisted to the point that they can mean anything and nothing at the same time. This requires critical thinkers to keep their spin-detectors finely tuned toward corporate and security elites promising to tackle the problems posed by climate change. More than that, we must simultaneously support the systems, structures, ideas and capacities that will genuinely contribute to a just adaptation while resisting those designed to entrench profiteering and authoritarianism.

One example is investment in, and large-scale adoption of, agroecology, proposed in the food chapter, that promises to produce far less carbon dioxide than current industrial farming practices, while building a more ecologically diverse food system that has a better chance of adapting to climate change. But its long-term success in terms of meeting the human right to food will depend also on redistributing land and democratising food supply and distribution chains.

In the field of energy, cities such as Berlin taking back control of their energy utilities are another important example. Not only have these initiatives to end privatisation allowed these cities to adopt bolder renewable-energy plans, they have also helped decentralise power (both electrical and democratic) that will be key to a more robust energy system. This initiative is also building community cohesiveness and participation – all invaluable assets for responding to climate changes.[33] Technology platform Ushahidi,[34] which has grown out of citizen journalism and the mapping of post-election violence in Kenya and offers a range of open-source tools for bottom-up, community-led crisis management and development, is another inspiring example.

In terms of resilience, we also need to revisit the letter and spirit of human and environmental security as developed in opposition to narrower, state-centric concepts. Various scholars have laid out in meticulous detail the way in which human security can be written into climate-change strategies, offering tangible alternatives to the hubris on offer from the military.[35]

Ally ourselves with those who suffer the most from climate change

Concomitant to the rejection of elite visions of how to profit from climate change, is our embrace and solidarity with those who will suffer its consequences most – the community that loses control of water to an agribusiness, the migrants seeking to cross the Mediterranean, the low-income neighbourhoods in our cities sited next to oil refineries. Actions of solidarity will often move the terrain and even focus of struggle, so 'climate change' will not always be the headline cause of social injustice. As the migration chapter explored, climate refugees will in practice be difficult to discern from other people who are forced to leave their homes, but in practice, if we don't resist EU policies predicated on military action against migrants, what kind of a world are we creating for future refugees, whether they seek protection across borders or internally?

There are, however, encouraging signs that environmental movements are more frequently joining the struggles against racism, inequality, injustice and in support of human rights – after a chequered history in which some environmentalists have either isolated themselves from other social struggles, or even taken the side of oppressive forces. In the US, for example, the leadership of major rallies and convergences of action, such as the massive Climate March that took place in September 2014, is increasingly led by indigenous, black and grass-roots community groups. The result has been greater collaboration with struggles against racism, corporate power and economic injustice, and acts of solidarity by environmental activists with anti-racist movements, responding to police killings of black men in Ferguson, New York and Baltimore. As Deidre Smith of the US climate activist group 350.org puts it: this cross-linking of movements comes from a realisation that the 'fight is not simply with the carbon in the sky, but with the powers on the ground.'

Ultimately, the only way to confront the injustice at the heart of the climate crisis – that those who had the least responsibility for the crisis will suffer the most – is for power and wealth to be redistributed at local, national and global levels. This will require taxation, financing for climate adaptation, and the (re)building of a strong social-welfare system for all. Public-public partnerships, where well-performing public utilities partner with their counterparts in other areas or countries, are initiatives that the climate-justice movement should support. Waternet, Amsterdam's public water utility is one such example: it has worked with cities in Indonesia, Egypt, Suriname and South Africa and could be a model for other public-sector solidarity initiatives.

Draw on commons-based, collective and ecologically rooted responses to climate change

In an accompanying online chapter, Henfrey and Kenrick provide an inspiring insight into the growing global movement for just transition and the role played by the Transition Towns movement.[36] They note that this is essential work aimed at creating a 'new commons' which they describe as 'the relationships that constitute a place, and the care we need to take to ensure that all (human and nonhuman) aspects of this place flourish'.

They cite examples of age-old commons-based regimes in Kenya, Australia and Guyana that successfully conserve forests and drylands, as well as more recent experiments by Transition Towns that are creating their own currencies, communi-ty-owned energy companies, and community farms; ideas and practices that are shared with a growing global movement. According to Kenrick and Henfrey, transition- and commons-based responses to climate change help us

> ... dis-identify from, and oppose, a system we are all to a greater or lesser extent implicated in and addicted to; and secondly [enables us] to build sustainable communities that can both prefigure and help set the direction we all need to take to diminish the climate and related crises, and to cultivate networks of cooperation among these.

In this book, we have also seen the power of commons-based responses to disaster. This book cited the incredible impact of the Occupy movement in responding to Hurricane Sandy – not because we want to endorse some kind of politics of apocalypse and rebirth – but because it offers an alternative vision of society than that posed by the dystopians and climate securocrats. Another telling example is that of Cuba, whose experience of Hurricane Sandy is often overlooked. Sandy hit Cuba even more severely than New York, yet the Caribbean nation lost very few lives and recovered more rapidly. The challenge is to take inspiration from these local initiatives and to replicate them at much larger scales. Studies of Cuba's success in responding to disaster show that it relies on a very successful collaboration between the state and well-organised communities to identify and minimise hazards to vulnerable populations, to encourage a culture of safety and solidarity, and then to implement good planning and successful mobilisation of community resources to respond to the disaster and to promote recovery.

In developing local responses, it is crucial, however, that we don't romanticise the local while failing to act globally, as this will not deliver the international governance or trans-formation we need.

Reclaim the state

Amidst all this, social movements will need to have a necessary but difficult relationship with the state. This may seem counter-intuitive. After all, many states are the prime agents of the militarisation of climate change and the dystopian security strategies and practices described in this book. It is the state that feeds the military-industrial complex, and the state that acts as the prime backer of the corporate takeover of land, water, food and energy, removing regulations and opening up markets to them, negotiating trade deals on their behalf, and creating what some scholars call an international legal 'architecture of impunity' for corporations, which has escalated human rights abuses and corporate crimes worldwide.[37] This is because corporations have in many ways captured states; populating their ministries with staff, designing their policies, lobbying against regulation, and threatening boycott and withdrawal if any state dares to challenge them. In today's world, we are no longer talking about states, but rather a hybrid: the corporate-state.

It is hardly surprising that many movements and civil-society actors – not just anarchists – choose to either reject or ignore states and their potential role for transformation and focus on building local alternatives. The trouble is that this strategy does not weaken or remove states from our lives, but rather leads them down a more and more repressive and corporate-directed route. It also ignores the fact that despite three decades of neoliberalism, the state is still one of the remaining guardians of the 'public sector' and of victories fought hard for in the first half of the twentieth century: the National Health Service in the UK, the welfare state in Nordic countries, state corporations in many countries in the South, to name just a few examples. More than 10 per cent of the world's biggest companies are owned by the state, with a turnover equivalent to 6 per cent of global GDP, exceeding the gross national product of countries such as Germany, France, or the United Kingdom.

The fact that state enterprises and services such as water, education and health for now still largely remain in the 'public' sector – and are still widely celebrated for this despite years of corporate attack – shows the importance for retaining a vision of the commons in the twenty-first century. It also heralds the possibility that they can be reshaped towards social and environmental purposes. Moreover, in recent years, there has even been a resurgence of companies returning to the public sector, particularly in Latin America, but also in the US and Europe. Many of these large state enterprises are highly corporatised and financialised, and some are also deeply embedded in the fossil-fuel industry, but there are small examples – such as the state telecommunications industry in Uruguay and the electricity supply industry in Costa Rica – of states that are effectively integrating social and environmental objectives into their work.

The truth is that we will need the state to develop the re-engineering of our economy and infrastructure that will be necessary to prevent worsening climate change. And we will need a state to respond to climate-change impacts, whether they are slow and drawn-out, such as the unfolding drought in California in 2015, or sudden and dramatic, such as Typhoon Haiyan in the Philippines. Localised adaptation and just transition are crucial parts of the puzzle, but it will require a state to ensure they boost and interconnect their efforts and most of all to provide the infrastructure, economic framework and policies that can enable them to flourish.

Reject dystopian and neo-Malthusian narratives

Perhaps the most important lesson of this book is that by portraying people as some kind of Hobbesian mass that will inevitably meet food shortages with violence, or as hordes of would-be migrants massing at our borders, we are giving succour to the security strategists and the politics of fear that make people more willing to contemplate giving up their freedoms. Instead of fuelling dystopia, we need to uncover the social basis of all that is truly horrifying and catastrophic about our world as part of a critical practice designed to change it.[38] And we only need scratch the surface of how elites are preparing for climate change to understand where the real 'threat multipliers' lies. We should then contrast this with the way people – as opposed in many cases to those in positions of power and authority – actually respond to disaster.

In her deeply important book, *A Paradise Built in Hell*, Rachel Solnit studied five major disasters in depth, from the San Francisco earthquake of 1906 to the flooding of New Orleans in 2005. While there is obviously nothing good about disaster itself, she discovered that crises, more often than not, lead not to civilisational collapse, but altruism and solidarity. The fear of disorder, mayhem and the justification for military responses is the instinct of the richest – those with most to lose. This is what Solnit describes as 'elite panic'. In contrast, what emerged from the disasters she studied, are mini ephemeral utopian societies built on precisely the solidarity, democracy and accountability that neoliberalism and authoritarianism have stripped from contemporary political systems: 'Disaster often reveals what else the world could be like – reveals the strength of that hope, that generosity and that solidarity. It reveals mutual aid as a default operating principle and civil society as something waiting in the wings when it's absent from the stage.'[39] Hurricane Sandy is a case in point. While *New York Post* correspondent Heather MacDonald wrote about stories of looting, and 'the Thin Blue Line' between 'civilization and anarchy',[40] New York's citizens were forming citizen brigades to rescue vulnerable people, hand out food and water, and provide love and care for a traumatised city.

As noted in Chapter 2, and in contrast to the 'perspective of Malthusian dog-eat-dog resource competition', the issues engendered or exacerbated by climate change have just as much potential to produce cooperation among peoples.[41] In other words, when you have lots to lose, you are more compelled to collaborate than compete.

Faced with the sure knowledge of worsening climate change, corporations determined to continue business-as-usual, and a security industry promoting a politics of fear and insecurity, humanity faces a critical choice. On the one hand, we can throw up our hands in despair and darkly predict our demise – in which case we will entrench the power of those thriving from the politics of dystopia and hasten some of the worst-case scenarios that they predict. Or on the other hand, we can reject their forecasts and believe in the power of popular movements to advance a different vision of the future, one that harnesses humanity's compassion, creativity and cooperation. As the chapters in this book on energy, water and food showed, countless communities are not sitting back but actively advancing a just response to climate change – showing that alternatives not only exist but are thriving. The environmentalist and author Paul Hawken, when asked if he was optimistic or pessimistic about the future, said:

> If you look at the science about what is happening on earth and aren't pessimistic, you don't understand data. But if you meet the people who are working to restore this earth and the lives of the poor, and you aren't optimistic, you haven't got a pulse. What I see everywhere in the world are ordinary people willing to confront despair, power, and incalculable odds in order to restore some semblance of grace, justice, and beauty to this world.[42]

Notes

1. Greenhough, C. (30 October 2012). Hurricane Sandy rages, but the lights stay on at Goldman Sachs. Retrieved from http://www.inquisitr.com/381743/hurricane-sandy-rages-but-the-lights-stay-on-at-goldman-sachs/.
2. Nessen, S. (24 January 2013). Thousands still cold and struggling months after Superstorm Sandy. Retrieved from http://www.npr.org/2013/01/24/170198110/thousands-still-cold-and-struggling-months-after-superstorm-sandy.
3. Wimer, C. and Raker, E. (2014). *New Yorkers Negatively Impacted by Hurricane Sandy: How are they faring since?* Columbia Population Research Center, pp. 1–10. Retrieved from https://courseworks.columbia.edu/access/content/group/c5a1ef92-c03c-4d88-0018-ea43dd3cc5db/Working%20Papers%20for%20website/Working%20Papers_2014/Working%20Papers_14-03_New%20York%20Negatively%20Impacted%20by%20Sandy_24oct14.pdf.
4. Hoarn, S. (30 October 2012). Hurricane Sandy military response: Preparation and early response. Retrieved from http://www.defensemedianetwork.com/stories/hurricane-sandy-military-response-l-photos/.
5. Kilkenney, A. (5 November 2012). Occupy Sandy efforts highlight need for solidarity, not charity. Retrieved from http://www.thenation.com/blog/171020/occupy-sandy-efforts-highlight-need-solidarity-not-charity.
6. Ambinder, E. and Jennings, D.M. (2013). *The Resilient Social Network.* Homeland Security Studies & Analysis Institute, pp. 1–103. Retrieved from http://homelandsecurity.org/docs/the%20resilient%20social%20network.pdf.
7. Goldstein, K. (4 November 2012). Is OWS outperforming the Red Cross in disaster relief? Retrieved from http://www.slate.com/blogs/the_slatest/2012/11/04/occupy_sandy_hurricane_relief_being_led_by_occupy_wall_street.html.

8. Rowley, J. (15 January 2013). House completes $60 billion in Hurricane Sandy relief. *Bloomberg*. Retrieved from http://www.bloomberg.com/news/articles/2013-01-15/house-supports-17-billion-in-hurricane-sandy-relief.

9. Haiti: UN appeals for $40 million to help people affected by Hurricane Sandy. (12 November 2012). Retrieved from http://www.unocha.org/top-stories/all-stories/haiti-un-appeals-40-million-help-people-affected-hurricane-sandy.

10. Ashton, J. (30 March 2015). Open letter to Shell's Ben van Beurden from John Ashton. *Guardian*. Retrieved from http://www.theguardian.com/environment/2015/mar/30/open-letter-shell-ben-van-beurden-john-ashton-climate-change.

11. Stirling, A. (2014). *Emancipating Transformations: From controlling 'the transition' to culturing plural radical progress*. STEPS Centre, 64, pp. 1–48. Retrieved from http://steps-centre.org/wp-content/uploads/Transformations.pdf.

12. Lee, M., Willmott, E., Le Courtois, A., Gallegos, J.B. and Datta, N. (2011). *Guide to Climate Change Adaptation in Cities*, pp. 1–106. Retrieved from http://siteresources.worldbank.org/INTURBANDEVELOPMENT/Resources/336387-1318995974398/GuideClimChangeAdaptCities.pdf. Approached more critically, however, municipal climate adaptation plans often contain little more than aspirational goals, with little in the way of concrete steps to prevent and deal with climate change: Gallucci, M. (20 June 2013). 6 of the world's most extensive climate adaptation plans. Retrieved from http://insideclimatenews.org/news/20130620/6-worlds-most-extensive-climate-adaptation-plans.

13. Lawson, N. (22 December 2009). Time for a climate change plan b. *Wall Street Journal*. Retrieved from http://www.wsj.com/articles/SB10001424052748704107604574607793379880698.

14. Zografos, C. et al. (2013) Sources of human insecurity in the face of hydro-climatic change. *Global Environmental Change*. Retrieved from http://dx.doi.org/10.1016/j.gloenvcha.2013.11.002.

15. Adger, N., Brown, K. and Waters, J. (2011). Resilience, in Dryzek, J.S., Norgaard, R.B. and Schlosberg, D., eds., *Oxford Handbook of Climate Change and Society* (p. 696). Oxford: Oxford University Press, p. 696.

16. Schlosberg, D. (January 2013). Political challenges of the climate-changed society. Retrieved from https://www.academia.edu/2372945/Political_Challenges_of_the_Climate-Changed_Society.

17. Dalby, S. (2014). Environmental geopolitics in the twenty first century. *Alternatives: Global, Local, Political* 39(1), 15.

18. Monbiot, G. (2000). *Captive State: The corporate takeover of Britain*. London: Macmillan.

19. Sivanandan, A. (16 October 2005). Why Muslims reject British values. *Guardian*. Retrieved from http://www.theguardian.com/politics/2005/oct/16/race.world.

20. Kingsnorth, P. (December 2012). Dark ecology. Retrieved from https://orionmagazine.org/article/dark-ecology/.

21. Douglass, F. (n.d.). 'If there is no struggle, there is no progress'. Retrieved from http://www.blackpast.org/1857-frederick-douglass-if-there-no-struggle-there-no-progress#sthash.O2JamUGR.dpuf.

22. Welzer, H. and Camiller, P. (2012). *Climate Wars: Why people will be killed in the twenty-first century*. Cambridge: Polity Press, p. 140.

23. Hartmann, B., Subramaniam, B. and Zerner, C. (2005). *Making Threats: Biofears and environmental anxieties*. Oxford: Rowman and Littlefield, p. 250.

24. Environmental Justice Foundation (2014). *The Gathering Storm: Climate change, security and conflict.* Retrieved from http://ejfoundation.org/sites/default/files/public/EJF_climate_conflict_report_web-ok.pdf.

25. Gilbertson, T. and Reyes, O. (23 November 2009). Carbon trading: How it works and why it fails. Retrieved from http://www.tni.org/tnibook/carbon-trading-how-it-works-and-why-it-fails.

26. Buxton, N. (May 2011). Time to be honest – Interview with Tim DeChristopher. Retrieved from http://www.redpepper.org.uk/time-to-be-honest/.

27. See www.climatesecurityagenda.org.

28. Buxton, N. (2 June 2014). The great divide: Exposing the Davos class behind global economic inequality. Retrieved from http://www.tni.org/article/great-divide-exposing-davos-class-behind-global-economic-inequality.

29. Phillips, L. (2013). Kick 'em all out?: Anti-politics and post-democracy in the European Union. *Statewatch*, 23(1), 9–19. Retrieved from http://www.statewatch.org/subscriber/protected/statewatch-journal-vol23n1-march-2013.pdf; Buxton, N. (2014). The Great Divide: Exposing the Davos Class behind global inequality, in *Civicus State of Civil Society Report 2014*, Civicus. Retrieved from http://www.civicus.org/images/The%20Great%20Divide%20Exposing%20the%20Davos%20class.pdf.

30. Phillips, L. (5 November 2014). The solution is democracy. Retrieved from https://www.jacobinmag.com/2014/11/the-solution-is-democracy/.

31. Stirling, A. (2014). *Emancipating Transformations: From controlling 'the transition' to culturing plural radical progress.* STEPS Centre, 64, 1–48. Retrieved from http://steps-centre.org/wp-content/uploads/Transformations.pdf.

32. Declaration of Nyéléni. (27 February 2007). Retrieved from http://www.nyeleni.org/spip.php?article290.

33. At times of disasters, localised systems built on renewable energy can be particularly important, as the Red Cross presciently discovered in April 2015 when their solar-powered blood bank (made out of recycled shipping containers) proved critical to its rescue efforts after the earthquake had knocked out power systems and killed several thousand people in Nepal: Burnett, C. (7 October 2014). Nepal's solar-powered blood banks will save lives after deadly earthquakes. Retrieved from http://blogs.redcross.org.uk/emergencies/2014/10/nepals-solar-powered-blood-bank-will-save-lives-deadly-earthquakes/.

34. See http://www.ushaidi.com for more details.

35. Redclift, M. and Grasso, M. (2013). *Handbook on Climate Change and Human Security*. Cheltenham: Edward Elgar. See also Matthew, R. and Floyd, R. (2013). *Environmental Security*. London: Routledge. See also Brauch, H.G. (2015) *Hexagon Series on Human and Environmental Security and Peace*. Berline: Springer.

36. See www.climatesecurityagenda.org.

37. Transnational Institute and Observatory on Debt in Globalisation. (24 June 2014). Reflections on the 'super-rights' and 'super-powers' of corporate capital. Retrieved from http://www.tni.org/briefing/impunity-inc.

38. Lilley, S., McNally, D., Yuen, E. and Davis, J. (2012). *Catastrophism: The apocalyptic politics of collapse and rebirth*. Oakland, CA: PM Press.

39. Solnit, R. (2009). *A Paradise Built in Hell: The extraordinary communities that arise in disasters*. New York: Viking, p. 312.

40. MacDonald, H. (5 November 2012). Looters & the NYPD. *New York Post*. Retrieved from http://nypost.com/2012/11/05/looters-the-nypd/.

41. Pan, W. (2 December 2013). More than local: How PHE can help solve humanity's biggest problems. Retrieved from http://www.newsecuritybeat.org/2013/12/local-phe-solve-humanitys-biggest-problems/.

42. Hawken, P. (3 May 2009). Commencement address to the Class of 2009, University of Portland, Oregon. Retrieved from http://www.yesmagazine.org/issues/columns/you-are-brilliant-and-the-earth-is-hiring.

NOTES ON CONTRIBUTORS

Editors

Nick Buxton is Communications Manager for Transnational Institute (TNI) and has been involved in global justice and environmental justice movements for over 20 years. He is editor of TNI's annual *State of Power* reports and the book *Shifting Power: Critical Perspectives on Emerging Economies* (2015). He also wrote 'Politics of debt' in *Dignity and Defiance: Bolivia's Challenge to Globalisation* (University of California Press, 2009) and 'Civil society and debt cancellation' in *Civil Society and Human Rights* (Routledge, 2004).

Ben Hayes is a TNI fellow who has worked for the civil liberties organisation Statewatch since 1996, specialising in international and national security policies. Ben also works as an independent researcher and consultant. He is the author of *NeoConOpticon: The EU Security-Industrial Complex* (TNI, 2009) and has written widely on the impact of counter-terrorism on human rights, peace-building and civil society; on border control and the development of 'Fortress Europe'; and on surveillance before and after Edward Snowden.

Contributors

Nafeez Ahmed is an author, investigative journalist and international security scholar. His books include *Zeropoint* (2014), *A User's Guide to the Crisis of Civilization: And How to Save It* (2010) and *The London Bombings: An Independent Inquiry* (2006).

Mark Akkerman is a researcher at the Campagne tegen Wapenhandel, the Dutch Campaign against Arms Trade. His reports in Dutch include *Piracy, Private Security and the Arms trade* (2013) and *The Rise of Mercenaries: Private services in the Military and Security Sector* (2011).

Zoe W. Brent is a researcher on agrarian justice issues and a fellow at Food First, Institute for Food & Development Policy in Oakland, California. Her recent papers include *Territorial Restructuring and Resistance in Argentina* (2015) and *Contextualising Food Sovereignty: The Politics of Convergence Among Movements in the USA* (2015).

Susan George is the President of the Transnational Institute, Honorary President of ATTAC-France, the author of 17 books and holds a doctorate in political science. Her latest book is *Shadow Sovereigns: How Global Corporations are Seizing Power* (Polity, 2015).

April Humble is a scientific researcher and a writer on climate change, border security, human security and migration. She currently works at the secretariat for the Earth League and the Climate Service Centre in Germany.

Mary Ann Manahan is a feminist researcher and activist at Focus on the Global South where she works on issues related to land, food, agrarian reform, water, and reclaiming the commons. She co-authored the book, *State of Fragmentation: The Philippines in Transition* (2014).

Christian Parenti is an author, journalist and teaches in New York University's Global Liberal Studies program. He has published four books, the most recent being, *Tropic of Chaos: Climate Change and the New Geography of Violence* (2011).

Oscar Reyes is an Associate Fellow of the Institute for Policy Studies and a freelance consultant focusing on climate finance. His published work includes the co-authored book *Carbon Trading: How it Works and Why it Fails* (2009).

Platform is an arts, activism, education and research organisation supporting and engaged in struggles for social and ecological justice. Contributors to the chapter include Emma Hughes, Anna Galkina, Mika Minio-Paluello, Mel Evans, Kevin Smith and the Platform Collective.

Silvia Ribeiro is a journalist, campaigner and the Latin America Director for ETC group and on the editorial committee of the Latin American magazine *Biodiversidad, sustento y culturas.* She writes regularly for the newspaper *La Jornada* in Mexico.

Annie Shattuck is a Fellow at Food First and co-author of *Food Rebellions! Crisis and the Hunger for Justice* (2010).

Kathy-Jo Wetter is a researcher for ETC Group and has contributed to their analyses of the ownership, control, social and environmental impacts of new technologies, including nanotechnology, synthetic biology and geoengineering.

Steve Wright is a professor at Leeds Beckett University and an expert on technologies of political control, including new policing systems such as sub-lethal weapons systems, torture technologies and surveillance. His books include *Cyberwar, Netwar and the Revolution in Military Affairs* (2006).

INDEX

Compiled by Sue Carlton

and social justice 222, 224–5
see also fossil fuels; renewable energy
    sources
enhanced weathering 146
Environmental Defense Fund, Corporate
    Partnerships Program 63
environmental degradation 5–6, 8, 40, 90,
    114, 194
Environmental Justice Foundation 236
environmental justice movement 40, 112,
    127
environmental regulations, harmonising
    76–7
environmental security 40–1, 46, 49, 153,
    231, 240
environmentalists/environmental
    movement
  alliances with military 161–2, 237
  continued resistance 235
  and effective action 237
  emphasis on democracy 238–9
  and greenwashing 237
  murdered activists 51
  seen as threat 12, 51
E.ON 218–19, 220–1, 223
essential services 97
ETC Group 135–6
Ethiopia 174
European Union (EU)
  Action Plan on illegal immigration
    117–18
  Air Traffic Management system
    (EUROCONTROL) 97
  border surveillance 123, 127–8
  containment strategy 2
  emissions trading schemes (ETS) 75
  energy efficiency standards 76–7
  European Convention on Human
    Rights 100
  European Critical Infrastructures
    (ECIs) Directive 97
  European Security Strategy 43

Global Approach to Migration 117
  migration policy 111–12, 115, 117–19
  Secure societies programme 52
  security implications of climate change
    43
EUROSUR 123, 127–8
extreme weather 6, 7, 24–5, 68, 88–9, 91,
    174, 180, 231
Exxon Mobil 10, 70

Faludi, Susan 99
Federal Emergency Management Agency
    (FEMA) 230
Feed the Future initiative 179, 180
Ferguson protests (2015) 50, 240
financial sector
  and fossil-fuel companies 64–5, 69, 72,
    77
  investment and market structure 72
  speculation in food commodities
    177–8
Finmeccanica 122, 125, 126, 160
First World War, and energy security 211
fishing 25, 172, 197
Fleming, James 136
flex crops and commodities 181
flooding 6–7, 25–6, 42, 88, 89–90, 96,
    174, 191
  companies profiting from flood
    protection 10, 201–2
food security 6, 9, 14–15, 40–1, 171–85
  and conflict 171–2, 173
  dependence on fossil fuels 91–2
  distribution and access 177–8
  food crisis (1997-08) 171
  food price increases 8, 173, 177–8
  food sovereignty 184–5, 239
  and global food regimes 174–5
  vulnerability of global food system
    87–8, 91
  and waste 178
fossil fuels 2, 5, 15, 24